Oscar P. Fitzgerald

Three Centuries
of
American Furniture

A SPECTRUM BOOK

PRENTICE-HALL, INC., ENGLEWOOD CLIFFS, N.J. 07632

Library of Congress Cataloging in Publication Data

Fitzgerald, Oscar P.
  Three centuries of American furniture.

  A Spectrum Book.
  Bibliography: p.
  Includes index.
  1. Furniture—United States—History.
I. Title.
NK2405.F58   749.213   81-17898
                                 AACR2

ISBN 0-13-920371-0

ISBN 0-13-920363-X {PBK.}

To my mother,
Anne Gordon Fitzgerald,
who inspired this book

This Spectrum Book is available to businesses and organizations
at a special discount when ordered in large quantities.
For more information, contact Prentice-Hall, Inc.,
General Book Marketing, Special Sales Division,
Englewood Cliffs, N.J. 07632.

Editorial/production supervision by Donald Chanfrau
        and Maria Carella
Interior design by Donald Chanfrau
Page layout by Elinor Koehlinger
Color insert designed by Christine Gehring Wolf
Manufacturing buyer: Cathie Lenard
Cover design by Mike Aron
Front cover photograph by Joseph C. Bomar

Prentice-Hall International, Inc., *London*
Prentice-Hall of Australia Pty., Limited, *Sydney*
Prentice-Hall of Canada, Ltd., *Toronto*
Prentice-Hall of India Private, Limited, *New Delhi*
Prentice-Hall of Japan, Inc., *Tokyo*
Prentice-Hall of Southeast Asia Pte., Ltd., *Singapore*
Whitehall Books Limited, Wellington, *New Zealand*

Contents

PREFACE

THREE CENTURIES OF AMERICAN FURNITURE grew out of a series of lectures developed for the Smithsonian Institution and several universities in the Washington area. No recent major textbook is available that incorporates the prodigious amount of new research produced at the Winterthur Museum and other centers for the study of American cultural history. Helen Comstock's *American Furniture: 17th, 18th, and 19th Centuries*, published in 1962, did an excellent job of synthesizing the research available to that date, but her book is long out of print and now outdated.

The work of a number of scholars, particularly graduates of the Winterthur program, has increased our knowledge of cabinetmaking far beyond the state of the art in 1962. The new research has permitted a fresh survey of the 17th- and 18th-century furniture styles. Recent scholarly interest in the period after the Industrial Revolution has made possible the first major synthesis of recent research by such scholars as Kenneth Ames since the landmark exhibition at the Metropolitan Museum of Art in 1970.

The history of American furniture is approached from both a cultural and aesthetic point of view. Furniture styles did not evolve in isolation but were determined by cultural and historical events, particularly political, economic, and intellectual ones. These influences are emphasized in the text, and more than 500 photographs and captions analyze the artistic merit of the furniture. Although a selection of familiar masterpieces serves as a touchstone, numerous seldom-seen pieces are illustrated as well. Many examples are not in the masterpiece category, but they are often more representative of the bulk of American furniture than the rarer pieces.

In response to the often-asked questions of when a piece of furniture was made and what its provenance is, the book describes what furniture types, designs, and ornamentation were typical in each period. The book explains the development of American furniture styles through the 17th, 18th, and 19th centuries as they evolved through the Jacobean, William and Mary, Queen Anne, Chippendale, Federal, Empire, and various Victorian sub-styles. Instead of the usual lumping of 19th-century styles into the single Victorian furniture category, the multiple sub-styles, such as the Renaissance and Rococo revivals, Eastlake, Mission, and the innovative Art Nouveau are identified and described. The emphasis is on the development of 19th-century shop practices, the growth of furniture factories, and the historical influences on furniture design.

The gradual evolution of styles frequently defies the traditional dating systems. Still, distinct forms and ornamentation characterize each style. Certain types of furniture rose and fell in popularity. Various periods saw such innovations as new concepts of construction, progressive specialization, and mechanization. The 17th century joiner was displaced by the cabinetmaker in the 18th century, and the factory gradually squeezed the individual cabinetmaker out of business in the 19th century. Even in the Victorian period, however, individual craftsmen continued to sell custom-made furniture to a few wealthy customers who could pay for the service.

Further insights into 18th- and 19th-century furniture practices are contained in two significant documents available in their entirety as appendixes. Benjamin Lehman's price book is an indispensable research tool, published in 1786. George Henkels' catalogue, which first appeared in Philadelphia in the 1850s, offers new perceptions of the furniture business at mid-century.

Collectors—and scholars as well—have usually focused on high-style urban cabinetmaking. This book will address both urban and nonurban furniture in such special topics as Southern furniture, Pennsylvania German and Shaker work, and country cabinetmaking. Although much research remains to be done, the work of Frank Horton and others at the Museum of Early Southern Decorative Arts has made possible a preliminary, overall survey of Southern furniture. The studies of Charles Parsons, Charles Hummel, and others have made it possible to speak with some confidence about furniture-making in the countryside, where over 95 percent of the population lived in the 18th century, and where about half

lived even at the end of the 19th century.

The book will prove of interest to the growing army of collectors, curators, and scholars and to a public increasingly aware of this valuable heritage. A brief description of the latest principles of furniture conservation will assist those people who are responsible for preserving this heritage. The book will provide a starting point for the study and appreciation of the legacy of three centuries of American furniture craftsmen.

ACKNOWLEDGMENTS

A book starts out as a very personal idea in the mind of the author, but as it grows it begins to involve other people. When it is finished it is still the author's book but it would never have been completed without the encouragement and assistance of an enormous number of people. A brief listing in the acknowledgments is a wholly inadequate way of expressing my appreciation to the many friends who made this book possible.

A special word of thanks is due Anne Golovin of the Smithsonian Institution for her early encouragement and many helpful suggestions on the manuscript. Ken Ames, Nina Statum, Jack McBride, and Joe Kindig also read major portions of the manuscript and the book is the better for their generous efforts. June Sprigg, Peter Hammell, Nancy Starr, James Goode, John Hill, Brock Jobe, Frank Horton, Donald Fenimore, Robert Trump, Christine Minter-Dowd, Lawrence Belles, Pat Kane, Wendy Cooper, Lorraine Pearce, Morrison Hecksher, Anne Sellin, Page Talbot, Robert Trent, and Monroe Fabian also read selected parts of the manuscript which related to their own special areas of interest and I am grateful for their comments.

No matter how descriptive the text, only pictures can capture the nuances of design. I was very fortunate to have met Joseph C. Bomar who took on the task as my photographer and is responsible for the largest number of pictures in the book. Night after night he worked his magic with the camera and the results are a vivid testimonial to his skills. Many of the pieces had never been photographed before and without his help it would not have been possible to illustrate them. Frank Jelenfy worked a similar magic with pen and ink and produced all the drawings.

I also wish to thank the individuals who opened their homes and allowed us to disrupt their lives for a few hours as we photographed pieces in their collections: Anne and David Sellin, Nancy Starr, Miriam Morris, Anne Alvarez, Richard Klank, Denys Peter Myers, Herbert Collins, James Goode, Annette Wattles, Perry Fisher at the Heurich mansion, and several private collectors.

I ordered a large number of photographs from several institutions that were extremely helpful. Lawrence Belles and Mary Kay Ingenthron at the Strong Museum put up with my requests over a period which spanned nearly a year. Nancy Goyne Evans and Karol Schmiegel were also particularly helpful at Winterthur, as was Frank Horton at MESDA. At the White House and State Department Clement Conger and his staff, including Camille Bradly, Kathy McCutchen, and Bill Allman were always willing to assist me in my search. Others who provided photographs included Joe Kindig III, June Sprigg, Rodris Roth, Nathan Benn, Randell Makinson, Beth Rahe, Pam Driscoll, Robert Trump, Richard Ahlborn, and William Elder.

A special word of thanks must go to Gertrude Frankel and Hedi Lieberman at the Alexandria Library who processed the prodigious amount of paper work to order nearly 50 books on interlibrary loan. Barbara Lynch at the Navy Department Library and Mary Rosenfeld in the Smithsonian Rare Book Library were also particularly helpful.

Typing the manuscript fell to Mary Palmer and to Linda Braemer who helped me out at the last minute to get the manuscript to the publisher on time.

As any author knows, a book is all-consuming and family life suffers. My wife, Toby, combined just the right amount of help, encouragement, and threat to keep the project moving along. The entire family helped with the final rush to press including my children, Michael and Molly, who duplicated and assembled the hundreds of captions, pictures and text.

OSCAR P. FITZGERALD
Alexandria, Virginia

CREDITS

The author would like to thank the following photographers for their contributions:

Joseph Bomar:
Figures II-8, II-9, II-15, II-19, III-2, III-4, III-22, III-25, III-31, III-35, III-37, IV-9, IV-10, IV-15, IV-16, IV-18, IV-19, IV-20, IV-21, IV-27, IV-28, IV-29, IV-33, IV-34, IV-36, IV-37, IV-39, IV-53, IV-54, IV-55, IV-56, IV-57, IV-58, IV-59, IV-61, IV-63, IV-70, V-4, V-7, V-13, V-15, V-20, V-48, VI-8, VI-10, VI-25, VI-26, VI-29, VI-32, VI-33, VI-34, VI-39, VI-41, VI-43, VII-8, VII-9, VII-11, VII-12, VII-16, VIII-18, VIII-29, IX-7, IX-20, IX-29, IX-31, IX-32, IX-33, IX-34, IX-35, IX-38, X-6, X-7, X-8, X-9, X-15, X-17, X-22, X-23, X-24, XI-7, XI-19, XI-20, XI-21, XI-33, XII-1, XII-3, XII-6, XII-7, XII-9, XII-16, XII-33, XII-34, XII-36, XII-37, XII-39, XII-40, XII-41, XIII-3, XIII-4, XIII-5, XIII-8 through XIII-27, color photo of Heurich Mansion.

Israel Sack, Inc.:
Figures II-3, II-7, II-13, II-14, II-23, III-11, III-19, III-21, III-29, IV-40, IV-51, V-1, V-19, V-27, VII-5, VII-6, VII-13, VII-14, VII-28.

Richard Cheek:
Figures I-8, II-10, II-16, III-9, III-10, III-12, III-17, III-18, IV-38, IV-46.

Joe Kindig III:
Figures III-15, IV-2, IV-8, IV-49, IV-65, V-38, V-43, IX-4.

Marvin Rand:
Figures XII-43, XII-44, XII-45, all copyright © 1980 by Marvin Rand.

J. David Bohl:
Figure I-13.

Bernard and S. Dean Levy:
Figure IV-25.

Harvey Patteson:
Figures VIII-60, VIII-61.

Ewing Waterhouse:
Figures VIII-62, VIII-63.

FOREWORD

A GOOD CAPSULE HISTORY OF American furniture has been needed for a long time. A rich and complex tale of dramatic change against a backdrop of impressive continuity, this story has been told only piecemeal, up until now; various periods, those covered in the earlier chapters in particular, have been written about before and written about well, but few books have attempted to capture the whole sweep of the story. Now Oscar Fitzgerald has made a significant attempt to present a comprehensive view of nearly three centuries of furniture in America.

Pictorially rich, yet verbally succinct, Fitzgerald's work should appeal to readers looking for that single volume to introduce them to the major design alternatives of three centuries of American furniture production. Drawing on an immense range of literature and the expertise of many, Fitzgerald has fashioned a readable and straightforward account charting the general contours of furniture in this country from the time of the early English settlers in the 17th century to the beginnings of modernism in the early years of the 20th. Fitzgerald has taken a long look and shared the most salient episodes with us. He has given us the gist of a lengthy and involved story without getting lost in the details. This is what a survey ought to do, and this one does it well.

A survey possesses distinct advantages over more intensive studies of shorter periods or narrower topics. The long view of the survey makes it easier to see dimensions that might be less obvious in a smaller sample; continuities and changes both become more pronounced. A detailed examination of a single style helps us see and appreciate its subtleties and nuances but may do little toward giving us a sense of its position in the stream of history, of its relationship to forms that precede and follow it.

A survey helps us understand that objects and styles are not created in a vacuum. Designers feed on the history of their trade; they work from what they know, from the ideas, forms, patterns, and models within their physical and intellectual reach. Most of what is available to them at any time is from the past, both recent and distant. The better we understand the whole sweep of furniture history, the better we can comprehend the varied and sometimes subtle ways furniture designers of every period have drawn upon the accomplishments of their predecessors.

Fitzgerald's text helps bring us closer to this comprehension. It helps us see that much of the explanation for an object's appearance lies in its history, in its place in a historical sequence. Oscar Fitzgerald's long view makes these sequences more apparent and helps us date individual examples of furniture chosen from the parade of possible historical pieces.

Oscar Fitzgerald's briskly paced survey illustrates a small but significant portion of the vast range of furniture options that have been available in this country over three centuries. We get a fuller sense of the design diversity that is part of the American past and a strong reminder that in furniture, as in so many other kinds of objects, ideas about how things ought to look have changed markedly over time. Sometimes they have changed slowly, as with Shaker and some folk furniture, and sometimes they have changed rapidly, but they have changed. When we leaf through the illustrations in this book, the cumulative effect of three centuries of different ideas becomes a compelling testimony to the powers of the human imagination.

It is important to remember that schools of furniture making have not always coexisted peacefully. Highly distinctive styles were sometimes designed against or in opposition to another. An important part of selling one style has often been the condemnation of another. We can say, then, that not only does this survey record three centuries of changing forms but also three centuries of changing tastes, meanings, and evaluations.

Oscar Fitzgerald's decision to bring his survey through the 19th century and into the early 20th is itself a reflection of changing meanings and of the continuing process of reevaluating the past. While there are still a few holdouts who think that only 18th century and Federal style furniture really matter, their number is small. Many more people find later furniture fascinating and are willing to pay considerable prices to own it. Any increase in the economic value of a category of goods usually accompanies and generates renewed respect for and interest in those goods. The range of furniture now viewed as a significant and valuable part of the American past has expanded greatly in recent years, a fact mirrored by Fitzgerald's text.

The extraordinary diversity of forms presented here should teach us caution or at least charity in evaluating design. Virtually all of the furniture in this book was originally owned by normal, competent individuals. Yet what a remarkable range of forms and shapes it represents. At various times in the past most of it was viewed as ugly, odd, or at least inconsequential. When, with Fitzgerald's guidance, we survey this sequence of conflicting alternatives, we can see that they all made sense, they all were appropriate in their time. Fitzgerald deserves credit for resisting facile condemnation of any of the objects he presents. Instead, he shares with us objects characteristic of many ages. From this progression of different and opposing formal ideas, all considered correct, all considered tasteful by someone at one time, comes the valuable lesson of the relativity of taste.

One last point not developed in Fitzgerald's text but suggested by the material he presents is that furniture is not merely utilitarian function decorated but often part of a social strategy. Put another way, a chair is more than something to sit on; it may also be a tool to express, convey, or enforce certain attitudes, values, or behaviors. I am not criticizing Fitzgerald for not developing this argument more fully since it is really beyond the scope of the book. However, readers should remember that furniture is part of an intricate and elaborate system of nonverbal communication and that the decorative details embellishing any given piece are units of meaning that conveyed something intelligible when those objects were new. It is also fair to remind readers that furniture may sometimes be part of a broader ideology or social campaign. Fitzgerald reminds us of this when he discusses Eastlake, Shaker, and Arts and Crafts furniture. These are among the most obvious examples. Other styles of furniture also have been products of and expressions of specific attitudes and values which, while not stated in well-articulated position papers, were very real nonetheless. Readers should keep this in mind as they peruse Fitzgerald's text, perhaps asking themselves what sort of attitudes and values different historical styles seem to endorse.

Oscar Fitzgerald's book suggests many other lines of thought. I mean this as an endorsement of the book and its approach. For while on one hand it is a tidy, compact survey of a topic, on the other hand it represents a rich collection of stimulating and suggestive artifacts that raise many questions reaching far beyond these pages to the basic conditions of American life.

This book is also an invitation. On one level it is an invitation to learn more about another aspect of human creativity, another aspect of life in the past. On another level it is an invitation to see, to think and to understand. Either way, it is an invitation well worth accepting.

KENNETH L. AMES
Winterthur Museum

I

THE JACOBEAN PERIOD:
JOINERS AND CABINETMAKERS
IN THE NEW WORLD

THE JACOBEAN STYLE, WHICH TAKES its name from Jacobus (the Latin name for James I), who ruled England from 1603 to 1625, was at the height of popularity in the American colonies between 1650 and 1690. The dates are only approximations, since furniture design changed slowly and numerous pieces with Jacobean characteristics were made after 1690. Nevertheless, by the last decade of the century the most fashion-conscious patrons in the largest cities of New England were demanding a new style that has come to be called William and Mary. Terms such as this were unknown until the late 19th century when writers conjured them up in an attempt to distinguish among the various styles of the 17th and 18th centuries. Our ancestors simply ordered furniture built in the "newest" manner, as distinguished from the "old" style.

No documented American furniture has survived from the period prior to the 1640s. The earliest settlers in the Massachusetts Bay Colony were forced to "burrow themselves in the Earth for their first shelter under some Hill-side, casting the Earth aloft upon Timbers,"[1] and conditions were little better in the Virginia colony. The Pilgrims brought with them a few pieces of furniture, such as chests, but mostly they brought tools, seeds, clothes, and other essentials that would not be available in the new land. A carpenter, who could have fashioned furniture, came with the first band of settlers in New England, but his skills were more in demand for building shelters. Much of the furniture of this early period would have resembled the crude benches and tables made from felled logs and similar to ones reproduced at the reconstructed

settlements of Jamestown and Plymouth. The dirt floors, wattle and daub walls and chimneys, and thatched roofs of the one- and two-room houses that began to rise in the wilderness matched this furniture quite well. In short, during the first generation of life in America the colonists were too busy building crude shelters, raising subsistence crops, defending against the Indians, and looking after the necessities of life to spend much time on stylish furniture. What little fine furniture might have been produced has not survived long years of hard use, fire, and other calamities.

By 1640 England had established seven successful colonies on the North American continent. Virginia was the largest, with 15,000 inhabitants living on agricultural plantations and small settlements scattered throughout the Tidewater. The

---

3

more urban colony of Massachusetts was a close second, with 14,000 inhabitants who, together with 3,000 in the Plymouth Colony, depended primarily on a mercantile economy. Tiny Rhode Island had only about 300 settlers, all of Maryland had 2,000, and the Connecticut and New Haven colonies had about 2,000. New England merchants were amassing fortunes by exploiting the riches of the new land—such as fish, timber, and furs through naval stores—all free for the taking from the most bounteous continent on earth. In the South, the cultivation of sugar and tobacco brought wealth to the planters settling there. Ships carried these goods to England and on return voyages brought the manufactured necessities and, increasingly, luxury goods, such as furniture, cloth, and fancy clothes.

Since the majority of the settlers in America came from Great Britain, the English culture was the dominant force in the emerging American culture. During the troubled reign of Charles I, from 1625 to 1649, nearly 30,000 Puritans immigrated to America, where they were free to practice their religion. But part of the uniqueness of the American culture was due to an infusion of other cultures as well. During the reign of Charles II, from 1660 to 1685, immigration to America by peoples from all over Europe was encouraged. Swedes and Finns settled in what is now Delaware. The Dutch and Flemish began to build New York City and pushed on up the Hudson River Valley. French Huguenots came to Virginia and the Carolinas along with Englishmen, and a few of all these nationalities turned up in the predominantly Puritan colonies of Massachusetts and Connecticut. The Dutch culture remained strong in New York, but the spread of its influence was curtailed after Peter Stuyvesant surrendered the settlement to an English fleet in 1664.

ARCHITECTURE

As the colonists began to amass some wealth by the middle of the 17th century and could support a small furniture-making trade, the old furniture from a difficult time was quickly discarded. In 1642 Edward Johnson, a joiner, wrote that "the Lord hath been pleased to turn all the wigwams, huts, and hovels the English dwelt in at their first coming, into orderly, fair, and well-built houses, well-furnished many of them...."[2] William Harris, an Englishman who visited Boston in the 1670s, wrote that "the merchants seem to be rich men, and their houses as handsomely furnished as most in England."[3]

By mid-century, the most common house was two rooms and a loft, but many people could afford a four-room, two-story structure built around a central stone fireplace, which had replaced the hazardous wattle and daub ones. Shingles or slate roofs began to replace thatch, and small diamond-shaped glass panes covered the windows, which earlier were sealed with oiled cloth or paper. More common than brick or stone, at least in New England, was the massive frame construction using exposed hand-hewn wooden posts and beams joined with mortise and tenon joints and pegged with treenails, which echoed the construction of the furniture. The overhang of the second story of many houses of the 17th century was similar to the curious overhanging upper section of cupboards ornamented with pendants (Figure I–1).

The finest New England dwellings had a parlor, or best room, where most of the finest furniture was displayed for use on special occasions and for entertaining guests. A hall, equivalent to our modern family room, contained the kitchen and was used also as a work area, dining room, and bedroom for the master and his wife. A buttery or

pantry plus one or two additional bedrooms, filled with beds in dormitory fashion, completed the house, which might shelter as many as 10 or 12 people.

THE 17TH-CENTURY FURNITURE TRADE

Between 1640 and 1650, the earliest documented piece of American furniture was made—a chest attributed to Thomas Mulliner, a joiner who worked in the New Haven Colony from 1639 to at least the 1650s. Until the end of the 17th century, the craftsman who made furniture was a joiner, not a cabinetmaker. In England, the first mention of a cabinetmaker was in 1625, when one marched in the funeral of James I, but cabinetmakers did not appear in America until the end of the century. The joiner produced furniture by joining pieces of wood together. Thus the joiner made the sides of a chest or the door of a cupboard by joining four pieces of wood together to form a frame and then fitting the frame around a panel of wood that was set into a groove cut into the edge of the frame. This method of construction had the advantage of allowing the wood to expand and contract as it absorbed and gave off moisture from the air. The joiner usually used the mortise and tenon joint to bond the wood. A projecting tongue or tenon, cut on the end of one member, fit snugly into a rectangular hole or mortise cut into the other member. The joint would then be secured with a peg (Figure I–2). Although early in the 17th century glue was used to secure the joint, the peg continued to be employed as a matter of custom.

In America, techniques of cabinetmaking appeared in the 1680s. The cabinetmaker constructed sides of chests with solid boards that were secured by dovetail joints at the top and the bottom (Figure I–3). The dovetail, like most other wood-working techniques, dates back to ancient Egypt and can be seen, for example, on boxes from the tomb of King Tutankhamen. The cabinetmaker also used veneering, which was not common in England until the early 17th century. This technique involved gluing beautifully grained woods, often either with matched figures or cut into geometric designs, to the surfaces of a coarser wood. Furthermore, they worked with sawn boards, which were a more efficient use of wood than the joiner's use of riven wood. Riven wood was split from a log in a pie-shaped slice using a mallet and froe. To obtain a fairly flat piece of wood, the craftsman had to discard the thin and thick ends. The disappearance of cheap, abundant wood in England at the end of the 17th century was a major factor in the eclipse of the joiner and the rise of the cabinetmaker who used mill-sawed wood. Mill-sawed boards, usually not oak, but the softer, more easily cut sycamore or pine, appeared in New England furniture by the 1670s and were common by the 1690s.

In the 17th century colonial carpenters also, on occasion, made furniture where demand for it was often greater than a small number of skilled joiners could supply. In 1661, Richard Jacob of Ipswich contracted with William Averell, Jr., to build a house and "allso to make a table and frame of 12 to 14 foot Long and joyned forme and a binch Behind the table."[4] However, it was only the joiner who possessed the superior skills for making more elaborate and finer furniture, such as chests and cupboards, but even joiners would do whatever work was available, which often included carpentry, coffin-making, and farming.

In addition to carpenters and joiners who made furniture, there were turners who specialized in operating a lathe or device for turning wood so that by

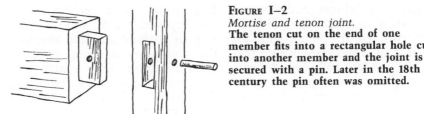

FIGURE I–2
Mortise and tenon joint.
The tenon cut on the end of one member fits into a rectangular hole cut into another member and the joint is secured with a pin. Later in the 18th century the pin often was omitted.

FIGURE I–3
Dovetail joint on drawer.

applying gauges and chisels the wood could be rounded and formed into myriad shapes, such as balls, rings, vases, and columns. By the end of the 17th century, these craftsmen made mostly seating furniture and were known primarily as chairmakers. Turners also made dishes, bowls, and tool handles and spent much of their time repairing broken chairs. They may even have made the applied spindle ornaments for chests or cupboards, which were often superior to the joinery used to construct the rest of the piece.

In medieval England, the functions of these trades were defined by craft guilds, which were established soon after the rise of the cities. Through the guild, which operated the apprentice system, designs and techniques were passed down from one generation to another. These organizations, representing master, journeyman, and apprentice alike, controlled the access to the trade in order to limit competition, regulate prices, and ensure quality workmanship. Except for the shortlived attempts of the cordwainers and coopers of Boston to establish guilds in 1648, the guild system did not flourish in America. For one reason, by the late 16th century, the guild system was beginning to break down even in England because the increased demand for low-priced goods grew beyond their control. For another, fewer than 10 percent of the settlers in the first half of the 17th century in New England came from London, where the guild system was strongest. The rest came from rural areas, such as Suffolk, where the guild system was not strong.

Although the guild system was not adopted in 17th-century America, the custom of apprenticeship was. In 1660, the city fathers of Boston lamented the lack of sufficient training of apprentices in the city and declared that "Itt is therefore ordered that no person shal henceforth open a shop in this Towne, nor occupy any manufacture or science, till hee hath compleated 21 years of age, nor except hee hath served seven years Apprentice-ship...."[5] The age requirements were in accordance with 17th-century rural English practice, as was the regulation of apprenticeship by the city rather than by the guild. However, in labor-short New England, even these regulations were often ignored. Nevertheless, in abbreviated form, apprenticeship was the primary means of transmitting woodworking skills and designs from one generation to another.

Just as the apprentice system in America was derived from English models, so too was the choice of wood for 17th-century furniture. The earliest furniture-makers selected oak, which had been the stylish and traditional furniture wood in England for centuries. Of the two most common varieties, red oak and white oak, the 17th-century American furniture-maker preferred the red because its long, knot-free trunk and less dense wood made it easier to work than the white oak. Red oak was never used in English furniture of the 17th century because it was not native to England and had acquired the reputation of being unsuitable for shipbuilding—which was the main reason for exporting the boards to England. It proved unsuitable because, unlike white oak, it did not swell to seal the joints when exposed to water. Thus, by microscopic analysis of the wood, it is possible to determine the provenance of a piece of 17th-century furniture. Indeed, because of the similarity of designs and techniques used by the recently arriving woodworkers from England, wood analysis is often the only definitive way of determining on which side of the Atlantic a piece of furniture was made.

THE FURNITURE

Thus, most of the furniture listed in the 1678 probate inventory of the estate of Peter Hobart, a well-to-do minister in Hingham, Massachusetts, was probably of oak. In the parlor, he had one bedstead "and all things thereto belonging," including curtains, valances, sheets, bolsters, pillows, mattresses, and coverlets, plus a table, a cupboard, two chairs, and four joint stools. The hall, which also served as the kitchen, contained a settle, two small tables, a small form (bench), two joint stools, and seven chairs, probably arranged against the wall. The bedchamber over the parlor contained a bedstead, a cupboard and cloth, two joined chests, a joined table, four joint stools, two chairs, a close stool and pan, and a looking glass. The hall chamber held a third bed, a table, a joint stool, and another looking glass. The garret contained one old featherbed and an old trundle bed.

Beds with their hangings and other accouterments were the most expensive and elaborate items in a colonial household. Most of the value was in the expensive hangings and the mattress; the bedstead or frame had only a relatively low value. This,

FIGURE I-4
Joint stool. Oak. New England. Ca. 1640–1680.
The heavy stretchers and legs with ball turnings are often considered an early feature, but that rule is not always reliable. Often sold in sets, the stool was one of the most common pieces of furniture found in the 17th-century home. Many 17th-century stools stood 23 or 24 inches high compared to the common 16- to 18-inch seat height for chairs. The additional height matched the extra height of dining tables in this period.
Smithsonian Institution Photo No. 42172.

along with the fact that many beds were built in, may explain why no American bedsteads have survived from the 17th century.

Chairs

Seating furniture, however, was made in such abundance that it is the most common survivor. Until the mid-17th century, the colonists had only a few chairs with backs; they sat, instead, on stools or benches, which were sometimes called forms. The turned stool, similar to five mentioned in 1676 in the kitchen of Thomas Hanley of Roxbury, Massachusetts, was usually made by a joiner—hence the name joined or "joint" stool (Figure I–4). Chairs with arms were less common. These chairs were throne-like in appearance and were used by the head of the family or were offered to an honored guest. The family would sit around the table, which may have been a board thrown across a trestle—hence the expression, "chairman of the board" for the most important person in a group. Simple joined tables, however, were much more common.

Of the three principal chair types in the 17th century—turned, wainscot, and Cromwell—the turned ones were the most common. These were turned on a lathe and were either armchairs, called "great" or "elboe" chairs in the inventories, or straight-backed chairs with rush seats. Modern writers refer to turned chairs as either Carver or Brewster types, named after chairs owned by early leaders of the Massachusetts colony. The Carver type has fewer spindles, with none under the arms or seat (Figure I–5). The few Brewster chairs that exist have double rows of spindles on the back and spindles under the arms and seat (Figure I–6). A third type of chair made by turners had more comfortable horizontal slats instead of vertical spindles across the back, a form that originated in Germany and the Netherlands (Figure I–7).

FIGURE I–5
Armchair. Maple. Chesapeake Bay area. Ca. 1690.
This turned chair is similar to New England examples from the 17th century. However, arms on Southern examples such as this one often extend over the front posts rather than over the front rails rising above the arms, as on New England chairs. The space between the seat and the spindles allows for a cushion. The splint seat is not original. Such seats usually lasted no more than a couple of decades.
Courtesy, Museum of Early Southern Decorative Arts, Winston-Salem.

FIGURE I–6 *(below, left)*
Armchair. Hickory and ash. Massachusetts. Ca. 1650–1690.
Largely because of Wallace Nutting's belief that heavier was earlier, this chair is often dated from the mid-17th century. However, documented examples of heavier turnings were made as late as the end of the century. The crisp turnings on this so-called "Brewster" chair indicate a turner with a high degree of skill. A plumper cushion would have enriched the chair in the 17th century. The knobs on the front posts are 20th-century replacements.
The Metropolitan Museum of Art, Gift of Mrs. J. Insley Blair, 1951.

FIGURE I–7 *(below)*
Armchair. Oak. Massachusetts. Dated 1691.
The date, 1691, and the initials "J P," for John Pickard, appear on the back of this chair made in Rowley, Massachusetts, about 30 miles north of Boston. The splint seat is a replacement, and the feet have lost an inch or more of height through years of scraping across the floor. Some floors had a stylish sand covering.
Smithsonian Institution Photo No. 46935J.

These chairs, made throughout the 17th, 18th, and 19th centuries, exhibited progressive simplification of the turnings. Descendents of these slat- or ladder-back chairs were made in the Appalachian region of America into the 20th century. Turners selected a combination of woods for the chair, such as ash for the posts; hickory for the arms; and hickory, ash, or birch for the spindles.

FIGURE I–8
Wainscot chair. Oak. Ipswich, Mass. Ca. 1665–1700.
This chair, one of the finest examples from the 17th century, was made by Williams Searle or Thomas Dennis, who married Searle's widow in 1668. The carving and form of this chair and a similar one in the Essex Institute recall examples in Devonshire, England, where Searle grew up and was probably trained. A sophisticated series of S-curves ornament the skirt and frame the paneled back on which is a vase holding stylized flowers. The primitive figures with elongated chins on either side of the back rarely appear on American 17th-century work, although the motif is more common in England.
Bowdoin College Museum of Art, Brunswick, Maine.

Wainscot chairs, made with plank seats and solid backs and fitted with a cushion, take their name from the designation for the large, oaken boards of fine grade exported to England from northern Europe. They were more expensive and much rarer than the turned chairs because of the elaborate carving that usually adorned the paneled boards making up the back of the chair (Figure I–8).

By the end of the 17th century, sets of upholstered side chairs, called backstools, were found in homes of prosperous merchants and other wealthy colonists. Fewer upholstered arm chairs were made, and only one example is known today. Since the late 19th century these chairs have been called Cromwell chairs (Figure I–9). Popular throughout Europe in the 17th century, they actually predated Oliver Cromwell's Commonwealth in England, which began in 1654. The chairs, usually made of maple and oak with ball-turned legs and stretchers, had upholstered backs and seats instead of the wooden ones on wainscot chairs. Occasionally spiral shaping was substituted for ball-turnings on New York and New Jersey chairs. Although the lathe could be used to rough in the design, a rasp or file was necessary to finish the work, a laborious and time-consuming procedure. This costly embellishment, which came to England by way of Holland, was more common in Europe than America, where labor was scarce and expensive.

Usually the chairs were upholstered in Russian leather, which was the name given to leather tanned with birch oil, rather than tannin or oak bark. A scored effect was left on the leather by a cleaverlike tool that broke the surface and allowed the oil to penetrate.[6] For an even greater show of elegance, a wealthy merchant might purchase "turkeywork" chairs that were upholstered with brightly woven cloth, the designs inspired by Near Eastern carpets but made under the cottage industry system in England, and on a limited scale in America. Brass nails on the frame and velvet, silk, and other brightly colored cloth with gold or silver fringe were also used to brighten the otherwise drab interior of many early American homes.

Chests

The chest, which dates from classical times, was an important piece of furniture in the sparsely furnished homes of the Middle Ages. London in the 17th century was still a medieval town, and the rural areas were also dominated by the ideas of the Middle Ages. When the settlers came to the New World, they tried, as much as possible, to surround themselves with familiar things. Since closets were not common until the beginning of the 19th century, the chest was essential for the storage of valuables, such as silver and money, as well as for clothing, linens, and woolens. Chests were also used as places to sit and as tables.

Medieval chests were elaborately painted, carved, and paneled, and this style was in use during the first hundred years of the settlements in America. These chests were made by

FIGURE I–9
Armchair. Oak and maple. Boston. Ca. 1660–1670.
The so-called Cromwell, or upholstered, back stool from the 17th century was fairly common among wealthy New Englanders, but this upholstered arm, or "Great," chair is the only known surviving American example. The high front stretcher first appeared on English chairs about 1660. A bulging, down-filled cushion, properly fitted with tassels, as on this chair, fills the gaping space between the seat and the bottom of the upholstered back. Bright brass tacks finish off the original "Russhia" leather upholstery. A red or brown stain covered up the use of two different woods for the front and side posts and stretchers.
Courtesy Museum of Fine Arts, Boston.

FIGURE I–10
Chest. Oak with pine. Massachusetts. Ca. 1680–1710.
This chest was probably made in Springfield for Priscella Warner whose initials appear on the front of the chest. The stylized vines, leaves, and tulips are typical of chests today called Hadley types. The scratch carved squiggles are also common, but the heart found above the initials is unusual. These chests were typically painted but only traces of the original paint remain on this example. The frequent appearance of initials indicates that these chests were made as hope or occasionally as wedding chests.
Courtesy, The Henry Francis du Pont Winterthur Museum.

joiners who framed panels of wood, usually oak, for sides and used pine for top and bottom boards. Occasionally even the lid was paneled, although this practice was more common in England where there was a scarcity of the wide boards found in abundance in the virgin forests of America. The chest often had one, two, or sometimes three drawers that ran on side runners and were fitted with wooden knob pulls. Drawers were usually nailed together, except in Boston, where the dovetail joint was commonly used. Most of the joiners who settled in Boston had been trained in London, where the dovetail joint was well known.[7] The bottom boards on Masschusetts chests usually ran front to back and were joined to each other with several types of joints—tongue and groove being the most common. These bottoms were simply nailed to the drawer edges. In Connecticut, they ran from side to side and were set into rabbets.

The most popular decoration on the earliest chests was shallow relief carving, which was highlighted most often with red, blue, white, black, brown, or green paint. The colonists were accustomed to bright colors, which were found in their tex-tiles and throughout their houses as well as on their furniture. Chests, with the carving probably done by a specialist other than the joiner who made the chest, were of three major types. The most elaborately carved chests, first discovered in the Hadley area of Massachusetts, hence the modern name Hadley chest, were made in a fifty-mile stretch of the Connecticut Valley from Hartford to Deerfield. Joiners used a template to create a double-petaled tulip design growing from a stem with leaves and adorned with incised scrolls (Fig. I–10). Over 120 of these chests, many with carved dates of manufacture and the initials of original owners, have survived. Another group of chests with less elaborate carving from the Wethersfield area of southern Connecticut are inaccurately called sunflower chests (Figure I–11). Actually joiners used a compass to lay out stylized English Tudor roses and tulips.[8] A third group of chests from the coastal Connecticut towns of Guilford and Saybrook featured painted decorations with tulips, thistles, urns, flowers, and roses—all based on stylized designs of Dutch and English origin. All of these designs had English prototypes, al-

FIGURE I–11

Chest. Oak with yellow pine. Wethersfield, Conn. Ca. 1680–1705.
The so-called sunflower chest with tulips is attributed to Peter Blin, who worked in Wethersfield, just outside of Hartford, in the late 17th and the early 18th century. Tulip and vine carving was popular in the northern counties of England east of Liverpool, and the sunflower, possibly a Tudor rose, has turned up in Sussex county, south of London. The two-drawer chest, however, is rarely found in England, where the chest of drawers was more popular. Stripping has left only raw wood where old paint once enhanced the carved and paneled facade. The lid has been replaced, and the feet have been pierced out.
Smithsonian Institution Photo No. 54484.

though the makers of Hadley chests seemed to have drawn on Wethersfield and Hatfield for their inspiration. The Guilford and Saybrook chests were decorated with designs similar to inlaid decorations seen on the backs of some English wainscot chairs that, in turn, were inspired by familiar textile designs, printer's devices, or other English sources (Figure I–12).

FIGURE I–12

Chest of drawers. Tulip and oak. Saybrook or Guilford, Conn. Ca. 1690–1720.
Tulips, roses, thistles, crowns, and fleur-de-lis characterize the decoration on a small group of case pieces made in towns along the Connecticut coast. The possible sources for these designs include the royal British coat of arms, 17th-century printer's book decorations, textiles, "turkey" carpets, and actual rural English furniture with similar decoration. Whatever the source, the design, painted in yellow, red, pink, and white on a black ground over red primer, was given a distinctively American flair with the addition of birds, vases, and vines. Charles Gillam of Saybrook has been identified as one of several possible decorators of this group of chests.
Courtesy Wadsworth Atheneum, Hartford, Conn.

By the 1660s, carving was still being employed, but with the Puritan austerity imposed on life by Cromwell's rule, more restrained applied decorations had become popular. These were in the shapes of lozenges, diamonds, Norman nailheads, triglyphs, and turned balusters. These last are today commonly called split spindles, but the term is misleading because they are turned as two separate pieces of wood, then glued together and split apart after working, with the result a symmetrical half-turning (Figure I–13). The use of applied ornaments was introduced to Europe by the Moors, who maintained a foothold in Spain until the end of the 15th century. Dutch and Flemish furniture imported to England in the 1650s stimulated an interest in the technique. Late in the 17th century, inlaid woods accentuated the effect of applied geometric moldings on a few pieces of American furniture. The 17th-century penchant for elaborate ornamentation was part of the Mannerist aesthetic, which demanded that every inch of a surface be decorated. This idea contrasted with classical principles of design that were more evident in the 18th century, when the relationships between the decorated parts and the transitions from one element to another were more important.

The chest continued to be made into the 18th century, and the interesting group of painted floral chests of the Taunton, Massachusetts, area carried on the tradition of decorated chests until the 1740s. The well-known Pennyslvania German painted chests continued the same traditions into the 19th century. But by 1700, the chest was gradually being replaced by the more stylish and practical chest of drawers (Figure I–14). Although inventories show chests of drawers as early as the mid-17th century, no American ones have survived from this early date despite the fact that they were often valued more highly than the elaborate press and court cupboards.

FIGURE I–13 *(above)*
Chest. Red oak, walnut, cedar, and white pine. Boston area. Ca. 1640–1670.
The applied spindles and moldings that enrich the facade of this chest reflect Dutch influence. These decorations were found on English furniture as early as the beginning of the 17th century, although carved ornamentation was more popular until the middle of the century. The layout of the applied spindles, triglyphs, octagon, circle, and other geometric forms is strikingly similar to the ornamentation of a chest with drawers found in Wiltshire, England. The triglyphs above the applied spindles appear on classical Doric friezes. The stiles of this chest probably extended several more inches to form feet for the chest.
Society for the Preservation of New England Antiquities.

FIGURE I–14 *(below)*
Chest over drawers. Oak with pine. Hadley area of Massachusetts. Ca. 1695–1720.
Using a compass and straight edge, the decorator of this chest has created a profusion of geometric and floral ornaments in blue, red, and black on a white background that has yellowed with age. The segmented circles suggest the carved sunflowers or Tudor roses of earlier Connecticut Valley chests. The drawers are constructed with one large dovetail joint on each side, and the drawer runs on a side runner. S. W. are probably the initials of the original owner.
The Sheldon Collection, Memorial Hall, Deerfield, Mass.

Boxes and Desks

Boxes, often elaborately
carved, served as storage containers, as did chests, but they
were smaller and were made
without legs to sit on tables or
chests (Figure I–15). These containers are today erroneously
called Bible boxes even though
inventories indicate that deeds,
letters, and other papers, rather
than Bibles, were kept in them.
The small portable box was a
convenient container for valuables, since it could be snatched
up quickly should the house
catch on fire, a not uncommon
occurrence in the 17th century.
Since medieval times, boxes
with sloping lids to support
books or papers for reading were
called desks. Late in the century,
these desks were at times placed
on frames made especially for
them, as indicated by the 1672
inventory of William Whit-
tingham, a Boston merchant,
which lists, "In the parlor
Chamber, 2 Standers & a desk
with a fframe. . . ."⁹ A new type
of desk in use by 1670 was mentioned in the inventory of
Nathan Rainsford, another
Boston merchant. A portion of
his inventory reads, "In ye porch
Chamber, 1 desk & some. de-
vinity books and some knives
and one scredoar. . . ."¹⁰ The
"scredoar," or scrutoire, was a
slant-front desk with drawers below, which came to England
from the Continent, but was
quite rare until the beginning of
the 18th century. The term
"desk" was also applied to the
new form in some inventories
but the French terms scrutoire,
or bureau, were more popular
until the 18th century.

Tables

Tables were less common
than chests in the 17th century,
although each home usually had
at least one. The earliest ones
were similar to the "Great table
bord" owned by Alice Jones in
1642 (Figure I–16). The practice
of resting a board on a trestle to
form a table dated from medieval times. By the 17th century
in England, this practice was
considered outdated, and there
are only a few references to such
pieces in American inventories.
The trestle table was replaced by
such forms as round, oval,
square, and drawing tables. The
latter was made to extend by
drawing out leaves, which were
pushed under the tabletop when
not in use. Only a few examples
of this form have been found in
17th-century inventories, and no
American examples have survived to the present. The chair-
table, whose top tipped up to
form a chair when not in use as
a table, dates also from the Middle Ages, when furniture was
portable and collapsible. A lord
and lady were expected to bring
their own furniture with them
when visiting the neighboring
manor. Such furniture also had
the virtue of saving space in the
cramped and overcrowded
houses of 17th-century America.
As a symbol of the Colonial Period, the chair-table was reproduced frequently in the 19th
century (Figure I–17). Tables in
the best houses were sometimes
adorned with Turkey carpets, a
very expensive luxury that
would never have been used on
the floor. By the end of the century, gateleg tables were coming
into use, but the earliest ones

FIGURE I–17
Chair table. White oak and pine. American. Ca. 1670–1690.
This piece has a rectangular top, but round ones were probably more common. The ogee scalloping on the bottom of the stretchers is repeated on the brace attached to the underside of the top. A drawer provides extra storage space under the seat. The ball feet have been worn down considerably from over 300 years of sliding across floors. Uncomfortable as a chair and inadequate as a table, the chair table appears in only a few 17th-century inventories, and even fewer examples have survived to the present. More of them seem to have been made since the 19th-century Colonial revival craze than in the 17th century.
The Metropolitan Museum of Art, Gift of Mrs. Russell Sage, 1909.

FIGURE I–18
Table. Black walnut with oak. Pennsylvania. Ca. 1675–1710.
Now called a gateleg table this form was variously referred to as a folding table or table leaf. This example has unusually heavy turnings even for the Middle Colonies, where heavier turnings were more common, in comparison to New England examples of the same period. Having a Chester County history, this table may be one of the earliest pieces surviving from Pennsylvania. The heavy stretchers, much stronger than necessary to support the table, echo the heavy exposed beams found in homes of this period. The hearts at the top of each leg are a common motif on Pennsylvania German painted furniture and may indicate the maker's Germanic background. The feet have lost several inches of height due to wear.
Courtesy, The Henry Francis du Pont Winterthur Museum.

still had the massive turnings and stretchers that echoed the huge, exposed beams and posts on the ceilings and walls of 17th-century houses (Figure I–18). Tables were made with legs as much as three and a half inches thick. Another type of table with or without a drawer, now called a tavern table, had no special designation in 17th-century inventories.

Cupboards

Although chairs, chests, and tables were necessities, the elaborate cupboards that graced the best rooms of many colonists by the middle of the 17th century were indeed luxuries intended to impress neighbors and to help perpetuate the status of their owners. Cupboards were made with or without drawers below

FIGURE I–19

Cupboard. Oak and maple. Plymouth County, Mass. Ca. 1670–1690.
Cupboards, such as this one with a drawer-filled bottom section, are today referred to as press cupboards. In 17th-century New England, however, the term press may have been used to describe cupboards with either open or closed lower sections. The applied moldings and turnings reveal the Dutch influence seen in English furniture after the mid-17th century. Several similarly ornamented cupboards with the saw-tooth moldings between the drawers and on the cornice have Plymouth histories.

Courtesy, The Henry Francis du Pont Winterthur Museum.

an enclosed upper section (Figure I–1 and I–19). They were used much like the 19th-century étagère, or whatnot, to display the trappings of wealth, which might include expensive silver, glass, or faience. The cupboard that William Francklin of Boston owned when he died in 1658 was valued at 16 shillings, a considerable sum for an old piece of furniture when the average carpenter in Massachusetts during the 17th century earned little more than two shillings per day. Bright decorative cloths or cushions of velvet, wool, or damask adorned the tops of cupboards, which together with the elaborate carving, and later fielded panels (beveled boards that fit into frames), applied bosses, and applied balusters on the cupboard itself made for an impressive show of elegance. Another distinctive feature of cupboards was the mammoth turned pillars, inspired by ancient Roman candelabra, which graced either side of the upper section.

The cupboard evolved from the medieval board for the display of cups and silver plate somewhat similar to our modern-day bar. In the 16th century, the ambry, which was an enclosed cabinet for the storage of food, began to be combined with the cupboard, giving it a superstructure. Even though the cupboard now had enclosed storage space, its old role as a place to display plate continued, which explains the use of a cloth with the cupboard. Cupboards largely went out of style by the end of the 17th century, but their function survived in the 18th- and 19th-century corner cupboards, which had both an open section for display and a closed section for storage.

Cupboards and other American furniture of the 17th century clearly reflected the style of the provincial English turner and carver. But even at this early date New England furniture began to show evidence of a distinct American character in such elements as the selection of woods and decorative motifs.

However, most Americans continued to look to England as their cultural model. Elements of the new continental fashions, introduced to England by Charles II and William and Mary, soon appeared on some American furniture as well. By the end of the century lighter furniture with a pronounced verticality had replaced earlier solid pieces with static, repetitive designs in homes of wealthy Americans trying to keep pace with the new styles sweeping their mother country.

NOTES

1. Marshall B. Davidson, ed., *The American Heritage History of Colonial Antiques* (New York: American Heritage Publishing Co., Inc., 1967), p. 9.

2. Davidson, *Colonial Antiques*, p. 19.

3. Davidson, *Colonial Antiques*, p. 13.

4. Benno M. Forman, "The Seventeenth Century Case Furniture of Essex County, Massachusetts, and Its Makers" (Master's Thesis, University of Delaware, 1968), p. 29.

5. Davidson, *Colonial Antiques*, p. 94.

6. This information was provided by Benno M. Forman, who is the acknowledged authority on 17th-century American furniture.

7. John D. Morse, ed., *Country Cabinetwork and Simple City Furniture* (Charlottesville, Va.: The University Press of Virginia, 1970), p. 12.

8. John T. Kirk, *Connecticut Furniture: Seventeenth and Eighteenth Centuries* (Hartford, Conn.: Wadsworth Atheneum, 1967), p. xiii.

9. Irving W. Lyon, *The Colonial Furniture of New England* (New York: E. P. Dutton, 1977), p. 114.

10. Lyon, *Colonial Furniture*, p. 116.

II

WILLIAM AND MARY:
THE YEARS OF TRANSITION

IN A SHORT TIME, THE ENVIRONMENT of the New World was putting a stamp on the culture that the English and European immigrants brought with them to America. The abundance of native woods from the vast and virgin forests of pine, walnut, cherry, and maple were altering the colonial cabinetmaker's choice of wood and his construction techniques. Economic necessity often required shortcuts: painted surfaces were substituted for imported woods, expensive inlay, and carving. Durable, simple, and unadorned furniture was more practical for the majority of the struggling colonists. In addition to economic factors, the growing diversity of the population also contributed to a divergence of American furniture from English tradition. Even in the 17th century, America was becoming the great melting pot of the world as substantial numbers of Dutch, French, Swedish, and German settlers brought their own special customs and traditions to the New World. Although they were only a minority in England, the Quakers in Philadelphia and the Puritans in New England dominated the cultural life of their colonies in the early years.

Although these subtle influences began to result in discernible differences between furniture made in England and in the colonies, most settlers in America still thought of themselves as Englishmen. By the end of the 17th century, a generation had been born and raised in America, but even these native sons continued to look to England as their mother country intellectually, culturally, and economically. A visitor to New England about 1700 observed:

*A Gentleman from London
would almost think of himself at
home at Boston when he observes the Numbers of People,
their Houses, their Furniture,
their Tables, their Dress and
Conversation, which perhaps is
as splendid and showy, as that of
the most considerable Tradesman in London. . . . There is no
Fashion in London, but in three
or four Months is to be seen at
Boston.*[1]

CLASSICAL AND ORIENTAL INFLUENCES

By the end of the 17th century, there was a new fashion abroad in the land. In England, the late Renaissance infatuation with the classical culture of Greece and Rome had peaked in 1603 with the death of Elizabeth I. Much of the 17th-century English culture and art, including the decorative

arts, represented a reaction to the late Renaissance in its experimentation, its lack of structure and relationships, and its exoticisms. In the production of furniture, this tradition was epitomized by the elaborate 17th-century cupboards of New England. Leone Battista Alberti, who wrote an important 15th century work on the theory of art, would not have approved the design of these monumental pieces because he defined the classical principles of beauty in very different terms: "Beauty is the harmony of all the parts, in whatever subject, fitted together with such proportion and connection that nothing can be altered but for the worse."[2]

Some of the 17th-century elements of disharmony persisted into the new interpretation of Renaissance classicism, often referred to as the Baroque. Baroque was a French term denoting irregular shapes and was first used widely in the mid-19th century as a term of derision. Today, it is understood to mean a return to classical harmony and motifs but with an exuberant, plastic effect and a dynamic sense of movement. It was sometimes applied to the rococo elements of mid-18th-century furniture, although by then art and architecture as well as the decoration on furniture had become lighter and more delicate.

The changes that were sweeping art, architecture, and the decorative arts in England were the results of momentous events that ended English isolation both culturally and politically and propelled the island nation into the modern period. England began to move out of its isolation in 1660 with the death of Oliver Cromwell and the passing of the austerity of the Interregnum. With the restoration of the monarchy in that year under the fun-loving Charles II, the period of austerity in the decorative arts ended. Charles II, who had spent the preceding decade traveling around Europe, brought with him to England a taste for the latest Continental styles. His wife, Catherine of Braganza, a Portuguese, was accompanied by Portuguese craftsmen who surrounded her with the richest, most stylish furniture from her native country, which was at the height of its influence and power.

She, like all Europeans, was fascinated with the products of the Orient, where Portugal had been trading since the end of the 16th century. Catherine brought with her the first Oriental cabinets to reach England, and her bedroom at Hampton Court was furnished in the Oriental taste. As part of her dowry, she gave England the right to trade in the Oriental ports opened by Portugal. Queen Elizabeth had established the English East India Company in 1600 but it could not compete with the Spanish, Portugese, and Dutch, who were already dominating the trade with the Orient. Catherine's dowry gave the English a foothold, and only after 1660 did the company begin to prosper.

England—and indeed all of Europe—was infatuated with the flood of Oriental goods, which included porcelain, lacquer work, painted fabrics, and rich wallpaper. Tea had been imported by the East India Company before Catherine ascended the throne, but it was considered "a rank poison far-fetched and dear bought." Catherine, however, popularized the tea-drinking habit, and by the end of the century, 20,000 pounds of it were imported annually. It was savored not only by the wealthy but by the common man as well. The tea ritual spawned specialized pots, cups, kettle stands, and tables for the serving of tea and the display of tea services (Figure II–2).

ARCHITECTURE

New ideals in the decorative arts were gradually percolating down to the lesser nobility as more and more people began to ape the court of Charles II. The process was sharply accelerated by the Great Fire of London in 1666, which destroyed most of the city. When London was rebuilt, the architecture and interior decoration were dominated by Renaissance ideas of design that drew on classical principles of symmetry, formal order, and classical motifs. English interest in Renaissance architecture dates from the mid-16th century when Henry VIII and Cardinal Wolsey commissioned Italian craftsmen to work in England. But not until the beginning of the 17th century did the Renaissance concepts of architecture and indeed of philosophy, learning, art, and culture gain widespread acceptance in England. The ancient Roman architect, Vitruvius, was the source for Andrea Palladio who, in the late 16th century, published his interpretation of the classical style. English editions were published by the mid-16th century, and architects such as Inigo Jones and patrons such as Lord Burlington popularized the style in England.

Wealthy Americans copied English models in their sumptuous country homes and townhouses. By the beginning of the 18th century, many of the finest houses built in America showed this Renaissance influence, which lasted until the Revolution. The house built by the wealthy Boston merchant William Clarke illustrated the new architecture. His three-story mansion of brick had 26 rooms.

The hall divided the house as a passageway rather than serving as the center of activity as earlier. Most 17th-century houses featured boldly exposed posts and beams, but in Clarke's house, elaborate plaster work and wainscoting hid the structural members within the walls. Although doorways, windows, and fireplaces in the 17th century stood as unadorned functional units, these elements in the classical style of the 18th century became elaborate focal points adorned with classical pilaster moldings and pediments taken from designs on Roman temples. The mantels in Clarke's house were fashioned of ornately carved Italian marble, and even the floors displayed intricately inlaid wood patterns. Sash windows replaced diamond-shaped, leaded, glass panes in casement windows.

The impressive mansions dotting the countryside were the most obvious manifestation of the wealth being amassed in the colonies and the new desire for comfort that this wealth made possible. Whether the wealth was based on the plantations of Virginia or South Carolina, the privateering business of Philadelphia, or the commerce of New England, the rich spent their money on commodious homes and furnishings. Whether it was Stratford, constructed by the Lees on the Potomac; the Archibald Macpheadris's home in Portsmouth; or Stenton, erected by James Logan in Philadelphia; they all exhibited the classical Georgian principles of symmetry, balance, and formal order. The influence of the architect was felt directly in the production of furniture; the more than 40 architectural design books known in America often served as models for elements in furniture. The sheer size, coupled with the specialization of rooms in the huge mansions of the day, stimulated the production of furniture and resulted in the invention of new forms to fill the space.

THE NEW STYLE

Accompanying the changes in architectural taste was a change in furniture styles. The influences that first began to appear in the reign of Charles II culminated in the emergence of a major style change by the time of William and Mary. They were invited to take the English throne in 1688 when the tyrannical James II was forced to abdicate after trying to impose his Catholic views on a largely Anglican country. William and Mary, who had occupied the Dutch throne, brought with them many Dutch artisans and designers. Many of these craftsmen, notably Daniel Marot, who became the court designer and architect at Hampton Court, had recently fled France. When Louis XIV revoked the Edict of Nantes in 1685, which had given French Protestants the freedom to practice their religion in a predominantly Catholic country, many of these Huguenots fled to a more hospitable Holland, and some even came to America. Many of these Huguenots were craftsmen who brought with them the Baroque ideas of design—"the unrestrained decorative orgy" that the French had adopted from Italy.

The rising English landed gentry of the late 17th century could afford the new styles, which included the use of rich veneers, inlay, and finer woods—particularly the beautifully grained Virginia walnut and elaborate carving. Lighter furniture with a pronounced verticality soon replaced the solid, static designs of the early 17th century. The prosperous merchants of New England and the planters of the middle colonies imitated their English cousins. New England had an established furniture-making tradition in the Jacobean style, but the wealthy merchants of Boston—and even those of the lesser port cities and commercial centers—sought and could afford the latest London style. This style has come to be called the

FIGURE II–3
Armchair. Maple. Massachusetts. Ca. 1700–1720.
The bold arms terminating in carved ram's horns relate to chairs by the Gaines family of Portsmouth, New Hampshire. Five bannisters instead of the usual four bannisters on side chairs, along with a central drop on the stay rail, create a strong vertical movement. The turnings on the bannisters repeat the shape of the stiles above the arms and part of the turnings on the arm supports. The old rush seat, which may be the first one, is a great rarity, since such seats typically wore out after several years of use. The wide space between the rush seat and the stay rail accommodated a cushion. The attenuated ball and ring turnings on the front stretcher are repeated on the side stretchers. The bold C-scrolls flank a plume, a common motif on chairs of this group.
Private Collection.

FIGURE II–4
Armchair. Oak and maple. Boston area. Ca. 1710–1725.
The C-scroll carving on the front stretcher, which is repeated on the crest, makes this one of the most expensive chair types produced in Boston in the early 18th century. The original imported "Russhia leather" is set off by a double row of brass tacks. The chair is similar to Russhia leather elbow chairs sold by the Boston upholsterer, Thomas Fitch, before 1725, when Russhia leather became scarce.
Courtesy, The Henry Francis du Pont Winterthur Museum.

to the English furniture tradition in Pennsylvania was a German element that resulted from the successful recruiting campaigns of William Penn's agents in the Palatinate region of Germany. These people, most of them poor peasants, came by the hundreds to Philadelphia and rural Pennsylvania, drawn by the promise of religious and political freedom and the lure of free land. So successfully was Pennsylvania promoted that by 1720 Philadelphia, the City of Brotherly Love, was the second largest city next to Boston in the colonies and was on its way to becoming the cultural center of America.

Chairs

The Oriental influence, one of the strongest elements of the new style, was most evident in chairs. The elaborate carving and turning were predominantly Baroque, but the frequent use of caning, and even the curved back that replaced the stiff, straight backs of Jacobean chairs, were all derived from China, where curved-back chairs were in common use by the 16th century (Figure II–1). Caned seats and backs, woven with rattan imported from Malaya, were so popular in England that the county of York petitioned Parliament on behalf of the upholsterers to suppress the burgeoning caning industry, but with little success. The popularity of caned chairs carried over to America. Jonathan Dickinson of Philadelphia, in 1722, owned 44 caned side chairs and 26 caned armchairs, or elbow chairs, as they were usually referred to in the 18th century. Many of these chairs were imported from England. James Logan, a wealthy Philadelphia merchant, wrote to a friend in London in 1718 requesting that he purchase "8 handsome but plain new fashioned Cane Chairs." Plain chairs of Virginia walnut have often been identified as American made, but Logan's "plain chairs," obviously made in England, merely exhibit Logan's

William and Mary style, and it was popular in America from about 1690 to 1730. Even in New York, where the Dutch tradition was still strong and was reflected in such pieces as the *Kas*, or wardrobe, newly prosperous Englishmen looked to London for cultural models. In Pennsylvania, which had been established in 1682 by William Penn, the new style predominated almost from the beginning. Added

22

Quaker conservatism. Adding to the difficulty of identification was the practice of exporting Virginia walnut for use by London cabinetmakers. Although more expensive and less durable than rush (commonly called flag in the 18th century), the popular cane gave resilience to the seat and back, thus eliminating the need for a cushion or upholstery, which usually was more expensive than the frame itself.

Less expensive bannister-back chairs, which, instead of being caned, repeated the shape of turned back posts in half-balusters across the back, were more popular in the colonies (Figure II–3). The first students of American furniture early in the 20th century thought that this form was a unique American invention, but subsequent research has confirmed English prototypes for these chairs and indeed for most American furniture forms once believed to be uniquely American.

Next to cane chairs, leather chairs with turned legs and stretchers, molded crest rails, and leather seats and backs were the most widely used seating furniture (Figure II–4). The five dozen leather chairs that Thomas Masters of Philadelphia owned in 1723 may have been made in Philadelphia or, just as likely, imported from Boston, where the prototype of this chair was first made. Indeed, Boston chairmakers exported the "Boston chair," as it was called, to all the colonies, and it was so popular that when local craftsmen copied the form, it was almost impossible to distinguish between the import and the locally made product (Figure II–5).

A new type of chair appeared in this period—called the easy chair—which had upholstered wings or cheeks to ward off the drafts drawn through the house by a raging fire in the fireplace (Figure II–6). The use of precious fabrics, such as serge, camlet, and shalloon, to cover the backs and arms of a chair as well as the seat was indeed a luxury, but

FIGURE II–5
Leather chair. Maple and oak. Boston. Ca. 1720–1750.
Known as a Boston chair, this inexpensive abstraction of an ornate William and Mary style chair with carved crest and cane back was shipped to colonial customers all along the Atlantic coast. Leather replaced cane and a turned stretcher and simple arched crest rail substituted for ornate carving found on the most elegant William and Mary examples. The frame was typically stained red or black and on this example a double row of brass tacks creates a flashy appearance. An advertisement of the Boston upholsterer, Thomas Fitch, in 1724 refers to a "crooked-back leather chair" which was probably similar to this piece.
The Metropolitan Museum of Art, Gift of Mrs. Russell Sage, 1909.

FIGURE II–6
Easy chair. Maple, oak, and pine. New England. Ca. 1710–1725.
The earliest known reference to an easy chair is in a 1708 New York inventory of household effects. This chair, with its flattened, arched crest, turned stretchers, and so-called Spanish feet, is the earliest type. The shaping of the skirt repeats the curves of the crest and may also have hidden a chamber pot, a standard addition to 18th-century easy chairs.
Courtesy, The Henry Francis du Pont Winterthur Museum.

it was a decided advance in comfort when compared to the straight-backed wainscot and Cromwell chairs that went out of favor by the beginning of the 18th century. These chairs, which were usually placed in the best room or parlor, continued to

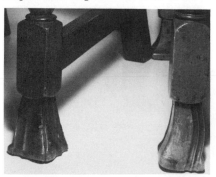

couch was derived from benches
of the Middle Ages, which were
fitted with cushions.

Chairs might have been made
by as many as four craftsmen: a
turner to shape the intricate
balls, rings, vase, trumpet spool,
and cup-shaped turnings of the
legs; a carver to ornament the
crest rail and front stretcher and
possibly the legs with C- and S-
scrolls; a joiner to make the
frame, and an upholsterer to
cover it. By the 18th century,
some craftsmen began to special-
ize in chairmaking. The most
elaborately carved and caned
chairs, usually of beech, were
generally imported from England, whereas a few leather-
upholstered ones, usually simpler and made of maple, with
turned legs and so-called Spanish
feet, were manufactured locally.
The characteristic foot, which
was introduced to the English by
Portuguese craftsmen arriving
with Catherine of Braganza, may
have been based on Renaissance
architectural scrolls (Figure II–8
and II–9). Foot binding, which
was practiced in Portugal as well
as in the Orient during the 17th
century, may also have suggested the Spanish foot form.
The Gaines family of furniture
makers in Portsmouth, New
Hampshire, carved their feet in
one piece, as did many Philadelphia chairmakers, but most
makers applied an extra piece of
wood to form the projecting toe
on the base of the foot in order
to save wood.

In this period, the most expensive chairs were made of walnut, which now replaced oak as
the most fashionable wood.
Abundant in America, walnut,
particularly that from Virginia,
was exported to England, and the
beautiful burl of some boards
were cut into thin strips of veneers. Veneering, however, was a
less common practice in the
colonies. Despite the availability
of many suitable cabinet woods,
such as cherry, maple, and pine,
which were often stained to look
like walnut, American cabinetmakers also used exotic imported woods, such as ma-

have a removable squab, or cushion, on the seat.

From the 16th century on,
well-to-do Englishmen owned a
daybed or couch, really an elongated chair for reclining. They
did not appear in America until
the end of the 17th century. The
most elaborate English examples
were upholstered in the manner
of the easy chair, but American
ones usually had a long cushion
laid upon them (Figure II–7). The

hogany, which began to arrive from the Caribbean, and olive wood from Africa, India, or Southern Europe.

Tables

Next to chairs, tables were the most common item of furniture. Oval ones are more frequently mentioned in inventories than any other type. They were sold by the foot, usually in lengths of three, four, or five feet. Round, square, and rectangular tables were made as well. The gateleg, a name assigned in the late 19th century, evolved: it had more lightly turned legs and less massive stretchers, which were often turned as well. Two leaves were supported on gates that folded out (Figure II–10). The inner edge of the leaves on the earliest tables were flat or formed a tongue and groove joint (Figure II–11), which was replaced about 1730 by the rule joint (Figure II–12). A variation of the gateleg table had gates in the shape of a butterfly supported from a single point on the stretcher (Figure II–13). This rare form was once thought to be an American innovation, but English prototypes have been found. Long banquet tables were rare until the 19th century. At large dinner parties, guests ate at

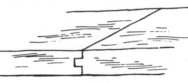

FIGURE II–11
Tongue and grove joint.

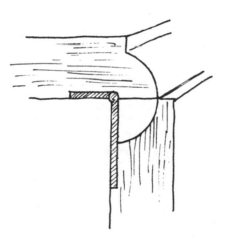

FIGURE II–12
Rule joint used to join drop leaves to table tops on 18th-century tables

FIGURE II–13
Table. Cherry. New England. Ca. 1720–1750.
Pieces such as this are now called butterfly tables because of the shape suggested by the gates that support the leaves. The turned stretchers, which echo the turnings on the legs, were made less often than plain, rectangular ones. The oval top is more common than the square variety, although some presently round tops may have been recut at a later date. The top is attached by means of pegs visible on the top, a technique acceptable on this less formal table but unacceptable on a high-style parlor piece.
Private Collection.

FIGURE II–14
*Dressing table. Walnut and maple.
Massachusetts. Ca. 1720–1730.*
The use of a long drawer above the
three smaller drawers, common in the
Queen Anne period, is rare on William
and Mary style dressing tables. By the
1730s, cabriole legs of the Queen Anne
style replaced the earlier turned legs
and stretchers, but the veneered case
often remained unchanged, as in this
example. The original engraved brass
pulls also herald the arrival of the
Queen Anne style. A herringbone inlay
surrounded by a double, arched molding
outlines the flush, veneered drawer
fronts. The herringbone inlay is
repeated on the top, which is veneered
with rectangular walnut panels with an
oval in the center. The stretchers, with
their double C-scrolls, add additional
movement to an already exciting piece.
As on high chests of the period, the
cup-turned legs are attached to the case
with dowels.
Private Collection.

FIGURE II–15
*Chest. Walnut. New England. Ca.
1700–1720.*
Arched or half-round moldings separate
the drawers. The sides are held within
a frame in a holdover from the 17th-
century joiner's method of construction.
The turned bun feet reflect the Dutch
fashion pervasive in England by the
mid-17th century. The period brass drop
pulls are typical of the William and
Mary style. The 17th-century beaded
box and looking glass are both English.
Courtesy Mrs. Miriam Morris.

several smaller tables scattered
around the room. Several specialized tables, such as ones fitted with slate or marble tops to
protect the wood from the ravages of spilled food or drink, began to appear in inventories at
the end of the 17th century.

The more genteel ladies and
gentlemen at the beginning of
the 18th century made frequent
use of the "toilet table" or
lowboy (Figure II–14). The term
toilet is derived from the French
word *toilette*, meaning a small
cloth that was placed on dressing tables where powderboxes,
salvers, brushes, combs, and
other dressing accouterments
were displayed. Because of the
difficulty of heating and transporting water and the lack of
knowledge of the importance of
hygiene, bathing was an infre-
quent affair. Benjamin Franklin
observed that men and fish stink
after three days; so in order to
mask the effects of lack of bathing, powders, perfumes, and
pomades were a necessity in po-

lite society. That, combined
with the custom of powdered
wigs and painted faces, made the
dressing table an important piece
of furniture for the refined lady
and gentleman.

Chests of Drawers

Another development dating
from the late 17th century—the
elaboration of dress—caused an
attendant need for more storage
space for the expanding wardrobe of the "better sort." Chests
of drawers, usually with ball,
turnip-shaped, or turned feet, or
feet formed by extending the
sides or corner stiles below the
bottom drawer, appeared in inventories of large estates (Figure
II–15). The chest of drawers appeared in inventories as early as
the 1640s in New England, but
examples were quite rare in the
Jacobean period. Those that have
survived were usually decorated
with carved paneling or applied
ornaments, the same decorations

FIGURE II–16
Chest of drawers. Pine. Eastern Massachusetts or New Hampshire. Ca. 1700–1730.
Pine furniture made in New England early in the 18th century was, almost without exception, painted originally. Unfortunately, few pieces have survived with their original finish. This chest is a rare exception. The paint job suggests the veneered drawer fronts and crossbanded inlay found on expensive, urban chests in the William and Mary style. The rural decorator has taken liberties, however, by stippling the top and base moldings as well as the drawer edges. The flush drawer surrounded by arched moldings, the drop pulls, and the ball feet are all characteristic of the William and Mary style.
Society for the Preservation of New England Antiquities.

that adorned the more elaborate cupboards. By the last quarter of the 17th century, the chest of drawers was being used as a dressing table as well as a place to store clothes, but as the chest of drawers began to be made higher and dressing tables appeared, this role became secondary.

A typical Pennsylvania chest of drawers configuration was two drawers side-by-side over two full-length ones. Three or four full-length drawers were common elsewhere. These pieces were made of local woods, such as maple and cherry, as well as the more exotic cedar, olive, and walnut. They were often adorned with japanning, veneers, or inlays. The drawers were typically outlined with single- or double-arched moldings. The earliest drawer pulls were usually of wood, but by the end of the 17th century, brass pear-shaped drops hung in front of rosette back plates, and matching cartouche-shaped brass escutcheons protected the wood around the key-

holes (Figure II–16). Variations, such as brass knobs or ring pulls, were also found. These pulls, along with nails, hinges, locks, couch chains for lowering the backs of daybeds, upholsterer's tacks, and even coffin handles, were usually obtained from merchants who imported them from England.

As the exterior of the early 18th century chest of drawers changed, so did the interior construction, particularly of drawers. The drawer no longer ran on grooves cut into the drawer sides but slid instead on the bottom edge of the drawer side or on strips of wood that formed bottom runners (Figure II–17). The bottom boards were less often nailed to the bottom edge of the sides but were now set into a rabbet or groove cut into the drawer sides (Figure II–18). Dovetails were commonly used to join drawer fronts to sides on 17th-century Boston case pieces, but by the end of the century, the dovetail joint was widely used elsewhere as well.

FIGURE II–17 *(below)*
Late 17th-century drawer construction in which a side rail nailed to the case fits into a corresponding slot cut into the side of the drawer.

FIGURE II–18 *(bottom)*
Bottom board of a drawer chamfered on the edges and fitted into a rabbet joint cut into the sides of the drawer.

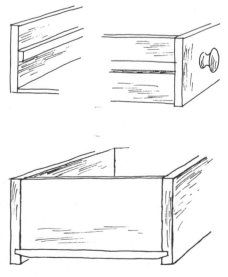

High Chests

The high chest of drawers, which was raised upon turned legs, also developed at the end of the 17th century. The term high-boy is a modern name, although "tallboy" is found in some 18th century inventories (Figure II–19). The popularity of this form may have persisted because of its utility but, contrary to conventional wisdom, it did not develop because people tired of bending over to open the bottom drawer of a chest. The high chest was modeled after the elaborate frames built for highly prized Oriental lacquered cabinets imported into England for London's wealthiest noblemen.

Few could afford the luxury of the real thing, and imitators quickly flooded the London market with locally made copies that were also sold with frames. The form itself became stylish, and many high chests were sold without the Oriental decoration at all.

The high chest supplanted the cupboard as the fanciest piece of furniture in English and American homes. The high chest, along with the corner cupboard, assumed the role of the court cupboard as a place to display glass, pewter, or other valuable objects. Some continued to be draped with cushions and cloths in the manner of the cupboards, and others were fitted with stepped pyramids on the flat tops in order to better display objects of wealth.

Although the high chest of drawers was very much a part of the English culture, the *Kas*, or armoire, was a product of a medieval Continental tradition (Figure II–20). Most of the examples surviving from the late 17th and early 18th century were made in the Hudson River Valley, settled primarily by the Dutch. Similar pieces called *Schranks* and made by Germans in Pennsylvania survive from the mid-18th century. Medieval in character, usually with massive cornices, both the *Schrank* and the *Kas* were painted and ornamented with geometric moldings.

Desks

Related to chests of drawers were slant-front desks, or "scrutoires," which developed when the so-called Bible box of the 17th century was placed upon a frame. Later, the frame was replaced with more serviceable drawers (Figure II–21). In fact, the earliest slant-front desks sometimes showed vestiges of a frame in a molding on the sides and front of the desk. A few slant-front lids opened upward, but most were hinged at the bottom, opened out, and were supported on slides or small drawers to form a writing surface. When closed, the slanted lid served as a convenient lectern for reading. As merchants expanded their accounts, the need for handy storage for ledgers was filled by the addition of a bookcase top to the desk. A few were essentially chest on chests with a fall-front writing lid that was supported by metal strips attached to the side of the upper section in the manner of some early 19th-century desks. Desks proliferated in

FIGURE II–20
Kas. Pine, maple, and gumwood. New York. Ca. 1690–1730.
Part of a small group of wardrobes with similar decorations, these pieces exhibit the earliest examples of American still-life painting. Carving on imported Dutch armoires of the early 18th century probably inspired the grisaille decoration. This technique involved the use of shades of one color to simulate marble cut in relief. Compass marks, visible on the surface, indicate the use of that instrument to lay out the design.
Van Cortlandt Manor, Sleepy Hollow Restorations.

FIGURE II–21

Desk. Maple and walnut. New England. Ca. 1700–1725.

An inlaid star on the lid and burl walnut veneer enlivened the facade of this desk. The space above the top drawers indicates the presence of a well, which was accessible from the interior of the desk. The arched moldings between the drawers, the protruding base moldings, the heavy, flattened ball or bun feet and the drop brasses are all characteristic of case pieces made in the early 18th century.

Courtesy, The Henry Francis du Pont Winterthur Museum.

FIGURE II–22

Tall clock. Walnut. New York. Ca. 1725.

The impressive walnut case is not matched by the poorly cast parts for the clockworks, which are signed by Anthony Ward. Such poor workmanship is one reason so few American tall clocks have survived from the early 18th century. Imported Dutch clocks with the high, stepped bonnet owned by Dutch families in the Hudson River Valley early in the 18th century may have served as the model for this case. Several tall clocks from Philadelphia also have stepped bonnets but are without the great height of New York cases in this period. This case stands nearly eight feet high.

Courtesy, The Henry Francis du Pont Winterthur Museum.

the 18th century as a result of growing prosperity but also because of the public postal system that developed in England and her colonies at the end of the 17th century, eliminating the need to send letters by expensive, private courier.

Beds

In the finer homes, even more valuable than the high chest was the bed with its expensive hangings and mattress stuffed with as many as 60 pounds of feathers. Mention of canopy bedsteads indicated the four-poster type; there were also tent and field bedsteads, which could easily be taken apart and folded. Cots, hammocks, and simple low-post frames were even more common. By the beginning of the 18th century, bed rails were fastened together with screws in a departure from the 17th century practice of using mortise and tenon joints, which could not easily be disassembled.

Clocks

Only clocks rivaled bedsteads, with their expensive hangings, as the greatest luxury a gentleman could own. Clocks were ticking away in the houses of New England and the middle colonies by the middle of the 17th century, but most were imported from London. Some of them may have been of the earliest design, with an hour hand

only. Minute hands were unnecessary, since the clocks were not accurate to the minute. By the beginning of the 18th century, longer pendulums were added to clocks, which had formerly hung on the wall, and a tall wooden case was required to protect the

pendulum from being disturbed (Figure II–22). By the early 18th century, clockmakers were turning out brass clockworks and faces in the major cities, such as Boston and Philadelphia, but most works continued to be imported from England. The diverse choices of imported clockworks available to a customer was indicated by the 1712 advertisement of the Boston clockmaker, Joseph Essex, "lately arriv'd from Great Britain," who advertised with Thomas Badley in Buttler's Building in King Street: "30 hour Clocks, Week Clocks, Month Clocks, Spring Table Clocks, Chime Clocks, quarter Clocks, quarter Chime Clocks, Church Clocks, Terret Clocks, and new Pocket Watches, new repeating Watches" and promised a 12-month money-back guarantee "if not liked. . . ."[3] The term grandfather clock originated with the popular song written by Henry C. Work in 1876 and called "My Grandfather's Clock."

Looking Glasses

Looking glasses to decorate the walls, as opposed to hand-held, polished metal mirrors, were also an extravagant luxury imported from England. The glass for large ones was usually in two parts because, until the late 18th century, most glass in England was hand blown. To fashion a large sheet for a looking glass, a large cone was blown and then cut off the end of the blow pipe. The cone was then laboriously formed into a cylinder that in turn was split, and the ends were cut off and flattened out. After a lengthy period of annealing, the glass was ground smooth with progressively finer grades of sand and then polished with powder. The glass was then silvered with tinfoil and quicksilver. A method for casting glass was developed in France late in the 17th century, but this procedure was not in widespread use in England until late in the 18th century. Little glass, either blown or cast, was made in the United States

until the mid-19th century. Although some frames were undoubtedly made in America, most were imported from England where cheaper and more abundant labor was available to perform the time-consuming work.

The William and Mary style looking glasses were usually square or rectangular with an angular or shaped crest and cyma curves, often pierced with hearts and geometric designs. Related to these earlier looking glasses, but mostly from the mid-18th century, were the so-called courting mirrors, which were probably purchased in the northern European ports of Holland, Germany, and Denmark and brought back to America by sailors and ship captains. These were square with angular hoods (Figure II–23). Looking glasses, although not made in America, were resilvered here, often by the same people who did japanning, such as William Randle in Boston, who in 1715 advertised a "Looking-Glass Shop in Queen Street."

The appearance of really unnecessary and expensive looking glasses, tall case clocks, and easy chairs to adorn the luxurious houses of wealthy colonial merchants and planters attested to the growing wealth of the colonists and to the desire to show off that wealth by displaying the most fashionable furniture. Not everyone chose to show off his wealth with furniture. Edward Shippen, Mayor of Philadelphia in the early 18th century, built the biggest house in the city before 1711 and purchased the largest coach. In that year his best parlor contained the following:

2 old elbow chairs, 6 small chairs and a broken child's chair, a cane couch cushion and squab all old and much torn, a clock out of order, ye key lost, an old fashioned glass, a pair of broken sconces, an old fashioned scrip-tors with some broken china, one large and one small oval table old and rotten, an old decanter and 1/2 dozen broken glasses on ye mantel piece, 10 glass pictures—many of which are broken, two lacquered framed pictures much spoiled by ye flys and smoke and a pr of old tongs, bent shovel, dog and broken fender.[4]

Still, furniture provided the most convenient and ostentatious way for the man of even modest means in the 18th century to show what he had accomplished, and the cabinetmakers stood ready to provide him with the latest fashions, simple or ornate, to accomplish just that.

NOTES

1. Marshall B. Davidson, ed., *The American Heritage History of Colonial Antiques* (New York: American Heritage Publishing Co., Inc., 1967), p. 61.

2. Frederick B. Artz, *From the Renaissance to Romanticism* (Chicago: University of Chicago Press, 1962), p. 17.

3. Irving W. Lyon, *The Colonial Furniture of New England* (New York: E. P. Dutton, 1977), p. 250.

4. Lita Solis-Cohen, "Don't Overdo, Kindig Says of Historic Restoration," *Antiques Monthly* 12 (July 1978): 4C.

III

QUEEN ANNE:
THE LINE OF BEAUTY

FIGURE III–1

High chest of drawers. Maple and pine. Boston. Ca. 1740–1750.
Raised gilt figures rest on a tortoise-shell background simulated by streaking red vermilion in lampblack. John Pimm made the case for Commodore Joshua Loring, but the japanner is unknown. An unusual survival from inlaid William and Mary furniture is the thin strip of mahogany applied to the skirt. The square paw feet are unusual departures from the more common pad foot. The urn finials are not original.
Courtesy, The Henry Francis du Pont Winterthur Museum.

THE SIGNING OF THE TREATY OF Utrecht in 1713, ending almost 25 years of costly war between Britain and France, ushered in a new era of prosperity. Britain benefited by the peace, which ended French domination of Europe, giving her trading concessions throughout the world. More capital was available for investment in her colonies, and trade between Britain and America grew to several million pounds a year. Hand in hand with economic prosperity came a dramatic increase in America's population—from about 650,000 in 1730 to about 1,600,000 in 1760.

As colonial merchants increased their wealth, they built grand houses and decorated them with luxurious furnishings in the latest style, which, by the 1730s, was the Queen Anne, a restrained style already popular back in Britain.

ARCHITECTURE

New houses proliferated, particularly in the five major port cities of Boston, Newport, New York, Philadelphia, and Charleston. The familiar 17th-century dwelling with two rooms built around a chimney and bed chambers on a second floor continued to be constructed, particularly in rural areas, but by the second quarter of the 18th century the fully developed Georgian style dominated the architecture of the finer houses. A symmetrical room arrangement and great attention to the interior characterized the new houses. The most popular floor plan—four rooms on the first floor divided by a central entrance hall, with a staircase leading to bedrooms upstairs—reflected the trend toward differentiation of rooms by function. Parlors, bedrooms, and kitchens had replaced the 17th-century halls that had served all these purposes. A profusion of classical detail in the entablature over doors and windows, the chimney pieces, and the decorative wall moldings enlivened the interior. Houses were built with more spacious rooms, higher ceilings, and larger windows, and the structural beams were hidden.

The modest Palladian houses of English gentry were imitated in America. Only a few, such as Tryon Palace in New Bern, North Carolina, built by a British royal governor, approximated grand English mansions. As a consequence, the ornate English Georgian furniture made for the nobility, with gilding and ornate carvings of lion masks and birds, was never popular in America. The carving, the gilt, and the larger scale of the English style simply would have overwhelmed the more modest American interiors. The more restrained Queen Anne style suited these houses best.

THE STYLE

The Queen Anne style had been popular in England for decades before it appeared in Boston, the largest colonial city in the first half of the 18th century. By 1730, the major elements of the new style—the cabriole leg, the compass seat, the vase-shaped splat, and the pad foot—were mentioned in Boston advertisements. The sensuous curves and restrained carving of the Queen Anne style gradually replaced the turned legs and angular appearance of the William and Mary style in other cities as well. The similarity of Queen Anne to modern furniture in its emphasis on form rather than on ornament explains the popularity of the Queen Anne style today. The new style began to be called Queen Anne in the 1870s, the same name that was applied to a late 19th century architectural style. Queen Anne ruled England from 1702 to 1714, but the new style had not eclipsed the William and Mary until after the ascension of George I to the throne in 1714. Although the style should more accurately be called Early Georgian, the Queen Anne name is used to avoid confusion with the English Georgian styles.

ORIENTAL INFLUENCES

Styles changed slowly. Cabinetmakers had an investment in templates or patterns and were comfortable with familiar designs and techniques. Only a pervasive new influence could stimulate demand for a change. Such was the growing impact of contacts with the Orient. Although the Oriental influence first appeared in the decorative arts in the William and Mary period, it became even more apparent in the Queen Anne.

The hallmark of the new style was the cabriole leg, called a "horsebone," or "crook'd," leg in the 18th century. The term cabriole is derived from the Italian word for a goat's leap and indeed the shape resembles the hind leg of a goat. William Hogarth, an 18th-century English artist and art critic, described the importance of the curved shape of the cabriole leg in 1753:

> There is scarce a room in any house whatever, where one does not see the waving-line employ'd in some way or other. How inelegant would the shapes of all our moveables be without it![1]

The S-shape, which he called "the line of beauty," was a universal form found in classical, European, and Oriental cultures. The shape appeared on ancient Egyptian chairs, complete with a bull's hoof and a break in the curve to suggest a knee joint. However, the smooth, uninterrupted curve of the Queen Anne leg was probably inspired by the legs on the low Chinese K'ang tables imported to Europe as stands for the highly prized, Oriental lacquered cabinets. The S-, or reverse, curve of the cabriole leg was repeated in all parts of the chair, including the stile, the stretchers, the seat, and the splat. The splat, called a bannister-back in the 18th century, suggests the silhouette of a large, turned architectural baluster or an Oriental porcelain vase.

In addition to the cabriole leg, the Queen Anne style borrowed other elements from the Orient, including the stylized double cloud form and, possibly, the ball and claw foot (Figure III–2). Most American Queen Anne fur-

FIGURE III–2
Cloud form on the base of a New England chest. Cherry. Ca. 1760–1780.
Author's Collection.

niture terminated in variations of a club, or pad, foot, but the most elegant pieces were purchased with the ball and claw foot, referred to as an "eagle's foot," or "crow foot." Although a paw foot appears on some Chinese lacquer work, the multi-clawed dragons that writhed across imported Oriental porcelain, textiles, and lacquer work may have been a more important inspiration for the claw foot. In Oriental designs, the claw is reaching for a pearl, but the Chinese dragon does not actually grasp the ball. Only vaguely familiar with the Orient, the American colonist saw no symbolic significance in the motif. Although the rationale of 18th-century designers may never be known with certainty, it is likely that the claw simply evoked the stylish novelty of the Orient, and the ball served as a structural element to support the inherently delicate carved talons.

One of the most obvious influences from the Orient was the growing importance of brass fittings similar to ones found in imported lacquered cabinets. The more restrained William and Mary drop pulls were replaced by brass plates following Oriental hardware designs. The earliest brass pulls with punched, or occasionally engraved, designs on the back plates were fastened to the drawer by cotter pins. After 1730, threaded posts, holding a bail between them, pierced the brass and were secured to the drawer by a nut. Although some brass was produced in America, English brass foundries produced most of the cast-brass pulls for the American trade. The light yellow color of 18th-century brass resulted from a higher proportion of zinc to copper in the alloy, as compared to modern brass.

But the most spectacular decorative influence from the Orient was japanning, an Oriental lacquer decoration that adorned furniture of all types from the end of the 17th century but reached its peak in the Queen Anne period. Japanning was probably practiced in all the major cities of the colonies but was especially favored in Boston, where most surviving examples were made (Figure III–1). Nehemiah Partridge and Thomas Johnston were among over a dozen japanners who worked in Boston before the Revolution, practicing their trade as described in *A Treatise of Japaning and Varnishing*, published by John Stalker and George Parker in Oxford in 1688. In the Orient, resin from the exotic *Rhus vernicifera*, or sumac, tree was applied in as many as 30 or more separate coats over a period of many months. Europeans lacked the resin and could not afford the time necessary for multiple coats, so they developed substitutes. First, the surface was made smooth by applying whiting, a chalk-like substance, over an oak ground. In America, however, the availability of close-grained woods, such as maple, obviated the need for the whiting base. A pigmented oil varnish was applied over the primed wood rather than the more expensive seed lac varnishes used in England. Black was the most common pigment, but white, red, yellow, green, and blue were also used. This surface was then painted wonderfully with bizarre interpretations of Oriental designs, such as boats, animals, mythical creatures, flowers, trees, and pagoda-like structures mostly copied from actual imported japanned pieces. On earlier examples, these decorations were sometimes built up in relief, using whiting. Japanners often gilded the figures with metallic dust or gold leaf and then painted the entire surface with several coats of varnish. In praise of the result, Stalker and Parker extolled, "Ancient and modern Rome must now give place: The glory of one Country, Japan alone, has exceeded in beauty and magnificence all the pride of the Vatican at this time, and the Pantheon heretofore."[2] The technique was at its height in the second quarter of the 18th century before the Revolution but continued in a debased form until early in the 19th century. The decoration was simply painted on and the figures were no longer raised as earlier.

CLASSICAL IDEAS

Even more important than the Oriental influence on the Queen Anne style was the strong classical strain, which was seen clearly in the restrained carving adorning the most expensive furniture. The acanthus leaf and the shell were the most common motifs. The acanthus plant, which grew in warm climates around the Mediterranean, was depicted on such classical Greek and Roman architectural elements as Corinthian and Composite columns as well as on Greek and Roman furniture. The scallop shell, appearing on chair legs and crest rails, was based on Phoenician coins, Greek vases, sculptured Roman thrones, and sarcophagi. During the Renaissance, Italians, such as the sculptor, Donatello, revived many of these motifs in the 15th century. Books based on the designs of the Roman architect, Vitruvius, which were owned by many wealthy patrons of the arts in America, illustrated many of the same motifs.

Not only was the surface ornamentation of furniture in the 18th century derived from classical inspiration but so was the system of furniture proportion. Proportion is the dimensional relationship between parts. The 18th-century system was grounded in complex mathematical relationships derived from nature and formulated by Greek mathematicians, such as Euclid and Pythagoras. Vitruvius rediscovered the Greek system of proportion and incorporated it into his architectural books. Architects and furniture designers alike drew on Vitruvius and the classical system for their own designs.

On well-designed 18th-century pieces, the dimensions of each

element related mathematically to other elements just as lines and ornaments echoed one another throughout a piece. These whole number relationships were usually based on geometric or arithmetic progression. In a geometric system, a given dimension was multiplied by a constant figure. Thus the length of a chest might be two times the height, the depth might be two times the width, and so on. In an arithmetic system, a fixed sum was added to a given dimension. Thus drawers might be five, seven, nine, and 11 inches wide, each one being two inches wider than the other.[3]

Conditioned by their classical training, customers unconsciously responded to these relationships. The aesthetics reflected the larger 18th-century world view as expressed by Sir Isaac Newton. In his *Principia* he had used mathematical formulas to explain the working of the universe. The highly regulated formulas used in furniture design illustrated, in microcosm, a similar belief in rational powers to solve such mundane problems as the dimensions of a high chest of drawers.

PERSISTENCE OF EARLIER DESIGNS

Elements of the earlier style persisted into the Queen Anne period. Stretchers continued to be found on chairs, particularly those made in New England, even though the broader seat rails and the wide knees on chair legs resulted in a strong enough joint to make them unnecessary. On a few transitional chairs, the knee blocks, which gave the chair a smooth movement from the vertical to the horizontal, were omitted, giving the chair the angular appearance of the earlier style (Figure III–3). Another important survival, the saddle shape of the crest rail on many Queen Anne chairs, was a provincial simplification of the double scrolls appearing on the crests of rural English William and Mary chairs. Similar shaping appeared on Chinese folding chairs exported to the West as curiosities.

Although the Queen Anne cabriole leg chair was the most fashionable after 1730, the cheaper leather-back chair with turned legs and Spanish feet survived to mid-century, either exported by Boston or imitated in most colonial towns (Figure III–4). Some Spanish foot chairs with pierced splats and an angular crest continued to be made until the end of the century. The more expensive cabriole leg was cut from a single piece of wood, using a template, and then shaped with a draw knife. Only the pad foot could be turned quickly on a lathe. In 1739, Plunket Fleeson of Philadelphia advertised in the *Pennsylvania Gazette* "black and red leather Chairs, finished cheaper than any made here, or imported from Boston" and argued that "in Case of any defects, the Buyer shall have them made good; an Advantage not to be had in the buying of Boston Chairs, besides the Damage they receive by the Sea."[4]

WOODS AND FINISHES

By the 1720s, walnut, with its beautiful color and figure and close grain, had replaced the coarser oak, once the most stylish cabinet wood. Virginia walnut, growing throughout the Middle Atlantic colonies, was used in America and exported to England because it was finely figured and was not susceptible to worms. Although walnut was the most popular wood until mid-century, maple, cherry, and other woods were also employed. Mahogany imported from the West Indies was found in cabinetmakers' inventories soon after 1700 but was not widely used until mid-century.

English cabinetmakers working in the new style depended on veneering, particularly with the burled walnut, to produce elegant furniture for the fine English Georgian mansions. In America, with an abundance of solid walnut and a lack of cheap labor, expensive veneering on the splats of chairs was not as common. Some examples of veneering and inlay in the form of cross banding, stringing, stars, and shells were found, however, particularly in Boston.

Varnish gave the close-grained woods, such as mahogany and walnut, a lustrous and hard finish. It was not used to any great extent until the end of the 17th century, since the open grained oak of that era did not lend itself to a smooth finish. Three common types of varnish were used in the 18th century. Spirit varnish, which was a resin, such as shellac or copal, usually dissolved in alcohol, and dried rapidly, but produced a brittle, easily cracked surface. Essential oil varnishes made with resins, particularly copal, dissolved in turpentine gave better results, but fixed oil finishes—usually made with copal dissolved in linseed oil—produced the most

durable and commonly used 18th-century finish. The cabinetmaker applied four to ten coats of varnish with a round brush of hog's bristles and rubbed down the final coat with ground pumice stone. Linseed oil was cheap and was easily extracted from the seeds of the flax plant, which grew abundantly along the Atlantic seaboard. On the finest pieces, more costly walnut or poppy seed oil was used, whereas on less expensive woods, painted finishes—or simply beeswax dissolved in turpentine—were popular.

THE UPHOLSTERER AND HIS WARES

Wealthy patrons spent considerable amounts of money for expensive upholstery. The upholstered slip seat, which first developed in France, was particularly popular in America because it was less expensive than fitting the upholstery to the seat rail. Heretofore, chairs had either

At first glance, this sofa appears to be the often reproduced "camelback" sofa of the Chippendale period. A closer look, however, reveals cabriole legs rather than the later Marlborough ones and the gentle serpentine curve to the back instead of the bold shaping of the Chippendale period. The arrow-shaped stretchers are rare features on Philadelphia furniture, but the paneled pad feet are fairly common.
Courtesy, The Henry Francis du Pont Winterthur Museum.

This chair is signed on the crest rail by "Gardner Junr," possibly Caleb Gardner, who was working as an upholsterer in Providence after the Revolution, or one of his relatives. The chair retains its original red, blue, green, and yellow bargello or flame-stitch embroidery. Instead of the usual wool or silk panel, the back is fitted with a needlework pastoral scene of birds, trees, deer, and a shepherd tending a flock of sheep. The customer stitched these panels and took them to the upholsterer for installation. The fat cushion outlined with cording, which also outlined the edge of the chair, is a common 18th-century upholstery technique.
The Metropolitan Museum of Art, Gift of Mrs. J. Insley Blair, 1950.

a cane, plank, rush, or splint seat that could be fitted with a cushion. The custom of upholstering the back of the chair between the stiles fell out of favor, and the splat typically rested on a shoe or block at the rear of the seat rather than joining a cross rail several inches above the seat.

The most properous of the furniture trades in the 18th century was that of the upholsterer.[5] He sold bedsteads, bedding, and upholstered furniture and often acted as a merchant by importing textiles and dry goods for sale (Figure III–5). Since he catered to the wealthiest merchants and professional people, the upholsterer tried to offer the most up-to-date fashions.

Customers generally requested English worsteds, including

cheyney, harrateen, camlet, or moreen, which came most commonly in crimson but also in blue, green, and yellow. These fabrics were decorated by watering, waving, or printing. Applying a water preparation and pressing the fabric under a hot iron produced a smooth, shiny surface. The waving technique was accomplished by rolling the material with a metal cylinder to produce a ripple pattern. Leather, which, after 1730, was made locally in New England of calf- and occasionally goat- or sealskin, offered a cheap and durable alternative. The furniture, stuffed with horsehair or cow's tails, was upholstered *en suite*, often to match the curtains.

The colonists used bright colors in their upholstery, in their painted furniture, in their curtains, and on their walls. The dull, drab, colorless image of the 18th century American, created by 19th-century writers such as Nathaniel Hawthorne in his popular Romantic novels set in New England, is simply inaccurate. The remnants of 18th-century upholstery that have survived disprove the image. The remains of original paint that has not darkened or faded on furniture and walls from the 18th century disprove it. The bright, almost gaudy, needlework panels done for upholstered easy chairs disprove it (Figure III–6).

The most lucrative items sold by the upholsterer were elaborately hung bedsteads, which became more common by the early 18th century as houses were built with more sleeping rooms. Low-post varieties were frequently surrounded by hangings that were hung from hooks in the wall. Field beds with arched canopies were also common, but the four-poster bedstead was the most desirable. Press beds continued in popularity until mid-century when houses became larger and there was less need for fold-up furniture. Octagonal posts, boldly scalloped head-

boards, and trestle feet indicated an earlier date, whereas round posts appear on beds throughout the century. Only rarely did the posts terminate in an expensive cabriole leg with pad or ball and claw feet because the hangings of such bright fabrics as chintz, calico, silk, taffeta, wool, or needlework embellished with lace, fringe, and tassels would cover them (Figure III–7). During the warm summer months, the heavy fabrics that enclosed the bedstead in wealthy households were replaced with muslin or dimity. The latter was often used

FIGURE III–7
Bed. Mahogany. Rhode Island. Ca. 1735–1750.
This is one of the few surviving Queen Anne bedsteads. The back feet on most bedsteads were left plain because the hangings usually covered them. This bed, however, rests on four cabriole legs. The summer hangings (winter ones enclosed the entire bed) were stitched in the 18th century, and the bedspread once belonged to John Hancock.
Courtesy, The Henry Francis du Pont Winterthur Museum.

FIGURE III—8
Easy chair. Mahogany. Philadelphia. Ca. 1760–1775.
Benjamin Lehman's price book describes chairs similar to this one as an "Easy Chair frame with Claw feet and Leaves on the Knees." Many easy chairs were fitted with an extra seat frame to support a chamber pot, but most of these have now been removed. The stump rear legs, the well-sculpted talons grasping a squashed ball, and the horizontally rolled arms are typically found on Philadelphia easy chairs.
Philadelphia Museum of Art. Membership Fund purchase from James Curran, subscription from Howard Reifsnyder.

FIGURE III—9
Easy chair. Mahogany. Rhode Island. Ca. 1740–1775.
The exposed frame reveals the cone-shaped arm supports typical of New England easy chairs. The legs are attached to the frame by means of a dovetail key, as in Philadelphia shop practices, but the rails are joined by a mortise and tenon in the typical New England manner. Although the corners of the seat rail are rounded, the front is flat. The back legs and stiles are made of solid pieces of mahogany; whereas in Philadelphia, the stiles are more often cut from a less expensive wood.
Society for the Preservation of New England Antiquities.

year round by less affluent families. A plain featherbed or bag, stuffed with moss or hair rested on canvas attached by cords to the bedstead and usually served as the mattress.

The fabric on the easy chair, which was typically found not in a parlor but in the bedroom, often matched the hangings. The William and Mary form, with an angular, high crest and turned legs and stretchers, was replaced by the smoothly curving crest and cabriole legs. Although the easy chair fell out of style in England by the 1740s, the form continued to be popular in America until the end of the century. By mid-century, carved acanthus leaves and ball and claw feet were sometimes grafted onto an essentially Queen Anne chair.

As with other furniture from the 18th century, the easy chair clearly announced its place of origin. Arms on New England chairs rested on vertical cones, whereas in Philadelphia they rested on a C-scrolled block (Figure III—8). For the most part, Philadelphia gave up stretchers by mid-century, but they persisted in New England. On all easy chairs with straight legs, the legs were fastened to the seat rail by means of mortise and tenon joints. Mortises were cut into the legs, which ex-

tended to the top of the rail in a block shape, to receive the tenon cut on the seat rails. Similar construction was used on cabriole leg chairs made in Boston, Newport, and New York. New York chairs were distinguished by rounded corners and bowed front rails in contrast to the squared-off seat rails more common in New England. Philadelphia legs joined the seat rail by means of a round, extended pin or a dovetail slot cut into the rails to receive the top of the leg. The rails themselves, which were shaped like a balloon, were usually joined by means of a lap joint in typical English fashion. In contrast, the rails on Philadelphia balloon-seat side chairs were usually joined by mortises and tenons. Some Newport and Connecticut chairs had rounded corners but were flattened across the front. The leg was attached as in Philadelphia, but the seat rails had mortise and tenon rather than lap joints (Figure III—9). The rear legs were either a continuation of the stiles, as is frequently found in New England, or were attached separately, as is more common in Philadelphia. Philadelphia rested the leg on a notch cut into the stile, and the back stile also rested on a notch cut into the seat rail for added strength. In a rather strange variation, found on some Connecticut and New York chairs, the stile was cut at a diagonal just above the seat rail.

OTHER FURNITURE

Case Furniture

Also in the bedrooms were bureau tables (called kneehole desks by the late 18th century), high chests, and matching dressing tables now called lowboys (Figures III—10 and III—11). The high chests had the familiar pilasters and heavy cornice moldings, often derived from the architectural design books available, or at least familiar, to most fashionable cabinetmakers. The

FIGURE III–10
Dressing table. Walnut with white pine. Boston area. Ca. 1730–1745.
The cabriole legs with the bold S-curves repeated in the skirt indicate the arrival of the new Queen Anne style. Veneering continued to be popular, however, and the facade and top of this piece are faced with rich burl walnut. To cut costs, the sides were left plain but stained to mask the omission of veneer. These brass pulls were examples of a variety of imported hardware available to the American craftsmen.
Society for the Preservation of New England Antiquities.

FIGURE III–11 *(far left)*
Bureau table. Walnut with white oak and pine. Massachusetts. Ca. 1740–1750.
Since the late 18th century pieces like this have been known as kneehole desks. However during the Queen Anne and Chippendale period they were known as bureau tables. These pieces were usually found in bedrooms. The center compartment slides forward on the base molding, and the door opens to expose three drawers. The light and dark string inlay outlining the drawers, the recessed door, the side, and the top in addition to the diamond inlay on the lower drawer indicate the Queen Anne style. The more delicate proportions and lines, compared to the similar but bolder pieces dating from the 1760s, also indicate an earlier date. Doors with similar rounded, Roman-arched panels appear on desk and bookcases of the period. The early 18th-century brasses contrast with more exuberant Chippendale ones.
Private Collection.

"bookcase heads" and similar to the arched bonnets on tall case clocks (Figure III–13). Cabinet-makers copied these arches from designs for mirrors and from drawings in architectural design

bold torus moldings on the William and Mary high chests gave way to the more fashionable ogee or cove moldings and frets that were popular until the end of the century. Triple-arched skirts fitted with drop finials were vestiges of the multiple, front legs on William and Mary style high chests (Figure III–12). About 1730, as higher ceilings became more popular, high chests were made with broken arches—sometimes referred to as

FIGURE III–12
High chest of drawers. Walnut with white pine. Eastern Massachusetts or New Hampshire. Ca. 1735–1760.
The heavy cornice moldings, the overhanging molding at the midsection, and the applied bead on the skirt are survivals from the William and Mary period. The absence of sharp knee brackets and the smooth flow of the legs into the skirt characterize Massachusetts tables and desks as well as high chests.
Society for the Preservation of New England Antiquities.

FIGURE III–13

FIGURE III–13
*High chest of drawers. Mahogany.
Newport. Ca. 1750–1760.*
**The skirt, minus the shell, and the
slipper-footed legs are identical to those
found on a flat-topped high chest of
drawers inscribed by Christopher
Townsend in 1748. The shell, confined
within an arc, is the earliest version, in
contrast to a later example, Figure
IV–41, where the edge of the shell is
scalloped. The original pierced brasses
suggest Chinese fretwork. The standard
Newport characteristics include
detachable legs, pointed knees, a
corkscrew finial, and panels beneath the
bonnet.**
Private Collection.

FIGURE III–14
*Spice chest. Walnut with tulip.
Philadelphia. Ca. 1740–1750.*
**Special locked chests or "nests of
drawers" appeared late in the 17th
century as repositories for expensive
imported spices. This chest, standing
five feet high on bold cabriole legs and
ball and claw feet, is a rare survivor
from the earlier period.**
*Courtesy, The Henry Francis du Pont Winterthur
Museum.*

FIGURE III–15 *(far right, top)*
*Desk. Walnut. Philadephia. Ca.
1740–1760.*
**The beading on the lively ogee-scrolled
skirt recalls the earlier practice of
applying a thin protective strip to
exposed edges, but the intaglio shell
carvings on the knees are found on
Chippendale style chairs attributed to
William Savery of Philadelphia. The
finely carved trifid feet are a five-toe
variation of the standard three-toe
variety. The serpentine curves of the
drawers are repeated by the moldings
over the pigeonholes, and the dividers
are cut out to repeat the ogee curves of
the skirt.**
Joe Kindig III.

books. The flat-top variety with
"square heads" continued to be
made as well and was sometimes still fitted with a stepped
pyramid for displaying pewter,
silver, or other riches. As late as
1762 in Philadelphia, John Ar-
mitt displayed "on ye Draws—9
China Bowls, 6 Plates & 1 Dish,
6 Cupps & Saucers." Thomas
Polegreen in the same city had a
"Chester Draws & Pyramid
China top of it."[6]

While the flush drawers of the
William and Mary style continued to be made throughout the
century, the lipped drawers were
introduced in the Queen Anne
period. In this technique the
drawer fronts overlapped the
drawer cavity, covering the crack
between the drawer and the
case, thus hiding any inac-
curacies in constructing the
drawer. Flush drawers in both
the Queen Anne and Chippendale styles were made with a
cock bead around the opening. In
Philadelphia, the bead was applied usually to the drawer itself,
whereas in New England, it was
applied typically to the frame.

Smaller chests, called nests of
drawers or spice boxes, contained valuable spices and sugar
imported from the Far East or
from the West Indies (Figure
III–14). The smaller ones sat on
tables, and a few larger ones
were placed on frames, much
like high chests of drawers.
These rare forms disappeared by
mid-century as spices became

more readily available and less expensive.

The number of desk and bookcases increased, along with the plain slant-front desk or desk on frame (Figure III–15). Glass panes or sparkling looking glass added elegance, but wooden paneled doors, usually with rounded Roman arches, were more common. Many desks rested on frames with short cabriole legs (Figure III–16).

Tables

The varieties of tables proliferated. Tables with cabriole legs and pad feet began to compete with the earlier turned gateleg tables (Figures III–17 and III–18). Tea tables grew more common as the price of tea dropped to a level where tea drinking was no longer confined to the wealthy. A raised molding on the edge of the table, strikingly similar to ones on Chinese K'ang tables, provided a little insurance against a valuable silver or porcelain tea service sliding off. Other tables, used for serving, were fitted with tile, slate, or marble, either imported or quarried in America. They were spread with a damask cloth and held knife boxes and glass decanters. Card and game tables, made in great numbers by the second quarter of the 18th century, confirmed the growing wealth and increased leisure time in the New World, when fortunes could be won or lost on the flip of a card. These tables with fold-over tops were common even in Philadelphia, where the Quakers frowned on gambling.

Looking Glasses

Looking glasses took on a decorative role throughout the Georgian style house as well as gracing the finest desk and bookcase. Import records show that thousands of frames made by cheap English labor arrived annually in America. Pier glasses, which appeared about 1735,

might hang on the wall in the best parlor between two windows—the space called the pier in architectural parlance. The solid walnut, veneered, or japanned frames were surmounted by hoods with carved and gilded shells or feathers. Larger looking glasses were usu-

FIGURE III–16
Desk and bookcase. Walnut with pine. Boston, Mass. Dated 1738.
The earliest documented blockfront, this piece was signed by Job Coit, Jr. in 1738. The unusual semicircular termination of the blocking pleasantly repeats the form of the arched door panels. These doors are fitted with mirror glass, which was the height of elegance in the 18th century, when glass was a luxury, but is less pleasing to the modern eye conditioned to prize polished, natural, wooden surfaces. The gently rounded bonnet contrasts with the sharply rising pediments of Chippendale case pieces. The interior is enriched with inlaid fans behind the arches of the door panels.
Courtesy, The Henry Francis du Pont Winterthur Museum.

FIGURE III–17 *(below, left)*
Table. Mahogany with birch and white pine. York, Maine. Ca. 1740–1780.
The cabriole-leg tables, such as this one, replaced the turned gateleg table popular in the first half of the 18th century. The beautifully figured mahogany for the single-board top and leaves was shipped by boat to the port of York, north of Portsmouth, New Hampshire.
Society for the Preservation of New England Antiquities.

FIGURE III–18
Detail of underside of table (Figure III–17).
The top is attached by means of glue blocks in the most common 18th-century manner. Not until early in the 19th century, when screws were produced less expensively, were table tops usually screwed to the frame. The rough chisel marks on the scalloped skirt indicate hand craftsmanship, in contrast to the band-sawn skirts of the mid-19th century.
Society for the Preservation of New England Antiquities.

FIGURE III–19
Looking glass. Walnut. Possibly New England. Ca. 1730–1740.
The detachable cresting with pegs that fit into holes in a crosspiece on the back is usually missing on these early looking glasses. This example, however, is intact. The original two-part glass was an imported luxury item. The frame may have been made in America, although the elaborate cutouts on the crest could have been done more cheaply in England, where labor was abundant.
Private Collection.

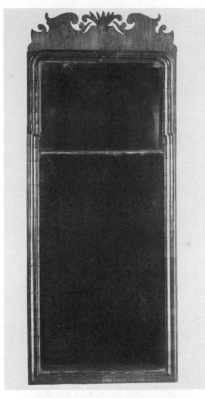

FIGURE III–20.
Daybed. Walnut. Philadelphia. Ca. 1740–1750.
The bold splats, with stiles that echo their shape, appear on a group of Philadelphia chairs. The trifid feet and the shape of the crest rail are other Philadelphia characteristics, but the presence of turned stretchers is uncommon in that area. The unusual width of 30 inches may explain the need for the additional support.
Courtesy, The Henry Francis du Pont Winterthur Museum.

FIGURE III–21 *(far right)*
Corner chair. Walnut and birch. Boston area. Ca. 1735–1765.
The corner chair was one of the most comfortable seats available, which accounts for its popularity throughout the 18th century. The vase-shaped, solid splats, cabriole front legs, and straight rear legs terminating in pad feet indicate a date before 1765, when the full-blown Chippendale style was popular.
Society for the Preservation of New England Antiquities.

in England in the late 17th century, as more attention was devoted to fireplaces.

SEATING FURNITURE

As in all periods, seating furniture was produced in great numbers. As large parlors became more common, sofas and settees proliferated, and the daybed declined in popularity (Figure III–20). Other types of chairs included slat-backs with two to seven slats and corner, or "roundabout," chairs, which appeared about 1740 (Figure III–21). Originally used almost exclusively in the bedroom, corner chairs were praised by Patrick Henry for their comfort over the hot easy chair and the stiff, uncomfortable side chair. The best corner chairs had balloon seats and scrolled, knuckled arms. Others, fitted with pans hidden

ally made in two parts (Figure III–19). The smaller upper section often contained diamond-engraved flowers or symbols of the English Crown. Since the glass was made in two parts, any slip by the engraver would ruin only a small piece of the valuable material. Diamonding or beveling was done from the late 17th century on. Some rare pier glasses were fitted with brass or glass candle arms so that they would magnify the faint glow of the candle. Chimney or "mantle tree" looking glasses for the wall above the fireplace first appeared

behind deep skirts, served as close stools or 18th-century toilets (Figure III–22). Stools were rarely found in America, although they were common in English parlors. It was considered impolite to sit in a chair in the presence of nobility in England. With no such strictures in America, the more comfortable side chair was preferred.

Windsor Chairs

American-made Windsors, which began to appear in Philadelphia by the 1740s, did not surpass the cheaper rush-bottom chairs in popularity until after the Revolution. The first Windsors in America were imported from England, where they were made as early as the 1720s. Furniture similar to Windsors was known from Egyptian times, but the English origin of Windsors is obscure. They may have been made by wheelwrights in the Windsor castle area outside London. The English version usually had solid or pierced splats with legs socketed close to the edge of the seat. Some were made with cabriole legs and stretchers in the shape of a cow's horns. Most English Windsors were of elm or oak, but a few stylish ones were made of mahogany, a wood rarely used in American Windsors.

Early American Windsors, once called Philadelphia chairs, because they first appeared in that city, had a distinctive lightness, since they almost never had splats or cabriole legs. Their strength, economy, and comfort made them ideal for public places and, lending themselves to prefabrication, their cheapness made them sell fast. The earliest ones, usually with seven or nine spindles and made with arms until the 1770s, were classified as "low back'd," "high back'd," and "sack back'd," also called "round top." The low-backed chair was the ancestor of the 19th-century captain's chair (Figure III–23). The high-backed chair had a horizontal crest, supported on spindles of the same

FIGURE III–22
Close stool. Walnut. New England. Ca. 1740–1760.
The close stool and the night table, a close stool on legs, began to appear in England by the 1740s. The night table was rarely found in America, but chairs fitted with chamber pots, concealed by a deep skirt, became common. The stool, however, is one of the rarest surviving American furniture forms.
Courtesy Mrs. Miriam Morris.

FIGURE III–23 *(above)*
Armchair. Maple. Pennsylvania. Ca. 1760–1780.
This early Windsor was known as a "low back'd" Windsor in the 18th century. The U-shaped seat and the ball feet are typical of Pennsylvania Windsors. The turned spindles, however, are unusual and are more often found on Rhode Island and, occasionally, on Connecticut chairs. The X-shaped stretcher is also a rare feature.
Courtesy, The Henry Francis du Pont Winterthur Museum.

height, rising from the seat through a rail that followed the curvature of the seat (Figure III–24). The sack-back was similar but had a rounded crest in the shape of a half circle (Figure III–25). In addition to chairs, the Windsor stick construction was used to fashion settees with as many as 38 spindles, three-legged stools, cradles, high chairs, and writing arm Windsors for both right- and left-handed customers (Figure III–26).

Windsors were usually constructed with several different woods readily available in America. The Windsor chairmaker shaped a two-inch thick piece of pine or tulip into a comfortable

FIGURE III–24
Armchair. Pennsylvania. Ca. 1755–1775.
The Pennsylvania characteristics of this high back Windsor chair include the cylindrical turnings on the lower part of the legs, which end in ball feet, the elongated vase-shaped turnings on the arm supports, and the horseshoe-shaped saddle seat. The serpentine crest rail ending in carved volutes also appears on documented Pennsylvania Windsors. The legs are inserted into holes bored through the nicely shaped seat and are secured with a wedge of wood driven into the top of the leg. With the exception of a different medial stretcher, this chair is quite similar to one in the Garvan Collection at Yale stamped by Thomas Gilpin I, who worked in Philadelphia in the 1750s.
Philadelphia Museum of Art: Charles F. Williams Collection, purchased by Subscription and Museum Funds.

saddle seat and chamfered the
front edge to lighten its appearance. He turned the legs
from durable maple, birch, ash,
or chestnut. The spindles—the
earliest ones were hand-shaped,
but later ones were turned on a
lathe—were fashioned from ash,
oak, or hickory. The availability
of diverse woods in America resulted in lighter chairs than
most English counterparts,
which depended primarily upon
oak.

Remnants of dried glue in the
joints of old Windsors dispel the
myth that only the shrinking of
green wood held the legs and
spindles in their sockets. A
wedge driven into the top of the
leg secured the joint. A coat of
paint hid the use of different
woods. At the end of the 18th
century, Benjamin Franklin ordered white ones and Thomas
Jefferson purchased black and
gold ones, but green was the
most common color earlier in
the century. In fact, Windsors
were often referred to as "green
chairs."

Windsor chairs exhibited certain regional characteristics. The
typical Philadelphia chair had a
U-shaped seat and button or
ball-turned feet surmounted by
cylinders and elongated vases
that were repeated in the arm
supports. This form was exported from Philadelphia to all
the colonies, as few Windsors
were made in New England until
after the Revolution. In New
York and Connecticut, Windsor
chairmakers produced the continuous armchair, unknown in
Philadelphia (Figure III–27).
Ebenezer Tracy of Lisbon, Connecticut, produced chairs typical
of that area, with swelling spindles and legs that did not completely pierce the seat. On these
chairs, the wedge was partially
inserted into the chair leg and
driven in as the leg hit the bottom of the hole drilled in the
seat to accept the leg. Rhode Island preferred the bow-back
form with scrolled, attached
arms, often of mahogany (Figure
III–28). The use of ornately
turned spindles usually indicates
a Rhode Island origin, but Connecticut and New York chairs
sometimes have those elements
as well.

REGIONAL CHARACTERISTICS

In 1928, when Wallace Nutting
published his monumental survey of furniture in America, *Furniture Treasury*, he was com-
pelled to add the caveat, "Mostly
of American Origin," to the subtitle.[8] With the state of knowledge of furniture design at that
time, it was difficult to distinguish between English and

FIGURE III–27
Left: Bow-back Windsor side chair. Southern New England or New York. Painted wood. Ca. 1785–1800.
In contrast to the turnings of the armchairs, these are rather flat and unexciting. The thick, soft-wood seat is chamfered on the front edge to lighten its appearance. The bow-back was made in Philadelphia, but the form was more common in New York and New England.
Virginia Museum.

Right: continuous-arm, bow-back Windsor armchair. Painted wood. New York or southern New England. Ca. 1785–1800.
Despite the bracing at the back, the single piece of wood that forms the back and the arms is easily broken, so that few examples of this form have survived. The turnings of the legs are repeated on the arm supports. The ungraceful transition from the bulb to the neck of the vase is rather abrupt and is known as clubbing. The bulge of the side stretchers provides enough room for a hole to hold the cross stretcher, and the bulge in the center stretcher repeats the motif.
Virginia Museum.

American furniture, much less between that made in Boston or Philadelphia. As more and more specialized studies appeared, some common characteristics of furniture produced in the six major 18th-century American economic and cultural centers— Boston, Newport, New York, Philadelphia, Charleston, and the Connecticut River Valley— were discovered. However, the assurances with which provenance was assigned, based on details of the woods used, construction techniques, and design, have been shaken. Further research has turned up exceptions to almost any statement about a particular detail appearing in only one place. And even assigning furniture of similar details to one area can be hazardous. The Boston chair, for example, which was exported to all the major cities in the colonies in the first half of the 18th century, was avidly copied by local cabinetmakers. It is virtually impossible to distinguish the copy from the import.

Regional variations in furniture design and construction can be explained in part by differing patterns of migration. Cabinet-

makers, immigrating from different parts of England, brought with them London techniques or various distinctive rural English cabinetmaking practices. To the principally English cabinetmaking tradition were added the designs and practices of several groups from other countries. The large number of Germans who

FIGURE III–28
Armchair. Painted wood. Rhode Island. Ca. 1790–1805.
The exaggerated splay to the legs on this bow-back Windsor gives great stability but has an awkward appearance. The slight swelling of the spindles is sometimes replaced by delicate turnings on Rhode Island chairs. The lack of the distinctive, sharply tapering legs, characteristic of many Rhode Island Windsors, might indicate a New York origin. Chairs with turned spindles, attached arms, and legs sharply tapering at the base are usually attributed to Rhode Island, although no documented examples with these characteristics have been found.
Smithsonian Institution Photo No. 76–9336.

FIGURE III–29
*Side chair. Walnut. Philadelphia. Ca.
1740–1750.*
The intaglio, leaf-carved knee is often attributed to William Savery, but it was used on chairs from other cabinet shops as well. The flat, serpentine medial and double-ogee side stretchers appear frequently on Rhode Island chairs but also occur on a group of Philadelphia chairs. The chamfering of the back posts is also a common Rhode Island characteristic. The applied three-piece rim, which supports the slip seat, is apparent on the seat rail of the balloon seat. A narrow tongue that continues into the leg accents the rounded slipper-front feet.
Private Collection.

FIGURE III–30 *(top, right)*
*Side chair. Mahogany. Philadelphia. Ca.
1750–1760.*
The S-curved stiles echo the outline of the splat. The same curve is repeated at least four times on the edge of the splat and again in the horseshoe seat and on the front legs. Two S-curves terminating in scrolls flank the scallop shell in the crest. This chair with trifid feet is part of a rare set of six that has survived together for almost 250 years.
Diplomatic Reception Rooms, U.S. Department of State.

FIGURE III–31
Detail of Philadelphia side chair (Figure III–30).
The wide rails provide a large surface to join the front and sides with a horizontal mortise and tenon joint. The legs are fastened to the seat with a dowel that secures the joint of the front and side seat rails. The trifid feet have tongues rising from the middle toes.
Diplomatic Reception Rooms. U.S. Department of State.

came to Pennsylvania influenced that colony's furniture. Between 1727 and 1740, over 50,000 Germans arrived in Pennsylvania, and by the end of the century they made up about one-third of the state's population. Another large group consisting of 20 percent of the population of Pennsylvania were the Scottish-Irish or Scottish Protestants, who had settled in Northern Ireland during the reign of James I early in the 17th century. Philadelphia

had fewer Scots and French Huguenots than did New York, but the Dutch influence in the latter colony was particularly strong. Both Massachusetts and Rhode Island had smaller numbers of these nationalities and were much more homogeneous than Philadelphia or New York.

Although disparate cabinetmaking traditions help to explain the strong regional characteristics in American furniture, the persistence of the apprentice system and the close-knit community of cabinetmakers in each center help to explain the perpetuation of these differences. Throughout the 18th century, circulating money was scarce, and business activity was carried on largely with credit or barter. Obviously, a craftsman would be more willing to deal with businessmen he knew than with newcomers. The business relationships might become further intertwined. In the construction of a high chest, for example, the seller of the piece might only have provided the raw materials, such as the wood, hardware, and nails. He may have engaged another cabinetmaker to construct the case; a turner to fashion the finials, the corner columns, and the drop ornaments on the skirt; as well as inlay specialists, carvers, and japanners to add gilded or inlaid shells. The community of cabinetmakers usually lived in the same section of the city, often intermarried, and took their fellow artisans' sons as apprentices. In Boston between 1725 and 1760 the community was relatively small, with about 200 craftsmen, including joiners, cabinetmakers, chairmakers, upholsterers, carvers, turners, and japanners. This figure was about one-third more than the next most important city of Philadelphia and about 50 more than the number of furniture craftsmen who worked in New York. In such a tight-knit community, design and construction practices changed only slowly.

Philadelphia

Despite the caveats and the realization that exceptions will turn up to every rule, some generalizations are possible about regional design and construction preferences. Chairs, which were relatively less expensive than other forms, were subject to hard wear, and were replaced frequently because of hard use, reflect the regional characteristics best although similar regional details appear on other furniture as well. Philadelphia Queen Anne chairs display a finely crafted series of curves in magnificent tension (Figure III–29). The plain, stump rear legs on many Philadelphia chairs contrast with the gracefully curved cabriole front legs, which end in a round or pointed club foot atop a thin disk, a ball and claw, or the distinctive Philadelphia trifid foot with three toes (Figure III–30). This three-toed foot introduced to America about 1745 reflects a strong Irish influence in Philadelphia. Legs are usually unencumbered with stretchers, which become unnecessary because the thick Queen Anne skirt joins the wide knees of the legs to form a strong joint. The seat rails are mortised and tenoned, and the legs are attached with large dowels projecting above them in the same manner that the legs are attached to William and Mary high chests (Figure III–31). Large quarter-round corner blocks are made up of two overlapping blocks. The technique of exposing the seat-rail tenon through the rear legs, for which the customer paid extra, is more common in Philadelphia than elsewhere (Figure III–32).

Boston

Chairs in Boston looked sparse, lean, and slender, particularly in the legs, back posts, and seat rails. These proportions characterized the simple vase-shaped splat, in contrast to the balusters with cusps of the Phil-

adelphia area. Although the rear legs are square in section, sometimes ending in the English pad foot similar to New York examples, the front legs terminated in a circular club form placed upon a thick pad. Stretchers continued to be used as a holdover from the earlier William and Mary style but were usually turned rather than flat, as in Philadelphia or New York (Figure III–33). The seat construction was similar to other areas in New England and New York in that the legs continued as one piece of wood to the top edge of the seat rails, which were tenoned into mortises cut into the legs; the joints were reinforced with triangular corner blocks. The compass seat, also called a horseshoe or balloon-shaped seat, was preferred in Massachusetts, but the square seat was found on less expensive chairs too. Brackets at the junction of the rear leg and the underside of the seat rail were common.

New York

Although Philadelphia and Boston chairs show distinct

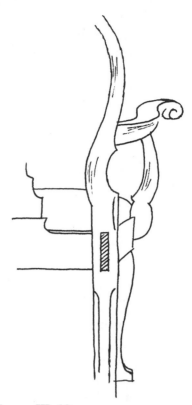

FIGURE III–32
Through tenon exposed on the back leg of a Philadelphia chair.

FIGURE III–33
Side chair. Walnut. New England. Ca. 1740–1760.
The curved stiles, the characteristic scrolled skirt, and the rounded back legs above the stretchers are found on chairs in Massachusetts and throughout New England. The side rails are cut out to lighten them, and the front rail is shaped similarly to the Newport chair in Figure III–37. The yoke crest, derived from Chinese examples, is found on chairs from other areas in America.
Virginia Museum.

characteristics, New York chairs were influenced by four separate areas: Philadelphia, Rhode Island, Holland, and England. The impact of the Dutch culture is apparent in the heavy lines and proportions of much New York furniture. The English influence was not surprising considering the presence of a Royal Governor and the large numbers of British troops, particularly during King George's War with France in the 1740s. The imported furniture owned by these native Englishmen served as models for the local craftsmen. Commercial and religious ties, particularly among the Quaker communities of Connecticut, Rhode Island, Philadelphia, and northern New Jersey, help to explain the influence of these areas. For example, Joshua Delaplaine, a prominent New York cabinetmaker, sold furniture made by his fellow Quaker, Christopher Townsend of Newport.[9] Philadelphia and Boston furniture was also sold in New York.

The seemingly unique New York characteristics, such as the cupid's bow on the shoe, where the splat attaches to the seat rail; the double reverse curves of the stiles; the bulbous ginger-jar-shaped splats; the volutes on the knee brackets; and the veneered splat, are all found on English chairs of the George II period (Figures III–34 and III–35). Rhode Island characteristics found on New York chairs include the square, or disk-shaped, foot on the rear leg, the configuration of the stretchers, and the single reverse curve on stiles of some New York chairs (Figure III–35). A few New York chairs have Philadelphia characteristics, such as the tenon extending through the back leg; the quarter-round, two-piece corner blocks; the pointed club foot; and the absence of stretchers.

Newport

A small group of Newport furniture exhibits very strong Chinese characteristics having a rectangular splat and rolled shoulders (Figure III–36). The baluster-shaped splat, similar to that of other areas, was more common, however (Figure III–37). The cabriole legs, often with flattened back sides, terminated in the familiar club foot, but the bottom portion, in contrast to the rounded Philadelphia foot, was cut away sharply. The eared splats, similar to the Philadelphia ones, were larger in scale. The rear legs terminated in a rectangular block surmounted by a turned

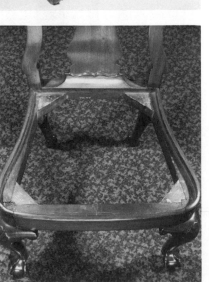

FIGURE III–34
Side chair. Walnut with pine. New York. Ca. 1740–1760.
Chairs with this form were owned by a number of prominent New York families. The rear stiles descend from the crest rail in reverse curves that generally follow the outline of the splat. An extra piece of wood is added to the bottom inside sections of the stiles opposite the base of the splat so that thinner stock could be used to form the stiles. The highly figured splat is set into a shoe at the back of the seat rail, which is topped with a bow-shaped molding. New York cabinetmakers followed common English practice by making the rear legs terminate in hoof-shaped blocks.
Diplomatic Reception Rooms, U.S. Department of State.

FIGURE III–35
Detail of New York side chair (Figure III–34).
Triangular corner blocks reinforce the seat rails, but their use as horseshoe-shaped seats is unusual. The molding on the top of the shoe that holds the base of the splat is shaped like a Cupid's bow.
Diplomatic Reception Rooms, U.S. Department of State.

cylinder, a formula based on English prototypes. The upper part of the stiles often had rounded, almost circular, shoulders, a feature that appeared only occasionally in Massachusetts and Philadelphia. As in Massachusetts, the stretchers persisted, but they were often flattened rather than turned and were similar, though heavier, than those found occasionally on Philadelphia chairs.

The Queen Anne style represented the culmination of the transition from the heavy medieval furniture of the 17th century to the classical furniture of the 18th century. The catalyst for the change was the impact of the Orient on furniture designs. The William and Mary style was much lighter than the 17th-century furniture and exhibited strong Oriental influence, but Queen Anne furniture showed the supremacy of the curve over the straight line. The graceful Queen Anne forms dominated furniture designs until the middle of the century.

NOTES

1. Walter Muir Whitehill, ed., *Boston Furniture of the Eighteenth Century* (Boston: The Colonial Society of Massachusetts, 1974), p. 77.

2. Marshall B. Davidson, ed., *The American Heritage History of Colonial Antiques* (New York: American Heritage Publishing Co., Inc., 1967), p. 148.

3. Timothy Philbrick, "Tall Chests: The Art of Proportioning," *Fine Wood Working* 9 (Winter 1977): 39–43.

4. William Macpherson Hornor, Jr., *Blue Book of Philadelphia Furniture from William Penn to George Washington* (Washington, D.C.: Highland House Publisher, 1977), p. 191.

5. Whitehill, *Boston Furniture*, p. 24.

6. Hornor, *Blue Book*, p. 69.

7. Nancy A. Goyne, "American Windsor Chairs: A Style Survey,"

FIGURE III–36
Armchair. Walnut with maple. Newport. Ca. 1725–1740.
The rounded shoulders and the Chinese-inspired rectangular dished splat are English features unknown on chairs from other areas in America except Newport. The veneered splat and detachable shoe are other English characteristics. The shaping of the front stretcher repeats the outline of the top of the crest rail.
Courtesy, The Henry Francis du Pont Winterthur Museum.

FIGURE III–37
Side chair. Walnut. Newport. Ca. 1740–1765.
The chamfered edges on the back legs and the distinctive shell carved on the crest, which is underlined with a double S-curve ending in scrolls, are typical Newport characteristics. The two ogee curves flanking the central drop on the front seat rail echo the lines of the stiles, the knee blocks, and the edges of the splat. The shell carving and splat configuration are sometimes found on New York chairs, but their proportions are usually fatter. A virtually identical chair is owned by the Rhode Island School of Design.
Courtesy Mrs. Miriam Morris.

The Magazine Antiques 95 (April 1969): 538–43.

8. Wallace Nutting, *Furniture Treasury* (New York: The Macmillan Company, 1963).

9. J. Stewart Johnson, "New York Cabinetmaking Prior to the Revolution" (Master's Thesis, University of Delaware, 1964), p. 62.

IV

THE CHIPPENDALE STYLE

FIGURE IV–1
*High chest of drawers. Mahogany.
Philadelphia. Ca. 1770–1780.*
**The carving on the Pompadour high
chest combines rococo and classical
motifs. The draped urns are derived
from a library bookcase design in
Chippendale's 1762 *Director*, and the
drapery against the diaper work on the
plinth and the allegorical bust itself are
all designed in the classical manner. In
sharp contrast is the swirling leafage on
the scrolls flanking the bust. The vines
beneath and the scrolls that curl up
each corner and ornament the knee,
skirt, and lower central drawer
illustrate the rococo at its best. The
carving of fighting swans confronting
the dragon on the lower central drawers
is derived from Thomas Johnson's *A
New Book of Ornaments*, published in
1760. A rich, mellow color is gradually
returning to the mahogany, which was
mercilessly stripped early in the 20th
century.**
*The Metropolitan Museum of Art, Kennedy Fund,
1918.*

BY THE THIRD QUARTER OF THE 18TH
century, the profitable trade
with England and the West Indies expanded the ranks of the
wealthy merchants and in-
creased the value of earlier fortunes. Drawn by the prosperity
and the promise of a better life,
new waves of immigrants, particularly Germans and Scottish-
Irish, flocked to American cities.
Bricklayers and carpenters fever-
ishly built houses to accommodate the new arrivals, and
cabinetmakers flourished by filling them with simple or ornate
furniture depending on the customer's pocketbook.

Philadelphia alone was adding
200 new houses a year after
1760, and this number more
than doubled by 1770. In the 15
years before the Revolution, the
City of Brotherly Love grew
from 23,750 to 40,000. During
the same period in Boston,

where the population remained
virtually stationary at about 16,-
000 inhabitants, cabinetmakers
and carpenters were kept busy
rebuilding and furnishing buildings destroyed by the city's
worst fire in 1760. Craftsmen
prospered in New York, too, as
the population of that city rose
from 18,000 in 1760 to 25,000 in
1775. In the same period, Newport grew from 7,500 to 11,000.

ARCHITECTURE

Notable exceptions of German,
Dutch, and Spanish influence
notwithstanding, the grandest
houses in America, and even ordinary dwellings, usually followed English provincial designs.
Georgian architecture by mid-
century had entered a new, more
formal, and elegant phase in the
pursuit of classical purity.

Touches of the Baroque persisted, but for the most part
American houses of the second
half of the 18th century were
more strictly classical in detail,
rigidly symmetrical, and based
on close readings of London architectural design books.

Wealthy patrons demanded as
much attention to interior decoration as to the exterior.
Jeremiah Lee of Marblehead
built a home in 1768 that was
typical of a wealthy merchant's
house and furnished it with expensive imported wallpaper,
painted paneling, and rich carving. The carved overmantel with
ornate garlands and swags was
drawn from Abraham Swan's
British Architect. William Buckland used the same source in
1773 and 1774 when he built his
masterpiece in Annapolis, Maryland, the Hammond-Harwood
House. Buckland's exquisitely

carved entrance and the exuberant rococo carving that graced the interior walls were among the finest in America.

The architectural design books promoted a richness of interior decoration that cabinetmakers matched in their furniture. The striking similarity of architectural detail, from that of cornices and chimney pieces to that of the pediments on high chests, and desk and bookcases, is easily explained by the carpenter's and cabinetmaker's dependence on common sources. Amateur architects in America owned a variety of books on architecture in addition to Swan's, including James Gibbs's *A Book of Architecture,* William Salmon's *Palladio Londinensis,* and William Pain's *The Builder's Companion,* all published in London in the 18th century. In addition to architectural details, these books suggested furniture designs to match interior decoration.

THE NEW STYLE

The subtle change in architecture at mid-century was paralleled in furnishings as well. It was not an abrupt change. Queen Anne curves continued to grace some chairs until after the Revolution even though the

more angular style, now called Chippendale, gradually gained ascendency between 1755 and 1790 (Figure IV–2). The rounded crest of the Queen Anne chair was replaced by an angular one with projecting ears similar to that of Chinese chairs. The pierced splat, or "cut-through bannister," had occasionally appeared on Queen Anne chairs, but the carvers of the Chippendale period turned the splat into a panoply of ribbons, cusps, arches, and scrolls. The richness of architecture was reflected in the carving, bold curves, and blocked facades of the furniture. As ceilings became higher, pediments on case pieces suggested the designs of windows, doors, and chimney pieces. As merchants and landowners built larger and more elegant houses, cabinetmakers filled them with an ever-increasing array of forms, such as firescreens; dumb-waiters; reading and corner tables; and candle, basin, and kettle stands (Figures IV–3, IV–4, IV–5, and IV–6).

Not until the mid-19th century was Chippendale's name used to describe the furniture style popular in the second half of the 18th century. Although he was one of the most fashionable cabinetmakers of his day, his fame rested on the publication of his furniture design book, *The Gentleman and Cabinetmaker's Director.* First published in London in 1754, it was so successful that a new edition came out the next year, and a third, expanded version with 200 designs appeared in 1762. The book was essentially a catalog to advertise his work. Chippendale operated one of the largest cabinetmaking establishments in London in the fashionable St Martin's Lane area, where he employed between 40 and 50 workmen. Pieces of furniture made in his shop still grace houses around London. Reacting to earlier criticism that his designs were too elaborate and impossible to execute, Chippendale declared in his 1762 edition:

these subtleties, the cabinet-maker could create his own designs.

Chippendale was not the creator of a new style but simply the recorder of the fashion that thrived at mid-century in London. His designs showed three major influences—the Chi-

Chippendale recognized the close relationship between furniture designs and architecture and began his book with an analysis of the five orders of ancient Greek and Roman columns. He admonished his fellow cabinet-makers to study them "since they are the very Soul and Basis of his Art." Chippendale included an explanation of the proportions of these columns along with instructions for designing architectural details, such as balusters, volutes, and moldings, for use in furniture. By mastering

FIGURE IV–4 *(far left)*
Kettle stand. Mahogany. Newport. Ca. 1770–1785.
Common in England, the kettle stand was not as popular in America. Most American kettle stands were made in New England. This one is attributed to John Townsend on the basis of his labeled Pembroke table, which has a pierced fretwork stretcher similar to the gallery on this example. The three legs are joined to a central block rather than to the banister, which is attached to the legs by means of a threaded dowel. The edge of the slide is cut on a diagonal to conform to the diamond-shaped incising on the edge of the top.
Courtesy, The Henry Francis du Pont Winterthur Museum.

FIGURE IV–5
Basin stand. Mahogany. New York. Ca. 1770–1780.
Chippendale, in his *Director*, illustrates several basin stands. By the third quarter of the 18th century, more and more wealthy households could afford the luxury of such specialized and elegant furniture.
Courtesy, The Henry Francis du Pont Winterthur Museum.

FIGURE IV–6
Fire screen. Mahogany. New York. Ca. 1766.
Fire screens were known from medieval times, but the tripod form was an 18th-century innovation. The blockish profile of the ball and claw feet indicates a New York attribution, which is confirmed by the original wool-on-linen needlework signed by Tanneke Pears of that city. Today, such pieces are mostly decorative, but in the 18th century they served the necessary function of protecting the bare skin from the heat of a roaring fire.
Courtesy, The Henry Francis du Pont Winterthur Museum.

Armchair. Mahogany. Boston. Ca. 1765–1775.

The popularity of Gothic motifs is clearly evident in the four columns rising to form pointed Gothic arches in the crest and in the four quatrefoils in the midsection of the splat. Touches of rococo carving adorn the center of the crest and intrude on the Gothic arches. Leaf carving also highlights the arms and arm supports. A gadrooned strip under the concave seat and a carved knee bracket are missing from this chair, whose mate is in the Winterthur Collection.

Diplomatic Reception Rooms, U.S. Department of State.

Side chair. Mahogany. Philadelphia. Ca. 1755–1775.

Extraordinarily bold carving is more characteristic of fine London chairs, but this chair proves that Philadelphia cabinetmakers could produce rich furniture too. The design is taken directly from a plate in Chippendale's *Director*, published in 1754. The splat combines rococo carving with a Chinese fret design. The scrolled French feet, rare in America, along with the straight Marlborough feet, were the most common ones found in Chippendale's design book. Although gadrooning was most prevalent in New York, it is seen in other areas, as on this Philadelphia chair.

Joe Kindig III.

nese, the Gothic, and the Rococo—that were grafted onto furniture with classical proportions. Additionally, the 1762 edition showed about a dozen plates with neoclassical elements. The Gothic and Chinese crazes that appeared in literature, architecture, and philosophy as well as in furniture reflected the 18th-century philosophe's passion to improve society by drawing on any available source. The exotic Orient and the idealized Gothic period of English history served as foils by which to criticize 18th-century English culture and as a relief to rigid classicism.

CHINESE, GOTHIC, ROCOCO

The Chinese taste had waned since the beginning of the 18th century, but reports by travelers, such as J. B. Du Halde's, published in England in 1741, revived the interest. The influence was apparent on furniture from about 1745, and in 1753 one writer in London observed that "According to the present prevailing whim everything is Chinese, or in the Chinese taste...."[2] Chippendale drew heavily upon *A New Book of Chinese Design*, published in 1754 and compiled by George Edwards and Matthew Darly, who engraved most of Chippendale's own plates in his 1754 edition.

The influence of the Gothic style was found throughout England in the churches and castles that dotted the countryside. Batty Langley's *Gothic Architecture, Improved by Rules and Proportions* published in 1742, first recommended Gothic designs in 18th-century architecture (Figure IV-7). Darly's *A New Book of Chinese, Gothic and Modern Chairs*, published in 1751, was the first pattern book of furniture designs to show the Gothic taste. One of the most enthusiastic exponents of this style was the son of Britain's prime minister, Horace Walpole, whose Gothic castle at Strawberry Hill was filled with furniture in the Gothic taste.

The most obvious influence on Chippendale, however, was the Rococo, which developed in Paris in the early 18th century (Figure IV-8). The word was derived from the French *rocaille*, which meant rock or grotto work. The style was based on the garden ornaments that Catherine de Medici, the wife of Henry II of France, used to decorate the grottos in the Tuileries in Paris in the 16th century. The style rejected the stiff classicism

of Louis XII. Although the asymmetrical motifs included rocks, shells, vines, leaves, and flowers, the highly regulated forms did not imitate nature. The style originated in France in the first quarter of the 18th century but not until the 1740s did Matthias Lock publish the first of numerous collections of designs of the French Rococo in England.

Like most cabinetmakers in the mid-18th century, Chippendale favored mahogany as the ideal medium for executing his creations, such as the intricately pierced chair splats. The Spanish had discovered the wood in the West Indies in the 16th century, and in the next century, it was employed to a limited extent in fine furniture. Not until after the heavy duty on imported woods was lifted in 1721 did it come into widespread use, replacing walnut as the preferred cabinet wood. Discriminating cabinetmakers prized it for its strength, fiery color, highly figured grain, resistance to warping and to worms, and suitability for carving. Gigantic mahogany trees, with trunks six to 12 feet in diameter, grew primarily in the Spanish colonies of Cuba, Santo Domingo, and Honduras and in the British colony of Jamaica, until it was exhausted there by 1750. The rich soil and tropical rainfall in Honduras pro-

duced a lighter colored and more highly figured wood than trees growing in the poorer, less watered soil of Cuba and Santo Domingo. The latter wood, because of its relative scarcity and more desirable color, cost up to twice as much. Because of its greater cost and the abundance of readily available substitutes, mahogany in America was used for the finest pieces, but it never supplanted native timbers, such as cherry, walnut, and maple, for less expensive work. Toward the end of the period veneers averaging an eighth-inch thick came into use for drawer fronts and desk and bookcase doors.

Chippendale's designs influenced cabinetmakers not only in England and America but also in Portugal, Spain, the Low Countries, Germany, and even in France, where a French edition was published (Figures IV–9 and IV–10). As the first of a number of English furniture design books, it inspired subsequent ones by Thomas Johnson, Robert Manwaring, and one by William Ince and John Mayhew. Chippendale's designs were particularly popular in Philadelphia, where the Library Company lent their copy to local cabinetmakers. Thomas Affleck, one of the most successful cabinetmakers in Philadelphia, owned a copy of "Shippendale's Designs."

FIGURE IV–9 *(far left)*
Side chair. Mahogany. New York. Ca. 1765–1775.
The back of the chair is based on Plate XII of the 1762 edition of Chippendale's *Director*. Most of the carving shown in the Chippendale plate is omitted on the American example. The seat slips out, in contrast to the one in the plate, which is upholstered over the rail; and the legs are cabriole, ending in ball and claw feet instead of the straight legs shown by Chippendale. The chair is one of a set of 12 that, incredibly, are still together. They once belonged to the Revolutionary War general, Matthew Clarkson.
Courtesy Mrs. Miriam Morris.

FIGURE IV–10
Plate XII from Thomas Chippendale's The Gentleman and the Cabinetmaker's Director. 1762 edition.

His competitor, Benjamin Randolph, was also familiar with the designs, some of which he copied for his elaborately engraved trade card. John Folwell hoped to publish a Philadelphia edition of Chippendale's *Director*, but the Revolution interrupted his plans. One of almost a dozen copies of the *Director* now known in America was found in Salem, Massachusetts. But not everyone was smitten with the new style. Isaac Ware, surveyor for the King of England, did not like

> to see an unmeaning scrawl of C's inverted and looped together, taking the place of Greek and Roman elegance even in our most expensive decorations. It is called French and let them have the praise of it! The Gothic shaft and Chinese bell are not beyond nor below it in poorness of imitation.[3]

ENGLISH INFLUENCE

As important as these design books were, only a very few cabinetmakers could afford their own copy. Instead, the new styles were transmitted to America primarily by imported English furniture and furniture-makers trained in Britain. Imports were as much as four times as expensive as locally made products. Advertisements by American cabinetmakers often claimed that English walnut, beech, oak, and other woods were more susceptible to devastating wood borers, and changes in humidity in the move from the damper English climate to America wrought havoc on the furniture. Despite the disadvantages, however, many Americans, reflecting their close cultural ties to the mother country, considered English furniture the most desirable and stylish. Even American craftsmen acknowledged this fact in their advertising, which claimed their products to be "in the latest London fashion" or made by craftsmen "late of London." In addition to furniture imported

for sale in the colonies, the royal governors and the horde of English bureaucrats sent to America in the 1760s brought English furniture with them. Immigrants sometimes arrived with pieces as well.

Despite the strong English influence, local craftsmen benefited by the increasing anti-British sentiment at mid-century. The implementation of the Non-Importation Agreements among merchants beginning in 1765 in Boston, Philadelphia, New York, and other colonial cities cut the flow of English goods appreciably. These agreements sought to overturn the heavy customs duties levied by the Stamp and Sugar Acts and, later, the Townshend Acts. Captain Samuel Morris of Philadelphia wrote to his nephew, Samuel Powel, Jr., in London in 1765:

> Household goods may be had here as cheap and as well made from English patterns. In the humour people are in here, a man is in danger of becoming Invidiously distinguished, who buys anything in England which our Tradesmen can furnish. I have heard the joiners here object this against Dr. Morgan & others who brought their furnishings with them....[4]

The English influence was still strong in Boston, which, unlike Philadelphia and Newport, had royal governors in residence. Boston had suffered economic distress as a result of King George's War in the 1740s and the French and Indian War which ended in 1763 and had lost out in a number of important markets to competition from neighboring towns, such as Salem and Marblehead. It ranked third in population and had fallen behind New York and Philadelphia. Nevertheless, the city continued to be one of the most important cultural and economic centers in the colonies.

Andrew Burnaby, Vicar of Greenwich, England, observed in 1760 that "The arts are undeniably forwarder in Massachusetts-Bay, than either in Pennsylvania or New York." John Adams, in 1766, noted in his diary that he dined with his friend Nicholas Boylston in Boston and then "Went over the House to view the Furniture, which alone cost a thousand Pounds sterling."[5] The local furniture market remained strong, and Boston cabinetmakers shipped their wares to all the colonial ports.

THE FURNITURE

Chairs: Regional Variation

Massachusetts chairs, although often revealing strong English influence, continued to exhibit distinctive regional preferences. While Philadelphians chose many designs from Chippendale's *Director* Boston patrons selected at least one chair design from Robert Manwaring's pattern book, *The Cabinet and Chair-Maker's Real Friend and Companion*, published in London in 1765. Chairs made in Boston in the second half of the 18th century manifested the light proportions of earlier styles, particularly in their thin seat rails and legs. Even the carving had a delicacy and softness in contrast to the bold and lively work on Philadelphia chairs. Stretchers continued to be used; corner blocks were triangular (Figure IV–11). One of the most common chair splats had four strap-like scrolls descending from the crest, two of them forming circles like owl's eyes. These circles were supported on four gently curving scrolls rising from the seat rail (Figure IV–12). Another group of chairs had an urn-shaped splat enclosing a series of scrolls (Figure IV–13). Many Massachusetts chair splats seemed to have a visual division at mid-section, but one group exhibited an uninterrupted movement from the shoe to the crest similar to one group of Philadelphia chairs. Gothic arches appeared on yet another group.

FIGURE IV-11
Typical triangular corner block with horizontal grain reinforcing seat rails at rear leg of mid-18th-century Massachusetts chair. The block was often omitted on the front corners (right).

FIGURE IV-12
Corner chair. Mahogany. Boston. Ca. 1760-1770.
The raked talons on the ball foot, the presence of stretchers, and the distinctive owl-like pierced splat all scream Massachusetts. The well-carved foot and reeded columns supporting the crest rail indicate a Boston maker. Since they wore full coats and dresses in the 18th century, men and women welcomed the comfort of the corner or roundabout chair, which offered arm support but did not bunch up their clothes.
Diplomatic Reception Rooms, U.S. Department of State.

FIGURE IV-13.
Side chair. Mahogany. Boston. Ca. 1760-1780.
A thin and delicate back and legs mark Massachusetts chairs. The delicate carving on the crest and splat heightens this effect. The smooth curve of the legs, which flow into the seat rail without interruption of a pronounced knee block, is another Massachusetts characteristic. The splat is based directly on English prototypes and is found on Massachusetts corner and straight leg chairs as well as on some New York examples. Chairs with the seat upholstered over the serpentine rail were rarely made and indicate an unusual degree of elegance for usually restrained American customers. The acanthus on the knees is carved with more definition than the usually wispy Massachusetts examples.
Diplomatic Reception Rooms, U.S. Department of State.

FIGURE IV-14
Side chair. Mahogany. Rhode Island. Ca. 1750-1760.
The pierced vase-shaped splat with dots in the midsection and the chamfered rear legs are among the elements that point to a Rhode Island origin. The cabriole legs, pad feet, and compass seat characterize the Queen Anne style, but the squared off crest and protruding ears confirm the influence of the Chippendale style. The crest relates to a similar design on York chairs. Marked number "III," this chair is part of a set of 12.
Courtesy, The Henry Francis du Pont Winterthur Museum.

The splats in the most common Rhode Island chairs resembled Massachusetts examples, with four curved straps rising from the base meeting the four curling ones descending from the crest. Instead of curving around in the shape of an inverted question mark as in Boston work, the two inner straps cross each other to form interlocking C-scrolls. Another common Newport splat was a vase shape formed with four straps tapering at the base and joined at the middle with two dots (Figure IV-14). Looping interlocking scrolls similar to those on New York chairs were also common. Legs on many Rhode Island chairs, and on tables as well, were straight and ornamented with stopped fluting (Figures IV-15 and IV-16).

On one of several popular Philadelphia types the splats bulged at the base to accommodate a trefoil, above which rose an elongated, pierced splat terminating in three irregularly shaped voids at the crest. The design was found on a group of chairs attributed to James Gillingham, a prominent Philadelphia chairmaker (Figure IV-17). The discovery of a simi-

FIGURE IV–15
*Easy chair. Mahogany. Newport. Ca.
1770–1780.*
The horizontally rolled arms are
associated with Philadelphia and early
New England chairs. However, the use
of stopped fluting on the front legs
indicates a Newport attribution. The
restrained lines of this chair are also
more typical of New England than of
Philadelphia, where curves and carving
were often more exuberant.
Courtesy Dr. and Mrs. Arthur Mourot.

FIGURE IV–16 *(right)*
Detail of easy chair (Figure IV–15) with
stopped fluting or cabling on the leg.
Found on many English chairs and
architectural details, stopped fluting was
most common on Newport cabinetry.
Courtesy Dr. and Mrs. Arthur Mourot.

FIGURE IV–17 *(far right, top)*
*Side chair. Mahogany. Philadelphia. Ca.
1770–1780.*
A group of chairs with an identical
splat are attributed to James Gillingham
on the basis of this chair with his
label. The splat design follows a plate
which appears in both the 1754 and
1762 editions of the *Director*, although
carving has been omitted on the crest
of this Philadelphia chair. The splat
with the four Gothic quatrefoils was
reproduced in so many different
variations in Philadelphia that it was
obviously a design favored by
chairmakers like Gillingham.
White House Collection.

FIGURE IV–18 *(far right, bottom)*
*Side chair. Walnut and maple.
Philadelphia. Ca. 1760–1780.*
A dark stain disguises the use of maple
in the seat rails. The pierced splat,
made of a single piece of walnut, is a
standard design favored in Philadelphia.
The carved scallop shell is also typical,
but the asymmetrical shell ornamenting
the crest is less common. The
repetition of the volutes on the crest in
the tips of the two C-scrolls sweeping
down from the crest and on the knee
brackets give rhythm and unity to the
design. The ovoid, stump, rear legs,
typical of Philadelphia, cant inward
since the back stiles rise at an angle
from the seat. The needlework seat
cover is a 19th-century addition.
Courtesy Mrs. Miriam Morris.

lar chair stamped I. Duncan indicates that other cabinetmakers in Philadelphia made the design as well. A more common Philadelphia splat had basically a Queen Anne vase-shape. When pierced, these were usually carved with ribbon-like scrolls (Figures IV–18, IV–19, and IV–20). Another splat design featured intertwined strapwork flowing into the crest rail to form Gothic arches, cusps, trefoils, and quatrefoils (Figure IV–21). Philadelphia chairs were rarely upholstered over the rail. On chairs with the more common slip seat, the splat entered a shoe that was, in turn, attached to the seat rail. The corner block was quarter round and made in two pieces (Figure IV–22). On many English chairs where up-

holstery tacked to the seat rail was more common, the splat joined the seat rail directly. The shoe was set in front of the splat so that it could be removed easily, and upholstery was tacked to the frame under it. As in the Queen Anne style, Philadelphia customers often paid the extra six pence to have tenons cut through the rear stump legs.

New York chairs followed English designs closely. They often had broad proportions, heavy splats, and bold crests. Cupid's-bow beading often outlined the shoes at the base of the splats, and gadrooning, called "toad's back" in at least one cabinetmaker's advertisement, frequently enhanced the front seat rail. The carved arms terminating in eagle's heads followed typical English Georgian designs (Figures IV–23 and IV–24). The tassel and ruffle, the looping scroll, and the diamond shapes

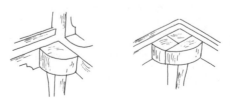

FIGURE IV–23
Armchair. Mahogany. New York. Ca. 1760–1770.
The carved, eagle's head, arm terminals are typical of English Georgian furniture and show the close affinity of New York to English designs. The squarish back legs are also common in New York, in contrast to the ovoid stump legs on Philadelphia chairs. The unusual drop on the front seat rail breaks up the broad expanse of the rail.
Diplomatic Reception Rooms, U.S. Department of State.

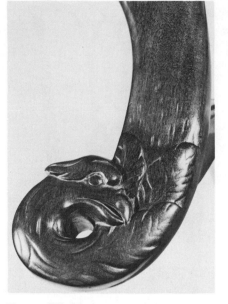

FIGURE IV–24
Detail of New York chair (Figure IV–23) showing the eagle's head on the arm termination.
Diplomatic Reception Rooms, U.S. Department of State.

FIGURE IV–25 *(far right)*
Side chair. Mahogany. New York. Ca. 1760–1775.
The tassel and ruffle carving on the splat is characteristic of several documented sets of New York chairs, although a related motif appears on some Philadelphia chairs. Irish chairs with the same motif may have served as the prototype for both areas. Gadrooning applied to the underside of the skirt and the hoof rear feet appear on other New York furniture.
Private Collection.

FIGURE IV–26 *(left)*
Armchair. Mahogany with red oak and pine. Philadelphia. Ca. 1760–1770.
Called "French Chairs" in both the 1754 and 1762 editions of Chippendale's *Director* and "Marlborough Feet Chairs" in the Colonies, the upholstered armchair was a luxury. This example has Gothic and Chinese frets on the front Marlborough legs, brackets on the bottom of the legs, and carved arms and arm supports. The double serpentine crest rail gives a great sense of movement to the back. This chair belonged to Governor John Penn and was probably part of the set he purchased from Thomas Affleck in Philadelphia.
Diplomatic Reception Rooms, U.S. Department of State.

were common splat designs (Figure IV–25). Knee carving showed acanthus leaves streaming down either side of the leg, forming a deep V that was cross-hatched, a technique found on two chairs signed by Gilbert Ash, who worked in Wall Street after 1756.[6]

The cabriole leg on easy chairs continued to be popular, but by the 1760s, the Marlborough leg, with or without "bases" and "brackets," was more fashionable. Whereas Philadelphia cabinetmakers often molded these legs or ornamented them with fretwork, fancy Newport legs were stop-fluted. Marlborough legs were illustrated in Chippendale's *Director*, which did not feature the then outdated ball and claw foot. The inspiration for the design may have been the square pillars in Marlborough Palace, designed by Sir Christopher Wren (Figure IV–26). The same Marlborough legs appeared on rare back stools described in a Philadelphia price book as "Chair frame for Stuffing over back and Feet with Marlborough Feet." These chairs and the "French chairs" with upholstered arm rests and backs, also with Marlborough feet, were designed for parlor use rather than for bedrooms, where easy chairs were found.

Although furniture designs and construction techniques varied from shop to shop, the carving that enriched the furniture in each city showed general consistency, particularly in the execution of the ball and claw foot. Even though each major city supported numerous cabinetmakers, they all depended on only a handful of carvers to embellish their work. In Massachusetts, the ball was rounded, the talons were delicate and attenuated, and the two side talons raked back sharply, a feature rarely seen elsewhere (Figure IV–27). In Philadelphia, carvers executed a slightly squashed ball, and the finely sculptured talons, joined by wide webs, flowed up into the leg (Figure IV–28). The ball and claw foot in New York work was usually squarish and apparently cut from a cube (Figure IV–29). The talons came straight down around the ball and were thicker, as in the Philadelphia ones, or very thin, as in Newport work. The web between the talons was omitted or not distinct, seeming to flow into the talon. The thick, poorly defined talons and round ball of some Rhode Island feet were similar to the New York foot. A second Rhode Island type, associated with the Goddard and Townsend cabinetmakers, exhibited a finely carved talon without a web, and an elongated ball. Occasionally the talon was undercut as on some English chairs (Figure IV–30).

FIGURE IV–27 *(top, left)*
Detail of Massachusetts ball and claw foot (Figure IV–60). The side talon rakes backward in the typical Massachusetts manner.
Diplomatic Reception Rooms, U.S. Department of State.

FIGURE IV–28 *(top, center)*
Detail of Philadelphia ball and claw foot (Figure IV 20). The Philadelphia ball and claw is characterized by a flattened ball and well-defined talons with a web between them.
Courtesy Mrs. Miriam Morris.

FIGURE IV–29
Detail of foot on New York desk and bookcase (Figure IV–69). The typical New York ball and claw foot seems to be cut from a cube, as in this example. The web between the talons is not distinct.
Diplomatic Reception Rooms, U.S. Department of State.

FIGURE IV–30
Detail of carved leg and foot of Newport dressing table (Figure IV–45). The undercut talon appears on only a few choice pieces of Newport furniture. The thin talons without a web between them and the attenuated ball are characteristic of Newport work.
Diplomatic Reception Rooms, U.S. Department of State.

FIGURE IV–31
Side chair. Mahogany. Massachusetts. Ca. 1780–1790.
The "Slatt back," or "Splatt back chair," as these were called in the 18th century, was popular until about 1810. The projecting rounded ears and the traces of rococo carving on the slats and crest indicate the earlier date. The carved central ornaments on the slats are anthemia or Greek honeysuckle, a popular neoclassical motif. The notation in *The Journeymen Cabinet and Chair-Makers Philadelphia Book of Prices* for 1795 of "Splatt back Chair, honey suckle pattern made for stuffing over the seat rail" indicates that this same pattern was made in Philadelphia as well as elsewhere.
Diplomatic Reception Rooms, U.S. Department of State.

FIGURE IV–32 *(below, left)*
Settle. Pine. American. Ca. 1725–1775.
Settles descended from medieval benches with high backs that usually were equipped with a locker below the seat. Although they were less common in England by the 18th century as chairs became more prevalent, the form continued to be made in America for most of the 18th century although usually without the locker. They typically stood in front of the fireplace in the great hall or kitchen. The hood on this example provided extra protection from cold winter drafts. The simple lines and lack of ornament which typified these pieces make it risky to assign a precise date or place of origin.
The Metropolitan Museum of Art, Gift of Mrs. J. Insley Blair, 1947.

Parlor Furniture

Numerous chairs lined parlor walls in typical 18th-century fashion. Chairs and tables were pulled out temporarily for dining, conversation, or other activities. Chairs were usually made in sets. Although James Logan at Stenton had 71 side chairs, three armchairs, and one easy chair, the parlor of John Cadwalader, with six side chairs and one armchair, was more typical. Some may have been elegantly carved mahogany or walnut slatbacks, which, for a short period at the end of the 18th century, assumed a formal role in the parlor (Figure IV–31).

Sofas, which evolved from settles, also lined the walls and added considerable elegance to a few extravagantly furnished houses (Figure IV–32). The straight seat rails on the earliest dated ones rested on cabriole legs. Later examples had a serpentine skirt or a carved fret below the seat and straight Marlborough legs (Figure IV–33). In a technique employed on some upholstered chairs, brass-headed nails sometimes accentuated the outline of the sofa.

FIGURE IV–33
Sofa. Mahogany. Philadelphia. Ca. 1765–1780
Sofas were rare luxuries in the 18th century, and few examples survive. The serpentine curve to the front seat rail echoes the sharply reverse-curved back. The heavy, plain legs provide a sturdy platform for the graceful curves of the seat, back, and arms. Although this form is clearly in the Chippendale style, a plainer documented example at Winterthur is dated 1812.
Courtesy Mrs. Miriam Morris.

Tall case clocks, several times as expensive as high chests, stood as ostentatious centerpieces in the best parlors. In widespread use only from the mid-18th century, they generally appeared in the parlor after the bedroom declined in importance as a public room. American clock cases had scrolled or bonnet pediments, similar to those on high chests. They housed brass works imported from London makers, such as Thomas Wagstaffe, or made in America by David Rittenhouse of Philadelphia or others in the relatively small group of American 18th-century clockmakers (Figure IV–34).

Game tables were standard fixtures in the parlors of most fashionable houses. New York examples were the most impressive. Even though New York's booming wartime economy turned to depression in the 1760s, when peace came and the British troops left after the French and Indian War, many New Yorkers were still able to purchase some fine furniture. Mahogany card tables were among the most impressive New York pieces. These had a gadrooned, serpentine skirt and square corners that rested on bold cabriole legs with richly carved acanthus leaves on the knees. A concealed drawer in the back skirt for cards and dice was not very secret, since most of the two dozen known examples had one (Figure IV–35). The New York card table may well be a uniquely American form; the most common English type had round turret-shaped corners and a straight skirt.[7] By comparison, Philadelphia game tables with cabriole legs were usually more reserved (Figure IV–36). The Philadelphia table—with a rectangular top and full-length drawer in the skirt, resting upon straight, molded legs with pierced corner brackets—was less common in New York.

Also gracing the parlors in all parts of the colonies were imported pier glasses and rectangu-

lar chimney glasses above the fireplaces. Chippendale's *Director* referred to some pier glasses, based on designs by William Kent, James Gibbs, Isaac Ware, and Abraham Swan, as taberna-

FIGURE IV–34
Tall case clock. Mahogany. Philadelphia. Ca. 1760–1775.
The dial is signed by Thomas Wagstaffe, a London Quaker who sent clockworks to his brethren in both Philadelphia and Newport. The brass face has rococo work in the spandrels. The applied panel on the base and the door are made of highly figured mahogany flanked by fluted corner columns. Two urn finials, or "blazes," and a central cartouche, or "shield," with the so-called Philadelphia peanut top the pediment.
Courtesy Dr. and Mrs. Arthur Mourot.

FIGURE IV–35 *(top)*
Game table. Mahogany. New York. Ca. 1765–1785.
The characteristic five-legged game table is fitted with a green baize top (old but not original), oval depressions for counters, and square corners for candlesticks. The shallow, serpentine skirt with a gadrooned edge nailed on contrasts with other New York card tables having deeper skirts and bolder gadrooning. The C-scrolls and acanthus leaves on the knees contrast with the plain rear legs. The fifth leg swings out to support the top as is typical of New York tables.
Diplomatic Reception Rooms, U.S. Department of State.

FIGURE IV–36
Card table. Walnut. Philadelphia. Ca. 1760–1780.
Card tables with round corners, such as this example, were more expensive than the cheaper straight-legged variety. The typical Philadelphia shell on the knees added additional expense. Candles stood on the corners, and the depression in the baize top held counters and chips used in various 18th-century card games. When not in use, the top folded over, and the rear leg swung back to the frame.
Courtesy Mrs. Miriam Morris.

cle frames because of their relationship to the architectural niches of Renaissance buildings. These looking glasses with gilt frames were surmounted with a triangular or scrolled pediment and either a central eagle or an Oriental phoenix bird. Carved leaves and flowers and, later, acanthus leaves and C-scrolls streamed down each side of the frame (Figure IV–37). Simpler versions were embellished by elaborate fretwork around the

frame and a simple phoenix bird, a sheaf of wheat, or feathers in the crest. In a variation of the architectural Chippendale looking glass usually found in Philadelphia, the surrounding frame was carved with elaborate rococo ornament (Figure IV–38). By 1775, oval looking glasses with rococo ornament were particularly popular. Some frames were even ornamented with papier mâché, a chewed paper technique that was also used on ceiling and woodwork to imitate plaster. This method was out of style by 1783, when it was derided as a "harbour for vermin." The development of glass-casting techniques, which supplanted glass blowing at the end of the century, facilitated the manufacture of large-sized looking glasses.

Looking glasses, along with most of the frames, continued to be imported, even though some bore American labels, such as those of John Elliott of Philadelphia. These labels were generally pasted onto imported English frames. In 1763, Elliott advertised that "He also quicksilvers and frames old glasses, and supplies people with new glasses to their own frames: and will undertake to cure any English looking glass that shews the face either too long or too broad or any other way distorted."[8] Not surprisingly, Elliott put his business up for sale on the eve of the Revolution when he foresaw that his source of supply would be cut off. There were no takers. Other merchants, such as Samuel Kneeland of Hartford, Connecticut, advertised in 1787, "Old Looking Glasses repaired, fram'd and gilt in the neatest manner, so as to look equal to new ones."[9]

Dining Furniture

A parlor usually served as a dining area, but meals were sometimes taken in the bedroom as well. Few people could afford to set aside one room exclusively for dining until late in the

18th century. Rooms exclusively for dining were not common until the 19th century. The dining area of Charles Willing's Philadelphia mansion, built in 1746, featured a large mahogany table, two "Fan back'd" armchairs, and 12 "Claw footed" chairs. Against the wall stood a marble-topped sideboard table and two tea tables, one a round, scalloped one. A large gilt looking glass and gilt sconces decorated the walls, along with seven bronze busts set on brackets. Crimson draperies added splashes of color at the windows.

The dining table was usually plain because it would be hidden under a cloth. The square-top table, often with notched or cut-out corners, was more popular in Philadelphia at mid-century than the round type. Tables had straight or cabriole legs with ball and claw or pad feet that matched the rest of the furniture. Tripod-base dining tables did not become popular until the end of the century. The sideboard table, from three to six feet long and fitted with a marble slab, provided additional serving space. The marble was imported or obtained locally—gray from nearby quarries in Pennsylvania, black from Vermont, and green from

the New Haven, Connecticut area (Figure IV–39). "Circular Side board Tables," which Thomas Affleck and others advertised, were less common. The sideboard tables were also used in drawing rooms and hallways as console tables. If the tally of surviving examples is an accurate guide, Newport and Boston favored the serpentine tops, Philadelphia preferred the rectangular ones (Figure IV–40).

Corner cupboards, either built in or free-standing, appeared about 1720 and were at first called buffets. Elaborate shell-carved hoods with single or double glass-paned doors in the upper section provided a fitting setting to show off family silver

FIGURE IV–41
Corner cupboard. Painted wood. New England. Ca. 1770–1780.
Cupboards such as this were frequently built in and required no rail beneath the lower doors. The shell is carved from a large block of wood made up of numerous pieces glued together. The vertical fluted molding above the door suggests the keystone in a Roman arch.
Diplomatic Reception Rooms, U.S. Department of State.

FIGURE IV–42 (below, right)
Tea table. Mahogany. Massachusetts. Ca. 1760–1780.
This tea table is one of several surviving examples with a multi-turreted top. The top is cut from one solid piece of mahogany. The table epitomizes the Chippendale style in which the contained and restrained Queen Anne lines explode as elements of the furniture burst their bonds and seem to fly off the surface.
Courtesy, The Henry Francis du Pont Winterthur Museum.

FIGURE IV–43 (far right)
Tea table. Mahogany. Philadelphia. Ca. 1765–1780.
The one-board top is dished by attaching it to the faceplate of a lathe and chiseling away part of the top, but the series of reverse curves, now called a pie-crust edge, must be done laboriously by hand. The top both tips and revolves by means of a bird-cage device under the top. The formula of a straight or slightly bowed line and a double-ogee curve flanked by two cresents is usually repeated eight times around the edge, but on this table, the series is repeated 10 times. The broad knees on the legs provide a surface that is exquisitely carved with asymmetrical acanthus leaves.
Diplomatic Reception Rooms, U.S. Department of State.

FIGURE IV–44
High chest of drawers. Mahogany. Newport. Ca. 1760–1770.
The corkscrew finials (these are replacement copies), the enclosed bonnet, and the flowing skirt with a stylized scallop shell are all Newport characteristics. The applied panels in the bonnet repeat the effect of the lipped drawers, unify the piece, and fill a visual void. The legs can be detached from the case for ease of moving, a convenience found on a number of Newport high chests. The back legs end in pads, in the usual Newport practice. Rare touches for the usually restrained Newport carving are the two tiny scrolls that curl out from the two bottom lobes of the shell along the skirt.
Diplomatic Reception, Rooms, U.S. Department of State.

their work to other craftsmen. In 1767 one specialist, Samuel Williams, advertised "mahogany and walnut tea table columns" for sale.[11]

Bedroom Furniture

Even though high chests were among the most expensive and ornate furniture owned by wealthy colonists, these pieces and their matching dressing tables were usually displayed, not

and china (Figure IV–41). The corner cupboard replaced the court cupboard for this purpose. In 1740, Captain John Hopkins of Philadelphia displayed "2 China Dishes, 2 Scolloped Basons, 6 Burnt China plates, Some delf Ware, 2 China Cupps, and 3 Glasses" in his cupboard.[10]

Square-top tea tables, popular from the Queen Anne period, or the newer round-top ones, were set with glistening silver services (Figure IV–42). The finest Philadelphia tables had laboriously scalloped rims, dished tops, carved pedestals, and bird-cages, or "boxes," to allow the top to turn as well as tip (Figure IV–43). The great number of balusters having the characteristic flattened ball with ring turning indicated that a few turners specialized in this form and sold in the best parlor, but in the bedroom (Figures IV–44, IV–45, and IV–46). The custom of receiving guests and even tradesmen in the bedroom had receded by mid-century, but the habit of placing the best pieces there had not completely changed. Besides, they provided a handy place to store clothing and linens in 18th-century houses built without much closet space. However, the addition of the small Pembroke, or breakfast, table to the bedroom about 1770 was a harbinger

FIGURE IV–45

Dressing table. Mahogany. Newport. Ca. 1745–1770.

The finest Newport dressing tables had less carving than their Philadelphia counterparts but no less elegance. The finely sculpted undercut talons, the acanthus leaves with anthemion pendants on the knees, and the typical Newport stylized scallop shell on the skirt indicate a high degree of cabinetmaking skill. The graceful curves of the skirt repeat the lines of the cabriole legs and lead the eye into the central shell. The molded top and the cove molding beneath it are almost identical to those on Figure IV–52. A similar dressing table was made by Job Townsend in 1746.

Diplomatic Reception Rooms, U.S. Department of State.

FIGURE IV–46

Dressing table. Mahogany with pine and poplar. Philadelphia. Ca. 1765–1775.

The dressing table is ornamented with the finest Philadelphia rococo carving. A swan, derived from illustrations in *Aesop's Fables*, swims on the central drawer. Even the corner columns are carved with vines instead of the more common reeding. A Chinese fret pierced with rosettes outlines the top. The veneered drawer fronts may reflect the increasing scarcity of mahogany toward the end of the Chippendale period, but the shimmering effect of the veneer could not be obtained with solid wood. A cloth for the top and a looking glass mounted on the wall or a dressing box completed the setting for the table.

Courtesy, Museum of Fine Arts, Boston, M. and M. Karolik Collection.

of the changing role of the bedroom from a public to a private room for family use (Figure IV–47).

If the owner could afford the lump sum expense, he decorated his bed chamber *en suite*. The woods of all the furniture would be the same. The style of the legs on the case pieces, such as dressing tables, high chests, and chairs, would match, and of course the draperies, bed hangings, and chair coverings would all be the same color.

Other furniture in the bedroom might include chests, kneehole desks, tables, or a bu-

FIGURE IV–47

Pembroke table. Mahogany. Philadelphia. Ca. 1770–1790.

The carved and gadrooned edge of the table top adds to the liveliness of this table. The corner brackets and stretcher are pierced in a Chinese fretwork pattern, but the tapered legs suggest a neoclassical influence. An astragal molding accents the skirt under the drawer.

Diplomatic Reception Rooms, U.S. Department of State.

FIGURE IV–48
Chest of drawers. Mahogany.
Philadelphia. Ca. 1770–1780.
Chests with chamfered corners, a serpentine facade, and massive ogee bracket feet are attributed to Jonathan Gostelowe, on the basis of a related chest with his label, although other Philadelphia makers undoubtedly sold similar forms—a documented Salem example is also known. This one is especially fine, particularly because of the fretwork applied to the chamfered corners, the unusual carved feet, and the ornate bail pulls.
Joe Kindig III.

reau, a chest fitted with a compartmented top drawer to hold toilet paraphernalia. The character of these pieces in the bedroom depended on the region where they were made. Philadelphia examples often had fluted quarter-columns, drawers surrounded with cock bead, and "swel'd," ogee bracket feet. The serpentine-front chest of drawers with canted corners is associated with the work of Jonathan Gostelowe of Philadelphia, although others no doubt produced the design as well (Figure IV–48).

Blockfronts: Boston and Newport

Whereas Philadelphia reveled in elaborately carved and ornamented case furniture, Boston and Newport favored Baroque blockfronts that depended on three panels, alternately concave and convex, for their pretensions to elegance. The blockfront conceit cost from one-half to two-thirds more than a plain piece. Splashy brass pulls often accented these pieces, as indicated by a 1756 Boston advertisement for a chest "brass'd off in the best manner."

The earliest documented blockfront, a walnut desk and bookcase signed by Job Coit and Job Coit, Jr., in 1738, was made in Boston, not Newport (Figure III–16). The younger Coit was involved in trade with the West Indies and may have seen examples of blockfront designs on Spanish furniture there. Although blockfront furniture was also made in Italy, Holland, Germany, and France, it is more likely that English examples served as his model.

Although the American blockfront concept first appeared in Boston, the idea was executed with paramount success by a talented group of craftsmen working in Newport (Figures IV–49 and IV–50). Blocking easily became known in Newport because of the migration of craftsmen and the close business ties between Newport and Boston. The designs may also have been passed among the New England Quaker community during their annual religious conclaves.

Newport blockfront furniture is commonly associated with the Quaker families of Goddard and Townsend. In the late 1740s, John and James Goddard moved from Massachusetts to Newport and were apprenticed to Job Townsend. They subsequently married two of Townsend's daughters. Job's brother, Christopher, was also a cabinetmaker, and together the two families produced more than 20 cabinetmakers who prospered in Newport until after the Revolution.

In 1763, John Townsend wrote Moses Brown of Providence asking if Jabez Brown wanted a "Case of Drawers," which was "a sort which is called a Chest on Chest of Drawers & Sweld front which are Costly as well as ornimental. . . ."[12] He was referring to the practice of enriching the facades of case pieces with concave and convex panels surmounted by richly carved shells.

The lobes of the shell radiated from an open loop or were centered on a carved palmette. The convex panels were either applied or cut from a solid piece of mahogany. Blocking sometimes enriched small items, such as dressing glasses, but it more commonly adorned case pieces, such as chests, high chests, chest on chests, and desk and bookcases.

Boston and Newport blockfronts differed significantly. In Boston, the blocking rose up to the underside of the top, which was shaped to conform to the contour of the blocked facade (Figure IV–51). Newport cabinetmakers terminated their blocking with sculptured shells and used a complex combination of moldings to direct the eye back onto the facade (Figure IV–52). Boston chest on chests and desk and bookcases often contrasted a blocked base with a plain upper

FIGURE IV–49 *(far left)*
Chest on chest. Mahogany. Newport. Ca. 1765–1780.
Although the blocking on this piece is cut from solid pieces of mahogany, other Newport blockfront furniture was made by gluing wood to drawer fronts. The boxes on either side of the pediment recall the stepped pyramids used to display china, silver, or other valuables on early 18th-century high chests. A similar pediment appears on a desk and bookcase probably made by John Goddard for Joseph Brown of Providence. The brass handles on the sides of the upper and lower sections facilitate the handling of the two parts.
Courtesy, the Henry Francis du Pont Winterthur Museum.

FIGURE IV–50
Detail of Newport finial (Figure IV–49). The corkscrew finial and fluted urn are typical of Newport work. The flutes do not continue around to the back of the urn. The urn has no lip, as do Massachusetts urn finals.
Courtesy, The Henry Francis du Pont Winterthur Museum.

FIGURE IV–51
Chest. Mahogany. Massachusetts. Ca. 1760–1780.
Typical of Massachusetts, the blocking continues up to the top, and the top board is shaped to conform to the blocked facade. The base molding also follows the same outline. The chest rests on straight bracket feet. The brass pulls date from the 18th century but are not original to this piece.
Private Collection.

FIGURE IV-52
Chest. Mahogany. Newport. Ca.
1765–1780.
**Although three-drawer examples are
found, the four-drawer chest was the
most popular. Less common is the
extraordinary blocking terminated by
finely carved Newport shells, the lobes
radiating from palmettes. Blocking is
sometimes applied, but as the grain of
this piece clearly indicates, this
blocking is cut from a solid piece of
wood. The cove molding under the top
is also characteristic of Newport work
and gives the piece a tight appearance.
The exposed dovetails for the drawer
dividers contrast with the Boston
practice of covering them with a thin
strip of wood.**
*Diplomatic Reception Rooms, U.S. Department of
State.*

FIGURE IV-53
Detail of foot from Newport desk.
Mahogany, Ca. 1760.
**On Newport pieces, blocking continues
down into the ogee foot and terminates
in a delicate scroll, which is almost the
signature of the Goddard–Townsend
school of cabinetmaking.**
*Diplomatic Reception Rooms, U.S. Department of
State.*

FIGURE IV-54 (far right)
**Detail of back of Newport chest (Figure
IV-52) showing the dovetail slot for
attaching the top to the sides.**
*Diplomatic Reception Rooms, U.S. Department of
State.*

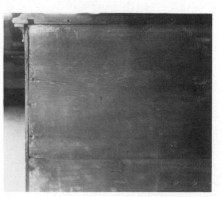

whereas on Boston work, the
feet were most commonly
straight brackets or carved ball
and claw (Figure IV-53).

Even the internal details of
construction differed between
the two areas. The dovetails that
held the drawer dividers to the
sides of the case in Boston examples were usually hidden with a
thin strip of wood in the English
practice, whereas they were usually exposed on Newport pieces.
The top of the Newport chest
was attached by means of a
dovetail mortise cut into the top
section, whereas the best Newport work employed blocking
throughout. The feet on Newport case pieces invariably carried the blocking to the ground
through ogee-curved feet with
the typical Newport volute,

FIGURE IV–55 *(far left, top)*
Detail of Boston desk (Figure IV–58). The pine bottom board is faced with a piece of mahogany that is attached by means of a giant dovetail in the typical Massachusetts method of construction.
Author's Collection.

FIGURE IV–56 *(far left)*
Detail of Newport chest (Figure IV–52). The Massachusetts method of construction contrasts with the Newport way of laying the mahogany drawer divider on top of the bottom board.
Diplomatic Reception Rooms, U.S. Department of State.

FIGURE IV–57 *(near left)*
Desk. Mahogany. Salem, Mass. Ca. 1770–1785.
The serpentine desk, which bows out in the middle, has unusually exaggerated gadrooning on the legs and a central drop on the skirt. As in most Massachusetts case furniture, cockbeading is applied to the case rather than to the drawer edge, as in Pennsylvania work.
Courtesy Mrs. Miriam Morris.

FIGURE IV–58
Desk. Mahogany with pine. Boston. Ca. 1770–1785.
The reverse serpentine, or oxbow, desk usually has a plain interior, but this example has unusual interior blocked drawers and carved shells. The choice of figured mahogany for the drawer fronts is expected on high-quality furniture such as this. Despite the highest quality of the desk, the carver followed established practice by not finishing the fourth talon on the two back feet, which sit against the wall.
Author's Collection.

FIGURE IV–59
Detail of the interior of Massachusetts desk (Figure IV–58) showing blocking and shell carving.
Author's Collection.

high chests and dressing tables were also made.

In addition to blockfronts, Boston, Newport and adjoining areas enjoyed undulating facades on desks, desk and bookcases, and chests. The serpentine facade bulged in the center and was flanked by concave curves, whereas the reverse serpentine front (shaped like an oxbow) had a concave center and convex panels on either side (Figures IV–58, IV–59, IV–60, and IV–61). Customers willingly spent money on the expensive, curved facade on desks but rarely paid extra for an elaborately carved or

and fitted into a corresponding tenon cut into a board running from side to side under the top to prevent warping (Figure IV–54). The Boston top was simply notched to rest on the top edge of the sideboards. The mahogany molding on the bottom of the case in Boston work was attached to the pine bottom board with a giant dovetail joint, whereas in Newport examples the mahogany was thicker and rested on top of the bottom board (Figures IV–55 and IV–56). Plain or shell-carved drops typically accented the skirts of Boston case pieces.

Not surprisingly, blockfronts made in nearby Concord, Charlestown, and Marblehead exhibited Boston characteristics, whereas those made in Rhode Island and Connecticut followed Newport practices. Salem work exhibited elements from both areas (Figure IV–57). Although blockfront desks, desk and bookcases, and chests were the most common forms, rare examples of

FIGURE IV–60
Desk and bookcase. Mahogany. Boston. Ca. 1765–1780.
From this extraordinary piece, the merchant and shipping magnate, Robert "King" Hooper, conducted his business in Marblehead just north of Boston. The smooth curves of the lower section are similar to those on the piece in Figure IV–58 and contrast with the angular facade seen in Figure IV–51. Fluted pilasters flank nicely shaped doors with highly figured wooden panels. The polished door panels reflect the light of candles resting on slides beneath the doors. The flaring rim and the corkscrew flame, or "blaze," as it was called in the 18th century, is characteristic of Massachusetts carving.
Diplomatic Reception Rooms, U.S. Department of State.

FIGURE IV–61
Detail of finial on Massachusetts desk and bookcase (Figure IV–60). In contrast to the Newport "blazes," the Massachusetts ones usually have a shallow urn with a flaring disk-like lip and a corkscrew flame.
Diplomatic Reception Rooms, U.S. Department of State.

blocked interior, which was hidden behind the closed lid.

Boston Bombé Furniture

The height of elegance in Boston was the coveted bombé chest or desk and bookcase, which was found nowhere else in America. The earliest dated example of the approximately 50 known is one signed by Benjamin Frothingham in 1753 (Figure IV–62). John Cogswell made the latest dated piece in 1782 for the wealthy Derby family of Salem. Bombé, a French word meaning to bulge or jut out, was first used in the late 19th century.

The 18th-century designation is unclear, but the first edition of Chippendale's *Director* referred to the commode shape to describe a bulging base on a tall clock. The form first appeared in architectural design books of the 17th century, and French cabinetmakers built prototypes in the early 18th century. The form arrived in England via Italy and France and may have been based on Renaissance versions of the medieval chest or *cassone*, which was shaped like a Roman sarcophagus. Boston cabinetmakers probably produced the first bombé piece by copying a bombé desk and bookcase owned by Charles Apthorp, a wealthy Boston merchant.

Cabinetmakers fashioned the bulging sides from solid mahogany boards. On the earliest examples made before the Revolution, the drawer sides were straight, and only the front of the drawer followed the curve of the side. More common is the later technique of shaping the sides of the drawers themselves to follow the outline of the case. The ogee curves of the case were repeated in the bracket, ball and claw, or hairy paw foot, in the door panels, and in the swan's neck pediment. On rare examples, the cabinetmaker shaped the bombé base with a serpentine facade—an incredible feat of workmanship. Even more common than the desk and bookcase were bombé chests. Occasionally dressing glasses and tea caddies also incorporated this design.

Philadelphia High Chests

Whereas Boston and Newport excelled in making essentially outdated Baroque forms, Philadelphia carried the rococo aesthetic to the highest pitch. A few wealthy Philadelphians ordered the stylish "drawers, case upon case" that first appeared in the 1730s, but most customers favored the old-style high chest, updated with the new Chippendale, rococo carving and pediment (Figure IV-63). The flat-top version continued to be made

FIGURE IV-62
Desk and bookcase. Mahogany with red cedar and white pine. Boston. Dated 1753.
This desk and bookcase, signed in pencil by Benjamin Frothingham in four places, is the earliest dated bombé example in America. The wide brim on the urn and the corkscrew finial are typical of Boston work. The drawer sides are straight, as they are on about fifteen percent of the surviving examples. On later, post-Revolution examples, the drawer sides usually follow the swelling outline of the case. *Diplomatic Reception Rooms, U.S. Department of State.*

FIGURE IV-63
Chest on chest. Mahogany. Philadelphia. Ca. 1765–1780.
The chest on chest was never as popular in America as in England, where the form had supplanted the high chest of drawers. Customers had the option to include a "desk drawer," but few chose to trade storage space for a writing surface. Most Philadelphia chest on chests rest on "swelled brackets" or ogee feet, as does this one. The cutout brass pulls are original. *Courtesy Mrs. Miriam Morris.*

79

FIGURE IV–64

High chest of drawers. Mahogany. Philadelphia. Ca. 1765–1780.

Although the pitched or triangular pediment cost less than scrolled ones, few pitched, pedimented high chests have survived. The typical rococo cartouche; the carved shell, leaves, and vines on the base; and the carved knees contrast with the classical lines of the pitched pediment. The rococo carving, preferred in Philadelphia, is more in harmony with the scrolled pediment.
Joe Kindig III.

FIGURE IV–65

High chest of drawers. Mahogany. Philadelphia. Ca. 1765–1780.

The exuberant rococo carving of vines, leaves, and shells, exemplifies the finest Philadelphia work of the mid-18th century. The carving on the central drawer, skirt, and tympanum is applied; the shell on the drawer is cut into the case. The fluted corner columns are common on the most expensive Philadelphia case furniture. This is one of the few high chests to be matched up with its similarly designed dressing table after 200 years.
Diplomatic Reception Rooms, U.S. Department of State.

FIGURE IV–66 *(far right)*

Detail of Philadelphia high chest (Figure IV–65). The high-quality, flowing carving is evident in this closeup of the pediment. If the carving were cut into the surface of the case, then the background would have been matte to disguise the marks of the carving knife. The original flame finials contrast to the corkscrews of New England case pieces.
Diplomatic Reception Rooms, U.S. Department of State.

until the end of the century, but the Philadelphia makers, such as William Savery and Thomas Affleck, added pediments for their best customers, who were willing to pay double for the added embellishment. These pediments were designed as scrolls, pitched in a triangular shape, or had a bonnet that covered the entire top (Figures IV–64, IV–65, and IV–66). Fluted columns on the corners of the case and richly carved architraves and skirts enhanced the finest high chests. Sculpturesque finials in the form of rococo cartouches, urns, flames, or baskets of fruits and flowers added unexcelled richness.

The so-called Pompadour high chest, attributed to the shop of Benjamin Randolph, was adorned with a bust, probably not of Louis XV's famous mistress, but because of the flowers in her hair, more likely Flora, the goddess of Spring (Figure IV–1). Busts of the heroes of the Enlightenment—Benjamin Franklin, John Milton, and John Locke—graced a small group of desk and bookcases (Figures IV–67 and IV–68). Hercules Courtenay, born in Belfast, Ireland, immigrated to Philadelphia after learning his craft in London and may have carved many of these busts.

Some of the furniture produced in Philadelphia conformed to one Quaker's description— "Of the best sort, but plain." At the same time, however, the

Quaker elders spoke out against the richness of the furniture filling the homes of other wealthy brethren. In a revival of religious fervor in the early 19th century, many Quakers stripped applied carving from 18th-century pieces.

The most common embellishments took the form of naturalistic leaves, vines, flowers, and allegorical figures. The carver traced the outline of his designs on a piece of paper that was then glued to a thin strip of wood and cut out. The rough design was placed on the surface of the piece of furniture and held in the proper position by sharp set pins surrounding the design. It was then removed and dropped on a board spread with hot glue. The outline of the carving, which had picked up the glue, was then replaced on the surface of the furniture, using the set pins as guides. Once the glue had dried, the carver could complete his work, which he sold by the foot for skirts, drawers, and other surfaces on the cabinetmakers' most elegant pieces. The carver used the same techniques to fashion fretwork in the geometric Chinese taste, which was then applied to the friezes of desk and bookcases and to the legs of tables and chairs.

New York Case Pieces

With a royal governor and his entourage in residence, New York furniture continued to follow English designs (Figures IV–69 and IV–70). The British chose that city as the central military supply depot for their troops in 1755. As a result, even more English officials flocked to the city in addition to those who already surrounded the royal governor. Whereas Philadelphia and New England favored the high chest form, many New Yorkers bought the chest on chest instead. Out of style in England by mid-century, the high chest was not even illustrated in Chippendale's *Director*.

The Revolution drastically curtailed the production of fine furniture, as the war distracted both cabinetmakers and their customers. Many of the best customers were wealthy Tories who fled to Britain or Canada. Supporters of the Revolution found

FIGURE IV–67 *(top left)*
Desk and bookcase. Mahogany. Philadelphia. Ca. 1765–1775.
Although most of the pieces with finial busts are attributed to the shop of Benjamin Randolph, the varying quality of the carving indicates several different hands. This piece is quite restrained and has carving only in the pediment. The leafy terminations of the scrolled bonnet rest on the surface instead of flying off, as on the Pompadour example. The muntins, which form an octagon surrounding a square, resemble a "Chinese chair" splat.
Diplomatic Reception Rooms, U.S. Department of State.

FIGURE IV–68
Detail from desk and bookcase (Figure IV–67). The likeness of John Locke is based on a ceramic basalt bust by Josiah Wedgewood. The colonists greatly admired Locke's works on philosophy and government.
Diplomatic Reception Rooms, U.S. Department of State.

FIGURE IV–69
Desk and bookcase. Mahogany. New York. Ca. 1770–1780.
The gilded eagle finial, the interior shells, the gilded door panels, and the carved feet make this piece one of the great achievements of New York cabinetmaking in the 18th century. Drawers are beaded in the New York and Philadelphia manner.
Diplomatic Reception Rooms, U.S. Department of State.

FIGURE IV–70
Clothes press. Red gum, or "bilsted." New York. Ca. 1760–1780.
Although Chippendale illustrates a clothes press in both the 1754 and 1762 editions of the *Director*, the form was rare in America. This example has chamfered corners terminating in lamb's tongues. A fluted pilaster separates the two arched doors. The stubby legs are typical of other New York pieces. The cornice recalls a similar treatment on a Hudson River Valley *Kas*.
Courtesy Dr. and Mrs. Arthur Mourot.

their extra money for furniture taxed away to finance the war effort. Typically, cabinetmakers turned their talents to supporting the war. John Folwell and Jonathan Gostelowe served with the Artillery Artificers. Captain Hercules Courtenay spent the war "recruiting for the artillery." Plunket Fleeson made drums, and James Gillingham supplied "98 splinters" for surgeons. Before he was arrested as a Tory, Thomas Affleck made "sundry Shott Moulds." David Evans made tent poles, camp chairs, cots, and a mahogany polishing wheel for a gun factory.

By the 1760s, England was developing the new neoclassical style, but in America the Chippendale fashion lingered, as Americans were preoccupied with the Revolution. As late as 1812, Adam S. Coe of Newport made a typical Chippendale-style sofa with straight, molded legs for Edward W. Lawton. Although the Chippendale style remained popular until early in the 19th century, the neoclassical taste found its way into the most stylish homes by the 1790s.

NOTES

1. Thomas Chippendale, *The Gentleman and Cabinet-Maker's Director* (New York: Dover Books, 1966), Preface.

2. Christopher Gilbert, *The Life and Work of Thomas Chippendale* (New York: Macmillan Publishing Co., Inc., 1978), p. 114.

3. Marshall B. Davidson, ed., *The American Heritage History of Colonial Antiques* (New York: American Heritage Publishing Co., Inc., 1967), p. 195.

4. William Macpherson Hornor, Jr., *Blue Book Philadelphia Furniture: William Penn to George Washington* (Washington, D.C.: Highland House Publishers, 1977), p. 81.

5. Walter Muir Whitehill, ed., *Boston Furniture of the Eighteenth Century* (Boston: The Colonial Society of Massachusetts, 1974), p. 77.

6. The signature on the Winterthur example had been questioned, but the discovery of a second signed chair by Roderic Blackburn at the Albany Institute seems to confirm its authenticity.

7. Morrison H. Heckscher, "The New York Serpentine Card Table," *The Magazine Antiques* 103 (May 1973): 974–83. Joe Kindig, however, contends that the Temple Newsam House table is in fact American rather than English, as Heckscher thought.

8. Joseph Downs, *American Furniture: Queen Anne and Chippendale Periods* (New York: The Macmillan Company, 1952), Plate 255.

9. "American Mirrors" in *The Complete Color Encyclopedia of Antiques* (New York: Hawthorn Books, Inc., 1975), p. 361.

10. Hornor, *Blue Book*, p. 67.

11. Hornor, *Blue Book*, p. 143.

12. R. Peter Mooz, "The Origins of Newport Block-front Furniture Design," *The Magazine Antiques* 99 (June 1971): 882.

V

FURNITURE
OF THE FEDERAL PERIOD

IN APRIL 1789, WHEN GEORGE Washington took the oath of office swearing to uphold the recently ratified Federal Constitution, he ushered in a new era in American history. The time coincided with the beginning of a new style in furniture that takes its name from the Federal period. The Federal style represents the first phase of neoclassicism in America. The earlier Chippendale style continued to be popular as late as the first decades of the 19th century, but by 1790, straight lines and delicate ornament had largely supplanted the rococo curves and exuberant carving of the earlier period. In 1790, Archibald Alison, in his *Essays on The Nature and Principles of Taste*, described the new style:

> ... *Strong and Massy Furniture is everywhere vulgar and unpleasing.... Some years ago every article of furniture was made in what was called the Chinese Taste.... To this succeeded the Gothic Taste.... The Taste which now reigns is that of the Antique. Everything we now use, is made in imitation of those models which have been lately discovered in Italy.*[1]

NEOCLASSICAL IN AMERICA

At least a dozen illustrations in the 1762 edition of Chippendale's *Director* show traces of the neoclassical in such elements as fluted, tapered legs; caryatid supports; classical figures; festoons and swags of husks; paterae; square, tapered legs; bellflowers; and lion's head masks. Although the neoclassical was firmly established in England by 1770, Americans were too busy with the Revolution to adopt new fashions, particularly those of the enemy. The earliest documented piece of American domestic furniture with Federal elements is a lap desk that Benjamin Randolph made for Thomas Jefferson in Philadelphia in 1776. The delicate satinwood band around the drawer and the inlaid escutcheon presaged the new style. With a few exceptions, like Jefferson's lap desk, Americans did not accept the Federal style until after the Revolution (see Figure V–2). Even then, a depression followed the war, and not until 1789, with the establishment of a strong Federal government, was there a promise of prosperity. Only then did large numbers of Americans begin to indulge themselves in new homes and stylish furniture. The demand for new furniture was also swelled by new waves of immigrants and an expanding population.

85

Figure V–2
Lap desk. Mahogany. Philadelphia. Ca. 1776.

Thomas Jefferson commissioned this delicate lap desk from Benjamin Randolph in Philadelphia. The inlaid escutcheon and the string inlay around the drawer, along with the overall delicate proportions, make this the earliest documented piece of American domestic furniture with neoclassical details.

Smithsonian Institution Photo No. 42116.

English Origins

The neoclassical, or "style antique," was derived from English sources. Robert Adam exerted a profound effect on architecture in England, and the English neoclassical style takes its name from him. In 1754, he traveled to Italy to study the ancient remains of the Romans. He decided that the early classicists, such as William Kent and Andrea Palladio, had misinterpreted classical designs. They had been influenced by the heavy exterior architectural elements, such as pediments and columns. Adam, however, concentrated on Roman interiors, particularly those of Diocletian's Palace at Spalato, which, he discovered, were much lighter than Palladian architecture and did not always follow 18th-century ideas of proportion. Although the symmetrical exteriors of Adam houses differed little from earlier styles, Adam abandoned interior symmetry and emphasized function. A random arrangement of ovals, rectangles, and circles replaced the rigid Palladian floor plan of four square rooms and a hall. These same shapes, along with delicate naturalistic and other classical motifs in plaster or wood, created a rich and airy interior. Adam wrote that "we have been able to seize, with some degree of success, the beautiful spirit of antiquity, and to transfer it, with novelty and variety, through all our numerous works."[2] American Federal architecture was even simpler and more delicate than its English prototype.

Hepplewhite, Sheraton, and Shearer

Adam custom-designed furniture to harmonize with his buildings, but only the wealthy could afford his services. However, his designs were popularized by George Hepplewhite, Thomas Sheraton, and Thomas Shearer. Hepplewhite, an obscure cabinetmaker in London, collected 300 designs for furniture, which his wife, Alice, published as *The Cabinet-Maker and Upholsterer's Guide* in 1788, two years after his death. Hepplewhite made no pretense to originality, stating that "we designedly followed the latest or most prevailing fashion" in selecting illustrations. He proposed only to make "English taste and workmanship" available to "surrounding nations" and to "our own Countrymen and Artizans, whose distance from the metropolis makes even an imperfect knowledge of its improvements acquired with much trouble and expence."[3]

Even more influential was Thomas Sheraton's *The Cabinet-Maker and Upholsterer's Drawing Book*, published in several parts between 1791 and 1794. Sheraton had been a journeyman cabinetmaker, but his primary interest was in drawing. His *Drawing Book* was primarily that—a lesson in drawing, using furniture as an example. However, his book had a much more important influence on furniture design. Sheraton designs were more avant-garde than Hepplewhite's but were still little more than variations on Adam's designs. Sheraton also admitted that he was only showing the "present taste of furniture, and at the same time to give [sic] the workman some assistance in the manufacturing part of it."[4]

The Federal style is sometimes referred to as Sheraton and Hepplewhite. Today, Hepplewhite connotes a square, tapered leg and an oval or shield-shaped chair back. Sheraton describes a round, tapered leg, usually reeded, and a square chair back with small columns. Although these characteristics reflect the preferences of the two designers, such generalizations ignore the fact that each showed examples of both styles in his book. Even though Sheraton and Hepplewhite would not have approved of the narrow characterization of their styles, their names are useful today in describing particular furniture designs.

A third publication, *The Cabi-*

net-Makers' London Book of Prices, and Designs of Cabinet Work, with illustrations by Thomas Shearer and first issued in 1788, also influenced furniture designs. American imitations of the London price book were published in several major American cabinetmaking centers. These books listed prices for each element of cabinetwork, such as carving, turning, inlay, or gilding.

SPECIALIZATION IN THE FURNITURE TRADES

Each of these cabinetmaking operations was performed by a specialist. Specialization in the woodworking trade was known even in the 17th century, but the trend accelerated at the end of the 18th century as shops grew larger. Rarely did a single craftsman working in a large urban cabinetmaking shop both design and construct a single piece of furniture. The efficiency of specialization allowed the cabinetmaker to meet the demands of a rapidly expanding population and a growing export trade.

The way Ephraim Haines of Philadelphia filled the order of Stephen Girard for a set of black ebony furniture illustrated the new trend (Figure V–3). At least seven craftsmen worked on Girard's order, but Haines, the master cabinetmaker, did none of the labor himself. Instead, he chose the design, supervised and warranted the work of his own journeymen, or contracted some jobs to specialists. Girard, a wealthy merchant, provided the ebony himself and imported the French red silk velvet upholstery. Haines paid one of his own journeymen to saw the ebony logs and employed his next-door neighbor, Barney Schumo, to turn the legs. John R. Morris charged a premium for carving the legs and spindles because of the difficulty of working hard ebony. Haines supervised the assembly of the furniture in his own shop before turning the furniture over to the upholsterer,

George Briedenhart. He charged $5.80 per chair, which included the curled hair, canvas, twine, tacks, and his own labor. His bill did not include the double row of brass-plated tacks that Robert Pullen provided to outline the seat rail of the chairs.

Since Girard's furniture was made of ebony, no veneer or inlay was necessary. The Federal style, however, generally required this specialty as well. The inlay maker first drew the designs on a piece of paper and then duplicated them as many times as necessary by pricking through the paper onto other sheets. He then pasted them to a piece of thinly sliced wood and pinned several different kinds of wood together, depending on the number to be used in the design.

FIGURE V–3
Armchair. Mahogany. Philadelphia. Ca. 1805–1815.
This is similar to the armchairs in the set Stephen Girard purchased from Ephraim Haines in 1807. The major difference is in the turned spade foot rather than the tapered foot below a bulb on the Girard chairs. The foot on the Girard chair is usually associated with Haines, whereas the foot on this chair is usually attributed to Henry Connelly. However, the distinction is not valid since both cabinetmakers probably purchased chair legs from turners who worked for many cabinetmakers. The turned rather than square rear legs on this example are unusual, though they are more often found in Philadelphia than elsewhere.
Courtesy, The Henry Francis du Pont Winterthur Museum.

Figure V–4

Side chair. Mahogany. Rhode Island or Connecticut. Ca. 1795.

Kneeland and Adams in Hartford, Connecticut and Robert Burrough of Providence, Rhode Island made chairs with similar backs in the 1790s. Mahogany was common on Rhode Island chairs, whereas birch and cherry were more frequently used in Connecticut. Chairs with similar splats were listed in *The London Chair-Makers' and Carvers' Book of Prices for Workmanship*, published in 1802. The molded stiles, crest rail, and legs cost extra, as did the carving on the urn and the rosettes.
Herbert Collins.

Woods included satinwood from the East and West Indies as well as holly, rosewood, snake, zebra, boxwood, yew, maple, and birch. The craftsman clamped the layers of wood in a vise and sawed out the design. He selected the appropriate piece from each layer of wood and discarded the others, which were identically shaped, but of different woods. The entire design fitted together like a jigsaw puzzle. To effect shading, the inlay specialists thrust the tiny pieces into hot sand, which browned or charred the wood. Once the design was laid out, a paper was glued over it to hold it together until a cabinetmaker bought it.

The cabinetmaker, in turn, spread the surface of his furniture with glue, which was allowed to dry. He laid the panel on the surface and clamped a heated wooden caul over the inlay, which remelted the glue. In an alternative method, the ground was heated and the veneer pounded into place with a veneer hammer. Once the glue dried again, the cabinetmaker removed the paper and smoothed and polished the panel. In a similar manner, veneer was applied to the surface of a secondary wood, such as pine. The eagle, emblem of the State Department, was particularly popular, even though Benjamin Franklin berated the bird as being "of bad moral character." Other popular designs included the bellflower, fan, fluting, paterae, swags, urns, and drapery.

NEWPORT

AFTER THE REVOLUTION

The ravages of the Revolution, the rapid growth in America's population after the war, and the prosperity that followed the ratification of the Federal Constitution caused a major realignment of cabinetmaking centers in America. Newport, the source of some of the grandest furniture of the pre-Revolutionary War period, declined as a result both of the destruction of the war and of the laws against Newport's lucrative slave trade, which crippled her economy after the war. Cabinetmaking declined as precipitously as the population, which fell by 40 percent during the war and never reached its prewar high until 1850. Some members of the Goddard–Townsend clan tried to make furniture in the new Federal style, but their work never approached the innovative genius of their 18th-century creations (Figure V–4).

BOSTON

Boston, too, suffered greatly from the Revolution. By 1790, it had fallen to third in population, behind New York and Philadelphia, and had watched its neighboring towns draw off much of its profitable business after the British closed the port. Still, after the Revolution, the population soon surpassed even prewar levels. As the city grew and prospered, Boston's furniture craftsmen earned a good living. The city's best-known cabinetmakers, John Seymour and his son Thomas, arrived in the city in 1794 from Maine, where they had first settled after immigrating from England in 1785. Their furniture is often characterized by the use of contrasting light and dark veneer and inlay, half-moon inlay, and light blue painted interiors. However, these same motifs were used by other cabinetmakers as well, so that an attribution based solely on the presence of these elements may be little more than wishful thinking.

SALEM

Even though it was less than half the size of Boston, neighboring Salem produced some of the finest Federal furniture. Her products were shipped to every major Atlantic coastal port, particularly in the South, and to many foreign ports as well. But the highest quality furniture was made for the prosperous home market, often for the first citizen of the city, Elias Hasket Derby, one of America's new millionaires. Derby, like many of his fellow merchants in Salem, turned his seafaring skills to lucrative privateering during the Revolution and quickly reestablished new commercial markets in the Orient, Spain, France, and the West Indies when peace was restored. The city prospered until President Jefferson issued his disastrous embargo on trade in 1807. Although the city's merchants recovered quickly after the embargo was lifted the next year, the War of 1812 dealt a fatal blow to the city's mercantile fleet, of which only a fourth survived the war.

During its heyday, Salem supported 60 cabinetmakers and 15 chairmakers in the three decades after 1790. Many of them, such as Elijah Sanderson, Nehemiah Adams, William Appleton, and William Hook, have been identified by the labels on their furniture, which was shipped as venture cargo to other ports. The most famous name associated with Salem furniture, Samuel McIntire, was actually better known for his architectural work. This talented craftsman did, however, do furniture carving that included work for the Derbys and for Elijah and Jacob Sanderson, who operated a large furniture-manufacturing business in Salem during the Federal period. The eagles, bellflowers, fruit baskets, wheat sheaves, and cornucopias on bureaus, sofas, card tables, sideboards, and bedposts associated with McIntire were derived from English source books available to most Salem carvers (Figure V–5). Other carvers besides McIntire used the technique of setting the carving off against a matte background, achieved by using a starshaped punch. Boston carvers, such as John and Simeon Skillin, also worked on Salem furniture, so that it is impossible to be sure that a particular piece was carved in Salem, much less by McIntire.

Distinctive carving, turning, or inlay does not necessarily distinguish an individual cabinetmaker, but these elements can be used to identify the geographical origin of a piece. In the Federal period, regional characteristics became less obvious and more subtle. The widespread familiarity with design books tended to homogenize furniture design. However, in the subtle differences in the work of specialists, some regional characteristics persisted. Thus the traditional attribution solely to Nehemiah Adams of the turned and reeded leg with a bulging foot is probably not valid. He employed Joseph True for much of his turning work, as did many other Salem cabinetmakers. Therefore, the distinctive leg is a Salem characteristic rather than an Adams one.

LOLLING CHAIRS AND SALEM SECRETARIES

Although the same designs were available everywhere, some forms tended to be favored in certain locales. Sheraton recommends a secretary "for a gentleman to write at, to keep his own accounts, and serve as a library"[5] (Figure V–6). This impressive form, commonly found in Salem, is generally referred to today as a Salem secretary. The carved pomegranates on desk and bookcases also indicate a Salem origin.

A distinctive American piece, the Martha Washington, or lolling, chair, was popular throughout New England. The chair, like the Chippendale high chest of drawers, represented a peculiarly American updating of an outmoded English style. Chippendale's *Director* shows a similar upholstered "French elboe chair," but the form does not appear in books by either Sheraton, Hepplewhite, or Shearer. The high back and the tapered, or

FIGURE V–5
Side chair. Mahogany with birch. Salem, Mass. Ca. 1800–1810.
One of a set of 19, these were purchased from Samuel McIntire, according to family tradition, by Benjamin Williams Crowninshield for his yacht, *Cleopatra's Barge*. The plain, tapered legs contrast with the exquisite carved eagle in the "tablet" on the crest and the leaves on the "upright splatts." The molded stiles and rails on the back of the chair and the "sweeping," or swelling, of the front of the chair would have cost extra.
Diplomatic Reception Rooms, U.S. Department of State.

FIGURE V–6

Library bookcase. Mahogany. Salem, Mass. Ca. 1790–1800.

According to *The Journeymen Cabinet and Chair Makers' New-York Book of Prices* for 1796, the library bookcase "with wings"—the name for the two sections flanking the central portion— was one of the most expensive items, one for which the journeyman would get about $40. The central section, faced with oval inlay, pulls out to form a writing surface. Slides above the drawers in the wings pull out to accommodate books taken down from the shelves. The pointed Gothic arches of the muntins echo the pointed ends of the oval inlay. The curves that form the arches echo the hollow corners of the double stringing on the drawers and central doors. The piece stands nearly eight feet high and is eight feet long.
Diplomatic Reception Rooms, U.S. Department of State.

FIGURE V–7

Lolling chair. Mahogany. Massachusetts or southern New Hampshire. Ca. 1800–1810.

These chairs were usually called lolling chairs. However, the label of Joseph Short of Newburyport, which advertises that he "makes Martha Washington chairs," indicates that this more common modern term was also used in the early 19th century. This chair has turned and reeded legs rather than the more common tapered ones, and the "crane necked elbows" found on the finest lolling chairs. The serpentine crest echoes the similarly shaped front rail.
Author's Collection.

more rarely, turned and reeded legs of the lolling chair reflected the Federal styling (Figure V–7). The hundreds of immigrants settling in Philadelphia and New York brought with them a preference for the newest furniture styles. Boston attracted fewer immigrants in the early 19th century, which may help to explain the conservatism in Boston Federal furniture.

PHILADELPHIA

Philadelphia continued to be an important cabinetmaking center into the 19th century. Cabinetmakers served a growing domestic market as the population of the city and surrounding areas doubled from about 50,000 to over 100,000 between 1790 and 1810. In addition, cabinetmakers reestablished their export trade, which had been disrupted by the

Revolution. Merchants, such as Stephen Girard, capitalized on the nearly continuous state of war between Britain and France before 1815 by trading with both countries as a neutral. A few newly rich merchants like Girard spent some of their wealth on fine furniture. But in comparison to Baltimore, which had few wealthy families before the Revolution, Philadelphia had a large portion of old, moneyed clans who generally saw no need to reconfirm their status with new furniture. Although the finest Philadelphia cabinetwork is related to Baltimore styles, the former is more conservative, particularly in the use of inlay.

Hundreds of cabinet- and chairmakers worked in Philadelphia between 1790 and 1810, but only a few can be linked to labeled or documented furniture. The giants of the Philadelphia Chippendale period had died or retired by the 1790s and were replaced by a new generation of furniture craftsmen, both native-born and foreign, principally from England, France, and Germany. Daniel Trotter is known for his mahogany ladder-back chairs with pierced and carved slats and molded, tapered legs, which were popular in the two decades after the Revolution. Although the ladder-back was found in other areas, Philadelphians alone seemed to prefer ones with rounded shoulders. The square-back chair with three or four turned colonettes and round spade feet has been attributed to Henry Connelly. Similar chairs with a bulb above a turned cylinder are assigned to Ephraim Haines. Both styles, however, were made by others as well. Similarly, the bulb-shaped foot associated with Haines and the round, tapered foot attributed to Connelly indicate only that they probably depended upon two turners who worked for many Philadelphia makers. The heart- or fan-backed chair that John Aitken advertised in 1790 as a pattern "entirely new, never before seen in this city"

became particularly popular in Philadelphia but was also made elsewhere[6] (Figure V–8).

NEW YORK

After surpassing Boston in population by the mid-18th century, Philadelphia enjoyed distinction as the foremost economic and cultural hub in America. After the Revolution, New York began to challenge that position and by 1815 had supplanted Philadelphia as the new nation's center of commerce and population. New York furniture of the 18th century was, with a few exceptions, relatively undistinguished, but in the early 19th century the city became the center of cabinetmaking in America. New York merchants benefited from the city's unique location. Its port was closer to European markets than Boston's, and its links with the interior via the Hudson River Valley gave it access to wide markets. As business expanded, so did the population, which more than tripled to reach 96,000 between 1790 and 1810.

The expanding population and the trade opportunities combined to support a large and prosperous group of cabinetmakers, chairmakers, carvers, gilders, and joiners that numbered more than 100 by 1805. Foremost among them was the Scotchman, Duncan Phyfe, who had arrived from Albany in 1792. From 1795 until his retirement in 1847, Phyfe operated a shop at 35 Partition (now Fulton) Street in the heart of New York's cabinetmaking district, where he employed several dozen journeymen and apprentices. Early in his career, Phyfe was fortunate enough to complete an order for John Jacob Astor, the wealthy New York fur trader, and he soon became known as the most fashionable cabinetmaker in the city. His fame spread, and he was even recognized in Alexandria, Virginia, where his name was used in a newspaper advertisement to endorse the varnish sold by P. B. Smith & Company

FIGURE V–8
Side chair. Mahogany. Philadelphia or Baltimore. Ca. 1790–1800.
Heart-back chairs were commonly made in Baltimore and Philadelphia, but similar ones have descended in New England and New York families as well. Chairs like this one were described in a 1795 Philadelphia price book as "A Heart back stay rail Chair, with a bannister and two up-right splatts...." They were made with or without stretchers. This example has spade feet with upholstery over half the rails and a "swelled" seat rail.
Philadelphia Museum of Art: Given by Mr. and Mrs. David H. Stockwell.

in 1840. He, like other New York furniture makers, did a thriving business with southern clients, who sold much of their cotton through the New York financiers. Phyfe's labeled work was probably made for export, since these marked pieces are not as fine as his work done to order. Sarah Huger did not exaggerate much when she wrote her brother-in-law early in 1816 that "Mr. Phyfe is so much the United States rage."[7]

In contrast to New England, which preferred sharply contrasting dark and light inlay, New York favored solid mahogany that was reeded or carved. New York shield-back chairs took the form of three or four rib-like splats, carved draped fans, or Prince of Wales feathers (Figure V–9). Later chairs exhibited square backs with a draped urn flanked by two colonettes, with a series of colonettes forming Gothic arches, or with three columns shaped like urns.

DRAWING ROOMS

Standing against the walls in drawing rooms were the best chairs, tables, and possibly a new piano (Figures V–10 and V–11). Sheraton advised that the parlor should "concentrate the elegance of the whole house, and is the highest display of richness of furniture.... The grandeur then introduced into the drawing-room is not to be considered, as the ostentatious parade of its proprietor, but the respect he pays to the rank of his visitants."[8] Also along the walls when not in use, were stands and pairs of card tables—either square, pedestal, circular, or tripod (Figures V–12 and V–13).

Cabinetmakers levied an extra charge for shaping the top of tables with hollows, double hollows, rounded ends, ovolo corners, elliptic or serpentine fronts, half-serpentine ends, or canted corners (Figure V–14). The tripod form, new in the Federal period, was called a "pillar and claw" table (Figure V–15 and V–16). The pedestal type, popular by 1815, had a wide base that supported columns, lyres, dolphins, or eagles.

FIGURE V–12 *(far left, top)*
Candlestand. Mahogany. New York. Ca. 1800–1810.
The eagle inlay on the top, a common Federal motif, serves as a focal point for this table. Stringing outlines the top and the edges of the legs, and a broad, inlaid band defines the feet. The double-elliptic- or cloverleaf-shaped top was commonly found on New York tables. The thick legs with little lift do not match the high-quality inlay and nicely figured wood used for the top.
Diplomatic Reception Rooms, U.S. Department of State.

FIGURE V–13 *(far left, bottom)*
Card table. Cherry. Connecticut. Ca. 1800–1810.
This table, with ovolo corners, is a standard configuration described in cabinetmakers' price books of the early 19th century. The use of cherry, the unusual X-shaped inlay on the skirt, and the inlay on the legs support a Connecticut origin.
Nancy and Fred Starr.

FIGURE V–14
(top, near left)
Shapes of tops for Federal-style pier tables.

FIGURE V–15 *(left, center)*
Card table. Mahogany. New York. Ca. 1810.
The richly grained mahogany top takes a double-elliptic shape. The top rotates to rest on the skirt, which encloses a storage space for game equipment. The molded legs are more common in Philadelphia work, but the carved drapery and leaves on the urn baluster are less florid than most Philadelphia work. The brass casters and paw feet were probably imported.
Mr. and Mrs. V. Thomas Jocelyn.

FIGURE V–16
Card table. Mahogany. Massachusetts. Ca. 1795–1805.
This table with ovolo corners, which Sheraton called "sash plan corners," is one of the most common card table shapes. The inlaid urns over each front leg and the extraordinary eagle with 18 stars were costly additions to this table. A checkered band of inlay on the table top, stringing on the legs, and inlaid bands above the feet add further interest. This version of the eagle and the sharp taper below the inlaid cuff on the legs are common in Massachusetts.
Diplomatic Reception Rooms, U.S. Department of State.

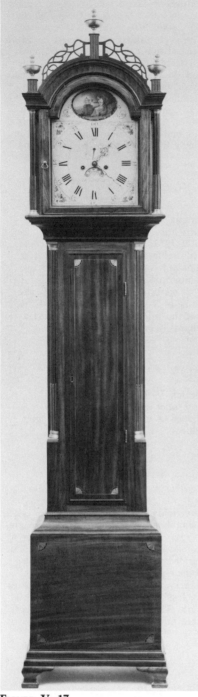

Tall case clocks continued to be the most expensive household item in the Federal period, and these handsome pieces were invariably displayed in the best parlor. The clocks of Simon Willard and other members of the Willard family, who worked in Roxbury, a suburb of Boston, were among the most outstanding (Figure V–17). The cases made by William Fisk, John Doggett, or other craftsmen living in Willard's neighborhood exhibited the spaghetti-like scrolls on the rounded bonnet, the brass finials, the fluted corner columns, and the inlaid cases. Similar cases were made throughout New England. Hand-painted faces, mostly imported from English dial makers, replaced the less legible brass dials used earlier. Craftsmen in Wilmington, Delaware, and Elizabethtown, New Jersey, made other well-documented tall case clocks (Figure V–18). Dwarf tall case clocks, although common in Europe, were rare in America because the more impressive tall clock cost only a fraction more. The tall case clocks continued to be made throughout the first half of the 19th century in rural areas, particularly in Pennsylvania, but in most other places the tradition rapidly died out.

Tall case clocks succumbed to the less expensive mass-produced wall or shelf clocks (Figures V–1 and V–19). In 1805, Eli Terry contracted to produce 4,000 clockworks over a three-year period. He produced none the first year while he geared up his plant in Plymouth, Connecticut. By the end of the second year, his water-powered machinery was turning out 60 clocks a day. Terry's clocks had wooden works. Benjamin Cheney and a few others had made wooden clockworks as early as 1745, but Terry applied the principle of interchangeable parts and assembly line techniques to manufacture his clocks. In 1810, he sold his thriving business to Seth

FIGURE V–17
Tall case clock. Mahogany. Roxbury, Mass. Ca. 1790–1810.
Simon Willard's name is painted on the dial, and his paper label is attached to the door. The fluted corner columns with brass bases and capitals, the columns flanking the hood, the three brass finials, and the spaghetti-like fretwork on the bonnet all characterize the Roxbury type of clock case. The dial is typical of many English faces, which American clockmakers imported from James Wilson of Birmingham and others to attach to their American-made works.
Courtesy, The Henry Francis du Pont Winterthur Museum.

FIGURE V–18
Tall case clock. Mahogany. New Jersey. Ca. 1790–1810.
A single New Jersey supplier may have sold the eagle medallion and light and dark inlay above and below the reeded corner columns, which are found on other New Jersey clock cases. The delicate scrolled pediment, the wide band above the clock face, and the serpentine door top are features common to a group of New Jersey clock cases.
Diplomatic Reception Rooms, U.S. Department of State.

Thomas and Silas Hoadly. In 1816, not content with retirement, he patented the widely copied Pillar and Scroll Clocks, which were much more stylish than his original box design (Figure V–20). By 1820, Terry faced numerous competitors, and Connecticut clocks were sold all over the country. No longer did a timepiece cost "a cow and a good calf." The low-priced shelf clocks with wooden works sold for about $15.00—one-sixth the price of a tall case clock. One of Terry's competitors, Chauncey Jerome, marketed a new style in 1825 that he called his Bronze Looking Glass Clock. He bragged that "It could be made for one dollar less, and sold for two dollars more" than the Pillar and Scroll Clocks.[9]

By 1840, New England clockmakers began replacing their wooden works with brass. Unaffected by changes in weather, these brass works were exported all over the world. By 1845, coiled springs were used to drive clocks. Since cases no longer had to accommodate weights, they could be made in an infinite variety of forms, such as steeples, beehives, and acorns.

Other luxury items in the best parlors were pier glasses. The tabernacle style, out of fashion in England, continued in popularity in America, enriched with Federal motifs, such as eagle inlay or delicate urns filled with bunches of exquisite flowers. The so-called rectangular Hepplewhite glass, surmounted by wispy plumes, urns, and vines made of gesso on a wire frame, actually predated Hepplewhite's designs (Figure V–21). The so-called Sheraton type, made with a rectangular frame flanked by applied columns, was surmounted by a cornice molding hung with balls (Figure V–22). The only similarity to a Sheraton design was his illustration of a mirror with acorns hanging from the frame. When ways were developed to produce convex glass cheaply and in quantity, the new style became popular in the Federal period.

The convex glass had a round frame that was often topped by an eagle. Sheraton called them mirrors, and the term soon began to supplant looking glass. Although the overmantle glass dated from the 1690s, it was at the height of popularity in the Federal period. Although Americans made more and more of their own frames, they continued to import the glass from Germany, Holland, and England until later in the 19th century.

FIGURE V–19
Wall clock. Mahogany. Roxbury, Mass. Ca. 1802–1805.
The iron pendulum plate is signed Elnathan Taber, and his signature is painted on the banner at the waist of the banjo-shaped clock. Taber was apprenticed to Simon Willard and later made clocks for both Simon and Aaron Willard in addition to clocks under his own name. The eglomise door and bottom panel add great elegance to this now rare form.
Private Collection.

FIGURE V–20
Shelf clock. Mahogany. Connecticut. Ca. 1816.
A paper label that reads, "PATENT./ INVENTED./ Made and Sold by/ Eli Terry./ Plymouth,/ Con," is pasted on the inside below the wooden works. The brass finials, turned columns, serpentine skirt, and French feet characterize the "pillar and scroll" clocks patented by Eli Terry in 1816.
Private Collection.

FIGURE V–21
Looking glass. Mahogany and gilt. Possibly New York. Ca. 1800.
Evolving from what Chippendale called "Tabernacle Frames," this looking glass is lightened by neoclassical details, such as the inlaid shells, and the reeded urn with a single flower, and sprigs of wheat.
Virginia Museum.

FIGURE V–22
Looking glass. Gilded wood.
Massachusetts. Ca. 1800–1810.
**This glass, which belonged to John
Quincy Adams, has an elaborate tribute
to George Washington painted on the
reverse of the glass panel in the
pediment. The United States flag shows
17 stars, which may indicate a date
after 1803, when Ohio was admitted to
the Union as the 17th state. The
columns are entwined with leaves and
topped with Ionic capitals.**
*Diplomatic Reception Rooms, U.S. Department of
State.*

Sofas and Tables

Before 1820, only the richest
homes contained sofas, couches,
or settees. They usually stood in
parlors but were found occasionally in bed chambers and halls as
well. Cabinetmakers in the
Federal period softened the bold
lines of the Chippendale sofa,
tapered the legs, and accented
the crest rail and legs with delicate carving, veneer, or inlay
(Figure V–23). More popular,
however, was a Sheraton-in-
spired square-backed sofa with
upholstered arms and turned, detached arm supports, which continued to the floor to form the
front legs (Figure V–24). Whether
with or without upholstered
arms, or occasionally with caned
sides and backs, these square-

FIGURE V–23
*Sofa. Mahogany with birch. Boston or
Salem. Ca. 1790–1800.*
**In the Federal period, the straight-back
sofa was more common than this form.
The bold, curved back and scrolled
arms of the Chippendale sofa have been
softened and the outline of the back
emphasized by a carved mahogany crest
rail under the influence of Robert Adam
who recommended "delicacy, gaiety,
grace and beauty." Elias Hasket Derby,
one of the richest men in America in
the early 19th century, owned this sofa.
Carved cornucopias similar to the two
that crown the crest rail appear on
several other pieces of Derby furniture.
The silk damask upholstery is a
reproduction of an early 19th-century
fabric.**
*Museum of Fine Arts, Boston, M. and M. Karolik
Collection.*

FIGURE V–24
*Sofa. Mahogany. New York. Ca.
1805–1810.*
**The scrolled or back-curving crest rail
is carved with drapery and tassels
flanking a central panel ornamented
with a sheaf of wheat tied with a bow.
Carved water leaves highlight the base
of the arm supports, and paterae top
the legs. Reeding on the crest rail,
arms, arm supports, legs, and seat rail
unify the piece in the typical New York
manner. The original brass casters cost
the customer extra. They appeared
occasionally on American furniture
from the mid-18th century but became
quite common by the early 19th
century. The sofa is attributed to
Duncan Phyfe, but other cabinetmakers
in New York produced similar work.**
*Diplomatic Reception Rooms, U.S. Department of
State.*

FIGURE V–25
Sofa. Mahogany with ash and birch.
New York. Ca. 1795–1805.
This piece was known as a cabriole sofa in price and pattern books of the early 19th century. The back on this sofa sweeps in a gentle arc from corner to corner. The arching crest rail repeats the curve of the back. The tapered, reeded legs ending in spade, or "therm," feet and the tiny rosettes carved at the termination of the crest rail are characteristics found on other New York furniture. The design is based on a sofa illustrated in Hepplewhite's *Guide*, but the arch of the back is bolder on this New York example.
Courtesy, The Henry Francis du Pont Winterthur Museum.

FIGURE V–26
Settee. Mahogany. Philadelphia. Ca. 1800–1810.
The double-curved arms are adapted from "Drawing Room Chairs" illustrated in Sheraton's *Drawing Book*. The lavish carving include leaves on the legs, arm supports, and balusters across the back, and Prince of Wales feathers over each of the four ovals in the back. Urns filled with leaves are inlaid in each of the four ovals. A pair of armchairs in the Winterthur collection has similar outline and carving, but upholstered, rather than carved and inlaid, splats.
White House Collection.

backed sofas usually had carved or veneered wooden panels above the crest rail. Some patrons preferred the delicately curved back of the cabriole sofa, which was based upon a Hepplewhite design (Figure V–25).

Since the sofa or settee was generally placed near the fireplace, a firescreen commonly stood nearby (Figure V–26). The tripod type, with delicate turnings and Federal ornament, replaced the heavier Chippendale style (Figure V–27 and V–28). A new design, the cheval, or horse screen, supported on a pair of two-legged pedestals, was less popular in America than in England (Figure V–29). Occasionally, a sofa table with short drop leaves supported by a pedestal was placed before the sofa (Figure V–30).

FIGURE V–27
Pole screen. Mahogany and satinwood. Boston. Ca. 1800–1810.
John Seymour made a commode for Mrs. Elizabeth Derby West with the same light and dark inlay. The hinged, half-circle shelf held a candle whose flame was amplified by reflecting off the polished wood. A scalloped base, spade feet, and a spiral finial further distinguish this striking piece.
Private Collection.

FIGURE V–28
Pole screen. Mahogany. New York. Ca. 1800–1815.
The design for the legs, or "standards," was based on Plate XIII in Sheraton's *Drawing Book* of 1793, but the carved pineapple finial is a unique addition. Sheraton designed his "Horse fire screen" to rotate "so that the screen may be turned to any position without moving the stand." However, the New York cabinetmaker used the common 18th-century version of the screen, which ran up and down on a pole, and put the stand on casters for ease in moving. The silk embroidery features a young maiden resting on an anchor, the symbol of hope.
White House Collection.

FIGURE V–29
Cheval glass. Mahogany. American. Ca. 1800.
Thomas Sheraton describes a horse, or cheval, glass in his *Cabinet Dictionary* as "a kind of tall dressing-glass suspended by two pillars and claws, and may, when hung by two centre screws, be turned back or forward to suit the person who dresses at them." The use of rosewood veneer on the frame and the fine turnings indicate an urban origin. The white oak found as a secondary wood was used occasionally in Philadelphia and New York during the early 19th century.
Courtesy, The Henry Francis du Pont Winterthur Museum.

FIGURE V–30 *(far right, top)*
Sofa table. Mahogany. New York. Ca. 1810–1820.
A rare form in America, most surviving examples of the sofa table were made in New York. Describing their use, Sheraton stated in his *Cabinet Dictionary* that "Ladies chiefly occupy them to draw, write, or read upon." The reeding on the legs, stretcher, and edges of the table top is typical of New York work. The lion's head pulls and the heaviness of the legs, stretchers, and balusters signal the advent of the Empire style.
Diplomatic Reception Rooms, U.S. Department of State.

FIGURE V–31 *(far right, bottom)*
Pembroke table. Mahogany. Baltimore. Ca. 1800.
The breakfast table, which first appeared in the 18th century, reaches its fullest development by the Federal period. This Baltimore example, with the distinctive Baltimore bellflower inlay on the legs, is exquisite. The eagle inlays above the legs are unusual and expensive additions. The sawtooth band around the skirt, sometimes executed in paint, is also typical of Baltimore work.
Diplomatic Reception Rooms, U.S. Department of State.

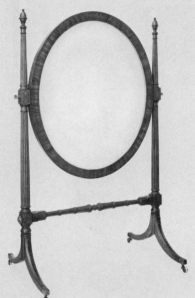

Two special-purpose tables, the work table and the Pembroke, were also found in the parlor and in bedrooms as well. The Pembroke, which first appeared in the Chippendale period was now fully developed and featured tapered legs, inlay, and often an oval top, was avail-able for tea, breakfast, cards, or writing (Figure V–31). Work tables, new in the Federal period, were variously fitted with a pouch for sewing, a writing drawer, a chess or backgammon board, or a mirror for dressing. Either four turned or tapered legs or a pedestal supported the table top. New Yorkers preferred the astragal shape although the square, oval, or canted tops were common also (Figure V–32).

BEDROOMS

Beds continued to carry a high value. Like other Federal furniture, the bedstead became lighter and had turned and reeded or carved posts and, occasionally, carved or inlaid cornices (Figure V–33). Most museums show their high-post beds with sparse summer hangings, but winter hangings surrounded the entire bed. Therefore, Stephen Collins' bill for "56 yd copperplate Furniture—cotton" to hang a bed was not surprising. The striking effect of matching bed hangings, upholstery, and curtains was an idea only the wealthiest could afford because of the huge single outlay of cash required.

Easy chairs were still used in the bedroom and continued to be fitted with chamber pots. The popular 18th-century form of the easy chair that had vertically or horizontally rolled arms remained popular in some areas as late as 1820. The wings and arms were simply lightened, and the legs either tapered or turned. Hepplewhite, in his *Guide*, shows a variation of the easy chair with a visual break between the arm and the wings. Other new forms of the easy chair were becoming fashionable, such as the "circular," or "tub" back; the bergère, with a lower, rounded back; and the fauteuil, with a low, square back (Figure V–34).

The bedroom was fitted with a number of other useful items. The basin stand was an important accessory in genteel bedrooms, since few benefited from running water. They came round, square, or triangular—for use in corners. A basin sat in a large hole, and two smaller ones held cups for soap. A high back protected walls from splashing water (Figure V–35).

In America the word "bureau" began to describe a four-drawer chest by 1792, although in England the term meant a slant-top desk. The typical chest and other case pieces had flaring French feet with a scrolled skirt and a straight, bowed, or serpentine front (Figures V–36 and V–37). On New England bureaus, turned legs often continued up each corner to the top. The veneered drawer front contrasted with the oval or angular brass pulls, which were often stamped with classical or patriotic motifs. Knobs of both mahogany and brass became popular after 1810. Also, by that time, the typical dressing glasses that rested on the chest in most bedrooms were supplanted by chests with the dressing glass attached, similar to modern dressers (Figure V–38).

A few bedrooms still had a dressing table, usually a square-topped one with turned or reeded legs and several drawers, the descendent of the 18th-century lowboy (Figure V–39). Much rarer was the dressing table shaped like a miniature sideboard, with a hinged top covering a mirror and compartments for bottles, boxes, and the other accouterments of a lady's toilet. The modern term for the pieces,

FIGURE V–35
Basin stand. Mahogany and birds' eye maple. Massachusetts. Ca. 1790–1810.
The lower shelf holds an ewer, and the large hole in the upper shelf accommodates a basin. The piece resembles Plate 42 in Sheraton's *Drawing Book*. However, the Massachusetts cabinetmaker has substituted a straight, inlaid skirt for the scalloped one shown by Sheraton and one small drawer for the three on the Sheraton design. The splash boards, which support the little shelf on the top, repeat the shape of the lower shelf in the Sheraton design. The changes result in a simpler but less elegant design.
Smithsonian Institution Photo No. 72-4421.

FIGURE V–36
Linen press. Mahogany. New York State. Ca. 1790.
Similar in form to a piece shown in a plate in Chippendale's *Director*, this press has been updated with neoclassical details, including the inlaid ovals on the doors, the stringing on the drawers, the pair of inlaid eagles, and the delicately pierced pediment. The flaring French feet and the scalloped skirt are also common on Federal furniture. Hepplewhite calls a piece like this a wardrobe, and Sheraton shows an illustration of a similar piece with "wings" added.
Diplomatic Reception Rooms, U.S. Department of State.

FIGURE V–38 *(opposite, bottom left)*
Chest of drawers with dressing glass. Mahogany. Boston area. Ca. 1810–1820.
This practical form, favored in New England in the early 19th century, has continued to be popular up to the present. The heavy, reeded, turned, and carved legs become delicately engaged columns with stopped fluting. Reeding is repeated on the mirror supports and in the concentric reeding on the scrolled buttresses flanking the mirror. Bands of half-moon inlay enliven the top and bottom edge of the lower drawer section. Cross-banding inlay completes the varied decorative techniques used to enrich this piece.
Joe Kindig III.

FIGURE V–39 *(opposite, bottom right)*
Chamber table. Mahogany. Salem, Mass. Ca. 1810–1820.
Small tables with two drawers are often called serving tables, but contemporary price books list "Chamber Tables" that fit the description of this example. The carved and reeded legs, which continue up the edge of the case, are often associated with Salem work. The star-punched background to the carving is often attributed to Samuel McIntire, but other carvers used the star punch as well.
Diplomatic Reception Rooms, U.S. Department of State.

FIGURE V–37
*Chest of drawers. Mahogany.
Baltimore, Ca. 1790–1810.*
The rich, dark mahogany veneer on the
drawer fronts contrasts with the light
crossbanded inlay around the drawers
and the light stringing with hollow
corners. The distinctively shaped skirt
with fan inlay is found on other
Baltimore Federal furniture. The
absence of applied moldings on Federal-
style furniture contributes to their lean,
sharp look.
*Diplomatic Reception Rooms, U.S. Department of
State.*

beau-brummells, conjures up the image of the impeccable arbiter of taste, the English dandy, George Bryan Brummell, who died in 1840.

DINING FURNITURE

Only by the end of the 18th century did one room begin to evolve for the exclusive use of dining. For the first time, large banquet tables could seat more than 20 guests. Pedestal-base "pillar and claw" tables with curved legs and brass feet are usually attributed to Duncan Phyfe, but others made them as well. These, along with another type with straight tapered or turned legs, were made in sections. The semicircular section with one large dropleaf could be joined to a similar table, or both could be attached to a third square section to form an even larger banquet table. When not in use, the sections were pushed back against the wall. These have rarely survived because of their fragile construction. Aside from the table, the most impressive piece in the dining room was the sideboard (Figure V–40). It developed from Adam's prac-

tice of placing urn stands at either end of serving tables. Hepplewhite extolled its virtues: "The great utility of this piece of furniture has procured it a very general reception; and the conveniencies it affords render a dining room incomplete without a sideboard."[10] Many English ones contained metal-lined compartments for chilling wine or washing glasses. Americans preferred a separate wine cooler, which usually stood under the sideboard. The sideboard contained drawers and shelves for the storage of liquor bottles, which had formerly rested on serving or side tables. In the South, where sideboards were rare, the cellaret served this purpose.

The large, bulky sideboard usually rested on tapered or turned legs, which lightened its appearance. The cabinetmaker further lightened the design by dividing the facade into sections that were unified by inlay or patterned veneer (Figure V–41). The more elaborate pieces displayed concave and convex facades similar to shapes found in architecture of the period. According to Robert Adam, the use of these shapes "gives great spirit, beauty, and effect to the compo-

FIGURE V–40
Sideboard. Mahogany. New Jersey. Ca. 1790–1800.
This serpentine front sideboard with rounded corners is highlighted with highly figured mahogany oval veneers, oval stringing, and inlay. Oval paterae and so called book inlay mark the tops of the front legs. The original oval brass pulls effectively repeat the inlaid ovals. Distinctive bellflowers stream down each leg. The richness of the veneer and inlay could indicate an origin around Elizabeth, which was a major center of cabinetmaking in New Jersey in the Federal period. The profusion of bellflowers that seem a bit cramped and overdone betrays the hand of a maker outside of New York or another major style center.
Diplomatic Reception Rooms, U.S. Department of State.

FIGURE V–41
Sideboard. Mahogany. New York. Ca. 1790–1800.
Oval and circular stringing in light and dark wood accents the richly grained mahogany veneer. The band of diamond inlay on the base of the case and the reed inlay over each of the front legs are typically found in the New York area. The inlaid spread eagle against a shield of 16 stars serves as a focal point.
Metropolitan Museum of Art.

sition." The sideboard largely supplanted the pier table of the 18th century. If a serving table were needed, a card table was usually employed rather than a pier table, which was smaller and less useful.

DESKS AND SECRETARIES

Desks and desk and bookcases were not new, but their design changed radically in the Federal period. The Chippendale slant-top desk and bookcase, updated with neoclassical carving or inlay and a delicate swan's neck pediment, continued to be made as late as 1810, but as Sheraton noted in 1803, slant-top desks "are nearly obsolete in London; at least they are so amongst fashionable people."[11] The fashionable desk was now fitted with a "secretary drawer" that pulled out, and the drawer front folded down to form the writing surface (Figure V–42). Another design had hinged flaps that folded down and rested on sliding supports. Rarer in America was the "Cylinder-fall desk," which had a curved lid that rolled back into the case when the desk was in use (Figure V–43). The appearance of lady's

FIGURE V–42
Secretary and bookcase. Mahogany. Salem, Mass. Ca. 1790–1810.
The straight bracket feet are an early feature, but the secretary drawer, the oval, stamped brass pulls, the lightened pediment, and the stringing around each drawer are all neoclassical details. Hepplewhite in his *Guide* calls this piece, with a writing section which pulls out, a secretary and bookcase, in contrast to the earlier desk and bookcase whose lid folded down to form the writing surface. The stringing on the frieze, the general shape of the pediment, and the configuration of the muntins are similar to features found on a piece labeled by William Appleton of Salem.
Diplomatic Reception Rooms, U.S. Department of State.

desks reflected a new emphasis on learning for women. Another new form was the tambour desk, or "Lady's writing table," which had shutters made by gluing thin strips onto a canvas backing (Figure V–44).

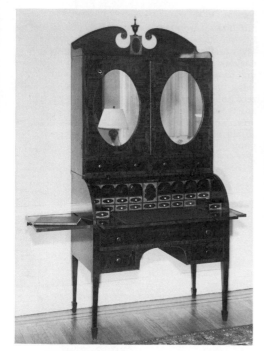

FIGURE V–43
Cylinder-fall desk and bookcase.
Mahogany. Maryland. Ca. 1790–1800.
The design combined elements of pieces illustrated by Sheraton and Hepplewhite. The slides each held candlesticks. The oval motif is repeated on the interior drawers, on the glass in the doors, and on the pediment. The flattened arch of the skirt repeats the arches over each pigeonhole. A cylinder slides over the interior to hide it.
Joe Kindig III.

FIGURE V–44 *(top, right)*
Tambour desk. Mahogany. Boston, Ca. 1795–1810.
Many of the details on this piece are similar to a tambour desk at Winterthur labeled by John and Thomas Seymour of Boston, including the use of inlaid bands above the tambours; the festooned husks on the tambour doors; the stringing around the drawers; the inlaid columns on either side of the doors, in the center, and on either side of the drawers; the bellflower inlay on the legs; the oval inlaid escutcheons; the corner brackets at the junction of the legs and the case; and the robin's egg blue paper on the interior. The unusual pediment offers additional storage behind a hinged door inlaid with a vase of flowers.
White House Collection

FIGURE V–45
Bow-back Windsor arm chair.
Philadelphia. Ca. 1790–1810.
Bow-back Windsors with arms attached are often associated with Rhode Island, but this chair is branded on the seat bottom by Joseph Burden of Philadelphia. The bamboo turnings on the legs, arm supports, and spindles began to appear on Windsors about 1790. At the same time, the seat grew thinner and showed less shaping.
Smithsonian Institution Photo No. 61011.

WINDSORS

Windsor chairs were used in every room of the house. The older forms, such as the sackback and the low-back, continued to be made, but new forms grew in popularity. The bowback or oval-back Windsor appeared in the 1780s (Figure V–45). In 1796, George Washington purchased two dozen of these from Gilbert and Robert Gaw in Philadelphia for forty-four dollars. Bow-backs usually had a cushion, but occasionally their seats were upholstered. The fan-backed form, favored in New England, also appeared in the 1780s (Figure V–46). Their backs were often braced by two spindles terminating in a block pinned to the back of the seat. Also, in the 1780s, Windsor chairmakers began to replace the bold vase- and ring-shaped turnings with simpler turnings that imitated bamboo. By the 1790s, customers ordered Windsor chairs in a wide variety of colors, such as white, yellow, black, and combinations of these. The New York Windsor chairmaker, Walter MacBride, advertised for sale in 1795, chairs "Japanned any colour and neatly flowered." Windsors were made by specialists, such as Ebenezer Tracy of Connecticut. This prosperous maker had 6,400 "chair rounds" and 277 "chair bottomes" on hand when he died in 1803.

By 1800, the square rod-back chair became popular, followed by arrow-back chairs in the next decade and by the ball-back chairs of the 1820s (Figure V–47). The stepped-up crest became popular after 1820. All these styles were related to the Sheraton fancy chairs of this period, particularly in their method of construction. Windsor chair parts were produced by the hundreds and shipped all over the country as "knocked down" or "shaken chairs." These chairs had less shaping in their seats and simpler, bamboo turnings so that they could be produced quickly and inexpensively to meet the burgeoning demand of

the growing population of America and for export to the Caribbean and South America. The stretchers were placed on the outside of the chair in tiers rather than under the seat in the earlier H-configuration.

The Boston and Salem rockers and the low-backed captain's chair, along with kitchen chairs, carried on the Windsor tradition throughout the rest of the century (Figure V–48). The Salem rocker, developed after 1810, was characterized by bamboo turnings, a flat, shallowly scooped seat, and a painted tablet for a top rail. The Boston rocker was developed in the 1820s and had spool turnings, a seat that rolled up slightly at the back, and scrolled shoulders on its tablet crest (Figure V–49).

All furniture forms—from chairs to sideboards—took on a neoclassical veneer after the Revolution. The first phase of neoclassicism in America drew primarily on Robert Adam and on English sources. After the War of 1812, which has been called America's Second War for Independence, the United States became more receptive to French cultural influences. Nowhere was the pro-French bias more obvious than in the preference for the new Empire style, which began to supplant the Federal style about 1815.

NOTES

1. Charles F. Montgomery, *American Furniture: The Federal Period* (New York: Viking Press, 1966), p. 9.

2. Marshall B. Davidson, ed., *The American Heritage History of American Antiques from the Revolution to the Civil War* (New York: American Heritage Publishing Co., 1968), p. 19.

3. George Hepplewhite, *The Cabinet-Maker & Upholsterer's Guide* (New York: Dover Publications, Inc. 1969), Preface.

4. Thomas Sheraton, *The Cabinet-Maker & Upholsterer's Drawing-Book* (New York: Dover Publications, Inc., 1972), p. 49.

5. Sheraton, *Drawing-Book*, p. 107.

6. The advertisement is reproduced in Morrison H. Heckscher, "The Organization and Practice of Philadelphia Cabinetmaking Establishments, 1790–1820" (Master's Thesis, University of Delaware, 1964), p. 70.

7. Berry B. Tracy, ed., *19th-Century America, Furniture and Other Decorative Arts* (New York: Metropolitan Museum of Art, 1970), p. xiii.

8. Thomas Sheraton, *The Cabinet Dictionary* (New York: Praeger Publishers, 1970), p. 218.

9. Brooks Palmer, *The Book of American Clocks* (New York: The Macmillan Company, 1950), p. 10.

10. Hepplewhite, *Guide*, p. 6.

11. Sheraton, *Cabinet Dictionary*, p. 111.

VI
AMERICAN EMPIRE

FROM THE 1790s TO THE 1840s, American furniture-makers interpreted and reinterpreted the classical designs found on architectural remains, fragments of sculpture, pottery, wall paintings, gravestones, and even on survivals of actual furniture, mostly sculpted in stone. The initial phase of the neoclassical influence, the Federal period, was followed about 1815 by a new interpretation of classicism called the "style antique," or Empire. The largely two-dimensional Federal style, with its subtle geometrical and classical inlay, had appealed to the intellect. The Empire style, with its three-dimensional sculptural figures, evoked an emotional response.

The change came gradually. As early as 1808, Duncan Phyfe made a set of furniture for Miss Louisa Throop in the Empire style. It included a Grecian couch; a console table with ormolu mounts; a *secrétaire à abattant* flanked by Doric columns; a lyreback chair; and a French bed with brass mounts in the Egyptian style. However, as late as the 1820s in urban areas and even later in the country, some furniture continued to show the Federal and in some cases, even the Chippendale influence.

Throughout the 18th century, furniture designers had used classical Greek and Roman motifs, such as the acanthus leaf, shells, and architectural pediments, but in the Empire period, classical designs were used with greater attention to historical accuracy. In fact, furniture manufacturers reproduced actual pieces of classical furniture. The new designs benefited from the continuing study of classical ruins, particularly those of Herculaneum and Pompeii. The work of Johann Winckelmann and Giovanni Piranesi, who first codified the findings of the archeologists, provided a ready reference for designers. Archeologists excavated several sites in Etruria in central Italy, and some furniture based on the finds at these digs was called Etruscan. Designers mistakenly thought that this was a separate style, but actually the Etruscans added nothing to the Greek models that they copied.

FRENCH EMPIRE

The Empire style was first developed in France. Jacques-Louis David, the French artist known for his paintings with such classical themes as "The Oath of the Horatii," included classical furniture in his compositions. He commissioned Jacob Desmalter, the largest Paris cabinetmaker

109

during the Napoleonic period, to make the props for his studio. When David became president of the National Convention, which met after the overthrow of the monarchy, he employed Charles Percier to design some furniture for the triumvirs of the French Republic. David also called upon Percier's friend, Pierre Fontaine, to design some furniture as well. Percier and Fontaine had met each other while studying architecture in Rome. Their work for the Convention launched their careers as designers whose services were sought by jewelers, upholsterers, carpetmakers, and cabinetmakers. They also designed sets for the popular classical dramas that were performed by the Paris opera. Napoleon Bonaparte employed them to restore and decorate Malmaison, St. Cloud, the Tuileries, and the Louvre. Their *Collections of Interior Decorations*, first published in 1801, which expounded their philosophy, served as a model for other designers.

The Empire style takes its name from the Empire of Napoleon. Seeing himself as a latter-day Roman proconsul, Napoleon surrounded himself with imperial furniture to reinforce this image. He took the Roman eagle, the bee, and the star as his own personal symbols. The swan was associated with his wife, Josephine. All these symbols were prominent on French Empire furniture and occasionally appeared on English and American work.

In addition to Roman and Greek motifs, the Empire style showed Egyptian influence as well. Napoleon's expeditions to the Nile between 1798 and 1801 stimulated interest in this part of the world. Lord Nelson's naval victories at the mouth of the Nile during this same period piqued English interest. Piranesi had shown elements of the Egyptian taste as early as 1753, and travelers had frequently written about Egypt, but Dominique Vivant Denon, who had accompanied Napoleon to Egypt, was mostly responsible for spreading the craze. He designed furniture in the Egyptian taste for his own home and for the Tuileries in Paris. His position as Director of Museums and of the Mint under Napoleon gave him an even greater influence on taste. Readers as far away as New York City enjoyed Denon's 1802 publication of *Travels in Upper and Lower Egypt*. The images of Egypt's mummies and the preoccupation with death tempered the craze, so that cabinetmakers incorporated only such elements as sphinxes and winged sun disks into their furniture. Palmettes, anthemia, and lion masks, which Empire designers copied from classical Greek and Roman sources, were in turn copied by these classical people from the Egyptians.

Soon after this, the Empire style in France was brought to the masses by Pierre de la Mésangère, who published periodicals on fashion between 1802 and 1835. During its more than 30 years of publication, his magazines touched on all subjects of taste and fashion, including over 400 engravings of furniture. Countless readers rushed to their cabinetmakers to order the latest designs, as depicted in La Mésangère's monthly magazine.

English Regency

The English architect, Henry Holland, first introduced the Empire style in England. He had sent his assistant, Charles Heathcote Tatham, to Rome to copy firsthand the classical buildings and artifacts as well as Egyptian antiquities there. Holland used these designs to redecorate Carlton House, the home of the Prince of Wales in London, in 1783.

Even more influential in spreading the taste for the Empire was Thomas Hope. This extraordinarily well-traveled man was a friend of Percier and had made on-site drawings of classical objects during his travels to Greece and Egypt. In order to house his own collection of classical artifacts, he remodeled and furnished a house in London in the Empire taste. His ideas inspired numerous imitators, but he became distressed when many of the copyists debased his ideas. In order to provide a standard, in 1807 he published *Household Furniture and Interior Decoration*, which depicted tripod tables, Egyptian sphinxes, lion monopodia, and center tables. George Smith, a prominent London cabinetmaker, used some of Hope's designs in his own publication of furniture "in the most approved and elegant taste" issued the next year, but without Hope's attention to historical exactness.

Other designers popularized the Empire or Regency style, as it became known in England after the Regency of George IV from 1811 to 1820. Thomas Sheraton showed elements of the Grecian taste in *The Cabinet Dictionary*, which he issued in 1803, and the *Cabinet-Maker, Upholsterer, and General Artist Encyclopaedia*, which he began publishing in 1804. Also showing Empire furniture was Rudolph Ackermann, who, like La Mésangère in France, published a monthly fashion magazine in London from 1809 to 1828 called *The Repository of Arts, Literature, Commerce, Manufacture, Fashions and Politics*. In 1808, the London Chairmakers' book of prices also began to show furniture in the Empire style, and by 1810 *The New-York Revised Prices for Manufacturing Cabinet and Chair Work* also included Empire designs.

Technological Innovation

Technology affected furniture construction in the Empire period. With the introduction of a circular veneer saw in America early in the 19th century, cabinetmakers could slice veneers 10 strips to the inch, much thinner than the seven to eight pieces per inch possible with hand saws. The thinner sheets could then be applied to curved surfaces and even to round columns without splitting. The thinner veneers were also cheaper, so that exotic woods, such as rosewood, amboyna, and zebra wood, became more widely used. The introduction of steam-driven lathes between 1820 and 1840 contributed to the popularity of turned Roman legs on American furniture.

As cabinet manufactures grew larger and turned out greater and greater quantities of furniture, cabinetmakers looked for ways to apply finishes more quickly. Early in the 19th century, furniture manufacturers increasingly adopted the French polish (called the English polish in France) as a substitute for the time-consuming application of the standard four coats of varnish. The technique employed several varieties of lac dissolved in a distilled alcohol solution. The solution was rubbed on in several stages, using more and more spirits and less and less lac, until a perfect gloss resulted.

AMERICAN EMPIRE

The Empire style came to America from both England and France. Most of the fashion books, particularly Thomas Hope's *Household Furniture* and Ackermann's *Repository*, were known in America. Even more important than books in the transmittal of the style was the importation of furniture. Thomas Jefferson greatly admired the French culture and, while serving as minister to France between 1784 and 1789, he purchased 86 cases of furniture and art. John Quincy Adams and George Washington also bought French furnishings. James Monroe even ordered French furniture for the White House. The importation of furniture was less important after the War of 1812, since a stiff tariff, that in 1820, for example, ran to 30 percent

on furniture and 50 percent on clocks, reduced imports considerably, but by then the new style was well established.

Countless immigrants brought their furniture with them. Philadelphia attracted the largest number of Frenchmen, but substantial numbers of the estimated 10,000 to 25,000 who came to America in the years after the French Revolution of 1789 settled principally in New York City, Baltimore, and Albany. Many of these immigrants were cabinetmakers and other artisans who were already trained in the latest European style.

ARCHITECTURE

The evolution of the Empire style in America paralleled the development of Greek revival architecture in the first half of the 19th century. After the War of 1812, the economy expanded as pent-up demand stifled by the war was satisfied. Further fueling the economy were the demands of a rapidly expanding population. These factors caused a great building boom, and neoclassical design affected architecture as it was affecting furniture design. The first American structure built entirely in the classical form was the Virginia State capitol in Richmond, completed in 1789. Thomas Jefferson designed this building using the model of the Maison-Carrée, a first-century Roman temple he had seen in France. Benjamin Latrobe's Bank of Pennsylvania, completed in 1801, combined Roman designs, such as a circular dome and steps ascending both ends, with Greek temple elements, such as Ionic columns. The first purely Greek revival building, William Strickland's Second Bank of the United States, completed in Philadelphia in 1818, imitated the Parthenon. After that, the Greek revival style of a temple with Doric or Ionic columns supporting an entablature encased coun-

try houses, southern plantation homes, government offices, schools, and prisons. Popularized by design books such as Asher Benjamin's 1827 edition of *American Builder's Companion*, the Greek revival virtually became a national architectural style. Americans symbolically associated the oldest democracy in the world with the newest. The Greek revolt against the Turks in the 1820s gave additional impetus to the Greek revival, which continued in popularity until the Civil War. Empire furniture, classically correct and often massive in scale, fit well within these replicas of Greek temples with spacious rooms and high ceilings.

THE BOSTON FURNITURE TRADE

The Empire style was often flamboyant and dramatic, but Boston furniture was more restrained when compared to Philadelphia or New York work (Figure VI–2). Since more of Boston's cabinetmakers were American born, foreign cabinetmakers did not introduce great change in the city's furniture industry. Conservatism, even in the choice of furniture, seemed to suit Boston's new rich, who felt a certain insecurity in the shadow of Boston's old elite. Bostonians preferred to buy locally or from surrounding towns, with the occasional exception of some furniture shipped from France. In 1823, for example, imports included only six cases of marble tables, eight packs of chairs, four cases of pianofortes, two bamboo couches, 48 cases of looking glasses and plates, and 23 cases of other furniture. Demand for furniture was great, and cabinetmakers in neighboring Newburyport, Ipswich, and Marblehead augmented the output of the more than 275 cabinet- and chairmakers working in Boston by 1835. On the other hand, Boston's large furniture export business of the 18th century had been largely usurped by

Figure VI–2
*Chest of drawers. Mahogany. Boston.
Ca. 1820–1830.*
**In America, these pieces were often
referred to as bureaus. As is typical of
the best Empire furniture, highly figured
mahogany veneers are relieved by
exquisite brass mounts, usually
imported from France. On this piece,
finely cast wreaths serve as keyhole
escutcheons, and brass pulls and collars
on the columns, with floral ornaments
above, add great elegance. A top drawer
overhanging three lower drawers flanked
by columns was a typical configuration
seen on the well-known Meeks
advertisement of 1833 and in Hall's
book of designs, published in 1840. The
use of a framed panel on the side of
the piece revives the 17th-century
joiner's technique that allows the wood
to expand and contract within a frame
without splitting.**
R. T. Trump and Company.

other centers, such as New York
and Philadelphia.

The most successful cabinetmakers banded together with
other artisans to establish the
Massachusetts Charitable Mechanics Association in 1795.
More than simply a charitable
and social organization, the Association began to hold annual
exhibitions in 1837 to encourage
fine craftsmanship and excellence of design. One outstanding
example of cabinetwork was the
center table that William San-
ford of Nantick, Massachusetts,
exhibited. The catalog described
the top as consisting "of 472
pieces of elegant mahogany,
carefully matched, and inlaid
with great precision and good
taste. . . ."[1]

Another sales outlet for cabinetmakers was the semiannual

auction held by the New England Society for the Promotion
of Manufactures between 1826
and 1832. The pieces sold
through these auctions were documented, but conspicuous labels
were prohibited, which may help
to explain the dearth of labeled
Boston furniture. The February,
1832 sale included 104 Grecian
couches, 15 French dressing bureaus with looking glasses, 81
French bureaus, 20 ladies' work
tables (some with silk bags), six
center tables, 23 pairs of card tables, 28 dining Pembroke tables,
18 French bedsteads, 108 Fancy
chairs with rush seats, 118 patent scroll-seat rocking and nurse
chairs, and 29 spring-seat rocking chairs. This long list indicates the volume and variety of
furniture available. The very
success of the auctions caused

the larger furniture warehouses to pressure the city to terminate the Society's free use of city space over Faneuil Hall Market in 1832.

PHILADELPHIA PRACTICES

Although Boston's population remained relatively constant during the first half of the 19th century, the city of Philadelphia grew from 64,000 in 1820 to 93,500 in 1840. Many of these new inhabitants emigrated from France, England, and Germany. The furniture manufacturers increased their output to meet the demands of the growing city and of the large export trade, which continued to expand in the first half of the 19th century. The expansion accelerated the growth of the large furniture warehouses and exacerbated the relations between the cabinetmakers and the journeymen.

The trend threatened the position of the journeyman. In the past, the cabinetmaker passed the journeyman's demands for higher wages on to his customers. However, when the cabinetmaker sold to a retailer, he was under great pressure to keep prices down. As a result, more and more shops employed only apprentice labor, which was considerably cheaper than the more skilled journeyman. The Society of Journeymen Cabinetmakers, established in 1806 as a benevolent association, had by 1829 become an instrument to maintain the journeyman's position in the face of the challenge of unskilled labor. By 1834, after attempts to force the cabinetmakers to cut back on the use of unskilled labor had failed, the society established its own wareroom to sell furniture made by its own members. In reprisal, the cabinetmakers fired all the participating journeymen. In announcing the establishment of the warerooms in 1834, the journeymen declared that "the history of the principle employing Cabinet-Makers of this city, for

the last five years, has been unhandsome in the extreme. They have endeavored to reduce us to a state of vassalege and poverty, below the meanest of our race....."[2] The journeymen argued that furniture could not be "as well manufactured by an inexperienced boy, as by an experienced man, who had spent his youth in acquiring a knowledge of the rudiments and the vigor of his man hood in perfecting himself in all the minutae of this difficult art."[3] The operation soon became the largest wareroom in the city.

Numerous small cabinetmaking shops competed with the journeymen. Some of their work continued to be "bespoke" or custom-made, although, increasingly, only the wealthiest customers could afford this luxury. Mostly these cabinetmakers produced "shop work" to be sold from their own shops. Even though the economy became increasingly money dominated, some cabinetmakers continued to engage in barter. Others even took old furniture in trade in order to stimulate sales. If a cabinetmaker's production could not justify a retail shop, he sold through an auction house or commission merchant for a fee of 10 to 12½ percent. One of the largest auction houses in Philadelphia, T. B. Freeman & Son, established in 1805, is now called Samuel T. Freeman, the oldest auction house in America.

The biggest firms did a considerable amount of "order work"—mostly for exporters or retailers who operated large warerooms (Figure VI–3 and VI–4). The order business grew as transportation improvements, such as roads, canals, and the infant railroads, opened up new markets for enterprising merchants. Middlemen, rather than the cabinetmaker himself, handled most of the large export trade in furniture. Some firms sent their own buyers to Philadelphia, but usually exporters based in Philadelphia shipped furniture on order or to commis-

FIGURE VI–3
Armchair. Walnut. American. Ca. 1830.
The carved lotus blossoms and leaves on the blocks supporting the arms and the anthemia on the crest are derived from classical prototypes employing Egyptian motifs. The cabriole legs foretell the arrival of the rococo. An identical leg is found on Figure VI–4, indicating the use of interchangeable parts at this early date.
E. J. Canton.

FIGURE VI–4
Armchair. Mahogany. American. Ca. 1830.
The legs are identical to those on the piece in Figure VI–3, but the variation of the gondole chair with arms is quite different from the square back of the other chair.
E. J. Canton.

sion merchants in ports throughout the South, the West Indies, and South America, and in the West as far as Pittsburgh. Chairs, usually knocked down in parts, were the most common item exported from Philadelphia, but shippers handled everything from bureaus, stands, and desks to wardrobes, sideboards, and even pianos.

The largest cabinetmakers in Philadelphia, including Joseph Barry and Anthony Quervelle, engaged directly in exporting furniture. The Irish-born Barry was trained in London before coming to Philadelphia in the 1790s. He moved from shop to shop in the decade before 1800 and finally opened his own shop by 1811. In January 1812, he advertised that he had recently returned from Europe with some new "selections of the Most Fashionable and Elegant Articles in Their Line," which were, no doubt, in the new Empire style.[4] Soon he opened branch shops in Savannah and Baltimore. His labeled, richly carved pier table is one of the best examples of Philadelphia Empire furniture.

Anthony Quervelle immigrated from France to Philadelphia in 1817 and by 1825 had opened a warehouse. He advertised "the largest and most fashionable assortment of furniture ever yet offered for sale in this city."[5] Like Barry, he did a large export business and sold locally as well. He even advertised that "the proprietors of Hotels, large Boarding Houses, &c. will find it greatly to their interest, in furnishing their establishments, to call and examine his extensive assortment."[6] His furniture business prospered in the 1820s and 1830s, and he invested the profits in Philadelphia real estate. He died a wealthy man in 1856. His furniture in the Empire style, animated by carving, avoided the heaviness and mechanical feeling of furniture by many of his less talented contemporaries.

NEW YORK: CENTER OF STYLE

Even more prosperous than Philadelphia was New York. After the Peace of Ghent, which ended the War of 1812, the British chose New York as the port in which to dump huge quantities of goods to flood the American markets and reestablish their trade dominance. Even before that windfall, New York was well on its way to becoming the busiest port in America. New York had strong trading ties with France as well as Britain. The opening of the Erie Canal in 1825 gave the port access to the interior. At the same time, the city solidified its position as the middleman between the South and Europe. Such firms as those of Duncan Phyfe and Charles-Honoré Lannuier benefited from this trade by shipping large quantities of furniture to the South. As the city grew in commercial importance, the population of the city and surrounding area rose between 1820 and 1840 from 123,000 to 312,000.

Despite the flood of English goods after the War of 1812, New York became increasingly fond of the French taste. The close commercial ties with France explained part of the fervor for French things, but the great number of émigrés who settled in the city after the War of 1812 also contributed to the feeling. A major figure in setting the fashion for French furniture in the Empire style was the French-trained Lannuier, who advertised in 1803 that "he wishes to settle himself in this city, and only wants a little encouragement." He traded on his French background and stated on one of his labels in his best French accent that "H. Lannuier, Cabinet Maker from Paris Kips his Warehouse" at 60 Broad Street. It was located in a typical New York row house, with his shop in the rear and the family quarters in front. Lannuier was indeed en-

couraged, and he counted among his customers some of the most distinguished families of New York. Lannuier specialized in tables but also made other furniture. His high-quality craftsmanship included the choice of exotic woods, such as ebony and rosewood.

Best known for his Federal furniture, Duncan Phyfe continued to make furniture throughout the neoclassical period. Taking advantage of the expanding transportation network, Phyfe sold furniture all over the country, but particularly to the South. Like most cabinetmakers, Phyfe also did many odd jobs relating to woodworking, but not necessarily to furniture-making. He refinished and reconditioned old furniture, put up and took down bedsteads, mended furniture, and even hung lamps. Many of his competitors sold cabinet woods and supplies, whereas others engaged in coffin-making.

CHAIRS

As in earlier periods, chairs continued to comprise a large portion of the business of large cabinetmakers such as Lannuier and Phyfe. One of the most popular was a commonly copied classical form, the klismos chair, based on actual fifth-century B.C. Greek chairs seen on vases recovered at Pompeii and Herculaneum (Figures VI–5 and VI–6). Some customers preferred the straight, turned Roman leg to the curved saber leg popular elsewhere. Percier and Fontaine introduced the klismos form after the French Revolution, and Thomas Hope illustrated them in 1807. Instead of the vertical splat common in the 18th century, the klismos chair had a horizontal stay rail that was often carved or painted.

New York chairs sometimes exhibit cornucopias on their stay rails, whereas simple carved

spread eagles or stylized, ancient Greek lyres, complete with strings, resting on the stay rails. Cheaper chairs with solid, lyre-shaped splats are sometimes misunderstood as poor renditions of the vase-shaped splats on 18th-century Queen Anne chairs (Figure VI–8). Some klismos armchairs attributed to Lannuier exhibited arm supports in the form of winged caryatids,

drapery adorns some Boston examples. Philadelphia chairs had a rolled lip on the crest rail, similar to those on Philadelphia sofas (Figure VI–7). Some Philadelphia chairs attributed to the workshop of Anthony Quervelle had leafy scrolls or paired volutes and anthemia. The common Empire motif, derived from the honeysuckle blossom, was frequently found on classical artifacts. Other chairs displayed

FIGURE VI–5
Vase. Terra cotta. Greece. Ca. 480 B.C.
The scene depicts a Greek woman seated in a klismos chair with bold, sabre-like front legs and a tablet crest resting on top of the back stiles. Designers in the early 19th century copied the Greek chair almost exactly.
Virginia Museum.

FIGURE VI–6 *(far left, below)*
Side chair. Rosewood. New York. Ca. 1815–1820.
This chair, in the *klismos* form, belonged to Chief Justice John Marshall. The crest rail is contained within the stiles, which is the most common New York construction method, as compared to a crest that rested on top of the stiles, as on most Philadelphia chairs. The inlay is done with brass, a rare technique on American furniture.
Smithsonian Institution Photo No. 10785A.

FIGURE VI–7 *(left)*
Side chair. Mahogany. Philadelphia. Ca. 1820–1825.
The maker of this chair has created a very close copy of an ancient Greek klismos chair with the sabre legs and tablet crest. Philadelphia chair makers, as illustrated by this example, usually rested the tablet on the stiles, in contrast to New York examples in which the crest rail is confined between the stiles. The brass inlay of stars and anthemia on the crest and skirt are found on work by Joseph Barry. Related chair designs with brass inlay were illustrated by Thomas Hope in 1807.
R. T. Trump and Company.

FIGURE VI–8
Side chair. Walnut. American. Ca. 1840–1860.
The overall form, with the sabre-front legs and the lyre-shaped splat, suggests the Empire style, but the hand-hold piercing the crest rail and the wavy outline of the top and bottom of the crest indicate the arrival of the Rococo revival. On these inexpensive chairs, the crest is applied over the face of the stiles and no attempt is made to integrate it with the rest of the chair.
Herbert Collins.

FIGURE VI–9
Sofa. Mahogany. New York. 1810–1815.
This sofa may have been purchased in suite with side chairs having "Grecian Cross Fronts." Duncan Phyfe sent a sketch of such a chair to a customer in Philadelphia about 1815. The leaf and cornucopia carving on the crest rail and arms, the caning, the reeding, the brass feet, and the lion's head medallions all made this sofa expensive, requiring about a month of labor to make. George Smith, Thomas Hope, and Ackermann's *Repository* all illustrated furniture with the Grecian or curule base, but only a small number of such pieces have survived from the early 19th century.
Boscobel Restoration, Inc., Garrison-on-Hudson, New York.

FIGURE VI–10
Side chair. Painted wood. American. Ca. 1825–1835.
This chair is similar to Figure VI–11 in overall design, but the differences in details, such as the turnings on the legs and seat, indicate another of the hundreds of imitators of Hitchcock's chairs. The silhouetted eagle appears on other fancy chairs of the period.
Herbert Collins.

inspired by ones found on the Erechtheum, a temple on the Acropolis in Athens. On Philadelphia chairs, as on most Baltimore chairs, a tablet surmounted the stiles, as shown by Hope, whereas in New York, the stiles typically rose above the crest rail or enclosed it. A less common chair, sometimes favored in New York, was the curule, or Grecian cross chair, based on a Roman magistrate's folding chair. The half circles forming the legs were often repeated in the back of the chair (Figure VI–9).

Fancy Chairs

Cheaper chairs substituted rush seats, turned legs and stiles, and stenciled decoration for expensive upholstery, carving, and brass mounts. Many firms throughout Massachusetts, New York, Rhode Island, and Ohio produced these "fancy," now called Hitchcock, chairs, named for their best-known manufacturer. Lambert Hitchcock began making chairs in Barkhamsted, Connecticut, in 1818, and in 1825 he opened a large factory in what is now Riverton, Connecticut. His factory employed over 100 workers, who turned out 15,000 chairs a year. He shipped most of them "boxed in good shipping order" by wagon to Hartford, where he sold some through a company store, but most were loaded aboard ships

destined for Boston, New York, Richmond, and Charleston. Over-expansion forced him to the brink of bankruptcy in 1829 and caused him to take on a partner, Arba Alford. The partnership was dissolved in 1843, and Hitchcock opened a new factory at Unionville, Connecticut, where he made bureaus, secretaries, washstands, and beds as well as chairs until his death in 1852.

Using paper stencils, Hitchcock and other "fancy" chair-makers applied their designs to their chairs, which were most often painted black, yellow, or green. Before the tacky varnish dried, a worker sprinkled the surface with bronze dust to suggest gilding or selected one of several other colors. Striping was added, and then the entire chair was painted with a protective coat of varnish. Using the same method, the slats—cut out in the shape of cornucopias, eagles, turtles, beehives, and butterflies—were decorated (Figures VI–10 and VI–11). The technique deteriorated after 1830, and fewer and fewer stencils were used on each chair. The designs became simplified and exhibited less detail and shading.

FIGURE VI–11
Side chair. Painted wood. Hitchcocksville, Conn. Ca. 1825–1830. **The chair is one of a set of eight, all with the Hitchcock label. The painted and stenciled stay rail cut in the outline of paired cornucopia was a common motif on chairs made in the Hitchcock chair factory. The multiple ring-turned legs tapering to tiny ball feet was also a common feature of Hitchcock chairs.** *Virginia Museum.*

SOFAS

The sofa, a rare luxury in the 18th century, had, by the Empire period, become relatively common. Most elegant parlors needed at least one sofa, which balanced the mandatory fireplace. Cabinetmakers sold three popular models. The "plain sofa," the cheapest and most common, based on the Roman sofa called a *fulcra*, had identically scrolled ends and a long, wooden crest rail. More expensive versions came with a carved tablet in the center of the crest rail. Reeding, carving, and veneer heightened the elegance. Many sofas rested on winged lion's paw feet, which were inspired by those of griffins, which had the body and feet of a lion and the wing and head of an eagle (Figure VI–12). The Romans frequently used the motif as a symbol of authority or exotica. Percier and Fontaine incorporated the idea into a table that they made for Madame Jeanne Récamier, a French socialite, in 1798, but by 1806, the carved foot lost favor to the turned Roman leg in France. However, in England, George Smith illustrated furniture with the carved paw foot in his 1808 design book, and the motif was widely used in America. One of the most dramatic variations of the

FIGURE VI–12
Sofa. Mahogany. Philadelphia. Ca. 1820–1830. **This sofa and its mate stood in the hall of the Hermitage when the state of Tennessee bought the house in 1856.** *The Philadelphia Cabinet and Chair Makers' Union Book of Prices for Manufacturing Cabinet Ware,* **published in 1828, lists a "plain sofa" for five dollars. This sofa, with its richly carved tablet flanked by carved scrolls on the crest, is the most elaborate version of the "plain sofa." The customer could choose from a variety of designs for the carved crest and carved or turned feet.** *The Ladies' Hermitage Association.*

"plain sofa" employed curling Roman dolphins to form the scrolled arms and feet of some New York sofas (Figure VI–13).

Sofas, like chairs, continued to manifest some regional differences. The wooden crest rails on New York sofas frequently terminated in rosettes. The overall appearance of the New York sofa was lighter than the much more exuberantly carved and heavier Philadelphia ones. New York sofas had more gently scrolled arms than their bolder, more florid Philadelphia counterparts. Philadelphia carving on the feet of sofas was usually confined to the two front feet, whereas turnings or uncarved blanks were used for the rear supports.

A second type, the "box sofa," became popular by the 1830s and 1840s. Vertical boxes formed the ends of these sofas, which rested on large, turned Roman feet (Figure VI–14). The 1828 Philadelphia book of prices called a third, more expensive type with complex scrolls on the back a "double scroll sofa" or, more commonly, a "Grecian couch." Often made in pairs, they usually flanked the fireplace (Figure VI–15). Cabinetmakers derived the form from Greek prototypes that evoked the romance of the antique and the suggestion of the highest beauty. Used for reclining, like the 18th-century daybed, they were related to the French Récamier couch, or meridienne. The modern term, Récamier, was derived from David's painting of Madame Récamier lounging on a small

FIGURE VI–13
Sofa. Mahogany with ash. New York. Ca. 1815.
Family tradition holds that Captain Charles Stewart purchased this sofa for the captain's cabin on USS *Constitution*. Holes for brackets that might have attached the sofa to the deck lend credence to the story. The extraordinary, writhing, gilt dolpins on whose heads the sofa rests make this one of the great American Empire creations. The carved crest adds additional elegance.
Navy Memorial Museum, Washington, D.C.

FIGURE VI–14
Sofa. Mahogany. Philadelphia. Ca. 1830–1840.
This sofa style with vertical ends listed in the 1828 Philadelphia book of prices as a "box sofa" that sold for $5.75. Seventy-five cents more expensive than the "plain sofa," the box sofa appears to have been less common, if the relatively fewer number that have survived is an accurate indicator. Richly grained mahogany veneers on the seat and crest rail and on the arm supports contrasted with a bold upholstery. The present floral upholstery, which tends to overpower the carving and veneer, is not the original covering. Boldly carved anthemia ornament the tops of the arm supports. The reeded and carved Roman legs rested on brass casters.
Philadelphia Museum of Art: Bequest of John W. Pepper.

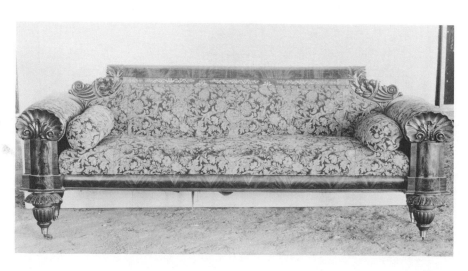

Figure VI–15
Sofa. Tulip and maple. New York. Ca. 1825–1835.
Cabinetmakers called this sofa a "Grecian couch" in the early 19th century. The design was inspired by an illustration in George Smith's *Guide*, published in 1826. It is also similar to a plate in the 1833 broadside by Meeks, but the proportions of the Meeks illustration are not as good as Smith's, which Meeks probably copied. A carved figure of a bearded, old man adds considerable interest to the crest rail, which is grained to simulate rosewood.
R. T. Trump and Company.

Figure VI–16
Bench. Painted wood. Baltimore. Ca. 1820–1830.
The heavy reeding and multiple-ring turnings on the legs and the intricate stenciling on the seat rail all characterize Baltimore work. Brass rosettes on the ends of the cylindrical headrests add additional interest to this classical form based on Roman couches. Stylized anthemia vines flow across the seat rail, and gilt trophies highlight the panels over the legs.
Ramon Osuna.

couch. Her couch had ends of equal height and no back, but the term stuck for ones with sloping backs because of the fashionable association. Also related to Grecian couches were the Ottoman sofas or benches made without arms, which were frequently used as window seats (Figure VI–16).

Parlor Furniture

In addition to couches and sofas, the parlor contained an assortment of card, work, and center tables (Figure VI–17). The center table first became popular in the Empire period and served much like the modern coffee table. Some of these tables showed the last gasp of the Sheraton influence in their reeded saber legs, but by 1820, these were replaced by heavy turned or carved pedestal bases, usually with lion's paw feet. The single carved and

Figure VI–17
Card table. Mahogany. American. Ca. 1815–1825.
The pedestal-base card table with double-elliptical top was found in Charleston, West Virginia, and was made outside the major style centers, possibly in Cincinnati, Ohio, which was tied to Charleston by way of the Ohio and Kanawha rivers. Drop finials appear on many card tables of the period, suggesting vestigial legs of earlier four-legged card tables. Carving rather than turning usually ornamented banisters made in the major cabinetmaking centers, such as New York. The table rests on four ball feet instead of on casters.
Glenwood, Charleston, West Virginia.

turned baluster sometimes had heavily carved feet directly attached, but usually the pillar rose from a hollowed triangular-, rectangular-, or circular-shaped plinth that rested on lion's paw feet (Figure VI–18).

FIGURE VI–18 *(above)*
Center table. Mahogany. American. Ca. 1835–1845.
The marble top is supported on a massive, fluted, classical column that rests on a platform supported by unusual cylindrical feet rather than the more common scrolled feet. The thin mahogany veneers are flexible enough to cover even the deep flutes on the pedestal. A series of graduated disks applied to the feet accentuate the circular form of the top, the pedestal, and the feet.
Ramon Osuna.

FIGURE VI–19
Card table. Mahogany. Salem or Boston. Ca. 1815.
Although the serpentine or elliptic front cost 10 shillings extra, according to price books of the period, it was one of the most popular shapes. The common, classical lyre motif in Boston was more often made with brass strings rather than more expensive ebony. The richly veneered skirt is edged with a beaded brass inlay. The scroll at the top of each leg is unusual.
R. T. Trump and Company.

FIGURE VI–20
Worktable. Mahogany. Philadelphia. Ca. 1815.
The top with "canted corners" lifts up to expose a fitted compartment. The tradition of fine carving in Philadelphia continues on the lyre and the legs. The acorn drops are a common motif on tables of the early 19th century. Typical lion's head brass pulls and brass paw feet relieve the richly grained mahogany veneers.
R. T. Trump and Company.

Some, with a triangular-shaped pedestal, were inspired by ancient Roman candelabra. On others, four scrolled supports called "standards"—or, more rarely, carved dolphins, caryatids, or lyres—held up the top (Figure VI–19). Figured veneers and inlay, as well as colored marble inspired by Roman precedents, enriched the tops.

A smaller version of the center table, the gueridon, developed during the Empire period. Used for basin stands, game tables, or tea tables, these small,

circular tables, often with marble tops, were based on ancient Greek and Roman examples (Figure VI–1). One version with three monopodia was derived directly from a table found in a garden at Herculaneum. Others were supported on three columns or on a single vase-shaped baluster. Tops on some tilted so that the table could be pushed out of the way when not in use.

Work tables, which were often made without silk bags by the Empire period, resembled the card and pedestal tables (Figure

VI–20). In one variation, however, trestle-like supports linked by turned stretchers supported the table tops. The trestles took the shape of lyres or carved dolphins, similar to those on English Regency sofa tables.

Pier tables, used as serving or hall tables, seemed to have been the most popular tables in the Empire period. A mirror often rose from a shelf near the base of the rear legs and the reflection gave the illusion of a double table. Cabinetmakers chose from a full vocabulary of Empire figures, including caryatids, dolphins, swans, lion-footed scrolls, eagle monopodia, and simple Doric or Ionic columns to support the tops (Figures VI–21,

FIGURE VI–21
*Pier table. Mahogany and marble.
Boston or Salem. Ca. 1820.*
The rare enclosed cabinet and white marble slab indicate a use as a serving table. The mirrored doors have the same arched shape as the doors on an upright piano forte illustrated by Thomas Hope. The elegantly carved and gilded caryatids, also related to plates in Hope, combine Egyptian and classical Greek motifs. The highly figured mahogany veneer is typical of other Boston work, but the elaborate carving is less common.
R. T. Trump and Company.

FIGURE VI–22 *(left, below)*
*Pier table. White pine and marble.
New York. Ca. 1830–1845.*
The gilded frame supports an original white marble top. The table is attributed to Joseph Meeks and Sons because the design matches a table depicted in the 1833 broadside published by that company. In London in 1826, George Smith published a similar design with lyres supporting a top in his *Guide.*
Virginia Museum.

FIGURE VI–23
*Pier table. Painted wood and metal.
Baltimore. Ca. 1820–1830.*
The two lion's head monopodal supports based on classical sources are cast from metal rather than carved from wood in the more usual manner. Similar lion's head monopodia or chimeras are illustrated on tables and chairs in Thomas Hope's *Household Furniture and Interior Decoration,* published in 1807. The plaster frieze of anthemia on the skirt is based on a similar one on the Erechtheum in Athens. The back supports flanking the mirror are gilded, and the background is grained to simulate rosewood.
Baltimore Museum of Art.

VI–22, and VI–23). Veneer, inlay, carving, stenciling, and brass or ormolu mounts relieved the broad expanses of rich mahogany.

The highest quality ormolu mounts, which added great richness to the Empire furniture, were usually imported from France. The ormolu was made by gold-plating brass, using the extremely toxic mercury method. Gold was combined with mercury and the mixture spread on the brass. When the piece was heated, the mercury vaporized, leaving the gold deposited on the brass. The popular designs of these miniature brass sculptures included bees, swans, Greek goddesses, flowers, and wreaths. The common star-shaped mount suggested the exposed bolts found on Roman furniture. However, beginning in 1807, Thomas Jefferson's Trade Embargo Act cut off the supply of imported mounts, and trade with Europe was interrupted off and on for eight years. As a re-

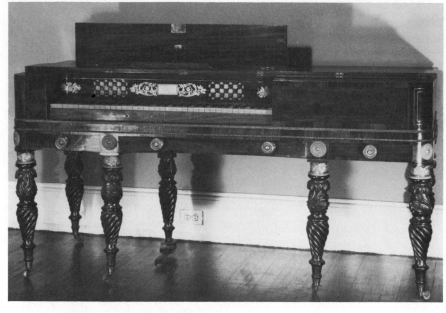

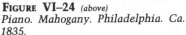

FIGURE VI–24 *(above)*
Piano. Mahogany. Philadelphia. Ca. 1835.
The case of this upright piano by Christian F. L. Albrecht exhibits all the best qualities of Empire furniture. The pleated cloth covering the sounding board is similar to the treatment of the glass doors in desk and bookcases or on the canopies of bedsteads. The veneered columns have brass collars on the bases and capitals. The stenciling above the sounding board is similar to designs on other Philadelphia furniture. The gilt lyres above the upper columns emphasize the musical theme. A curved lid with a collapsible music rack folds over to cover the keyboard.
Smithsonian Institution Photo No. 56381.

FIGURE VI–25 *(top right)*
Piano. Mahogany. New York. Ca. 1825–1835.
H. and W. Geib, who patented the first metal frame for piano strings in 1826, made the works. The firm purchased the case, possibly from Duncan Phyfe, whose shop was nearby. The brass mounts were imported. The spiral turnings appear on furniture about 1815 and become progressively heavier. The brass knobs on the skirt are decorative, but they also allow access to drawers for music.
Anne and David Sellin.

FIGURE VI–26
Mirror. Gilded wood. American. Ca. 1820–1830.
This is a common form with turned half-columns surrounding the glass. The blocks with carved rosettes at each corner solve the problem of mitering the balusters moldings. The unidentified ship painted on the top panel flies the American flag. The entire frame is gilded.
Herbert Collins.

sult, furniture manufacturers turned more to stenciling and gilding.

A major addition to the parlor of many middle- and upper-class homes in the 1820s was the pianoforte. The name is derived from the French *piano et forte*, or "soft" and "loud," from the sounds that can be made when the hammer strikes the strings. During the 1820s and 1830s, the manufacture of pianofortes boomed. Jonas Chickering, Gilbert and Osborne, Christian F. L. Albrecht, and others sold hundreds of instruments to middle- and upper-class families attempting to gain a little bit of culture (Figures VI–24 and VI–25). Other makers included the Loud Brothers, who began selling pianofortes in Philadelphia in 1816, and John Geib and Sons of New York. Chickering, the most famous name in the American pianoforte business, began working for John Osborne in 1819 in Boston. Osborne, in turn, had learned his trade from Benjamin Crehore, who made one of the first pianofortes in Boston about 1792. Chickering and James Stewart set up their own business in 1823 until Stewart returned to Britain to join the well-known firm of Clementi and Collard.

In 1830, Chickering took John

Mackay, a ship captain and astute businessman, as his partner. Mackay promoted and sold the pianos, freeing Chickering to manufacture and improve the product. To overcome the disastrous effects of low humidity in the coal-heated homes of the mid-19th century, Chickering, in 1840, patented an improved iron frame for the square piano. Various other makers developed better methods of stringing the piano to achieve the optimum tonal quality. Chickering bought his cases from cabinetmakers, such as Jonathan W. Felt and Ruggles Slack and Company, and used the services of the carver, Calvin Allen.

In nearly every room of Greek revival houses hung a mirror. The more fashionable, heavier, sculptured creations of the Empire replaced the delicately carved architectural mirrors of the Federal period. On those that still had a pediment, such as the Sheraton style ones, heavy gilded, turned or spiralling half-balusters accented the frame. These often had a painted glass panel in the upper section (Figure VI–26). Mantel mirrors in three sections had the same heavy turned balusters. On others, the pediment disappeared, and carved cornucopias or foliage ornamented the frame. On the most exquisite looking glasses of the 1830s and 1840s, cornucopias, dolphins, lyres, fruit, and the whole range of Empire ornament surrounded the glass (Figures VI–27 and VI–28).

SIDEBOARDS

One of the most impressive and expensive pieces of furniture in the house during the Empire vogue was the sideboard, which dominated the dining area as the sofa dominated the parlor. These pieces gradually grew in size un-

FIGURE VI–27
Girondole mirror. White pine. Probably English. Ca. 1800–1820.
The convex mirror glass reflects and amplifies the light of candles in the three sconces on either side of the frame. The carved dolphins on the crest were a common Empire motif derived from classical examples. As is typical of mirrors of this type, the frame is gilt, but the reeded border surrounding the glass is ebonized. At the base are leaves entwined by a ribbon.
University of Virginia.

FIGURE VI–28
Mirror. Poplar. Probably New York. Ca. 1825–1835.
The gilt cornucopias are related to carving on a mirror labeled by John H. Williams of New York and may have been made in his shop. Carved cornucopias appear on other New York furniture, including a desk and bookcase attributed to Joseph Meeks and Sons. The earliest looking glass frames were inspired by Renaissance architectural tabernacles. This frame represents the other extreme, of the completely sculptural frame.
R. T. Trump and Company.

FIGURE VI–29
Sideboard. Mahogany. Philadelphia or Baltimore. Ca. 1825–1835.
The depressed marble mixing surface is found on a number of Philadelphia and Baltimore sideboards. The angled pedestals topped by gadrooned caps and resting on lion's paw feet show an Egyptian influence. They are derived from a plate in an October 1822 edition of Ackermann's *Repository of the Arts* that shows a similar sideboard "suitable for the mansions of the great and opulent." One pedestal houses the original, pierced, revolving rack for the storage of wine bottles. Above the pedestals, double volutes slash through carved leaves, and cornucopias spill their bounty of fruit, suggesting the prosperity and abundance appropriate to a dining room. The ball feet on which Empire furniture frequently rest recall similar feet on 17th-century furniture.
James M. Goode Collection.

FIGURE VI–30
Detail from an October 1822 issue of Ackermann's *Repository*.

til cupboards filled the space below the top, and the piece came to rest on short turned or carved legs. Four classical columns projected from a finely veneered facade, which was sometimes relieved by stenciling or brass fittings. On Philadelphia sideboards, drawers usually flanked a marble-topped center section that had a carved or plain back, whereas New York and Boston ones were often made with a broad, flat top (Figures VI–29, VI–30, and VI–31).

Dining tables, similar in design to card and center tables, did not commonly stand permanently in the center of the room, as is the modern practice (Figure VI–32). In the Empire period, as in the 18th century, they were set against the wall or removed from the room altogether and placed in an adjacent hall when not in use.

FIGURE VI–31
Sideboard. Mahogany. Boston. Ca. 1820.
The reeded and turned legs and the fluted panels above each front leg relate to other examples attributed to John and Thomas Seymour. The shape of the backboard repeats the lines of the facade and also echoes the shaping of the skirt. The carving on the feet and the anthemia on either side of the central drawer are exceptional. The bright brass lion's head pulls contrast with the dark veneered drawer fronts.
R. T. Trump and Company.

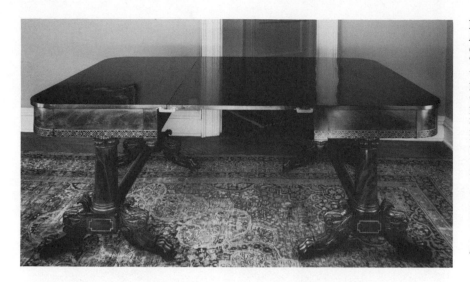

FIGURE VI–32
*Dining table. Mahogany. New York.
Ca. 1820–1830.*
The most common form of the dining
table in the Empire period was the
pillar and claw or pedestal type. This
configuration, with two separate
pedestals joined by the stretcher, was
more often found on library tables. As
is common in New York furniture,
highly figured mahogany veneer is
relieved by a gold, stenciled band
around the skirt of the table and on the
base of each pedestal. The well-
executed carving adds additional
interest and cost. The brass clips that
fit into brackets on the underside of the
table hold two leaves that could be
added to extend the table.
James M. Goode Collection.

BEDROOM FURNITURE

Bedchambers contained the
standard dressers, wash stands,
and chests, but the bed was the
most expensive piece (Figure
VI–33, VI–34, VI–35, and VI–36).
These were English-style bedsteads—massive four-post bedsteads, often with spiral turnings
or carvings and tall, carved headboards that were perfectly in
scale with the high ceilings of
the Greek revival mansions (Figure VI–37). A new type, the
French bed, now called a sleigh
bed, became popular in America
about 1815. A baldachin attached
to the wall often crowned the

bed, whose head and footboards
were of equal height (Figure
VI–38).

Other furniture in the bedroom included large wardrobes,
or armoires, descendants of the
medieval storage cabinets for ar-
mor. These pieces, often fitted

FIGURE VI–33 *(far left)*
*Basin stand. Mahogany. Baltimore. Ca.
1830–1840.*
The feet, turned in a beehive shape,
indicate a Baltimore origin. The lid
with a torus molding lifts up to expose
a circular cutout for a washbowl. The
cylindrical lower section rotates to
expose two shelves. The cylindrical
shapes play effectively against the flat
squares of the skirt and base.
James M. Goode Collection.

FIGURE VI–34
Open view of basin stand (Figure
VI–33).
James M. Goode Collection.

FIGURE VI–35

Dressing table. Mahogany. New York State. Ca. 1830–1840.

Dressing tables with mirrors attached became common in the Empire period, but ones resting on a pedestal base are unusual. Glass knobs were often found on Empire furniture but these are replacements, probably for brass ring pulls. The mirror with an ogee frame is similar to rectangular ones hung on walls during this period. The well-carved scrolls with anthemia, which support the mirror, contrast with the plain, veneered surfaces. The use of gadrooning recalls a similar 18th-century ornament on New York furniture.

Margaret Woodbury Strong Museum.

FIGURE VI–36

Chest of drawers with dressing glass. Mahogany. Salem. Ca. 1835–1845.

The dressing glass became attached to the bureau early in the Federal period. Some of the finest examples of this form were made in Salem, where the carved, engaged column was a hallmark. This piece derives from that tradition, but the heavy turned and carved columns indicate a late Empire date. The carving is skillfully repeated on the corners of the upper drawers and on the vertical supports for the mirror. Sheraton illustrates spiral turnings for chair legs and bed posts in his *Drawing Book.* This carver, however, has lavished extra work on the turnings to give a shimmering effect that contrasts to the regular spiral on the mirror supports.

E. J. Canton.

with drawers, augmented the bureau as a container for clothes. In his design book, Chippendale showed clothes presses, but few American examples have survived from the 18th century other than the great Hudson River *Kas* and the Pennsylvania German *schrank*. By the Federal period, clothes presses in two parts, with drawers in the lower section and shelves above, became popular. By 1820, the wardrobe resting on ball feet was fitted with large doors that often concealed drawers as well as space to hang clothes (Figure VI–39). The wardrobe, popular in the 16th and 17th centuries, gave way to the press by the 18th century as clothing styles became less bulky. The new clothing fashions made with thinner material could be folded away. Sheraton illustrated a wardrobe with four doors above drawer sections in the 1793 edition of his *Drawing Book*. The middle sections had shelves, and the end ones were fitted with rods for coat hangers.

Next to the bed, the most impressive items found in a bedroom were French desk and bookcases. These pieces usually had flat tops with a sharply projecting cornice, glass doors, and a fall-front writing section flanked by Roman or Greek columns. Most had shelves behind doors in the lower section rather than the drawers common on most earlier ones (Figure VI–40). The 1815 New York book of prices showed 28 different patterns for the muntins, which

126

FIGURE VI–37
Bed. Mahogany. Philadelphia. Ca. 1836.
After his Tennessee home, the Hermitage, burned in 1834, Andrew Jackson's adopted son bought this and five other bedsteads from George W. South of Philadelphia for $240. The hangings are reproductions of the originals. The mammoth bed stands just under nine feet tall and is more than six feet wide. The C-scroll ornaments on the front and sides of the canopy match similar ones over the bedroom windows.
The Ladies' Hermitage Association.

FIGURE VI–38
French bed. Mahogany. New York. Ca. 1815.
This bed is labeled 10 times by Charles Honoré Lannuier. Two paper labels are written in French and English, and eight are stamped with C. H. Lannuier and J. B. Cochois (who worked with him). Wheels attached to a metal brace allow the bed to roll on the floor without danger of breaking the carved paw feet. The dotted brass inlay, the brass molding around the base, and the stamped medallion emphasize the lines of the piece. The gilded eagle heads are carved with the same high quality typical of the more than 50 pieces attributed to Lannuier.
R. T. Trump and Company.

FIGURE VI–39

Wardrobe. Mahogany. Baltimore or Philadelphia. Ca. 1815–1825.

This wardrobe "with wings" is a rare and handsome survival from the neoclassical period. The beehive turning above the ball feet relate to Baltimore work, although this piece does not have the flamboyance of other examples from that city. A similar wardrobe owned by Edgar G. Miller, a Baltimore native, was pictured in his *American Antique Furniture.* Both Thomas Sheraton in 1793 and George Smith in 1808 illustrate a wardrobe with the same basic design. Smith, in *A Collection of Designs for Household Furniture,* describes wardrobes as "very useful appendages to the dressing room and bed chamber. . . ." The center section is filled with drawers in the bottom half and sliding shelves for clothes above. The wings "are usually calculated to hold dresses, to be suspended on arms sliding on an iron rod." The seven-foot-wide piece is made in five sections—a cornice, a base, and three case sections—which are all screwed to each other.

Tingey House, Washington Navy Yard, Washington, D.C.

FIGURE VI–40

Desk and bookcase. Mahogany, rosewood, and maple with poplar. Baltimore. Ca. 1835–1850.

The stenciled label reads, "John Needles/Cabinet Maker/54 Hanover St. Balto." Needles, who opened his shop in 1810, used that label between about 1835 and the end of his career in 1852. The light maple and richly figured rosewood veneers contrast with the dark mahogany. The angular pattern of the door muntins and the applied four-pointed stars are distinctive features found on other work attributed to Needles. The glass drawer pulls are original.

Private Collection.

were highlighted against bright silk that was tacked to the frame behind the glass doors. Less popular were the squarish fall-front desk and bookcases based upon the French *secrétaire à abattant* (Figures VI–41 and VI–42). A common form had veneered classical columns rising to a flattened Roman arch flanking a fall-front writing surface. Others had columns in the upper half over pilasters below the writing surface. More scarce was the cylinder-fall writing table.

PILLAR AND SCROLL

By the 1830s, neoclassicism in furniture design entered a third and final stage in a reaction to the exaggerated carving and sometimes bizarre decorations of the 1820s. Gone were the exciting carved winged lion's paws, caryatids, eagles, and dolphins. The simple classical lines re-

FIGURE VI–41

Secrétaire à abattant. Mahogany with pine and poplar. Philadelphia. Ca. 1820–1830.

Several elements support a strong attribution to Anthony Quervelle. Similar grape and acanthus carving flanking the lower section appears on documented Quervelle worktables. Burl ash columns like the ones flanking the fall-front are found on his labeled secretaries. The gilt, stenciled decorations on the door recall designs on Quervelle pier and center tables. The "plain veneered arch" flanked by bird's eye maple veneered drawers cost 15 cents more than a simple square pigeonhole. A drawer as well as a secret compartment below are hidden in the bonnet.

James M. Goode Collection.

turned but became massive pillars and scrolls. Brass ormolu mounts, gilding, and stenciling no longer enlivened the broad expanses of mahogany veneer. Only an occasional wooden rosette, beading, lotus leaf, or anthemion relieved the plain dark surfaces (Figures VI–43 and VI–44). Carved capitals replaced the brass rings and imported French ormolu mounts that had capped the classical columns in the early phases of the Empire style. On the best work, matched veneer heightened the design, and scrolls gave a sense of movement. Less sensitive designers, however, used veneer for veneer's sake and overwhelmed their furniture with massive curved blocks that could be

FIGURE VI–42

Secrétaire à abattant. Rosewood with pine and tulip poplar. Philadelphia. Ca. 1815–1825.

Based on illustrations published by Pierre de La Mésangere in the 1820s, this American *secrétaire à abattant* was as elegant as most French examples. Rosewood veneer faces the facade, and the sides are ebonized. White marble across the top, gilt paw feet, brass inlay, and imported ormolu mounts create a rich effect. On the theory that they do not show, the rear feet on even this elegant example are turned rather than carved.

Decatur House, Washington, D.C., a Property of the National Trust for Historic Preservation.

easily executed by the steam-driven scroll saws in use by the 1840s.

The new style developed in France in 1815 after the restoration of the monarchy in the person of Louis XVIII. The Duchess du Berry, niece of the King, was particularly fond of the new style, which included lotus carving, scrolls, and cavetto molding. Both the Frenchman, La Mèsangére, and Ackermann, the Englishman, popularized the designs in their magazines. George Smith, in his *Cabinet-Maker and Upholsterer's Guide*, published in 1826, also showed several pieces of the new style, including the archer's bow outline for the bases of pedestal and pier tables.

By the 1830s many fashiona-ble furniture manufacturers offered the new pillar and scroll style in America. The advertising broadside of the New York firm of Joseph Meeks and Sons', published in 1833, illustrated a number of pillar and scroll pieces. Meeks had taken several designs directly from George Smith's *Guide*, but a number of them represented uniquely American designs. Beginning with Chippendale, a number of designers had published books of European furniture designs, but the Meeks' broadside contained the first depiction of American furniture.

The Meeks firm claimed that it was "now the largest in the United States," and when the founder of the firm, Joseph

Meeks, died in 1868, his obituary noted that he had "supplied the markets from Boston to New Orleans with the most expensive, elegant and durable cabinet work made in America."[7]

Another prominent furniture designer, John Hall, a Baltimore architect, cabinetmaker, and draftsman, also drew on Smith, as well as on the *New-York Book of Prices for Manufacturing Cabinet and Chair Work* of 1834, when he published, in 1840, an entire book of pillar and scroll designs in *The Cabinet-Makers' Assistant, Embracing the Most Modern Style of Cabinet Furniture*. Hall wrote in the preface that "Novelty, simplicity and practicality, are blended with the present designs, in which originality mostly prevails. . . . As far as possible, the style of the United States is blended with European taste, and a graceful outline and simplicity of parts are depicted in all the objects" (Figure VI–45).

In 1837, Samuel A. Foot, a New York lawyer, ordered a suite of furniture from Duncan Phyfe that was in the latest style. It consisted of a meridienne, or sofa with half back, a window bench resting on large scrolls, a stool with a curule base, and a gondola chair. Percier and Fontaine first introduced this chair with rounded back and sloping arms, and by 1826, Smith had illustrated it in England. It became one of the most popular American chairs in the 1830s and 1840s (Figure VI–46). Foot chose not to buy the armchair with arms terminating in huge volutes, which was based on English prototypes rather than French. In this period Phyfe offered yet another chair design, a "Voltaire," an easy chair with a curved upholstered back and padded arms.

In the 1840s and 1850s, rococo and Gothic ornament began to encrust Empire furniture (Figure VI–47). The designs published by Robert Conner in 1842 confirmed this trend. To those steeped in classical principles of design that demanded unity and harmony in each part, the increasingly eclectic furniture of this period just prior to the Civil War was disturbing. Shortly before he retired in 1847, Duncan Phyfe referred to the current styles as "butcher furniture," and Benjamin Silliman, Jr., of Yale University in 1854

FIGURE VI–45
Pier table. Mahogany with white pine. Alexandria, Va. Ca. 1840–1845.
H. Bradley and Sons, whose paper label appears on this table, have created a distinctive interpretation of the popular pillar and scroll style. Highly figured mahogany veneers compare well with the best Philadelphia or New York work, but the oval shapes at the base of the scrolled supports, or "consoles," are similar to examples in John Hall's *Cabinet-Makers' Assistant*, published in Baltimore in 1840. The unusual splay to the front scrolled supports, the use of buttons of mahogany on the feet and scrolls, and the applied oval panels embellish Hall's basic design.
Richard H. Howland.

FIGURE VI–46 *(far left)*
Side chair. Mahogany. New York. Ca. 1830–1840.
This chair, part of a set of three, contains John Jay's coat of arms on the back. Another unusual feature is the compartment for papers hidden under the seat. Chairs such as this, in which the rear stiles curve down and forward, are known as gondole chairs. Two versions were illustrated in the 1833 Meeks broadside.
Diplomatic Reception Rooms, U.S. Department of State, on loan from William S. Patten and Peter A. Jay.

FIGURE VI–47
Chair. Mahogany. American. Ca. 1840.
This is a high-backed, fully upholstered version of the popular Empire gondole chair. It is also related to the French bergère chair with a tub-shaped, upholstered back. The beaded molding on the skirt and the scrolls flanking the circular shape on the crest add interest to an otherwise plain chair. The reverse curve of the rear legs, typical of Victorian chairs, prevents the chair from tipping over backwards.
Margaret Woodbury Strong Museum.

railed against the "ponderous and frigid monstrosities" of late Empire furniture.[9] Its popularity, however, was so great that it continued to mark furniture throughout the 19th century, but by the end of the 1840s, it had to compete with a number of revival styles, which characterized American Victorian furniture.

NOTES

1. E. Page Talbott, "The Furniture Industry in Boston, 1810–1835" (Master's Thesis, University of Delaware, 1974), p. 19.

2. Kathleen M. Catalano, "Cabinetmaking in Philadelphia 1820–1840: Transition from Craft to Industry" *American Furniture and Its Makers, Winterthur Portfolio, 13* (Chicago: University of Chicago Press, 1979), p. 89.

3. Catalano, "Cabinetmaking in Philadelphia 1820–1840" (Master's Thesis, University of Delaware, 1972), p. 37.

4. Robert T. Trump, "Joseph B. Barry, Philadelphia Cabinetmaker," *The Magazine Antiques* 107 (January 1975): 163.

5. Robert C. Smith, "The Furniture of Anthony G. Quervelle: Part I: The Pier Tables," *The Magazine Antiques* 103 (May 1973): 985.

6. Robert C. Smith, "The Furniture of Anthony G. Quervelle: Part IV: Some Case Pieces," *The Magazine Antiques* 105 (January 1974): 193.

7. John N. Pearce, Lorraine W. Pearce and Robert C. Smith, "The Meeks Family of Cabinetmakers," *The Magazine Antiques* 85 (April 1964): 417.

8. John Hall, *The Cabinet Makers' Assistant* (Baltimore: John Murphy, 1840), p. 3.

9. Berry B. Tracy, ed., *19th-Century America: Furniture and Other Decorative Arts* (New York: Metropolitan Museum of Art, 1970), p. xii.

VII

THE COUNTRY CABINETMAKER

COUNTRY CABINETMAKERS CREATED some of the most delightful and unique furniture produced in America. In the major cities, wealthy merchants and land-owners aped their London cousins as closely as their pocket-books would allow. Cabinet-makers vied with one another to produce furniture in the latest style. The country craftsman, on the other hand, frequently enjoyed the enviable position of a monopoly, and his clients preferred different concepts of furniture design and construction from their urban counterparts. Whereas the city cabinetmaker responded to the height of London fashion, the country craftsman often worked within alternate constructs that were based on an entirely different heritage, such as Dutch, German, Scottish-Irish, or rural English.

COUNTRY FURNITURE

The simplest definition of country furniture is work produced outside major style centers, which, in 18th-century America, were Boston, New York, Newport, Philadelphia, and Charleston, South Carolina. In 1790, these five cities supported a combined population of only 110,000 out of the four million people living in the United States. Since most Americans lived in a predominantly rural environment until well into the 19th century, more furniture was produced in the country.

Perhaps because Americans lived mostly in a rural setting, not until late in the 18th century did they perceive a distinction between country and city. By the 19th century, the image of the country bumpkin reinforced a growing conception of country

furniture as crude and poorly designed. That image was perpetuated by William Hornor's *Blue Book, Philadelphia Furniture,* which described high-style furniture, and Russell Kettell's *Pine Furniture of Early New England,* which illustrated the simpler cabinetwork. More recently, Charles Hummel's *With Hammer in Hand,* about the Dominy craftsmen of Long Island, alters the distinction by referring to furniture as either traditional or fashionable.

Perceived or not, a distinction existed between country and city work from the 17th century until about 1820, when the rural handcraft tradition began to fade. In the 17th century, Boston furniture-makers, for example, constructed drawers with dovetail joints. Outside Boston, the sides were nailed to the front and no dovetails were used. Design and

135

construction techniques continue to diverge in the two areas throughout the 18th century. By the 1820s, however, many country cabinetmakers began to disappear, put out of business by competition from major furniture manufacturers in the larger cities. The rural craftsmen working alone or with a few apprentices could not compete with the furniture warehouses in such cabinetmaking centers as Boston and New York. The former advantage of price disappeared as roads, canals, and coastal shipping companies carried furniture into the remotest villages.

Country furniture is not kitchen furniture. The same simple, unadorned, utilitarian furniture, such as dough troughs, wash benches, and work tables, were used in the city as well as in the country (Figure VII–2). Devoid of carving, painting, veneers, brass fittings, or any other touches of elegance, kitchen furniture served only a utilitarian rather than an aesthetic purpose. Today, it is appreciated because of the aura of antiquity and the patina of age that years of use have imparted. Such pieces are relics of the past but cannot be compared to furniture with ornament and style produced in both the city and the country.

At the same time, plain, simple furniture is not always country-made. Cabinetmakers, whether working in an urban or a rural economy, produced several grades of furniture. A middle-class customer in the city might prefer a simple, uncarved

FIGURE VII–2
Pie safe cupboard. Pine. Virginia. Ca. 1840–1860.
Pie safes such as this were commonly found in kitchens in the country and in the city. The pierced tin in a sugar-bowl pattern ventilated the shelves and facilitated the cooling and storage of pies and other food. The form descends from medieval food cupboards. The pierced tinwork, the turned legs, and the shaping of the gallery around the top provide the only relief for an otherwise plain and strictly utilitarian object.
Smithsonian Institution.

piece in the cheaper cherry or maple rather than mahogany, whereas a wealthy merchant might demand rich carving and expensive details. Some simple city furniture is less ornate than country masterpieces.

Much of the country furniture produced in America showed the strong imprint of a nearby style center, such as Boston, Newport, Philadelphia, or New York. The styles diffused outward in a series of concentric circles. Paris was the center of European design throughout much of the 17th and 18th centuries. The farther away from a style center, often the paler the design became. Thus, in comparison to the best Paris cabinetry, London work was less refined. Compared to London, Philadelphia work was often provincial. Compared to Philadelphia, Lancaster work was country[1] (Figure VII–3).

In cabinetmaking and, indeed, for most of the decorative arts in America, London was the style center until the early 19th century. However, some groups of cabinetmakers, particularly those in rural areas, learned their trade, not in London, but in rural parts of England or in other countries, such as Scotland, Ireland, Germany, or Holland. Many of what were once thought to be unique American creations are, in fact, derived from rural British or other European cabinetmaking traditions. These same influences affected city craftsmen as well, but most of the city patrons were oriented toward London by commercial and cultural ties. Differing traditions were soon assimilated by the predominant London tradition. In isolated rural areas, variations persisted for a longer time without challenge. In comparison to the large body of research on furniture craftsmen of the major American cities in the 18th and early 19th centuries, much less is known about rural craftsmen. However, important studies of craftsmen from several rural areas, including Lancaster in Pennsylvania, the Connecticut River Valley, Long Island, and southern New Hampshire, give at least a preliminary indication of the character of the rural furniture industry.

LANCASTER, PENNSYLVANIA

Lancaster furniture showed the strong influence of Philadelphia, only 60 miles away, but the Germanic heritage of most of the local cabinetmakers was also evident. The town's economy was based on its position as a gateway for trade between Philadelphia and the Pennsylvania frontier. The upwardly mobile Lancaster merchants and other wealthy style-setters had frequent contacts with Philadelphia and quickly adopted the trappings of the successful Philadelphia merchant, which included fine furniture in the latest taste. In fact, a few, such as Jasper Yeates, the attorney and judge, purchased most of their furniture from Philadelphia before the Revolution. However, the 160 cabinetmakers who worked in Lancaster between 1760 and 1810 enjoyed a considerable price advantage over their Philadelphia counterparts. Since Lancaster furniture sold for an average of 20 percent less than comparable Philadelphia work, men like Yeates were persuaded to purchase at least some of their furniture locally.

The Lancaster style is an understandable mix of the old Germanic Baroque tradition and the newer English styles. The Lancaster relief carving, cut directly into the wood on the pediments of high chests, has a Baroque heaviness when compared to the more delicate applied rococo carving in Philadelphia. The carving is closely related to designs shown in Chippendale's *Director* and in architectural design books, but touches of the Germanic folk tradition sometimes appear in the use of carved tulips. A similar mixture of traditions is apparent in the coexistence of English and Germanic construction techniques. The Germanic method of securing

FIGURE VII–3
High chest of drawers. Walnut with poplar. Virginia. Ca. 1760.
The configuration of this chest with three drawers, over two, over four long drawers, was favored throughout Pennsylvania and down the Shenandoah Valley into Virginia. On this chest a single top drawer is faced to imitate three. The ogee bracket feet are pierced in an unusual tear shape. A thin strip of wood covers the dovetails of the drawer dividers attached to the side of the case. The piece stands 64 inches high.
Private Collection.

drawer bottoms with tiny pegs is used along with the English technique of fitting the bottom into a rabbet cut into the drawer side.

As was typical of rural areas, old styles continued to be popular long after they were outdated in the cities. At the same time, some patrons demanded the most stylish pieces the local cabinetmaker could make. The earliest documented product of Lancaster woodworkers exhibiting the Chippendale taste was an organ case completed by George Burkhart in 1770. This case followed closely the designs in the 1762 edition of Chippendale's *Director*. The bellflower carving on the canopy is the earliest evidence of the neoclassical style on American cabinetwork—a full 20 years before the style became widespread.[2] On the other hand, Conrad Doll was commissioned by the Peace Church in Hampden Township, about 40 miles northwest of Lancaster, to make an organ case in 1807. The vine and leaf carving on its canopy is unrestrained by the neoclassical tradition that swept the country after 1790.

The only domestic furniture known to be signed by Lancaster makers is a simple desk by Michael Lind and a carved high chest, also by a member of the Lind family; both were made between 1770 and 1800 (Figure VII–4). Until the discovery of the Lind pieces, most Lancaster furniture was attributed to John Bachman II. He had a large business, employing at least 10 people in his shop between 1775 and 1810. Bachman's account book indicates that he divided his time between carpentry, furniture repair work, and cabinetmaking. His business records do not indicate that he made the pedimented high chests with distinctive 12-pointed rosettes that were once attributed to him. Coffins and low post beds were his most common products, followed by utilitarian pieces, such as tables, chests, cupboards, dough troughs, and cradles. Occasionally, he made clock cases, desks, tea tables, and desk and bookcases. The majority of his work was in walnut.

Connecticut

Although some rural Pennsylvania furniture betrays a strong Germanic tradition, the imprint of Philadelphia is unmistakable. In Connecticut, the influence of the adjacent areas of New York, Massachusetts, and Rhode Island is readily apparent. With such a diversity of choice, it is no wonder that "if it's different, it's from Connecticut." To this potpourri was added the strong rural English background of many Connecticut cabinetmakers. Numerous prototypes of Connecticut oddities have been discovered in English country houses. The similarity of some

Connecticut, and Philadelphia furniture is partially explained by the discovery that many rural English towns sent immigrants to both Connecticut and Philadelphia (Figure VII–5).

These similarities were further reinforced by several Connecticut cabinetmakers who were apprenticed in Philadelphia. One of the best-known Connecticut makers, Eliphalet Chapin, fled a marriage of necessity in East Windsor, Connecticut, and apprenticed for three years in Philadelphia. The distinctive X-shaped splat associated with him was based on the Gothic splat designs of Philadelphia chairs (Figure VII–6). Benjamin Burnham, known for his desks with an amphitheater

Figure VII–5
Table. Cherry. Connecticut River Valley. Ca. 1772–1774.
The 37-inch-wide, two-board top indicates a use as a tea or breakfast table. The execution of the feet relates this table to work by Eliphalet Chapin. The flattened ball with the ring found on this and other Connecticut tables relates to balusters on Philadelphia tea tables. The birdcage at the top of the baluster is not as common in Connecticut as it is in Philadelphia. Although family tradition indicates that this table, as well as the chair in Figure VII–6, were given to Anna Barnard of Northampton, Massachusetts, as wedding furniture, the serpentine top denotes a later date than the wedding in 1772.
Private Collection.

Figure VII–6
Chair. Cherry. Connecticut River Valley. Ca. 1772–1774.
Like the table in Figure VII–5 this chair is, by tradition, part of the wedding furniture of Anna Barnard and is attributed to Eliphalet Chapin. The flattened ball and sculptured talon, the spring of the legs, the two-piece, quarter-round corner blocks, the rounded stump legs, and the through tenon all relate to Philadelphia shop practices. The X-form in the splat creates an unusual design that appears on several other Connecticut chairs. The beautifully scrolled handholds with knuckles repeat the line of the scrolled ears on the serpentine crest.
Private Collection.

FIGURE VII–7

Desk. Cherry with pine and tulip poplar. Colchester, Conn. Dated 1769. The inscription reads: "This desk was maid in the/year of 1769 buy Benjn Burnam/that sarvfed his time in Felledlfay." The extraordinary interior has 28 drawers. The blocked facade is similar to typical Boston blockfronts, and the stopped fluting is found on Newport work. The inlaid stars on the desk lid are exaggerated survivals from the Queen Anne style. Such combinations of style are expected on rural furniture. Although Burnham was trained in "Felledlfay," he was responding to the desires of a conservative local clientele.
The Metropolitan Museum of Art, John Stuart Kennedy Fund, 1918.

FIGURE VII–8 *(below, left)*
Chest. Cherry with pine. Connecticut. Ca. 1760–1780.
The fluted quarter-columns are found on many Philadelphia pieces. Beading is suggested by a scratched line around each drawer. Bold knee brackets flank well-carved feet. On the underside of the chest, heavy braces nailed to the bottom add extra strength to the legs. The brass pulls are not original.
Author's Collection.

FIGURE VII–9 *(below, right)*
Detail of ball and claw foot of Connecticut chest (Figure VII–8). Each knuckle is finely carved. The ball is squashed, and the talons rise into the leg in the Philadelphia manner.
Author's Collection.

of drawers on the interior, also apprenticed in Philadelphia (Figure VII–7). Other Connecticut characteristics similar to Philadelphia work include a foot with a flattened ball and sculptured claw and the use of stump rear legs ovoid in section. Although fluted corner columns on chests and other case pieces, which served to lighten their appearance, were found in other areas, the technique was particularly popular in Philadelphia and Connecticut. Sometimes these columns resembled twisted rope, a typical Connecticut adaptation (Figures VII–8 and VII–9).

Connecticut case furniture offered the cabinetmaker great opportunity for expressing the diversity of his training. Eastern Connecticut blockfront furniture strongly recalls Newport work except in such details as the tendrils, which sometimes flow from the carved shells surmounting the blocked panels (Figure VII–10). The reverse serpentine chests were similar to Boston work, although they were executed in cherry, which was the preferred wood for much Connecticut furniture. The popularity of the chest on chest in Connecticut imitated English preferences and may have been inspired by similarly favored pieces in New York. Like the

Connecticut high chest, distinctive shell carving often set off by gouge work, distinctive brush-shaped finials, and rope-twist columns stamped them with an unmistakable Connecticut origin.

Architectural design books, which inspired the doorway pediments on Connecticut Valley houses, often inspired similar bonnets and scrolled tops on high chests. Skirts on tables, desks, chests, and desk and bookcases delighted the eye with dynamic series of reverse curves (Figure VII–11). On a small group of chests from the upper Connecticut River Valley, the scrolled tops impart an extraordinary sense of motion and excitement (Figure VII–12).

Carving is much less exuberant than the lively Philadelphia creations, but its simplicity and idiosyncrasy are appealing. Since the thinly populated Connecticut Valley could support few full-time carvers, cabinetmakers did most of their own carving. Most Connecticut carving consisted of easily designed and executed geometrical fans, sunbursts, and pinwheels (Figures VII–13 and VII–14). Elongated shells, looking like noses, accen-

FIGURE VII–10
Tall clock. Mahogany with pine. Norwich, Conn. Ca. 1775–88.
An inscription on the dial and a handwritten note inside the door indicate that this clock case was made by Abishai Woodward and the works by Thomas Harland. Although working in a non-urban area, these craftsmen produced as sophisticated a tall clock as any made in Newport. The influence of that city is seen in the carved shells and ivory stopped fluting on the corner columns, but the distinctive scrolls on the skirt of the base and the spiral reeding are found on other furniture from the Norwich and Colchester areas. Interpretations of the four seasons are engraved in the spandrels of the brass face.
The Detroit Institute of Arts.

FIGURE VII–11
Tea table. Cherry. Connecticut. Ca. 1740–1775.
The candle slides are a rare touch on an already elegant table. The delicate legs, characteristic of much New England furniture, terminate in thin pad feet resting on even thinner disks. The raised, molded rim with indented corners adds some protection against a valuable tea service slipping off the table. The volutes on the knee block make a beautiful transition from the legs into the curves of the skirt.
Dr. and Mrs. Arthur Mourot.

FIGURE VII–12

Chest. Cherry. Connecticut. 1780–1800.
A number of dressing tables, tea tables, and chests made in the Connecticut River Valley exhibit the exciting scalloped top, consisting of a series of ogee curves. The scalloping on this example continues around the back corners. Major construction differences among the group indicate more than one maker. This chest is signed in chalk by Libbeous Hill, Jr., who may have been the Lebbeus Hills, Jr. born in Colchester, Connecticut in 1761. On this example, the short cabriole legs are made separately and mortise and tenon joints attach them to the frame. The dovetail joints of the drawer dividers are exposed in typical Connecticut fashion.
Dr. and Mrs. Arthur Mourot.

FIGURE VII–13

High chest of drawers. Cherry. Connecticut. Ca. 1750–1800.
The shape of the free-standing scrolled pediment, the carved pinwheel rosettes in the shaped skirt, and the boldly formed knee brackets are similar to documented high chests from the Colchester and Norwich areas of Connecticut. The three arches on the skirt are a reminder of the early six-legged William and Mary high chests.
Private Collection.

tuated the central plinth of a large group of high chests and chest on chests often found in the New London area. The wispy central cartouches on several high chests attributed to Eliphalet Chapin captured the essence of the more elaborate Philadelphia cartouches (Figure VII–15). Knee carving is often straight and stylized.

FIGURE VII–14

Detail of high chest pediment (Figure VII–13).
The carved fan underlined by a concave strip contrasts with the convex lobes of the fan, which have incised lines halfway through them. The pinwheel rosettes with flower centers and chisel marks between the blades are also distinctive.
Private Collection.

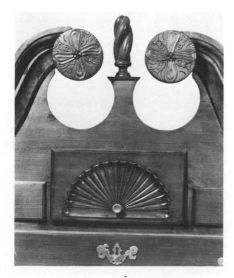

Connecticut chairs exhibit elements from neighboring style centers. Like Massachusetts ones, the baluster-splat is lean and simple, and the back is canted but not curved, as in Newport work (Figure VII–16). An exception to the simple splat is the sharply protruding bulges at the midsection of the splat on one group of Connecticut chairs, a design common to some Philadelphia and Irish examples. The distinctive ring at the neck of the splat usually indicates a Connecticut chair, but the feature is found on one New York example as well. The seat is often square and finished with a scalloped skirt. Generous ball-turned stretchers persisted, as elsewhere in New England.

The Connecticut "crown" chairs, or heart-and-crown chairs, as they are called today, illustrate the response of some country craftsmen to new styles.[3] These chairs were first produced in the Stratford area about 1725 and later in the Norwalk, Milford, and Guilford areas. How could the rural turner in the early 18th century compete against chairs available from Boston with upholstered backs and elaborate carving on the crest and stretchers? Even the cheaper bannister-backs with rush seats presented stiff competition. Boston chairs themselves were altered versions of the imported English caned-back chairs, which displayed a profusion of carving on the crest, surrounding the splat, and on the stretchers. Boston chairs could not be imitated in Connecticut because few upholsterers were living in Connecticut in the 1720s. Even if a carver had been available, an elaborately carved crest would have been too expensive. So the originator of the style, probably Thomas Salmon of Stratford, Connecticut, simplified the design. He eliminated the rake to the back legs, which took extra time to turn on a lathe, using an off-set chuck. He simplified the turnings on the front and rear legs and replaced the upholstered back panel by straight, reeded bannis-ters. Then he added a distinctive crest, similar to those on grave-stones and doorway pediments (Figure VII–17). These, in turn, may have been based on looking-glass frames imported from England in the early 18th century. Salmon's apprentices, such as Andrew Durand, carried the tradition to other areas, such as Milford. Norwalk and Guilford craftsmen made related chairs. The heart-and-crown chair was the country chairmaker's response to the high-style William and Mary leather-upholstered chair.

By the 1730s and 1740s, the Queen Anne style was becoming popular. Chairs with vase-shaped splats; rounded-yoke crest rails; and straight, conical versions of cabriole legs ending in pad feet were produced in New York and exported to Connecticut in such great numbers that they were referred to as "York" chairs. These chairs, which today are called Hudson Valley chairs because of their widespread popularity in

FIGURE VII–15
High chest of drawers. Cherry with pine. Connecticut. Ca. 1760–1800.
This piece is attributed to Eliphalet Chapin on the basis of similarity of the legs and feet to those on a chair with a Chapin bill of sale. Chapin worked in East Windsor until he died in 1807, but his Philadelphia training is apparent, particularly in the pediment with the diamond pierced strapwork and the scrolled bonnet. The wispy, central cartouch, which nicely echoes the double S-scroll carving on the upper and lower central drawers, is an inspired abstraction of florid Philadelphia cartouches.
Wadsworth Atheneum, Hartford, Conn.

FIGURE VII–16
Side chair. Cherry. Connecticut. Ca. 1730–1760.
The configuration of the stretchers, the shaping of the skirt, and the baluster are found on Newport, Connecticut, and Massachusetts chairs. However, the use of cherry favors a Connecticut Valley origin.
Dr. and Mrs. Arthur Mourot.

143

FIGURE VII-17

Armchair. Maple, poplar and ash. Stratford, Conn. Ca. 1730–1740.

The presence of reel turnings below turned cylinders at the top of the back posts indicates a Stratford origin compared to Milford chairs, which have a thin disk at this point. This is an early example of chairs attributed to the shop of Thomas Salmon as indicated by the turned side stretchers. In later examples they were left plain. Some drift away from the earliest design has begun, however, as evidenced by the addition of a third reel on the front posts below the arms. As with many early chairs three or four inches have been restored to worn feet.

Wadsworth Atheneum, Hartford, Conn.

FIGURE VII-18

Armchair. Maple, oak, and cherry. New York. Ca. 1750–1770.

Although many of these "York" chairs descended in Dutch families, the prototype for the design can be found in rural English chairs of the 18th century. The turnings on the legs and stretchers and the scrolled shape of the arms are all holdovers from the William and Mary style, but the arched, saddle, crest rail and the bold, vase-shaped splat are clearly Queen Anne characteristics. The sharply sloping pad foot above a disk is a New York characteristic. A grained finish simulates walnut.

Courtesy, The Henry Francis du Pont Winterthur Museum.

that area, were also imitated by local chairmakers (Figure VII–18). When the Chippendale style became fashionable by 1760, local chairmakers added ears to the crest to capture the essence of the new style. The shape of the unpierced splat suggested the name "fiddle back," which appeared in some late 18th-century inventories.

By 1810, many rural Connecticut craftsmen found that they could not compete with the large-scale cabinet shops of Hartford, New York, and Boston. These enterprises offered a wider selection at cheaper prices, made possible because of their specialization and the economics of scale. Even the cheaply made York and fiddle-back chairs fell to the competition of the fancy-chair factories, such as Lambert Hitchcock's at Riverton, Connecticut.

DANIEL CLAY OF GREENFIELD, MASSACHUSETTS

The furniture-making career of Daniel Clay, born in New London in 1770, was illustrative of numerous craftsmen earning a living in the Connecticut River Valley in the late 18th century. In 1794, Clay opened his Windsor chair shop in Greenfield in the upper Connecticut River Valley, which is now part of northwestern Massachusetts. The town, established in 1753, was the center of a rich agricultural region. Clay started his business with tools, many of which he purchased from William Bull, a blacksmith in nearby Deerfield. From John Breck, a Northampton merchant, he bought sandpaper, hinges, bed screws, and brass pulls mostly imported from England. By 1800, his Windsor chair business was so prosperous that he advertised for a journeyman to help him.

As in most rural areas like Greenfield, Clay was the sole maker of Windsor chairs and had only one or two other competitors in his cabinetmaking business. After 1802, Clay was the only professional cabinetmaker in town, but he faced some competition from craftsmen in nearby Northampton, which was about a day's journey from Greenfield. These craftsmen even advertised in the Greenfield

FIGURE VII–19
Pembroke table. Cherry with white pine and basswood. Greenfield, Mass. Ca. 1800–1810.
Daniel Clay labeled this table twice. He used a template to produce the distinctive stretchers, whose form appears on several other Pembroke tables. On most high-style tables, the stretcher is omitted by the Federal period. The tapered legs prove an awareness of the new Federal style, but expensive inlay was not used as was the case for most furniture made in rural areas. An original black stain approximated the look of mahogany.
Historic Deerfield, Inc., Deerfield, Mass.

paper. Five or six other villages in the area, including Deerfield, also supported cabinetmakers who catered to the inhabitants of Greenfield. However, Clay's proximity to his clients and his ability to fill their needs in a timely fashion, since he engaged in chairmaking full time, gave him a decided advantage. Most of the other rural cabinetmakers were only part-time workers and had their hands full meeting the needs of local residents.

In addition to Windsors, Clay made "fancy chairs" with bamboo turnings and, by the 1820s, Grecian chairs. He also sold Pembroke tables, card tables, candle stands, and dressing tables with either straight Marlborough legs or the tapered leg of the Federal style (Figures VII–19 and VII–20). He even made a few clock cases that had architectural pediments and side windows with Gothic arches (Figure VII–21). Like most cabinetmakers, both rural and urban, Clay sold a large number of coffins. In fact, when factories killed the handcrafts in the 19th century, many cabinetmakers became undertakers.

Even in Greenfield, style was important. Ansel Goodrich, who worked in Northampton in the late 18th century, stated that he had "worked among the French," and Elijah Tryon of Greenfield in 1822 boasted that his furniture was "made of the best materials, and by workmen who are well acquainted with the latest New York and Boston fashions."[4] Aside from learning the latest styles while apprenticed in urban centers, the cabinetmakers also depended on architectural design books, which were available for sale from booksellers in Greenfield. They clearly influenced Connecticut furniture with fluted columns, heavy moldings and dentils, and broken scrolled pediments.

Clay constructed his furniture with strength and durability, as was typical throughout the Connecticut River Valley. He used wide dovetails; thick wood, particularly on the drawer liners; and large proportions overall. At the same time, his furniture was

FIGURE VII–20
Card table. Cherry with pine and basswood. Greenfield, Mass. Ca. 1792–1794.
No trace of the new neoclassical style is apparent in this table, which is signed on the bottom by Daniel Clay. The handwritten signature probably predates Clay's use of paper labels. The table has a drawer in the frame and a gate that swings out with the rear leg in order to support the top. The legs are chamfered to lighten their appearance.
Historic Deerfield, Inc., Deerfield, Mass.

FIGURE VII–21
Tall case clock. Cherry. Greenfield, Mass. Dated 1799.
The tall case clock, labeled by Daniel Clay in 1799, clearly shows the influence of the neoclassical style in the brass finials, the string inlay, and the inlaid fans. The leafy sprigs carved on the rosettes confirm that Clay was not a highly skilled carver. The unusual scalloping around the base of the case is an individual expression that urban makers would not have ventured to attempt. The dial, marked by James Wilson, was imported from the English dial-maker who supplied numerous New England clockmakers during the Federal period. Clay sold the clock to Jerome Ripley of Greenfield who, according to family tradition, placed it "on the stairs."
Historic Deerfield, Inc., Deerfield, Mass.

rarely adorned with carving or inlay, although he seemed to favor gadrooning on the skirts of chests and tables (Figure VII–22).

Like most Connecticut cabinetmakers, Clay usually employed cherry and selected mahogany only for his particularly expensive creations. Occasionally, he used maple, butternut, pine, bass, ash, and oak. In 1806, a prosperous Clay decided to add carriage-making to his furniture business. This decision was typical of other rural craftsmen who combined different crafts, such as carpentry, joinery, trunk-making, wheelwrighting, and even clockmaking. The chaise-making business became less important after 1808, when Clay's first cabinetmaking competitor in six years arrived in Greenfield. In that year, Clay began to sell a general line of hardware from his cabinetmaking shop. The hardware business expanded, but he continued to produce furniture as well. By 1812, the carriage business failed, and Clay acquired an apothecary shop the next year. That business failed too, and by 1823, Clay was back in the cabinetmaking business but now faced new competition. Not only were other cabinetmakers established in Greenfield, but he also had to compete against shipments of ready-made furniture, including fancy chairs, which were advertised for sale as early as 1814. During this period, Clay associated with several cabinetmakers in partnerships of short duration. Clay even had to survive a disastrous fire that burned his shop to the ground one cold winter night in 1826.

Clay continued in business and was advertising "A Handsome Assortment of WINDSOR CHAIRS" in the late 1820s. However, in 1829, Clay gave up chairmaking and opened a pail factory in Algiers, Vermont. When that venture failed, he moved back to Greenfield for a short time before leaving the crafts altogether in 1832 to become a druggist in New York City. He died in 1848.

FIGURE VII–22
Chest of drawers. Cherry with white pine. Greenfield, Mass. Dated 1794.
Labeled by Daniel Clay, this chest of drawers gives little indication of the new Federal style that was popular in major population centers from about 1790 on. The earliest known chest by Clay, this example, with its reverse serpentine front, original bail pulls, ogee bracket feet, fluted corner columns, and gadrooned skirt, is in the Chippendale idiom. The stiff gadrooning contrasts sharply with the more sophisticated rounded lobes on New York gadrooning.
Historic Deerfield, Inc., Deerfield, Mass.

THE DOMINYS
OF LONG ISLAND

Another family of rural cabinetmakers working on Long Island had many similar experiences. On the eve of the Revolution, East Hampton, near the tip of Long Island and over 100 miles from New York City, had a population of about 1,250 people. The Dominy family of craftsmen, particularly Nathaniel IV, born in 1737; his son Nathaniel V, born in 1770; and his grandson Felix, born in 1800, served this rural community for more than 80 years.

The Dominys had few competitors before 1810 and they seldom saw the need to advertise. Dominy furniture had a key price advantage over goods from New York; the latter had to include transportation costs and took longer to receive. The Dominys also accepted credit or barter, which included blankets, spoons, food, tools, and lumber. By receiving most of their necessities in this way, the Dominys needed little cash.

Neither price nor the availability of credit explained why John Gardiner, the wealthy landowner who lived on Gardiner's Island just off the end of Long Island, purchased furniture from the Dominys. He could have afforded to buy all his furniture from New York, but instead, he purchased much of it locally from the Dominys. He apparently felt more comfortable with traditional designs rather than the fashionable furniture produced in New York. The Dominys themselves traveled to New York from time to time, but their knowledge of New York styles did not noticeably affect their own work. With a substantial investment in templates for furniture parts, such as legs, feet, and arm rests, the Dominys chose not to change their designs. With no competition and with a satisfied clientele, which included customers in adjacent towns and places as far away as Hartford, they had little reason to change.

FIGURE VII–23
Tall case clock. Pine with cherry. East Hampton, N.Y. Ca. 1824–1825.
Nathaniel Dominy V made the pine case for the silent clock manufactured by his son, Felix. In 1825, Jonathan Osborn was billed $25 for a "time-piece" that was probably this clock. The case, standing just over seven feet tall, relates to earlier Dominy examples with its plain case and simple, arched molding that forms the feet. The intricately cut cresting first appears on Dominy cases made in the 1820s. The hand-painted dial is cherry rather than the more often used brass or iron.
Mrs. George P. Morse.

The Dominys passed their trades down from father to son and did not serve formal apprenticeships. Whereas in the cities, apprentices learned only one trade, the Dominys taught their sons several. The country craftsmen needed to provide the community with as many different services as possible in order to prosper.

Between 1768 and 1840, the Dominys produced about 890 wooden objects, from furniture to buttons and trenchers. Obviously, they could not have supported themselves on woodworking alone, even if their sizeable furniture-repair business were included. As a result, the Dominys learned to provide the full range of woodworking skills, including those of house- and mill-carpenter and wheelwright. They could also do metal work, such as clockmaking, toolmaking, and gun repairs. Between 1768 and 1828, the Dominys made about 90 clocks (Figure VII–23). Even though they were twice the price of the next most expensive pieces of furniture, clocks were not enough to support them. Still, clockmaking provided a lucrative addition to their income. Ship captains and stagecoach drivers carried clocks and watches to the Dominys for repairs and then delivered them back to the owners. The Dominys also made housecalls to work on bulky tall case clocks. In addition to their main profession of wood- and metal-working, the Dominys, like most rural craftsmen, also engaged in farming, either on their own or on rented land.

The Dominy shop contained over 1,000 different wood- and metal-working tools. Some were obtained locally from blacksmiths, often as repayment for debts, but the best and most expensive were imported from England. So expensive were their tools that, as they wore out, they converted them to other uses. The tools often exhibited personal touches reflecting the toolmaker's personality. The types of tools used by the Domi-

Three Centuries of American Furniture

Criss-Cross Hall. Late 17th century, southern furniture.
Courtesy, Museum of Early Southern Decorative Arts, Winston-Salem, North Carolina.

The Wentworth Room. First quarter of the 18th century, William and Mary furniture. *Courtesy, Henry Francis du Pont Winterthur Museum.*

The Readbourne Parlor. Second quarter of the 18th century, Queen Anne furniture. *Courtesy, Henry Francis du Pont Winterthur Museum.*

(opposite page) Parlor. Mid-19th century, Rococo revival furniture.
Courtesy, Rosedown Plantation, St. Francisville, Louisiana.

(above) Duncan Phyfe Drawing Room.
Early 19th century, Federal furniture.
Courtesy, Museum of the City of New York.

(left) Trustees Dining Room.
Mid-19th century, Shaker furniture.
Courtesy, The Shaker Museum, Old Chatham, New York.

(above) The Blue Parlor. Late 19th century, Louis XV revival furniture.

Courtesy, Christian Heurich Mansion, Columbia Historical Society, Washington, D.C.

(right) Bedroom. Early 20th century, Mission furniture.

Courtesy, Glensheen, University of Minnesota, Duluth.

nys were similar to those described in the great French encyclopedias of the 18th century, showing the universality of woodworking techniques and tools.

The Dominys made the full range of furniture, including beds, bookcases, bureaus, chests, coffins, clothes presses, and tables. Chairs, representing one-third of their total furniture production, included fiddle-back; slat-back; and, after 1804, rocking chairs (Figures VII–24 and VII–25). Much of the furniture exhibited elements from earlier 18th-century styles drawn from Rhode Island and Connecticut. Some tripod stands had turnings similar to those of the 17th century, with drops below the point where the legs joined the baluster. One of their grandest pieces, a high chest with a skirt cut in the shape of a fleur-de-lis, was made with a flat top in the Queen Anne style. Only the original Chippendale brass pulls dated the piece from the end of the 18th century. Much of their work, repeated time after time over the years, is devoid of style, but it appealed to their conservative clientele. The Dominys used some mahogany, but mostly they worked in local woods, such as maple, pine, and cherry. The light-colored woods used for clock cases were usually painted or stained dark to imitate mahogany. In some cases, the country origin of their work was revealed in the multiple use of woods—for example, a breakfast table might have mahogany top and legs but a pine apron (Figure VII–26).

The design of an elaborate maple desk and bookcase, which John Gardiner ordered from the Dominys, is typical of country work. Virtually devoid of carving, the piece depends on a bold molding in the bonnet for dramatic effect. Fielded panels in the bonnet resemble Rhode Island work and may have been inspired by a Rhode Island desk and bookcase owned by Gardiner. Sliding candle rests below the bookcase section, a detail

usually found on the most expensive high-style desk and bookcases, add to the utility of the desk.

In the cities, the richest people usually owned the finest furniture.[5] In East Hampton, this was not always the case. John Gardiner, the wealthiest resident

FIGURE VII–24

Side chair. Maple, hickory, and pine. East Hampton, N.Y. Ca. 1790–1830.
The wooden template used by Nathaniel Dominy V to cut out the crest rail and the vase-shaped splat is in the Winterthur Museum. The sausage and ring turning on the front legs and the elongated ball and spool turnings on the front stretcher are also common Dominy designs. The chair is similar to other "Hudson Valley side chairs" made in the 18th century, but the tradition survived in conservative rural areas, such as eastern Long Island, into the early 19th century.
Mr. and Mrs. Gail Wilson.

FIGURE VII–25

Rocking chair. Maple and oak. East Hampton, N.Y. Ca. 1800–1825.
This chair is attributed to the Dominys on the basis of wooden patterns found in their shop which match the slats and arm supports. The rockers, however, are later additions, bolted to the legs which have been notched to receive them. The Dominys typically fitted their rockers into slots and pegged them in place. The urn finials on the rear posts indicate a late 18th- or early 19th-century date as do the arched slats and the turned tenon which joins the arms to the back posts. In 1809 the Dominys sold a similar chair to Thomas Baker for 14 shillings.
Mr. and Mrs. Gail Wilson.

FIGURE VII–26

Breakfast table. Mahogany with pine, cherry, and tulip. East Hampton, N.Y. Ca. 1815–1830.
This table, found in the Dominy house in East Hampton, was probably made for family use although account books indicate that the Dominys made at least 13 "breakfast" tables for sale as well. The top, leaves and legs are solid mahogany and the front and back of the skirt are veneered with 1/16 inch thick mahogany strips. The Dominys charged almost twice as much for mahogany tables of this type than for ones made of other woods. The casters and brass pulls are original.
Courtesy, The Henry Francis du Pont Winterthur Museum.

in the area, did in fact purchase two tall case clocks, an expensive desk and bookcase, and a mahogany desk. However, Mulford Hand, at the lower end of the economic scale, also purchased a mahogany desk similar to Gardiner's and paid the same price. Thomas Baker, who ranked 84th on a list of more than 150 in the amount of local taxes he paid, bought not one but three chest on chests. Captain David Fithian, who ranked 15th on the tax list, bought the simplest clock from the Dominys. In a barter economy, the Dominys could only pay their debts by producing goods and services in like amounts. They might not be in debt to John Gardiner, but they might owe a blacksmith at a lower end of the economic scale. An expensive desk and bookcase discharged the debt nicely.

By the second quarter of the 19th century, most rural cabinet shops like the Dominys's had disappeared in the face of factory-produced goods. The introduction of steamers on Long Island Sound destroyed the price advantage that the Dominys had enjoyed over New York furniture. Packets brought furniture of all sorts to cabinet warehouses, such as Nathan Tinker's in Sag Harbor, for sale to the rural population. By 1840, the use of interchangeable parts and the introduction of manufacturing processes lowered the price of clocks to the point that the Dominy handcraft methods could not compete. By 1834, Felix had given up the crafts. He became a lighthouse keeper on Fire Island and, later, a hotel manager.

THE DUNLAPS
OF SOUTHERN NEW HAMPSHIRE

A similar story was played out in New Hampshire. That state had a predominately Scottish-Irish population of about 142,000 in 1790. At least 150 joiners or cabinetmakers worked in the state before 1790; the majority lived in Portsmouth, its largest city, founded in 1623. Only a few of these makers are known, such as Thomas Dennis, who worked there in the 1660s before moving to Ipswich, Massachusetts, and John Gaines, who worked there from 1724 until his death in 1743. By the 1770s, Portsmouth had developed a large export trade, shipping hundreds of chairs, desks, tables, and chests, principally to the West Indies. Philadelphia, its closest competitor, claimed only half as much of the West Indian market.

Generally, New Hampshire furniture exhibited few distinct regional characteristics. Only the Dunlaps, particularly Major John Dunlap who died in 1792, and his brother Samuel, who lived until 1830, have been linked to furniture with highly individualistic elements. Dunlap furniture reflects a Scottish heritage combined with traditional designs from larger coastal New England cities such as Portsmouth. As in other rural areas, once the Federal style became known Major John's sons abandoned the distinctive furniture of their father and adopted the new Federal style.

The Dunlaps worked in several towns of 1,000 to 2,000 inhabitants, including Goffstown, Bedford, Henniker, and Salisbury, where they initially had no competition. They sold furniture to customers in the surrounding area up to 25 miles away.

John employed as many as seven men at one time to help him. Some of them were formally apprenticed to him from two to five years each. In 1775, William Houston's apprenticeship began with the stipulation that after two years, John would "help him to make the Wooden part of a set of tools fit for the trade. . . ."[6]

The Dunlaps produced all the furniture forms to fill the needs of their customers. They made chests, both high and low; desks; chairs; clocks; bedsteads; and a variety of tables, including candlestands, chamber, kitchen,

FIGURE VII–27
Side chair. Maple. New Hampshire. Ca. 1775–1790.
Major John Dunlap made over 500 chairs before his death in 1792, and this upholstered side chair may have been among the most expensive ones. The high stay rail, found on many early 18th-century banister-back chairs, allows for a seat cushion. The abrupt transition from the vertical to the horizontal plane is also a holdover from the William and Mary style. The carved fans and pierced splat are typical of the Queen Anne period. The pronounced ears and the molded legs and stiles typify the Chippendale period.
Courtesy, The Henry Francis du Pont Winterthur Museum.

breakfast, and square and round tea tables (Figure VII–27). The Dunlaps started with a typical ball and claw foot but gave it their own distinctive stamp. The talon was delicately carved, the half ball was egg-shaped, and the knee was fat and sharp. The geometrical or linear carving could be laid out with simple rulers and compasses. They modified the standard New England fan so that the lobes looked like spoon handles, and their carving on cornices resembled basket weaving. Many pieces had an intricate kind of gadrooning that they called the "flowered ogee" (Figure VII–28). The same design appeared on several church pulpits that the Dunlaps built in Temple and in Londonderry, New Hampshire. The bold, paired S-scrolls, separated by a heart-shaped cutout on the skirts of high chests, exaggerated Hogarth's line of beauty. Heavy architectural cornice moldings showed the influence of the Dunlaps as house carpenters. The chest on chest, perched on short legs, was topped with a gallery (Figure VII–1).

As with most rural cabinetmakers, the Dunlaps pursued a number of jobs in addition to making furniture. John Dunlap built houses and barns and did general painting. He replaced sash windows, laid floors, and installed paneling and woodwork. He also made tools, looking-glass frames, barrels, wheels, wagons, coffins, and spinning and weaving equipment. A prosperous farmer, he supplemented his income by raising corn, wheat, rye, and flax. His customers frequently paid him in farm produce or services. Some customers let him use their oxen to plow his fields as payment for furniture.

The Dunlaps chose to make their furniture primarily of maple, a wood that grew abundantly in southern New Hampshire. Since it was well seasoned, the wood in their furniture shows little warping or cracking, even after almost 200 years. The Dunlaps invariably stained the honey-colored maple to resemble mahogany, but they also used green and orange finishes as well. The Dunlaps embellished a few of their pieces, including a clock case and a high chest, with simple vine inlay.

SAMUEL GRAGG

Samuel Gragg also worked in New Hampshire in the late 18th century, but the details of his early life are unknown. He was born in Peterborough, New Hampshire, in 1772, and his father was a wheelwright and farmer. What training Samuel received is unknown, but about 1800 he arrived in Boston and established a chairmaking business. In 1808, Gragg advertised that he "calculates to make and have constantly on hand, all kinds of Fancy and Bamboo CHAIRS, of the newest fashion, which he offers for sale on as good terms as can be purchased in Boston."[7]

In 1808, Gragg was issued a patent for an "elastic chair." Gragg's springy innovation took the form of the familiar klismos chairs of ancient Greece, but they were executed in a unique manner. In some examples, single strips of bent wood formed the back, seat, and legs in one continuous, undulating curve. In others, the legs were made of a separate piece of wood. In both versions, slats across the back bent down into the seat. Gragg used heat and moisture to bend the wood, a process dating from Greek and Roman times. It was the same process used in forming wheels, in shaping slats in ladder-back chairs, and in the construction of Windsor chairs. Gragg painted and decorated his pieces like Sheraton fancy chairs. The most unusual ones were ornamented with peacock feathers, a motif foreign to the neoclassical vocabulary (Figure VII–29). However, Gragg may have copied examples that appeared on a wall illustrated by Thomas Hope, or he may have seen a piece of English furniture,

FIGURE VII–28
Chest on chest on frame. Maple. New Hampshire. Ca. 1780–1800.
This piece has many of the characteristics associated with Dunlap furniture found in southern New Hampshire. These include the use of maple, the spoon-handle rays of the fan, the double S-scrolls on the skirt, and the saw-tooth carving on the cornice. The pronounced curves of the legs, which terminate in unusual square pads, repeat similar curves on the skirt. The deep bottom drawer is faced with two false drawer fronts. The original brasses indicate a late 18th-century date.
Private Collection.

Figure VII–29
Side chair. Birch, oak, and beech. Boston. Ca. 1808–1815.
This distinctive design by Samuel Gragg of Boston was made almost a half-century before Michael Thonet patented his bentwood furniture. Few of the delicately curved slats have survived unbroken the stress placed upon them by the bending. The bright peacock feathers painted on the center slat and crest are scarcely needed to enliven this extraordinarily innovative design. The front legs end in hoof feet, whereas in other variations they are plain. On other Gragg chairs, the back legs are continuations of the stiles and seat rails.
E. J. Canton.

which occasionally sported the peacock motif.

Few chairmakers thoroughly immersed in the latest techniques of a stylish Boston or New York shop would have departed so radically from the accepted chairmaking norm. Growing up in a rural area, however, Gragg was less encumbered by tradition. He was also familiar with his father's wheelwright trade, which may have inspired his new construction methods. Gragg created one of the outstanding American furniture designs fully 75 years before the widespread popularity of bentwood furniture.

COUNTRY AND HIGH-STYLE FURNITURE

The best furniture produced by the Dominys on Long Island, the Dunlaps in New Hampshire, the Bachmans in Lancaster, and Clay in the Connecticut River Valley differs significantly from the fashionable work sold by Affleck, Townsend, or Frothingham. Part of the difference resulted from isolation, both geographical and cultural. Although travel in the 18th century was hard, it was not impossible. Much more difficult was the movement of heavy loads of goods. Even in the early 19th century, when transportation was beginning to improve, it cost as much to carry a ton of goods all the way across the Atlantic Ocean to America as it did to move that same ton of goods 30 miles inland to rural towns. As a result, country furniture was generally constructed of a local species of wood, such as cherry, maple, or walnut. Few customers asked for mahogany because of the added expense of transporting the lumber from a port to the rural village. Frequently, however, the local wood was stained or painted to imitate more fashionable cabinet woods, such as mahogany.

The frontier was also isolated from stylish new furniture. New designs were often spread by the actual example of new furniture, either imported or made locally. Transportation costs precluded the introduction to rural areas of much imported furniture. Few cabinetmakers with new ideas settled in small rural towns, which could support only one or two cabinetmakers who, in addition to making furniture, had to depend upon farming or other activities to make a living. A rural cabinetmaker's clients usually shared his heritage and felt comfortable with his work. His traditional furniture was in demand for a longer time than styles in the cities, where new furniture, new craftsmen, and new customers exposed to the "latest English taste" were constantly forcing change. The unique cabinetmaking heritage of the country cabinetmaker, which reflected the taste of his clientele, survived relatively unchallenged as the norm in the country. The community passed on their heritage to their children, just as the cabinetmaker passed on to his son the special techniques demanded by his customers.

Some distinctive schools of country cabinetwork reflect the perpetuation of alternative craft traditions, but others resulted from deficiencies in training or ability. Although many country craftsmen displayed a good sense of classical design and proportion, others seemed not to have received a thorough grounding in these principles. The mechanics of using tools could easily be learned, but the classical ideas of proportion and design were more subtle and less easily understood. Country cabinetmakers were often aware of the basic elements of fashionable furniture, but these ideas were not always thoroughly assimilated. They often simplified or exaggerated elements of conventional city designs. If one shell is good, five are better; if one small fan is pleasing, a larger one will be more impressive (Figure VII–30).

Simplification may have been due to a poor understanding of the design, but it was also due to

FIGURE VII–30
Desk. Maple with pine. New Hampshire. Ca. 1780–1820.
The giant carved shell relates to similar work on other southern New Hampshire furniture, though few others compare with this shell in size. The pinwheels, fans, and hearts, as well as the shell, were easily laid out with a compass and carved with a modest amount of skill. The brass knobs are strictly decorative, since the entire bottom section is a single deep drawer opened by means of brass pulls on either side of the shell. The exaggeration of the decoration and the odd combination of the bold fan with the delicate fans, pinwheels, and hearts betrays the hand of a provincial designer.
Courtesy, The Henry Francis du Pont Winterthur Museum.

the absence of the specialists, such as carvers, gilders, japanners, upholsterers, and veneer and inlay dealers, who supported cabinetmakers in the city. Indeed, the country craftsman frequently fits the myth of the cabinetmaker building each piece of furniture by himself. In the cities, many specialists were employed to make the elaborate masterpieces that are so often erroneously attributed to a single man. In general, then, country furniture is plain, and what carving there is is simple. A carver could not make a living working for only one or two rural cabinetmakers. Only the cities supported enough cabinetmakers to keep the carvers and other specialists busy.

Like some city furniture, country work could be poorly made and poorly designed or plain. At its best, however, country furniture was a strong, individualistic statement that

was applauded as enthusiastically by its contemporary customers as it is today by discriminating connoisseurs. The country craftsman did not simply copy design books, as did many of his colleagues in Boston or Philadelphia. Indeed, he could not copy these designs without the help of specialists. Instead, he was forced to rely on his own resources and personal training. The Dunlaps in New Hampshire, the Chapins in Connecticut, the Dominys on Long Island, and the hundreds of other frontier craftsmen maintained their own traditions, which often differed from English tradition. Although Boston, New York, Philadelphia, Newport, and Charleston continued to copy English culture even after the Revolution, American cabinetmakers on the frontier were pursuing their own cultural heritage.

By the second quarter of the

19th century, however, most of these craftsmen were driven from their trades by the arrival of cheaper furniture produced in the large-scale furniture manufactories. Those who survived were forced to abandon their unique heritage and adopt the latest urban style that was finding its way into the country market.

NOTES

1. John D. Morse, ed., *Country Cabinetwork and Simple City Furniture* (Charlottesville, Va.: The University Press of Virginia, 1970), p. 261.

2. John J. Snyder, Jr., "Carved Chippendale Case Furniture from Lancaster, Pennsylvania," *The Magazine Antiques* 107 (May 1975): 965.

3. Robert F. Trent, *Hearts & Crowns* (New Haven, Ct.: New Haven Colony Historical Society, 1977), p. 33.

4. Peter M. Rippe, "Daniel Clay of Greenfield, 'Cabinetmaker' " (Master's Thesis, University of Delaware, 1962), pp. 16, 58.

5. Morse, *Country Cabinetwork*, p. 56.

6. Charles S. Parsons, *The Dunlaps & Their Furniture* (Manchester, N.H.: The Currier Gallery of Art, 1970), p. 18.

7. Patricia E. Kane, "Samuel Gragg: His Bentwood Fancy Chairs" *Yale University Bulletin* 33 (Autumn 1971): 32–33.

VIII

SOUTHERN FURNITURE

WITH THE EXCEPTION OF CHARLESton, the southern states did not have major urban cities before the Revolution. Instead, a rural agrarian economy characterized the South. Since only Virginia, Maryland, and the Carolina low country were settled early in the 18th century, pre-Revolution furniture has survived mostly from these areas. Georgia, Kentucky, Tennessee, and Louisiana all had small populations at the end of the war but expanded rapidly in the years after the Revolution. As a result, most of the furniture produced in these southeastern states dates from the Federal and Empire periods.

Although cabinetmakers in cities, such as Charleston, Williamsburg, and Annapolis, drew heavily on English sources, the rural cabinetmakers, isolated in the countryside, expressed their individuality and cultural heritage much as did their rural counterparts in the north.

Southern furniture ranged from the highly sophisticated, English-inspired, ceremonial furniture of Williamsburg to the sometimes crude pieces with a German flavor made on the Texas frontier. Because of this diversity, only a few valid generalizations are possible. The cellaret, an English form, appeared in the North Carolina Piedmont and spread into Virginia and Georgia (Figure VIII–2). The origin of the huntboard, a form of the sideboard with high legs, is less clear, but it is also a distinctive southern piece. The armoire, common in Louisiana and Texas, reflects a strong French and Spanish influence in those parts of the country. In addition to these few distinctively southern forms, unique inlay, such as commas and jonquils, can also indicate a southern origin.

Southerners generally preferred simplicity in their domestic furniture. Peter Manigault,

one of Charleston's wealthiest merchants, ordered furniture and silver from London in 1771 and requested "to have them out as soon as possible & the plainer the better so that they are fashionable."[1]

Southern cabinetwork can also be distinguished by the woods employed. Although mahogany predominated for the best Charleston pieces, most southern furniture was made of walnut and sometimes of cherry, maple, or birch. The use of yellow pine, characterized by red streaks running through it, usually guaranteed a southern origin, although it appears on some Pennsylania pieces as well. Cypress, however, is a uniquely southern wood.

THE WILLIAMSBURG SCHOOL

The first English settlement in America was at Jamestown, near Williamsburg, in 1607. Although

FIGURE VIII-2
Cellaret. Walnut with yellow pine and poplar. Halifax County, N.C. Ca. 1792-1796.
It is unusual to find both a drawer and a mixing board on a cellaret. The inverted shield and scroll are carved in relief and stained. Putty inlay spells out TLL, probably the initials of the first owner. Slightly tapering legs confirm a date within the Federal period. Since the piece is finished on all four sides, it was probably meant for use at a table.
Museum of Early Southern Decorative Arts.

Virginia became the wealthiest and most populous English colony, little furniture has survived from the first 100 years of its existence (Figure VIII–3). By 1700, the colony supported 40,000 inhabitants, who depended for the most part on tobacco farming for their livelihood. Hundreds of plantations flourished along the numerous tributaries that flowed into the Chesapeake Bay. Ocean-going ships sailed up to private docks at these plantations and loaded the lucrative tobacco. By selling their crops in England, the Virginia aristocracy obtained credit for the purchase of English goods, including furniture and furnishings.

These planters regarded themselves as Englishmen and naturally preferred London-made products. Thus, furniture made in Virginia often follows English construction practices. The six-legged table commonly found in Virginia was an English form (Figure VIII–4). Virginians also spurned the out-dated high chest that continued to be popular in northern cities in the Chippendale period. Instead, Southerners preferred the more stylish chest on chest.

English construction techniques are seen in the use of a one-piece rear seat rail and shoe as well as the use of knee blocks attached over the seat rails rather than under them. However, certain construction techniques on Virginia furniture

FIGURE VIII–3
Cupboard. White oak with yellow pine. Tidewater, Virginia. Ca. 1645–1680. **This example is the earliest known piece of southern furniture. The open shelf at the top differs from most New England examples, where the open space is at the bottom. The applied walnut bosses and split spindles are stained to imitate ebony. Although several English examples are known, the form is extremely rare.** *Museum of Early Southern Decorative Arts.*

indicated the cabinetmaker's awareness of local conditions, such as extremes of humidity. The composite foot made up of several layers of wood stacked together, backboards held within panels, and cuts in the supporting strips backing base moldings were all calculated to counter the expansion and contraction of wood caused by changes in humidity.

Furniture production in Tidewater, Virginia, centered in Williamsburg, the capital after 1699. About 3,000 inhabitants lived in the town on the eve of the Revolution, but the population swelled considerably when planters arrived from all over the colony for the meetings of the House of Burgesses and the sessions of the courts. These planters, such as Thomas Jefferson and Robert Carter, did a brisk business with Williamsburg merchants during these periodic visits to the capital. As a result,

Williamsburg was second only to Charleston as a center of cabinetmaking in the South before the Revolution.

Williamsburg furniture was made in quantity beginning in the 1720s and 1730s when the George I and early George II styles were popular in England. Erroneously called Queen Anne in America, this style incorporated simple curves and cabriole legs ending in pad feet. One of the earliest Virginia pieces is the famous House of Burgesses' Speaker's chair with cabriole legs, William and Mary style arms, and an architectural hood (Figure VIII–5). Other furniture from the early 18th century includes an elegant tea table with characteristic bulbous pad feet. Often the molding of the top is set into a rabbet cut into the top edge of the table. Applied to an oak skirt is a pine wedge covered by a curved piece of mahogany (Figure VIII–6). Early gateleg ta-

FIGURE VIII–4
Dining table. Walnut with yellow pine. Central Virginia. Ca. 1760. **Derived from English prototypes, six-legged tables were prevalent throughout Virginia in the mid-18th century. The extra legs provide added stability. Variations of this form have rectangular tops and straight legs. The top is held to the frame by means of screws instead of glue blocks, a technique more commonly used early in the 18th century. This piece was found in the Petersburg area.** *Private Collection.*

FIGURE VIII–5
Speaker's chair. Walnut with yellow pine, poplar, and oak. Williamsburg. Ca. 1730.
Originally finished on all sides, this chair was intended to stand in the center of the chamber where the Virginia House of Burgesses met. It is patterned after a similar ceremonial chair that sat in the British House of Commons. The architectural back and pitched pediment give the sitter an aura of importance. The scrolled arms are the only documented survival of the William and Mary style in Virginia. The bulbous pad feet relate to other Williamsburg furniture.
Commonwealth of Virginia.

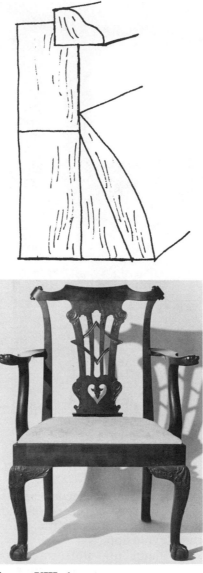

FIGURE VIII–6 *(top)*
Cross-section of the skirt of a Williamsburg tea table showing the pine wedge covered with a strip of mahogany.

FIGURE VIII–7
Armchair. Cherry with poplar. Williamsburg. Ca. 1745.
With its distinctive, carved, dog's head arm terminals and hoof rear feet, the chair closely resembled George II English chairs. The controlled, symmetrical carving on the legs reflects a date prior to the asymmetrical and exuberant Rococo style of mid-18th century. The one-piece shoe and rear seat rail, the dovetail joint fastening the arms to the rear stiles, the chamfering of the edge of the splat, and the practice of applying the knee blocks over the seat rail, which extends down behind the blocks, are characteristic of a group of chairs attributed to the shop of Peter Scott.
Mr. C. Hill Carter, "Shirley" Plantation, Charles City, Virginia.

bles have the same characteristic bulging pad foot with a squared-off upper section of the leg enhanced by a lamb's tongue molding. Later pieces substitute a lathe-turned pad foot for the bulbous hand-carved one.

By the 1730s and 1740s in both England and Williamsburg, the early Georgian style gave way to the late George II style, which featured elaborate carving, a precursor of the rococo. During this phase, paw feet, animal heads on arms, and geometrically pierced splats became common. Case pieces rested on straight bracket feet, and drawers on the interior of desks had fronts flush to the case.

One of the major cabinetmakers in Williamsburg was Peter Scott, who worked in a shop across from Bruton Parish Church as early as the 1720s. His work closely followed English practices in such details as a rear rail and shoe of one-piece construction, a hoof-pad rear foot on chairs, knee brackets applied to seat rails, the insertion of dust boards, and the use of composite feet. A chair made by Scott with ball and claw feet on both front and back legs is rare in America, though such a design was common in England. The dogs' heads on the arm terminals of another chair are also rarely found in America, though such animal forms are common in England (Figure VIII–7).Other Scott characteristics include the use of panels on the doors of desk and bookcases; such panels were let into a rabbet and held by a molding applied over them. Corners are often indented. The interior arrangement includes four drawers and a row of pigeonholes on either side of a central door.

The Rococo style arrived in Virginia as early as the 1750s and is seen on a chair made in 1755 for the Governor's use in the General Court at Williamsburg (Figure VIII–8). Anthony Hay, who made the chair, operated the most influential shop in Virginia. The uneven quality of the carving suggests that at least two carvers worked on the chair, and one of them may have been James Wilson, who worked in Hay's shop in the 1750s. Some of the most elaborate furniture ever produced in the colonies was made in the Hay shop (Figure VIII–9). Hay established the shop in the 1750s, and his success allowed him to become the proprietor of the Raleigh Tavern in 1767. Benjamin Bucktrout, for a time in partnership with William Kennedy, rented the shop for several years. Its next tenant was Edmund Dickinson.

Hay's work is identified by a number of individual characteristics. The interiors of many of his desk and bookcases had a center drawer flanked by two smaller drawers set one on

FIGURE VIII–8
Armchair. Mahogany with beech. Williamsburg. Ca. 1755.
Since beech was used in Virginia, it is not necessarily an indication of English provenance. Probably used by the Royal governor in the General Court, this chair, with its 12 inches of extra height; its extraordinary carved lion's paw feet on both front and rear legs; and a canopy, which no doubt hung above the chair, gave the sitter a great aura of authority. The acanthus leaf carving on the knees is similar to carving on Massachusetts and New York chairs, and the realistic paw feet and lion's heads show a thorough understanding of the animal's anatomy. Like other Williamsburg pieces with paw feet, this chair is attributed to the Anthony Hay shop. An unfinished chair leg with a paw foot was excavated from the site of that shop.
Colonial Williamsburg Foundation.

FIGURE VIII–9
China table. Mahogany. Williamsburg. Ca. 1770.
The intricately pierced legs are cut from a solid piece of mahogany rather than using the English practice of lamination. The bird carved in the skirt may confirm the family tradition that the table was owned by Susan Lewis, who married William Powell Byrd of Westover. The extraordinary table, attributed to Anthony Hay's shop, is one of three similar examples that are the finest of their type known. Chippendale's 1762 edition of the *Director* illustrates a similar form—but without the elaborate piercing—which he calls a "China Table" and was meant to hold a China tea service.
Private Collection.

top of the other and a central door flanked by three pigeonholes (Figure VIII–10). The upper section of the legs on several tables attributed to Hay has a carved intaglio shell that is similar to work by William Savery of Philadelphia and is also found on London work. Other London techniques used on chairs included lion's heads on the arm terminals and animal feet.

Bucktrout's most important production was the signed, intricately carved Masonic chair found at the Unanimity Lodge No. 7 in Edenton, North Carolina (Figure VIII–11). This Masonic chair relates to five similar ones with a Williamsburg attri-

FIGURE VIII–10
Desk and bookcase. Mahogany with yellow pine. Williamsburg. Ca. 1760.
The interior arrangement of pigeonholes, drawers, and prospect door is found on a number of other Williamsburg pieces. The shape of the bracket feet is also similar, suggesting that the same template may have been used as a pattern to construct the feet of all the furniture in this group. As with other pieces in this group, the bookcase section rests on a frame on top of the desk, and a molding is attached to the base of the bookcase to form an interlocking joint.
Private Collection.

FIGURE VIII–11
Armchair. Mahogany with walnut. Williamsburg. Ca. 1767–1770.
This Masonic Master's chair stamped by Benjamin Bucktrout is one of the outstanding American ceremonial chairs. A simulated stone arch that forms the crest rests on two Corinthian columns with stopped fluting. A carved sun and moon flank a bust of Matthew Prior, an English poet. The splat contains many Masonic symbols, such as a trowel, a hammer, a square, and a compass. The dolphin feet are copied from the 1762 edition of Chippendale's *Director*.
The Unanimity Lodge No. 7, Edenton, North Carolina.

bution. These chairs are among the richest and most elaborate pieces of furniture produced in America in the 18th century. They contrast sharply with the relatively simple furniture produced for private use and provide graphic proof of the importance early Virginians attached to public ceremony.

Although Virginia cabinet-makers produced domestic furniture with a characteristic simplicity, they were attuned to the latest style changes in London. One of the earliest examples of the neoclassical taste in America was on the three-tiered cast iron "warming machine" imported by the royal governor for the House of Burgesses in 1770. As early as 1774, a Williamsburg newspaper advertisement of George Hamilton, a London-trained gilder and carver who worked for Anthony Hay, touted the "New Palmyrian Taste" and confirmed the popularity of the new style. As in other cabinetmaking centers in America, however, the neoclassical style had to await the end of the Revolution before it

FIGURE VIII–12
Tall case clock. Cherry with poplar. Valley of Virginia. Ca. 1809.
Extraordinary inlay and veneer combine with an unusual design in a highly personal statement. The oval inlay on the base rests on a concave oval boss. The exaggerated, flaring French feet terminate in hooves. Hand-like scrolls from which hang balls adorn the bonnet. The many unrelated inlays of vines, flowers, and eagles give the clock a charming but provincial character.
Private Collection.

gained widespread popularity (Figures VIII–12 and VIII–13).

On the eve of the Revolution, the furniture of Norfolk, Virginia's largest city—with 6,000 inhabitants—showed the strong influence of Williamsburg cabinetmakers. Since Norfolk was burned by the British in 1776, little furniture has survived from the earlier period. However, the work by such men as John Selden shows the characteristic paneled back, detachable cornice, and composite feet also common on much Williamsburg furniture (Figure VIII–14).

Williamsburg's influence also stretched into rural Virginia villages as well, but generally the sophistication of rural workmanship suffered in comparison. Dovetails on case pieces were exposed, dustboards were omitted, and single blocks rather than the composite foot were more common.

A manufacturing center at the falls of the Rappahannock River, Fredericksburg was known for tall case clocks by such makers as Thomas Walker. Fredericksburg corner chairs, with a three-piece arm rail, were distinctive. The middle piece was supported on a turned column surmounted by a crescent-shaped support that gently curved into the splats on either side of a turned column[2] (Figure VIII–15).

Other distinctive cabinetwork came from Martinsburg, in what is now West Virginia. John Shearer worked in a transitional style between Chippendale and Federal from 1790 to 1810. Born in Scotland, Shearer never lost his loyalist sympathies. Inside one of his chests, he scrawled "From a Tory/Vive le Roy/1804/God Save the King/by me John Shearer." An inlaid crowned lion rampant on one of his desks is the only known American example of the British symbol. The eccentric placement of his drawer pulls in a vertical position must have appealed to his clients, since he repeated the unique practice on a number of his desks and his desk and bookcases (Figure VIII–16).

Figure VIII–13
Sideboard. Mahogany veneer with white pine, ash, and poplar. Virginia. Ca. 1800.
Ovolo corners and a serpentine mid-section are a standard configuration found on sideboards from New York and elsewhere. The play of ovals on rectangles and circles on squares epitomizes the intellectual compositions favored in the Federal period. Bold paterae, stringing, and bellflowers add further interest. The one-piece bellflowers without shading and the overdone use of nine of them on each leg betrays a provincial hand.
Private Collection.

Figure VIII–14
Clothespress. Mahogany with yellow pine. Norfolk. Dated 1775.
The piece is signed J. S., for John Selden of Norfolk. The stacked glue blocks, the detachable cornice, and the paneled backboards show the influence of Williamsburg work. However, the double-ogee spandrels at the top corners of the doors and the flare at the base of the bracket feet are distinctive Selden characteristics. The piece is closely patterned after a plate in the 1762 edition of Chippendale's *Director*.
Mr. C. Hill Carter, Jr., "Shirley" Plantation, Charles City, Virginia.

Figure VIII–15
Roundabout chair. Walnut. Fredericksburg, Va. Ca. 1760–1770.
This is one of a group of chairs that have the same basic characteristics, particularly the three-piece arm rail and rounded arches cut into the crest rail. Although the carving relates to Williamsburg work, a Fredericksburg attribution seems more convincing, since similar examples are found in the area.
Museum of Early Southern Decorative Arts.

FIGURE VIII–17
Corner cupboard. Cherry with poplar and white oak. Maryland. Ca. 1800.
A form, common in the 18th century, has been updated by a rural cabinetmaker, who has added carved paterae and inlay. In keeping with the more delicate neoclassical style, the pediment is flattened. The carved muntins, rather coarsely executed, arc a holdover from the rococo carving of the Chippendale period. The stiles, extending to the floor, form the feet.
Historical Society of Frederick County, Maryland.

FIGURE VIII–18 *(below)*
Desk and bookcase. Cherry. Maryland. Ca. 1760–1780.
Richly carved and expensive furniture, such as this, was more common in the larger cities, such as Philadelphia. However, the six-petaled flowers punched into the pitched pediment and the playful shaping of the frame around the central door on the interior of the desk indicate an origin outside a major style center. The interlocking circle fret beneath the pediment is repeated on the chamfered corners of the upper and lower case. The muntin pattern is found on a library bookcase illustrated in Chippendale's *Director*.
Courtesy, Mrs. Miriam Morris.

FIGURE VIII–16 *(above)*
Desk and bookcase. Cherry and walnut, with oak and yellow pine. Martinsburg, W. Va. Ca. 1801–1806.
John Shearer, who immigrated to Berkeley County, West Virginia, from Edinburgh, Scotland, signed the desk in 1801 and the bookcase section in 1806. In fact, Shearer signed the piece 20 times and wrote the name of the customer, Even Pendleton, as well. The pediment is related to designs shown in Sheraton's *Drawing Book*. The muntin configuration is illustrated in a plate of Chippendale's *Director*. The florid shells on the interior relate to Pennsylvania desks. The serpentine facade appears on Boston work, but there it usually encompasses the entire drawer. Shearer has left a sizable portion flat. The feet appear clumsy compared to high-style furniture, but they are certainly sturdier than the feet with thinner ankles on city work. The vertical placement of the drawer pulls is pure Shearer and just as serviceable as the more conventional horizontal placement.
Museum of Early Southern Decorative Arts.

Maryland Furniture

Maryland, like Virginia, had close ties to England, and many Marylanders purchased their furniture from the mother country. However, by 1776, Baltimore and Annapolis were emerging as major urban centers, with nearly 7,000 inhabitants each. Although cabinetmakers in these towns produced furniture that closely followed English designs, craftsmen in the rural towns of Frederick and Hagerstown produced furniture that betrayed a German inspiration (Figure VIII–17).

In the 1760s and 1770s, Marylanders built some of America's finest houses at Annapolis, which had replaced St. Mary's City as Maryland's capital in 1693. These homes included the Upton-Scott House, the Chase-Lloyd House, the William Paca House, and the Hammond-Harwood House. Although some of the furnishings were imported from England, much of the furniture was made by Baltimore and Annapolis craftsmen (Figures VIII–18 and VIII–19).

Maryland's furniture shows the strong influence of Philadelphia in the through tenon, rear stump legs, and characteristic ball and claw foot, but there are some local variations. Maryland cabinetmakers usually selected the cheaper local walnut rather than imported mahogany for their best pieces. They employed a carved, inverted shell on the skirts of high chests and preferred chamfered corners with lamb's tongue capitals instead of the reeded corner columns found on Philadelphia work. The usual three small drawers in the upper and lower parts of these high chests typically measured the same height. Chairs had broad, elaborately pierced splats and upholstery that continued over the rails. Saddle seats and serpentine seat rails were also common.

John Shaw, who immigrated to Annapolis in 1763 from Scotland, was Maryland's best-known cabinetmaker. More than

Figure VIII–19
Side chair. Mahogany. Baltimore. Ca. 1770.
This chair is attributed to Gerrard Hopkins of Baltimore, based on the similarity of the shell and acanthus leaf carving on a high chest signed by him. Like most Maryland furniture, this chair relates to Philadelphia shop practices, particularly in the rounded, stump rear legs and squashed ball feet, but the carving does not have the liveliness and complexity of the finest Philadelphia work.
Diplomatic Reception Rooms, U.S. Department of State.

50 pieces of furniture are signed or documented as made in his shop. After the Revolution, Shaw supervised the construction of the state capitol and made furniture for both the House of Delegates and the Senate chambers. A shrewd businessman, Shaw imported stylish furniture and hardware as well as producing his own furniture for sale. His reputation spread to Philadelphia, and the wealthy merchant, John Cadwalader, purchased a "True Madam" billiard table from him in 1775. Working mostly in the Federal style, Shaw frequently used geometric inlay as well as conch shells, acorns, fans, and eagles.

After the Revolution, Baltimore became the fastest growing city in America. It benefited from its location at the hub of the tobacco and grain trade in the upper Chesapeake Bay. Its cabinetmakers produced some of the most elegant Federal furniture, particularly sideboards, dressing tables, and lady's writing desks. Baltimore cabinetmakers frequently enriched these pieces with the distinctive bellflowers or "husk and drop" inlay suspended from a loop (Figure VIII–20). Chair seats were usually upholstered over the rails like New England chairs,

FIGURE VIII–20

Sideboard. Mahogany with poplar. Baltimore. Ca. 1800.

The "hollow round" ends and serpentine center follow a common sideboard design. The tapered legs terminate in spade feet. The four shells above each leg, the two eagles on either side of the central arch, and the typical boldly flaring Baltimore bellflowers add considerable interest to the facade.
Private Collection.

FIGURE VIII–21

Side chair. Mahogany. Baltimore. Ca. 1800.

The racket-shaped splat is derived from designs of "Backs for Parlour Chairs" in Sheraton's *Drawing Book*. The splat is often found in Baltimore, although variations appear in Philadelphia and New York as well. The serpentine seat, upholstered over half the rail, is also a frequent Baltimore characteristic.
Baltimore Museum of Art.

FIGURE VIII–22

Desk and bookcase. Mahogany with tulip poplar and cedar. Baltimore. Ca. 1800.

In the typical Baltimore technique, eglomise panels on the doors are painted on the reverse side of the glass with gilt musical trophies against a dark blue background. The central door on the interior and flanking letter drawers are also decorated with eglomise panels. The usual classical subjects of urns and arabesques enliven the letter boxes, but a unique helmeted knight adorns the door. It is based on a print attributed to Salvator Rosa that must have found its way to Baltimore.
Baltimore Museum of Art.

and the tennis-racket-shaped splat was common, although it was also found in New York and Philadelphia (Figure VIII–21). Many of the most elegant Baltimore case pieces sported inset eglomise panels or glass with painting and gilding on the reverse side. The technique, developed in ancient Damascus, takes its name from Jean Baptiste Glomy, an 18th-century French art dealer (Figure VIII–22). Other Baltimore Federal furniture continued to relate closely to Philadelphia work. At least one Philadelphia cabinetmaker, Joseph Barry, opened a branch shop in Baltimore in the first decade of the 19th century.

Although the art of painted furniture was popular everywhere in the early 19th century the technique produced spectacular results in the hands of Baltimore painters (Figure VIII–23). Painted furniture is often associated with country work, but in the Federal period, that decoration was considered quite stylish. Hepplewhite recommended the technique, stating that "for chairs, a new and very elegant fashion has arisen within these few years, of finishing them with painted or japanned work, which gives a rich and splendid appearance...."[3]

Painted decorations suited the two-dimensional character of the

Federal style. Of the 50 fancy chairmakers working in Baltimore in 1800, John and Hugh Finlay, late of Ireland, were the most famous. They specialized in painting "views adjacent to the city," primarily the numerous townhouses that circled Baltimore in the early 19th century (Figure VIII–24). One of their advertisements claimed that they had "an exclusive right for that species of ornament," although no document has been found to support their assertion. The more expensive painted chairs usually had cane seats, a technique that once again regained popularity. Chairmakers substituted painted rush on cheaper chairs.

Early in the 19th century, Baltimore turned out a huge amount of furniture, even though it had a relatively small population. During the height of the Empire style, no other area produced as large and distinctive a group of furniture as did Baltimore. The Finlays and other Baltimore furniture decorators painted dazzling, gilded designs, such as winged thunderbolts, anthemia, Grecian scrolls, and acanthus leaves, often against a simulated rosewood background. The Baltimore wheelback chairs copied Roman camp chairs, except that they did not fold up (Figure VIII–25). Mixing, pier, and card tables—often with

FIGURE VIII–26

Fire screen. Poplar. Baltimore. Ca. 1820–1830.

The beehive finial and ball turning on the pole characterize a large group of Baltimore furniture. The scrolled base is painted with anthemia springing from applied brass rosettes. The pie-shaped feet suggest antefixes, which were placed at the eaves of classical buildings. The fabric displayed on the screen depicts other classical motifs.
Private Collection.

X-shaped bases and hub-like pedestals—were also painted, as were fire screens (Figures VIII–26 and VIII–27).

CHARLESTON AND ALBEMARLE SOUND FURNITURE

The largest city in the South in the 18th century was Charleston, which, together with Savannah, dominated the culture of the Carolina low country. Settled in the late 17th century, Charleston, by the middle of the 18th century, thrived on the lucrative rice, indigo, and cotton trade. Although English culture predominated, Charleston was a cosmopolitan city with large groups of French, Dutch, German, Irish, Scottish, and West Indians.

Charleston cabinetmakers, such as Abraham Pearce, sold their wares to country plantations. In 1768, Pearce advertised that "orders from the country, or any of the southern provinces, will be punctually complied with." Plantation owners dealt through factors who lived in Charleston. One factor wrote that "with respect to the Chairs, I am quite at a loss what to do,

FIGURE VIII–27

Card table. Painted wood. Baltimore. Ca. 1820–1830.

The barrel-turned baluster and X-shaped pedestal are found on a large group of Baltimore furniture. The extravagant use of no less than 17 brass rosettes on the pedestal and baluster, the brass dolphin feet, the gilt, and the painted decoration create the flashy effect that characterizes much Baltimore furniture. Gilt acanthus leaves, winged thunderbolts, and stylized anthemia are standard Empire motifs. The top swivels open to expoe a red, velvet-lined storage compartment.
Baltimore Museum of Art.

Figure VIII–28
Library bookcase. Mahogany. Charleston, S.C. Ca. 1770.
The figure-eight fret pierced by diamonds in the frieze under the pediment is described in the account books of Thomas Elfe. On that basis, this piece is attributed to his shop. It is a modified version of the "Library Bookcase" illustrated in Chippendale's *Director*. The bookcase sits on bracket feet, whereas the Chippendale design calls for a base molding only. The Charleston piece stands taller, which is in harmony with the high ceilings found in houses there. The verticality of the piece is heightened by turning the inlaid ovals on end.
Museum of Early Southern Decorative Arts.

there is such a variety both in Pattern and Color that I wish you had mentioned the circumstance when you were in Charleston that you might have chosen the Pattern yourself."[4]

As was common throughout the South, wealthy planters and merchants obtained much of their furniture directly from England or New England. John Drayton wrote in 1802 that "before the American war, the citizens of Carolina were too much prejudiced in favor of British manners, customs, and knowledge, to imagine that elsewhere than in England anything of advantage could be obtained."[5] But they also patronized local workshops, which often copied the latest imported furniture. Richard Magrath advertised in 1772:

Carved Chairs, of the newest fashion, splat Backs, with hollow Seats and Commode-Fronts, of the same Pattern as those imported by Peter Manigault, Esq.— He is now making some hollow seated Chairs, the Seats to take in and out, and nearly the Pattern of another Set of Chairs imported by the same Gentleman, which have a light, airy Look, and make the Sitting easy beyond Expression.[6]

Even locally made products exhibited a strong English flavor. Instead of the out-of-date high chest, Charleston residents preferred the more stylish chest on chest. The use of full dustboards and a cross brace on the bottom of drawers also indicated English influence. Much of the work attributed to Thomas Elfe, Charleston's best-known cabinetmaker, closely follows the English precedents illustrated in Chippendale's design book (Figures VIII–28 and VIII–29). In the seven years before he died in 1775, Elfe produced over 1,500

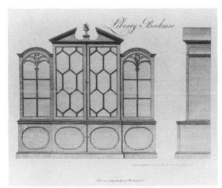

Figure VIII–29
Plate XCIII from the 1762 edition of Thomas Chippendale's *Director* showing the design source for the library bookcase made in Charleston (Figure VIII–28).

Figure VIII-30
Pembroke table. Mahogany with ash and poplar. Charleston, S.C. Ca. 1770–1780.

The lattice-like piercing on either side of the figure eights is derived from Chinese lattice designs. The pierced stretcher, related to a plate in Chippendale's *Director*, is screwed to blocks that have been tenoned into the legs. The C-scrolls surround the cutout skirt. Although the table displays impressive workmanship, the design elements do not relate well.
Charleston Museum, Charleston, S.C.

Figure VIII-31
Double chest with secretary drawer. Mahogany with cypress. Charleston, S.C. Ca. 1770.

The fretwork below the cornice, with figure eights pierced with diamonds, is attributed to Thomas Elfe. The stopped fluting in the upper and lower sections as well as on the pilasters flanking the prospect door is a feature often associated with Newport work but is derived from English precedents. The pilasters rest on double-ogee feet.
Museum of Early Southern Decorative Arts.

pieces of furniture, but only one piece, a chair, has been positively identified. Many pieces may have been destroyed by the periodic fires, hurricanes, and earthquakes that swept the city. However, based on entries in Elfe's account book of charges for figure-eight-shaped fretwork pierced with diamond shapes, a number of pieces with this motif are attributed to him (Figures VIII–30 and VIII–31).

Elfe and other Charleston cabinetmakers often used locally abundant cypress as a secondary wood. Massive four-poster bedsteads usually had removable headboards to allow full circulation of air around the bed during hot southern nights. The carvings of rice plants on bed posts were inspired by the locally grown crop (Figures VIII–32 and VIII–33).

Charleston furniture employed three-line string inlay with a black-stained wood flanked by two lighter woods. Details on bellfowers, sometimes of ivory, were scratched in, rather than shaded in by scorching, as was common in Baltimore and elsewhere (Figure VIII–1). By the Federal period, Charleston furniture came under the influence of New York, which replaced England as the city's major source of imported furniture.

The Albemarle Sound area, the most densely populated territory in North Carolina in the late 18th century, produced a group of elegant furniture (Figure VIII–34). As in most rural areas, the local craftsmen, such as cabinetmaker Thomas Sharrock, worked part-time as farmers (Figure VII–35). Sharrock owned 125 acres in the Roanoke River Valley by 1766. The Sharrock school of cabinetmakers, which included six of his sons, was

FIGURE VIII–32
Bed. Mahogany with yellow pine. Charleston, S.C. Ca. 1800.
This piece has many of the typical Charleston characteristics, including the detachable headboard and mahogany rails notched for slats. The carved posts with thin, pointed leaves; rice stalks; and fringed crescents at the base of the reeding are also typical. The inlaid cornice with finials marks the bed as an expensive one even when it was new.
Charleston Museum, Charleston, S.C.

FIGURE VIII–33
Detail of post of bed (Figure VIII–32) showing rice stalk carving.
Charleston Museum, Charleston, S.C.

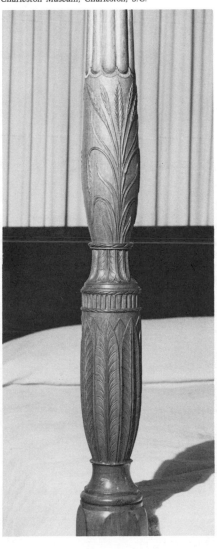

FIGURE VIII–34
Armchair. Mahogany with cypress. Edenton area of North Carolina. Ca. 1760.
The splat relates to designs of mid-18th-century English Chippendale chairs, but the rounded crest and symmetrical carving indicate a date at the end of the Queen Anne period. The cabriole rear leg ending in a hoof is also an English characteristic often seen on New York chairs. The ball and claw foot with little web between the talons and a knife-like back talon are characteristic of other chairs from northeastern North Carolina area.
Museum of Early Southern Decorative Arts.

characterized by a particular drawer construction. The drawer bottoms were beveled on three sides and nailed at the back. The beveled sides fit into grooves on the drawer sides and were reinforced by strips of wood fitted to the bevel (Figure VIII–36). Comb finials on desk and bookcases

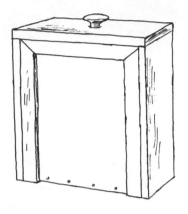

FIGURE VIII–35
Desk. Walnut with poplar and yellow pine. Albemarle area of North Carolina. Ca. 1760–1780.
The unusual center foot that appears on case furniture of Eastern Pennsylvania, and on some examples of Pennsylvania German chests, is found also on work by Thomas Sharrock and several other makers who lived in the Roanoke Valley area. It is likely that Sharrock was exposed to that technique— probably of German origin—during his apprenticeship in Norfolk County, Virginia. The brasses are replacements.
Private Collection.

FIGURE VIII–36 *(top, right)*
Drawer bottom construction typical of case furniture attributed to the Sharrock family of cabinetmakers. Strips of wood along each side and across the front serve as glue blocks to reinforce the bottom of the drawers.

FIGURE VIII–37
Corner cupboard. Walnut with pine. Northeastern North Carolina. Ca. 1790–1795.
This piece exhibits a number of characteristics found in Roanoke River Valley furniture and may have originated in a shop in either Halifax or Northampton county. These characteristics include the cutout flame cartouche; the whirling star rosettes with bone button centers; the black-stained shallow leaf and vine carving on the tympanum; the initials inlaid with putty; and the scrolls over the doors. The glass panes are backed with muslin, a common practice in the 18th century.
Historic Hope Plantation, Windsor, North Carolina.

and a third foot on fronts of chests were found on other furniture in the area attributed to the Sharrock school of cabinetmakers (Figure VIII–37).

CAROLINA PIEDMONT

Although the coastal areas of the Carolinas drew heavily on English sources for furniture, Piedmont furniture was influenced by Pennsylvania practices because many of the settlers there had come down the Great Wagon Road from Philadelphia. However, sophisticated Pennsylvania practices were often modified by the influence of local cabinetmakers such as Jesse Needham. Born in the northeast corner of North Carolina, Needham worked in that area from 1793 to 1839 and produced a large group of distinctive furniture that included many pieces with triangular pediments (Figure VIII–38).

Although the majority of the craftsmen in the North Carolina Piedmont came down the Shenandoah Valley from Pennsylvania, William Little arrived in Charleston directly from England and moved inland in 1800 to Sneedsborough, North Carolina, on the Pee Dee River. He also took up farming and owned a plantation with 112 slaves before he died in 1848. Little was one of the few Carolina Piedmont cabinetmakers to use mahogany. Other characteristics of his work included a distinctive capped tear-drop inlay and a four-petal flower inlay. His inlay was marked with neither shading nor scratching (Figures VIII-39 and VIII-40).

One of the best-known groups of rural Carolina Piedmont cabinetmakers was the Swisegood school, which was concentrated in the Yadkin Valley, 20 miles north of Salem. Like other rural makers, John Swisegood farmed a 400-acre tract until he moved west in 1848 to enjoy "cheap living." He died in Illinois in 1874. Swisegood produced a large group of furniture, and 40 pieces have been attributed to him. Swisegood's furniture is easily identified by the distinctive comma, barberpole, and vine inlays. He also employed the unusual method of attaching runners to the middle of the dustboards, which fit into a groove cut into the thick drawer bottoms (Figures VIII-41 and VIII-42).

James Gheen, who came from Pennsylvania to settle in the Yadkin River Valley, also owned a farm as well as a cabinetmaking shop. The extended bracket feet and one-piece board that supported both feet on each side of his case pieces typified his work.

Although the English tradition dominated the furniture of the Carolina Piedmont, a Moravian enclave in central North Carolina produced furniture with a strong German Baroque flavor. Moravian chairmakers typically attached drawer bottoms in the German fashion—with wooden pegs instead of nails. Their *schranks*, or wardrobes, resembled those made by Pennsylvania-German craftsmen, except that they did not come apart. Moravian cabinetmakers sometimes installed a double set of seat rails, as was the common German practice. In the prefer-

FIGURE VIII-38
High chest of drawers. Walnut with poplar. North Carolina Piedmont. Ca. 1795–1810.
But for the original Federal style brass pulls and the inlaid brass escutcheons around the keyholes, this chest could date from the Chippendale period. The configuration of drawers, with three across the top, over two, over four full drawers, was typical of high chests throughout the Shenandoah Valley and into Pennsylvania. The triangular, pitched pediment is an unusual embellishment on a number of pieces attributed to Jesse Needham.
Private Collection.

FIGURE VIII-39
Desk and bookcase. Mahogany with yellow pine and poplar. Sneedsborough, N.C. Ca. 1805.
The piece is marked WL, for William Little. It is in the full-blown Federal style with the exception of the straight bracket feet, which survive from the earlier Chippendale period. A flared French foot would have been more stylish.
Museum of Early Southern Decorative Arts.

FIGURE VIII-40
Pembroke table. Mahogany with poplar, yellow pine, and oak. Lower Piedmont area of North Carolina. Ca. 1805.
This table is attributed to William Little, largely on the basis of the four-petal inlay and the use of mahogany, which was uncommon on furniture made in the Piedmont of North Carolina. Other features found on pieces by Little include the triple bands of inlay on the skirt and outlining the table top and the low, inlaid cuff on the legs.
Museum of Early Southern Decorative Arts.

FIGURE VIII–41
Corner cupboard. Walnut with poplar. Davidson County, N.C. Ca. 1820.
The straight bracket foot of an earlier era is retained, but the delicately scrolled pediment and extensive inlay indicate an early 19th century date. The imaginative use of reeding substitutes for carving on the capitals of the pilasters and on the plinths beneath the central urn finial. The vine inlay topped with a tulip, the light and dark "barber pole" inlay, and the distinctive commas in the corners of the drawer are typical of work by John Swisegood.
Private Collection.

FIGURE VIII–42 *(above, right)*
Detail of inlay on corner cupboard (Figure VIII–41).
Private Collection.

FIGURE VIII–43
Dining table. Walnut with poplar, oak, and yellow pine. Salem, N.C. Ca. 1780–1790.
The straight, turned leg with pad foot and no disk characterizes many dropleaf and side tables made by the Moravians at Salem. A batten on the underside of the leaf prevents the top from warping. The technique is a holdover from 17th-century methods of construction.
Old Salem, Inc.

ence for Windsor rather than ladder-back chairs, which were more common in Germany, the Moravians betrayed the inroads of English culture.

In 1753, the Moravian Church purchased 100,000 acres in North Carolina and named the area Wachovia. By 1800, the 650 people in the area centered around the towns of Salem, Bethabara, and Bethania. Cabinetmakers like Joseph Bulitschek, Johannes Krause, and John Vogler came, not from rural villages in Germany, as did most of the Pennsylvania Germans, but from small towns. These artisans brought with them the 18th-century Baroque preferences common in the small towns of eastern Germany, in contrast to the rural folk tradition of the Pennsylvania Germans or the rococo pretenses of the German aristocracy in the larger cities. As a result, their furniture is not the painted folk art typical of the Pennsylvania German work. Usually lacking carving, inlay, or paint, the solid Moravian furniture appears stark (Figure VIII–43). Heavy Baroque turnings on bed posts as well as on table and chair stretchers were common.

Moravian desk and bookcases and corner cupboards show the

Baroque character best. Proportions of one to one in the height to width of both the upper and lower sections result in a massive appearance. The continuous ogee bonnet, or "dome top," is unbroken, in imitation of some 17th-century European architecture. Protruding stepped drawers on the interior of desks is also a Baroque characteristic often found on Pennsylvania work (Figure VIII–44). Corner cupboards have no feet and rest on base moldings. Arched doors and heavy muntins over a solid paneled door in the lower section complete the Baroque vocabulary.

Although, by the Federal period, imports from New York, New England, and Pennsylvania increased substantially, some furniture-making continued in the Piedmont. It was often characterized by a mixture of 18th-century construction techniques and new Federal decorations. Thomas Day, a freed black, employed a dozen people and used steam-powered equipment to produce furniture in the 1850s. He was one of the largest manufacturers in the state by 1850. Others, such as John W. Nelson of New Bern, imported furniture parts for local assembly. He advertised in 1830 that he had the following available:

Carved and Bronzed Sideboard Columns, Carved Sideboard Feet and Table Legs, Glass and Brass Sideboard and Bureau Knobs, Iron and brass Sideboard, Bureau and Portable Desk Locks, Together with a variety of other Mountings. [7]

By the end of the 19th century, furniture-making, centered around High Point, had again become a major industry in the Piedmont. Near cheap labor and abundant wood supplies and with good rail and highway connections, High Point was a natural location for large-scale furniture manufacturing. The High Point Furniture Company was established in 1889, and in the 1890s a number of other firms sprang up to make cheap furni-

ture to sell throughout the South, which was flush with income from the sale of cotton. By the mid-20th century, North Carolina was the largest producer of furniture in the country.

GEORGIA

Georgia had a population of only about 80,000 in 1790 compared to a combined total in the Carolinas of more than half a million. However, in the years after the Revolution, the state rapidly expanded. Most of the surviving Georgia furniture was made in this period and is a plain version of the Federal style. By the 1820s, Empire furniture, originating mainly in northern cabinet-making centers, was imported into Georgia.

Augusta, Georgia, was the southern terminus of the Great Wagon Road that ran down the Shenandoah Valley from Philadelphia to Salem, North Carolina, and into Georgia. As with many of the craft centers along this road, Georgia felt the influence of Philadelphia, even if only faintly. High chests of drawers with heavy cornice moldings and particular drawer configurations showed the Pennsylvania influence most clearly (Figure VIII–45). Georgia variation employed a scrolled pediment on the high chest form. Desk and bookcases and corner cupboards also had reeded corner columns but added an applied, scroll frieze around the top of the crest and in desk interiors.

Georgians preferred the typically southern pieces, including cellarets and huntboards. Few huntboards retain their original painted finish. Typical Georgia inlay of native holly, dogwood, or maple distinguished the finest cellarets. Similar inlay of fans, stars, vines, bellflowers, jonquils, tulips, and thistles enlivened other Georgia furniture, such as chests and tables. Barberpole and triple-line stringing was also commonly found. When used to outline drawer fronts, the string-

FIGURE VIII–44
Desk and bookcase. Cherry with yellow pine. Salem, N.C. Ca. 1795. **Made for Rudolph Christ, a Salem potter, this piece is attributed to Johannes Krause. The domed pediment, the fielded panels on the doors, and the wide cherry and mahogany cross-banding on the drawers and the side panels are more often found on furniture of the early 18th century than on furniture made during the neoclassical period. The use of veneer to cover the entire lower section is unusual on Moravian furniture.** *Old Salem, Inc.*

FIGURE VIII–45
High chest of drawers. Walnut with yellow pine and poplar. Athens, Georgia area. Ca. 1780–1790.
High chests with similar drawer configurations are found from Pennsylvania to the Georgia Piedmont. The simple cavetto cornice with a dental molding and the unique urn-shaped ogee bracket feet make this piece unique. The brasses have been replaced.
Stone Mountain Memorial Association, Georgia.

FIGURE VIII–46
Chest of drawers. Walnut with poplar. Athens, Georgia area. Ca. 1790.
The distinctive thistle inlay in maple and the intersecting stringing, which forms ovals, seem to be preferred by an unknown Georgian cabinetmaker. The cutout skirt and the unusual applied molding around the top relate to several pieces from the same area as on other southern pieces. The backboards are nailed on horizontally and are joined with tongue and groove joints.
High Museum of Art, Atlanta.

ing often had hollow round corners or intersecting lines forming pointed ovals (Figures VIII–46 and VIII–47.

Although the back country depended primarily on local craftsmen for their furniture, Savannah purchased much of its furniture, not from England but from American sources—mostly in Massachusetts and Rhode Island before the Revolution and from New York and Philadelphia after the war. New York City cabinetmakers captured a large share of the Savannah market because of the triangular trade that grew up after the Revolution. Cotton and other agricultural crops raised in the South were sent to New York for transshipment to England because only that city had the commercial contacts and financial resources to insure the shipments. With credit arrangements in New York, southern importers exchanged cotton for manufac-

tured goods, such as furniture. Similar trading relationships were established by northern businessmen in Charleston and other southern ports. In 1798, a typical advertisement by Joseph Meeks in a Georgia newspaper read: "Cabinetmaker from New-York informs the public that he has lately arrived, and has for sale, a handsome assortment of mahogany furniture and will dispose of it at very reasonable prices."[8] At the same time, furniture importers, often local cabinetmakers, sold boatloads of venture cargo from northern shops.

Much furniture was made in the south as well, since it was cheaper and more convenient than imported work. As in the rest of the south, relatively little furniture came from England. The seven and one-half percent tariff on furniture levied in 1789, a tax that increased over the years, and the tax on ships of

FIGURE VIII–47
Sideboard. Walnut with yellow pine and poplar. Athens, Georgia area. Ca. 1800.
Although made in the Federal style with the string inlay forming rectangles with hollow-round corners, this piece shows survivals from the 18th century in the reeded quarter-columns terminating in lamb's tongue molding top and bottom. The three-petaled flowers at each corner of the central door and the chamfered molding applied to the top are unusual features.
Private Collection.

FIGURE VIII–48
Sugar chest. Walnut with poplar. Kentucky. Ca. 1790–1810.
The curve of the cabriole legs continues into the skirt in the manner of many Louisiana armoires and tables. The identical skirt is found on several other chests found in the Lexington area attributed to Peter Tuttle. The playful inlay is easily laid out by a compass and straight edge. The hearts hanging on the vine are easier to design than flowers.
Private Collection.

foreign register landing in American ports, discouraged foreign imports. Only looking glasses, shaving stands, dressing boxes, and pianos were imported in great numbers, since these items were not readily available in America.

by water up the Mississippi and Ohio Rivers from New Orleans. Holly and dogwood were used for inlay, which was often characterized by wavy vines growing from tiny pots (Figures VIII–48, VIII–49, VIII–50, and VIII–51). The most sophisticated furniture

KENTUCKY AND TENNESSEE

Like Georgia, Kentucky had a relatively small population before the Revolution, but both states experienced a rapid increase after the war. Kentucky was settled by soldiers who had been granted land for their service in the Revolution. Most came from Maryland and Virginia, and Kentucky furniture often follows styles in those areas. Allen F. Macurdy, for example, advertised in Frankfort in 1810 that he had "just established a CABINET SHOP in Frankfort next door below the Bank. The foreman of the shop is a Mr. Simmons, lately from Baltimore—He has a complete knowledge of the newest fashions—and as a mechanic and a man of steady habits, he is inferior to none in Kentucky."[9]

Cabinetmakers selected local woods, such as walnut and cherry, until about 1810, when some mahogany began to arrive

FIGURE VIII–49 *(top)*
*Chamber table. Walnut with poplar.
Kentucky. Ca. 1800–1820.*
**A strong English influence is apparent
in this table with arched skirt flanked
by drawers. The design was rarely
found in America, but at least one
other similar table, probably by the
same maker, is known. The backsides
of legs are usually chamfered, but here,
the front side has also been cut away
to provide a surface for string inlay and
a single bellflower and diamond. The
inlay on the legs has little relationship
to the vines, circles, rectangles, quarter-
circles, and dots on the skirt and
drawers.**
Private Collection.

FIGURE VIII–50
*Card table. Cherry with poplar.
Kentucky. Ca. 1790–1810.*
**The plain, sturdy table with a skirt of
finely grained cherry is typical of much
southern furniture, but the concave
shaping on the skirt with triple bands
of light inlay on its edge gives this
piece great distinction.**
Private Collection.

was produced for the impressive Greek revival mansions that sprang up during the 1830s and 1840s. At the same time, Kentucky became accessible to ready-made furniture from Cincinnati and other midwestern cabinetmaking centers, and local cabinetmaking began to die out.

Although the eastern mountainous sections of the state made relatively crude pieces, the central blue-grass area, particularly around Lexington, produced more stylish furniture. Robert Wilson, recently arrived from England, set up his shop in Lexington about 1792 and produced distinctive furniture in the largest shop in town. A double band of inlay just under the tops of chests, reeded pilasters, and a characteristic turned foot that rested on a peg identified his work. Like other rural cabinetmakers, he supplemented cabinetmaking by farming a 300-acre tract 10 miles outside town.

Tennessee furniture is closely related to western Carolina, Virginia, and Kentucky styles. James B. Houston of Knoxville reminded his clients in 1810 that "the acquaintance he has formed in Philadelphia, Baltimore, and Norfolk, will enable him to obtain, at any time, patterns of the newest fashions."[10]

Tennessee furniture is constructed mostly of local woods, such as cherry and walnut, and only a small group of furniture has carving or inlay (Figures VIII–52, VIII–53, and VIII–54). A group of furniture from the Greeneville area of East Tennessee was characterized by inverted bellflower inlay and a rope and tassel motif. The sugar chest and the so-called "Jackson press"—a bookcase top with drawers and a cupboard section below—were particularly popular in Tennessee.

By the 1820s, large amounts of furniture from Baltimore, Philadelphia, Pittsburgh, and Cincinnati flooded the state. Local cabinetmakers struggled to survive. Powhatan Shumak of Greeneville advertised in 1824

that "Cabinet Furniture . . . shall not be excelled by any brought from the eastern cities or elsewhere."[11] But they simply could not compete with the large efficient factories that employed mass-production techniques and steam and water power to produce furniture that was still considerably cheaper than locally made products even when transportation costs were figured in.

Cabinetmakers outside the major population centers hung on longer than their urban counterparts, but they eventually succumbed to competition. N. Bell of Lebanon, Tennessee, complained in 1840 that he was "aware the good people of this town and county have generally thought that fine tasty furniture could not be had without going to Nashville or somewhere else at a distance—that superior Mahogany work was not executed here. . . ."[12] His complaint was echoed by craftsmen throughout the rural south.

LOUISIANA

Although English culture dominated most of the South, Louisiana was proud of its French heritage. Even though Louisiana was a Spanish colony from 1762 until just before France regained sovereignty over the territory in time to sell it to the United States in 1803, the majority of the settlers looked to France as their cultural model. The campeachy chair, named after the city of Campeche in Mexico, has a hammock-like bottom and is one of the few forms of Louisiana furniture to show the Spanish influence (Figure VIII–55).

Tables and armoires show the French influence quite clearly. The sprightly tables, with bold cabriole legs merging into the skirt, recall the Louis XV taste. Many Louisiana armoires followed French prototypes and had rounded cornice moldings, cham-

Figure VIII–51

Desk and bookcase. Walnut with poplar. Kentucky. Ca. 1790–1810.

The stylized vase and vine inlay, stars, and shells and the quarter-fans were very likely cut by the maker of the piece himself rather than purchased from an inlay specialist. The wide rail at the top of the bookcase door provides a large surface for the stylized shell inlay, which is derived from 18th-century carved shell motifs.

Private Collection.

Figure VIII–52

Corner cupboard. Walnut with poplar. East Tennessee. Ca. 1790–1810.

The proud inlaid roosters on the lower doors of the cupboard raise this piece above the ordinary and provide a vivid image that rural customers related to. The roosters are surrounded by the standard string inlay with hollow corners found on high-style Federal furniture.

University of Virginia.

Figure VIII–53

Detail of rooster on corner cupboard (Figure VIII–52).

University of Virginia.

Figure VIII–54

Miniature chest. Walnut with poplar. Tennessee. Ca. 1820.

The extraordinary two-story house with chimney is so unexpected that the unusual dots and diamond inlay are hardly noticed. The chest stands little more than 16 inches high.

Museum of Early Southern Decorative Arts.

179

FIGURE VIII–55
Campeachy chair. Mahogany and satinwood inlay. Alabama. Ca. 1810–1820.
The term is derived from the name of a major Mexican port on the Yucatan Peninsula. The chair form may have been based on Mexican examples from this area. In Louisiana, they were often called "bautac" (Bootjack) chairs. The beautiful play of curves is based on the Roman curule seat or Grecian stool. The half-circle crest, veneered and inlayed with a basket of flowers, repeats the line of the legs. The stretchers pierce the legs and are held by a wedge driven into them. The tops of the arms are also veneered and inlaid.
Private Collection.

FIGURE VIII–56
Armoire. Walnut with cypress. Louisiana. Ca. 1770–1800.
Many similar armoires with scrolled skirts, chamfered corners, and cabriole legs ending in hoof feet were owned by Louisiana residents in the late 18th century. The general form of the armoire is French, and the brass hinges and ornamental escutcheons were imported from France, but the woods are American. The false center panel and the lefthand door are joined and open as a unit. Scrawled in chalk on the bottom is "Glapion," probably the maker. The name of Celestin Glapion, a free black carpenter, appears in an 1838 New Orleans directory. The Glapion family has a long tradition of producing cabinetmakers, and the maker of the armoire may have been one of Celestin's ancestors. The cornice is a replacement.
Louisiana State Museum.

FIGURE VIII–57 *(far right)*
Armoire. Cherry with cypress. Louisiana. Dated 1815.
Provincial French elements, such as the armoire form itself, the shape of the feet, and the imported keyhole escutcheon, combine with unique inlays of vines, paterae, and stringing in geometric patterns. Fitting loosely into a joined frame, the wooden door panels and the sides expand and contract with changes of humidity without splitting. This method of construction, common in the 17th century, again became prevalent in the 19th century.
Mr. and Mrs. Chester A. Mehurin.

expanses of wood on large pieces (Figure VIII–57). Feet on armoires became either straight or turned, and a few elegant ones were fitted with brass balls like some found on New York furniture.

The slat-back chair, based on traditional French forms, was made in Louisiana throughout the 18th and early 19th centuries. Shaped slats and acorn finials added some style to an otherwise plain form. Upholstered furniture was seen rarely. C. C. Robin, who traveled through Louisiana in the early 19th century, offered one explanation: "I have found one or two upholsterers here, but they can do nothing. The climate is not compatible with this type of furniture"[13]

Beginning in the early 19th century, New Orleans became a major destination for New York furniture. From there, it was trans-shipped to customers all over the Mississippi River Valley. Francois Seignouret and Prudent Mallard dominated the fine furniture trade in New Orleans, and furniture with their shipping labels is still found in plantation homes throughout the lower Mississippi River basin (Figures VIII–58 and VIII–59). Both Seignouret and Mallard were born in

fered or rounded corners, hoof feet, decorative brass or iron hinges, and false central door panels (Figure VIII–56). Inside, armoires usually had three shelves and a row of three drawers at the mid-section. By the early 19th century, the Federal influence had straightened out the skirt and legs on many pieces, and the chamfered corners disappeared. Solid mahogany, cherry, or walnut gave way to veneered surfaces, but cypress continued to be used as a secondary wood. Inlaid paterae, ovals, vines, and bellflowers, often similar to Kentucky or Tennessee work, relieved the plain

France. Seignouret opened his shop in New Orleans in 1822 and sold furniture in the Empire and Rococo revival styles until 1853, when he returned to France. Mallard was employed for nine years in New York before coming to New Orleans, where he opened a furniture and upholstery business near Seignouret on Royal Street in 1838. He advertised furniture made-to-order and sold massive Empire, and Rococo and Renaissance revival furniture until his death in 1879. Both entrepreneurs specialized in high-quality furniture of mahogany and rosewood, or pal-

FIGURE VIII–58
Armchair. Mahogany. New York or Louisiana. Ca. 1840.
Called a "Seignouret chair" throughout the lower Mississippi Valley region, this form was found in the North as well. Scrolled arms have been added to an Empire gondola chair form. The lyre-shaped splat and plain, uncarved surfaces are characteristic of the late stages of the Empire style.
Louisiana State Museum.

FIGURE VIII–59
Sideboard. Mahogany. New York or Louisiana. Ca. 1821.
Andrew Jackson purchased this impressive sideboard from Francois Seignouret in New Orleans in 1821, who may have imported it from New York. Seignouret had served under Jackson in the Battle of New Orleans. The rarely found rounded pedestals are supported by richly carved lion's paw feet topped with cornucopias, acanthus leaves, and anthemia. At least one other sideboard with circular pedestals has been attributed to the New York cabinetmaker, George W. Miller.
The Ladies' Hermitage Association.

asandre, as it was called in New Orleans.[14]

TEXAS

Little stylish furniture was made in sparsely settled west Texas, which was populated by isolated ranchers and cowboys. However, soon after Mexico became independent from Spain in 1821, a wave of immigrants from the southern states as well as from Germany, France, and Scandinavia flowed into the Mexican provinces of east Texas. Settling in isolated enclaves, at least one local cabinetmaker in each county supplied the furniture needs of these small settlements. The difficulties of transporting furniture long distances ensured the survival of local artisans. When Sam Houston ordered furniture from Galveston for his home in Huntsville, he complained that "one of the bedposts [was] split at the top and roughly filled with wax or putty—no side rails, and further I have not looked at the thing."[15] The other pieces were in equally bad shape. For the privilege of receiving damaged, and in some cases unusable furniture, Houston had paid a steep 25 percent premium. Under such circumstances, the survival of the local craftsman was assured.

During their halcyon years from about 1840 to the 1880s, east Texas cabinetmakers, working in several different centers, turned out some highly individualistic furniture. Most imported furniture from New York and other eastern furniture-making centers entered Texas through the port of Galveston. Usually the furniture arrived "knocked down" in parts and was assembled by German cabinetmakers, who dominated the local market. Accessible only by wagon, the frontier town of Austin, established as the capital of Texas in 1839, depended on local cabinetmakers, such as J. W. England and Joseph W. Hannig, for most of its furniture. In the Piney Woods area along the Texas–Louisiana border, cabinetmakers had access to major stands of wood and benefited from a rapidly expanding population. To the north, along the border with the Oklahoma Territory, lay the Backland Prairie region, which was settled by families from the upper South, the North, and the Midwest. There, cabinetmakers used hardwood, such as oak, ash, and hickory. In this area, Willet Babcock and James W. Rodgers operated two of the largest steam-powered furniture factories in the state.

Germans dominated both the

FIGURE VIII–60
Bed. Walnut with pine. Texas. Ca. 1861.
This is the most impressive 19th-century Texas-made bed known. It was made by Johann Umland, a German immigrant who worked in Washington County from 1854 to 1880. Giant anthemia flank Gothic quatrefoils on the head and footboards, and the anthemia are repeated on the side rails. The severe posts and the massive cornice reflect the late Empire style, whereas the headboard with carved scrolls recalls the Rococo revival. The combination of stylistic ornament is typical of late Biedermeier furniture made in Germany in the mid-19th century.
Winedale Museum, Roundtop, Texas.

Brazos and Colorado River Valley areas east of Austin and the Hill country on the frontier, west of the capital. However, a sizeable number of settlers from the South and the Midwest brought with them an English heritage that diluted the German's culture. Johann and Heinrich Umland, who came to Texas in 1849 from Hamburg, Germany, were typical of the cabinetmakers in this area who produced stylish furniture with Renaissance and Gothic revival elements (Figure VIII–60).

On the other hand, the settlements in the Hill Country remained isolated, and their German culture remained strong until the 1870s. Typical German cabinetmakers there were Johann Martin Loefler and Johann Peter Tatsch, who settled in Fredericksburg in the 1850s, and Johann Michael Jahn, who worked in New Braunfels from its founding in 1845. Jahn's furniture reflected the strong influence of the Biedermeier style, a version of the Empire style popular in Germany before 1850. Jahn also hauled the first load of New York-made furniture into New Braunfels from the port of Indianola (near Port Lavaca) in 1866.

Some furniture produced in Galveston and Houston was as elegant as any from New York or Philadelphia, but most Texas furniture was primarily utilitarian. Mary Austin Holley observed that "tables are made by the house carpenter, which answer the purpose very well, where nobody has better, and the chief concern is to get something to put upon them. The maxim here is nothing for show, but all for use."[16] However, personal touches added by the cabinetmaker gave Texas furniture a distinctive character.

Walnut and pine, usually painted, were the most common woods. Wardrobes were as popular in Texas as they were in Louisiana (Figure VIII–61). Chairs were made in the klismos form for parlors and the Voltaire style for rockers. Ladder-backs usually had cowhide seats, and upholstered furniture, such as sofas, was rare (Figure VIII–62). The medieval German *Brettstuhl* form, with a plank back and legs dowled into a plank seat, was found occasionally. Many beds had the square posts typically found on rural German examples. Beds as well as chairs and tables often had the flaring, curved legs typical of the Biedermeier furniture. The center-pedestal table was also popular in Texas but was used primarily as a tea table. Pie safes, usually called tin or wire safes, assumed a distinctive local form with their open panels on the doors and sides. The bottom held drawers and a cupboard section (Figure VIII–63).

FIGURE VIII–61
Wardrobe. Cypress. Texas. Ca. 1870.
This piece was owned by Andreas Haby, an early settler of Castroville, Texas. Family tradition holds that this wardrobe was made by a carpenter named Bachmann who was employed to add a new wing to the Haby house. The Gothic arches on the doors are repeated on either side of the skirt below the doors.
Mr. Robert Quill Johnson.

FIGURE VIII–62
Sofa. Oak with pine. Texas. Ca. 1860.
Christofer Friderich Carl Steinhagen made this fascinating sofa for his own home in Anderson, Texas. The two fish that lie on the crest have no known precedents, but the swans' necks that adorn the ends of the sofa match similar ones on a rocker that was part of Steinhagen's parlor set. The shallow, acanthus leaf carving on the skirt is typical of other work by Steinhagen.
Winedale Museum, Round Top, Texas.

FIGURE VIII–63
Pie safe. Pine. Texas. Ca. 1880.
The configuration of a ventilated upper section for food storage, a lower section with doors, and a long drawer dividing the two parts is typical of Texas pie safes. The use of two vertical, beveled panels to form the back is also a typical construction technique found on Texas case furniture.
Winedale Museum, Round Top, Texas.

By the 1880s, railroads, which began to tie the state together after the Civil War, overcame the difficulties of transportation, and Texans turned to Grand Rapids companies and other large manufacturers for inexpensive furniture. Local cabinetmakers struggled to compete. Some mechanized their small shops with such equipment as mortising machines, but to little avail. Most eventually succumbed to the efficiency of the large factory. As transportation improved, local craftsmen lost their last advantage.

The transportation revolution reached Texas later than most of the south. As early as the 18th century, southern cabinetmakers in cities located along the coast and on major rivers felt the competition of northern centers of furniture-making. Other sections of the south faced the same competition as railroads and highways began to push into the interior in the years before the Civil War. Even the disruption of wartime did not delay for long the demise of local cabinet shops, which disappeared in the face of competition from the efficient factories and improved transportation available after the Civil War.

NOTES

1. Helen Comstock, "Southern Furniture Since 1952," *The Magazine Antiques* 91 (January 1967): 102.

2. Ann W. Dibble, "Fredericksburg–Falmouth Chairs in the Chippendale Style," *Journal of Early Southern Decorative Arts* 4 (May 1978): 1–24. Wallace B. Gusler, *Furniture of Williamsburg and Eastern Virginia, 1710–1790* (Richmond: Virginia Museum, 1979), pp. 36–38 and 56 attributes these chairs to Williamsburg but admits that "it is entirely possible, if not probable, that some production of these chairs occurred in that area. . . ."

3. George Hepplewhite, *The Cabinet-Maker and Upholsterer's Guide* (New York: Dover Publications, Inc., 1969), p. 2.

4. E. Milby Burton, *Charleston Furniture, 1700–1825* (Columbia, S.C.: University of South Carolina Press, 1955), pp. 18–19.

5. Burton, *Charleston Furniture*, p. 14.

6. Jan Garrett Hind, *The Museum of Early Southern Decorative Arts* (Winston-Salem, N.C.: Old Salem, Inc., 1979), pp. 9–10.

7. Robert E. Winters, Jr., ed., *North Carolina Furniture, 1700–1900* (Raleigh, N.C.: North Carolina Museum of History Associates, 1977), p. 47.

8. Katharine Wood Gross, "The Sources of Furniture Sold in Savannah 1789–1815," (Master's Thesis, University of Delaware, 1967), p. 36.

9. Hind, *Museum of Early Southern Decorative Arts*, p. 14.

10. Ellen Beasley, "Tennessee Furniture and Its Makers," *The Magazine Antiques* 100 (September 1971): 429.

11. Beasley, "Tennessee Furniture," p. 430.

12. Beasley, "Tennessee Furniture," p. 431.

13. Jessie J. Poesch, *Early Furniture of Louisiana, 1750–1830* (New Orleans: The Louisiana State Museum, 1972), p. 53.

14. According to Vaughn L. Glasgow, Curator of the Louisiana State Museum in New Orleans, the latest research indicates that Seignouret and Mallard imported most, if not all, of their furniture rather than making it themselves. The numerous labels showing their names on furniture throughout the Mississippi Delta were probably shipping labels. William Seale, however, has discovered one Mallard advertisement that states Mallard manufactured furniture.

15. Lonn Taylor and David B. Warren, *Texas Furniture: The Cabinetmakers and Their Work, 1840–1880* (Austin: University of Texas Press, 1975), p. 10.

16. Taylor and Warren, *Texas Furniture*, p. 8.

IX

FURNITURE OF THE FOLK:
SHAKER AND
PENNSYLVANIA GERMAN

FIGURE IX–1
Schrank. *Walnut. Pennsylvania. Dated 1779.*
About 20 pieces of Pennsylvania German furniture have been found with the same sulfur inlay that enlivens this wardrobe. Similar decorations and construction characteristics found on a chest in the Smithsonian Institution (Figure IX–13) and the Emanuel Herr wardrobe probably indicate that these three were produced in the same shop. The use of panels to form the doors and sides as well as for decoration indicates a surviving medieval tradition. The pinwheel motif on the bottom of the doors resembles similar designs on the rosettes of some Connecticut high chests. As with most *schranks*, this massive piece disassembles for ease of movement.
Philadelphia Museum of Art.

COUNTRY CABINETMAKERS WORKED IN relative isolation throughout rural America in the 18th and early 19th centuries. Although some of them interacted to form schools of cabinetmaking, their sphere of influence was usually confined to one town. However, two groups of people living in America's hinterland developed distinctive furniture styles even though their members were more widely scattered. In the case of the Shakers, their common religious beliefs and the leadership of a central ministry resulted in a relatively uniform Shaker style. The Pennsylvania Germans drew on a common cultural heritage to produce a large group of related furniture. Both peoples fell under the influence of the dominant English tradition in America. Ultimately, both lost their identity as their isolation broke down and as furniture became easier to obtain from commercial sources rather than from local craftsmen.

PENNSYLVANIA GERMANS AND THEIR FURNITURE

Although both Shaker and Pennsylvania-German furniture show the influence of the English tradition of cabinetmaking in their basic forms, Shaker furniture developed its own particular character independent of a European heritage. On the other hand, the Pennsylvania Germans, coming from rural areas far removed from the major German style centers, brought with them a largely medieval tradition in furniture design. Those who settled in rural parts of Pennsylvania, isolated from the major American style centers, carried on that tradition into the 19th century.

The Germans who settled in the major American cities rapidly became Anglicized, and their furniture differed only subtly from that of their English brethren. Certain Germanic techniques, such as the use of pegs to attach drawer bottoms and the cutouts beneath the arms of ladder-back chairs, contribute to the particular regional flavor of Pennsylvania furniture. Only the Germans who settled in rural areas, particularly Pennsylvania, retained their distinctive culture for a long period.

The majority of the Pennsylvania Germans came from the upper Rhine River Valley region of southern Germany and neighboring Switzerland. During Europe's Thirty Years War in the first half of the 17th century, French and German armies fought over this rich farm region, which included the Palatinate. The war devastated the area and made the poor German peasants susceptible to the glow-

FIGURE IX–2

Plank chair. Walnut and oak. Pennsylvania. Dated 1770.

Chairs were rare in rural Pennsylvania German homes; benches, either free-standing or built-in, were more common. The plank chair is derived directly from German prototypes. The date and initials, probably those of the original owner, are carved into the back along with a deer. The stick legs pierce the seat and are secured with wedges in the manner of Windsor chairs.

Courtesy, The Henry Francis du Pont Winterthur Museum.

FIGURE IX–3

Schrank. *Walnut. Pennsylvania. Dated 1781.*

This wardrobe was found in the Hottenstein home near Kutztown, Pennsylvania. The inlaid initials are those of David Hottenstein. The grasshopper and the flower buds inlaid on the central panel are similar to inlay on a chest made by the same craftsman for Maria Kutz in 1783. The heavy architectural pediment, the rounded arches and panels in the doors, and the ball feet are all commonly found in 17th- and early 18th-century furniture. These techniques survived in the conservative communities of rural Pennsylvania Germans.

Courtesy, The Henry Francis du Pont Winterthur Museum.

ing tales of land agents from America, mainly those from William Penn's land grant of Pennsylvania. Others, such as the Lutherans, Moravians, Amish, Mennonites, and Schwenkfelders, came to America to escape religious persecution. Beginning with the founding of Germantown outside Philadelphia in 1683, the number of German immigrants to Pennsylvania swelled to an estimated 75,000 before the Revolution. Settling primarily in Lancaster, Berks, Chester, and Bucks counties, they made up about one-third of the population of the state. Others streamed down the Great Wagon Road that traversed the Shenandoah Valley and led to the Georgia and North Carolina Piedmont.

Chairs, Wardrobes, and Cupboards

Few pieces of Pennsylvania-German furniture made before the middle of the 18th century have survived. The poor immigrants brought most of their belongings with them packed in chests. These chests served as seats and tables as well as stor-

age containers, and most of the first generation of immigrants could afford little else. By the mid-18th century, however, a new generation had become established and could afford to replace their old chests with locally made furniture. The distinctive forms of Pennsylvania-German furniture reflected their medieval origins. Chairs were rare, since Pennsylvania Germans often stood while they ate or sat on built-in benches. The few chairs that were used took the medieval form and had stick legs and a plank seat (Figure IX–2). Laboring from dawn to dusk, the German farmer found little time for lounging in chairs. The Pennsylvania German *schrank*, or wardrobe, was a traditional European form. Revealing its medieval origins in its heaviness, the *schrank* was often made to be disassembled for ease of movement (Figures IX–1, IX–3, and IX–4). The chest, dating from classical times, had been replaced by the chest of drawers early in the 18th century in most stylish English homes, but it remained one of the most common pieces of furniture in rural Pennsylvania-German houses. Although it was not a medieval form, the cupboard, which appeared in Pennsylvania-German homes early in the 19th century, reflected its isolation from the mainstream of furniture styles (Figure IX–5). Cupboards with glass doors in the upper section were no longer considered stylish in most urban homes.

Chests

Although the *schrank* was used by the whole family, the chest belonged to one individual. It was the most common form of Pennsylvania-German furniture. Fathers usually gave chests to sons and daughters when they were about the age of 14 and began to need a place to store their personal belongings (Figure IX–6). Girls usually took the chests, often filled with their trousseaux, to their new households after their marriages. However, the terms dower or dowry chest are misleading, since men owned chests as well.

The chest was usually kept in a bedchamber and was used to store clothes. However, on the long voyage across the Atlantic, they often held a several weeks' supply of food as well as clothing. The till, which was usually built into one end of the chest, frequently contained money. Socks or other small items were sometimes tied to a string and tacked to the underside of the lid so they could be easily found. Often, the lid served as a frame for *fraktur*, or decorated documents, such as birth and baptismal certificates.

The dimensions of many chests were surprisingly close to a clothes chest illustrated in Chippendale's *Director*, which measured 24 inches deep, and 48 inches long (Figure IX–7). Sometimes the drawer section projected beyond the ends of the chest in the English manner, a technique not seen on German chests. Chests rested on straight bracket feet or, more rarely, on turned or ogee feet. Some chests sat on runners that often left no trace of their presence when they became separated from the chest. A few had no feet at all.

The four sides of the chests were dovetailed together at the corners. On the rare chests with

FIGURE IX–4
Schrank. *Painted wood. Pennsylvania. Ca. 1775–1800.*
The motif of flowers sprouting from pots is common on many Pennsylvania-German chests. Painted designs other than graining on *schranks* are rare. This composition is particularly interesting in that each panel shows a different flower.
Joe Kindig III.

FIGURE IX–5 *(right)*
Cupboard. Pine. Mahantango Valley, Pennsylvania. Dated 1830.
The inscription, "Concortia," does not indicate a guild of craftsmen, as once thought, but is taken from a popular broadside poem about a maiden named Concordia. The angels below the inscription were copied from an identical one that adorns the broadside. The piece is painted ochre with red graining. The base moldings, corner columns, and central panel in the upper section are a dark blue-green. The upper doors are ivory, and the panels on the lower section are a pale salmon. The angels, birds, and tulips are painted blue, yellow, salmon, and red. The ogee feet and the corner columns are commonly found on 18th-century Philadelphia furniture, but the 1830 date shows the survival of these elements in rural areas well into the 19th century.
The Philadelphia Museum of Art.

FIGURE IX–6
Chest. Walnut. Virginia. Dated 1801.
This unusual chest was made by Godfrey Wilkin for Jacob Wilkin in Hardy County, Virginia, now part of West Virginia. In sulfur inlay, Wilkin has written "Read thes up" and "thes down." On either end are inlaid the words, "Wel Don." The front is hinged above the drawers and lets down to rest on slides similar to those found on slant-front desks. Drawers are built into the interior.
Greenfield Village and Henry Ford Museum.

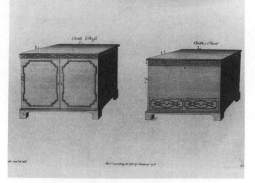

FIGURE IX–7
Plate CXXVI from Chippendale's 1762 edition of the *Director*. The same design appeared in the first edition of 1754. The dimensions of Chippendale's clothes chest are similar to the dimensions of most Pennsylvania-German chests of the 18th and early 19th centuries.

FIGURE IX–8 *(top, right)*
Chest. Tulipwood. Pennsylvania. Dated 1764.
In a rarely found feature, the bottom board projects to form a base molding. The construction of the chest is very much in the European manner, but wood analysis indicates the presence of American woods. The open top reveals the iron strap hinges and a till with a lid that holds up the top when the lid is open. Thin boards have been applied to the face of the chest to create the arched panels.
Smithsonian Institution Photo No. 75–13605.

FIGURE IX–9 *(right, center)*
Detail of original crab lock with engraved design on the back (Figure IX–8). The lock is attached with hand-wrought rose-head nails.
Smithsonian Institution Photo No. 75–13604.

FIGURE IX–10
Chest. Tulipwood. Berks County, Pa. Ca. 1750–1800.
The paneled top relates to 18th century German shop practices, but the use of American tulipwood indicates an American origin. The notched corners of the panels on the chest are also a traditional German feature and are found on the window frames of the Golden Plough Tavern in York, Pennsylvania.
Smithsonian Institution. Photo No. 80–48.

arcaded facades found in the Lancaster area, five pieces of wood were applied to the front of the chest. A board with three semicircles formed the top of the three arches, and four vertical strips divided the arches (Figure IX–8). The form, based on European prototypes, often had the ogee foot popular on English and German high-style furniture. Rare in the 18th century, the form fell completely out of favor in America by the beginning of the 19th century.

The forged-iron strap hinges often provided unexpected interest on the interior of chests. These straps usually terminated in tiny triangles, but sometimes they were fashioned into flowers, hearts, or tulips. File marks on the edges of the metal strips indicate the early date of forged hinges, whereas later hinges were often cut out of sheet metal. Butt hinges became common after 1820. The crab lock, with two arms closing on an arrow-shaped hasp, usually secured the chest, but the box lock with a horizontal bar was seen as early as the 1740s (Figure IX–9). Locks with bars sliding vertically into a slot replaced the crab lock by the 1820s. Drawer pulls and carrying handles were either forged locally or pur-

FIGURE IX–11
Chest. Walnut. Pennsylvania. Dated 1741.
This is the earliest dated Pennsylvania-German chest. The inlaid initials ITI may stand for Isaac Taylor of Gap in Lancaster County. The herringbone inlay confirms the early date in the Queen Anne period when much high style English furniture had similar embellishments. However, the stylized floral and animal forms are outside the English tradition.
Courtesy, The Henry Francis du Pont Winterthur Museum.

chased from a merchant who had imported them from England. By the second quarter of the 19th century, wooden or even glass knobs were common.

American-made chests were invariably constructed with one-board tops of tulip poplar. Paneled or domed tops, which are typical on European chests, are rarely found in America (Figure IX–10). Likewise, oak was rarely used, since it was hard to work, and its coarse grain did not lend itself to painting. Walnut, usually left unpainted and sometimes enhanced by inlay, was

found occasionally (Figure IX–11).

Carving was seldom used on Pennsylvania-German furniture. The North Germans were known for their carving, but painted furniture was preferred in the south of Germany. Since the majority of the Pennsylvania Germans came from the south, the tradition of painted furniture predominated (Figure IX–12). Only a few pieces, such as the extraordinary *schrank* made for George Huber in 1779, display carving. In addition to carving, the Huber *schrank* is also decorated with a profusion of inlaid

FIGURE IX–12
Chest. Pine. Lebanon or Berks County, Pa. Ca. 1795.
Realistic flower buds combine with geometric designs on the vines springing from the pots. Flowers even sprout from the top of the painted panels. Hearts, another common Pennsylvania-German motif, rise from each front corner of the chest. The chest rests on the straight bracket feet commonly found on other Chippendale furniture of the period.
Virginia Museum.

vines, crowns, and swastikas— the ancient good-luck symbol. Instead of painstakingly cutting out tiny bits of inlay to set into the wood, the cabinetmaker filled his intaglio carving with molten sulfur (Figure IX–13). The technique was largely confined to the Lancaster area. Holly, box, and other locally available wood were also cut for inlay, and there was an occasional use of pewter.

Painted Furniture

But the great glories of Pennsylvania-German furniture were the painted creations—mostly chests but also small numbers of chairs, chests of drawers, cupboards, desks, and clock cases. The tradition of painting furniture reached its height in the late 18th and early 19th century and coincided with a similar fashion in Germany. However, the tradition died out in America by the 1830s because of the breakdown of isolation and the upward mobility of middle-class Americans of German origin. These factors were not as strong in Europe, so the folk tradition persisted longer there. By the 1830s, graining to imitate veneer took the place of painted flowers, hearts, and birds. Although a few decorators continued to paint in the typical Pennsylvania-German manner into the 20th century, the tradition had largely disappeared by mid-century, when factory-made furniture became available.

Chests were usually made by farmers and decorated by the maker or a member of his family. They selected from a bright palette of red, blue, green, brown, black, white, and orange. They used powdered paints in an oil vehicle until milk-based paints came into use after 1800. Ready-mixed paints were not marketed until the middle of the 19th century. Most painters scribed the design into the wood before applying the decoration. Some 18th- as well as 19th-century chests were decorated by using wooden blocks with the design carved in them. Other painters used templates to achieve the decoration. Stencils were rarely used until the 1820s. A few chests were decorated in the sgraffito technique, in which the design was scraped into the top coat of paint, leaving the different-colored base coat showing through.

Decorations included birds, hearts, lions, mermaids, and geometric shapes. So-called hex signs, easily laid out with a compass and ruler, were quite common (Figure IX–14). However, they had no mystical significance. The Pennsylvania Germans did have a strong belief in the supernatural, and in the late 17th century, witch trials were held in Pennsylvania, although no one was executed, as some were in Salem, Massachusetts. Pennsylvania Germans protected their barns from evil spirits, not by hex signs but by special configurations of nails. The hex-sign story probably originated in an article written in the 1920s by a Philadelphia newspaper reporter, who either completely fabricated it or was gulled by the tall tales of the Pennsylvania Germans themselves.[1]

Decorators copied most of the designs from familiar models. Several examples of women's heads have been traced to pictures of Martha Washington. Horse and riders recall the German nobility or are portrayals of the 18th-century Prussian King Frederick the Great himself. Horsemen depicted on some chests are dressed in uniforms of the American Revolution. The unicorn, found on a number of chests, is copied from the creature on the British or the Pennsylvania coat-of-arms. Unicorns were usually depicted reared up on a tulip stem (Figure IX–15).

FIGURE IX–14
Chest. Pine and tulipwood. Pennsylvania, Ca. 1800–1840.
The so-called hex signs were one of the most common decorations on Pennsylvania German chests because of the ease of executing them with compass and ruler. Similar designs were used on barns as decoration, but they had no mystical significance. The inverted hearts, also a common motif that suggests tulip bulbs, flank the two drawers. The reeding is quite unusual on Pennsylvania German chests.
Courtesy, The Henry Francis Du Pont Winterthur Museum.

FIGURE IX–15
Chest. Soft-wood. Pennsylvania. Dated 1784.
The owner, Heinrich Faust, and the date are inscribed on the lid. The vivid reds and blues of the paint are still bright after nearly 200 years. Only the top, which served as a bench and table, shows substantial wear. The unicorns assume their usual position, reared up against a stem.
Reading Public Museum and Art Gallery.

When the lion and the unicorn fought, the lion won by tricking the unicorn into sticking his horn into a tree. The colorful tulip, which the German immigrants brought with them to Pennsylvania, provided another common motif for decorators.

Many of the motifs had symbolic significance. However, few decorators or their customers, who had little formal education and in most cases could neither read nor write, were familiar with the literary symbolism. Rather, they simply copied what was familiar and pleasing to them. In the case of the mermaid, however, the decorator might well have known the German folk tale surrounding the variation of the stork story in which the midwife received a newborn child from a mermaid who lived in a river or spring (Figure IX–16).

THREE SCHOOLS OF CABINETWORK

Of the hundreds of Pennsylvania-German cabinetmakers who produced chests, fewer than a dozen are known. A group of craftsmen in the Jonestown area of Dauphin (now Lebanon County) routinely scratched their signatures into the paint.

The names of Christian Selzer or his son John appear on many chests made in that area in the late 18th and early 19th century. Two or three panels showing vases of flowers characterize the decoration on their chests (Figure IX–17). In one of the most unusual painted designs, a chest by Christian Selzer has a genie-like woman springing from the vase of flowers. The brothers, John and Peter Rank, produced similar designs in the area.

Although German immigrants were concentrated largely in Pennsylvania, other pockets lived in Maryland, Virginia, North Carolina, and Ohio (Figure IX–6). The Moravians who settled in North Carolina did not practice the art of painting furniture. However, other Germans who settled in the valley of Virginia enjoyed painted furniture just as did their brethren in Pennsylvania. Johannes Spitler, who lived near Massanutten Mountain in the Shenandoah Valley, typified these rural farmers who produced extraordinary painted chests. He favored painted geometric designs with stags, birds, flowers, and upside-down hearts painted in red and black on a blue ground. Many of his designs were inspired by the work of a local *fraktur* artist (Figure IX–18). Spitler moved to

FIGURE IX–17
Chest. Pine. Dauphin County, Pa. Dated 1794.
This chest is signed and dated on the right and left panels by John Selzer, the son of Christian. The pots with flowers springing from them were a common motif on chests decorated by this family of craftsmen.
Baltimore Museum of Art.

Ohio about 1805 and probably continued to paint similar furniture there.

A group of furniture from the Mahantango Valley in central Pennsylvania represents one of the last significant flowerings of the Pennsylvania-German tradition of painted furniture. German immigrants settled the area in the 1770s, but the earliest documented piece of furniture from there is dated 1798 and the latest 1834. A number of painters, rather than just one, produced the distinctive stenciled figures and flowers on brightly painted grounds. A desk, probably made for Jacob Masser, is the best-known example in this group, which included chests, chests of drawers, cupboards, and desks. These pieces are ornamented with birds, trees, fans, flowers, hearts, horses, and stars (Figures IX–5 and IX–19).

THE SHAKERS

At the same time that the Pennsylvania-German culture, isolated in rural areas, such as the Mahantango Valley, began to lose its distinctiveness under the influence of the dominant English culture, the Shakers were at the peak of their prosperity. The United Society of Believers in the First and Second Appearing of Christ—or Believers, as they called themselves—sprang theologically from the French

FIGURE IX–18
Tall case clock. Yellow pine. Shenandoah County, Va. Dated 1800.
The initials, JSP, painted on the door are probably those of Johannes Spitler, whose name appears on another tall case clock with related decoration. Predominately red, blue, and white, the decorations represent a leaping deer, love birds, inverted hearts, and a tulip springing from a geometrical design. The motifs are related to *fraktur* by Jacob Strickler, who lived near Spitler in the Shenandoah Valley. In an unusual technique, the carved rosettes on the bonnet of the case are tacked to wooden cylinders that are attached to the tips of the scrolls on either side of the turned wooden finial.
Collection of Abby Aldrich Rockefeller Folk Art Center, Williamsburg, Virginia.

Camisards, who prophesied the coming of an earthly millennium. Some members of the sect had fled to England in the late 17th century in order to escape persecution. The group attracted many English Quakers, including James and Jane Wardley, who

Figure IX–19

Desk. Tulipwood. Mahantango Valley. Dated 1834.

The desk was made for Jacob Maser, whose name appears above the top two drawers. The red and yellow birds, flowers, horses, and geometric shapes, applied with stencils or freehand to a green ground, were derived from fraktur. The decoration is typical of the last flowering of the Pennsylvania-German tradition in the Mahantango Valley. The painted fans in the corners of rectangles, which outline the drawers, the lid, and the sides, suggest inlay of the Federal period, but the turned feet and paneled sides confirm the later date of 1834. Subtle differences on the more than three dozen related pieces from the Mahantango Valley suggest a number of decorators for this group of furniture.

Courtesy, The Henry Francis du Pont Winterthur Museum.

joined the sect in 1747. The Wardleys soon became the leaders of the group and preached that Christ's second coming was at hand.

Raised in the Manchester slums, Ann Lee turned to the Wardley group in 1758. Periodically persecuted even in England, the Shakers were often imprisoned for their beliefs. While in prison for disturbing the Sabbath with dancing and chanting, Ann received a vision that the Christ spirit had returned to earth through her. When she was released, the group recognized her as their leader. In a later vision, she was called to lead a small band to the New World. Mother Ann and eight followers set out for America on the ship *Mariah* in 1774. John Hocknell, who had financed the trip to America, also purchased land for the first set-

tlement at Niskayuna (Watervliet) near Albany, New York.

Benefiting from the religious revivals that swept America in the late 18th and early 19th centuries, the little band of Shakers converted large groups in nearby New Lebanon, New York, and in Hancock, Massachusetts. Other centers were established in Enfield, Connecticut; Canterbury and Enfield, New Hampshire; Sabbathday Lake, Gorham, and Alfred, Maine; and Tyringham, Harvard, and Shirley, Massachusetts. When Mother Ann died in 1784, her work was carried on by James Whittaker and, after his death in 1787, by the converted Baptist preacher, Joseph Meacham. Under these two dynamic leaders, the Shakers gathered together into communal families, and by 1794, eleven different communities prospered in New England. A central ministry at

New Lebanon, renamed Mount Lebanon in 1861, coordinated the work of all the rest.

To fulfill another prophecy of Mother Ann, the elders at New Lebanon sent missionaries out west to take advantage of the religious revival sweeping that area in 1805. John Meacham, Benjamin Youngs, and Issachar Bates were the first of several missionaries sent to establish communities, including Pleasant Hill and South Union in Kentucky and Union Village in Ohio. A settlement at Busro, Indiana, suffered Indian raids and malaria and was abandoned in 1827.

Shaker Furniture

Before 1800, little distinctly Shaker furniture was constructed. Craftsmen newly converted to Shakerism brought with them the standard designs of the World, as the Shakers called outsiders (Figure IX–20). It was a time of experimentation in which worldly designs were adapted to the Shaker ethic. The majority of Shaker furniture was produced between 1800 and 1860. After the Civil War, furniture production ceased almost entirely in the western communities, which rapidly lost population. Some furniture was made for Shaker communities in New England, but the largest production was at Mount Lebanon and was intended mostly for sale to the world.

In its simplicity, utility, and communal character, Shaker furniture epitomized the Shaker philosophy. The simplicity in furniture derived in part from the humble background of most members. Even before they became Shakers, they had been trained to make simple furniture. The early converts worked hard enough for the simple things and had no time to waste on frills. Simplicity was reflected not only in their furniture but in their architecture, their dress, their food, and even their theology. In the 1790s, Joseph Meach-

am set the tone for Shaker work when he enjoined the deacons to ensure that "all work done, or things made in the Church for their own use ought to be faithfully and well done, but plain and without superfluity."[2] These ideals were reiterated in the *Millennial Laws*, which evolved in the second quarter of the 19th century. These laws cautioned against manufacturing articles "which are superfluously wrought, and which would have a tendency to feed the pride and vanity of man...."[3] In a strict interpretation of the laws, the elders of New Lebanon directed Brother David Bowley to remove brass knobs, which were "considered superfluous," and replace them with wooden ones.

Related to simplicity was a desire for utility. A half-century before Louis Sullivan declared the essence of the modern style in his famous statement in 1891, "Form ever follows function," the Shakers had written that "any thing may, with strict propriety, be called perfect which perfectly answers the purpose for which it was designed." The Shakers believed that "beauty rests on utility. That which has in itself the highest use possesses the greatest beauty."[4] On this basis, highboys, lowboys, upholstered chairs, tea tables, cabriole legs, canopy beds, splat-back chairs, card tables, daybeds, and sofas were rejected

Figure IX–20
Candlestand. Painted wood. Alfred, Maine. Ca. 1820–1830.
The use of paint, red over black, indicates an early date. The table also has the characteristic snake foot of some early 19th-century tables of the World. Shaker craftsmen have completely stripped the baluster of the typical turnings of the World, but the legs have not yet taken on the spider-like appearance of later tables derived from Federal examples.
Richard Klank.

as not being useful. The Shakers, struggling to make a living in their early years in America, could not afford the luxury of useless ornament, and the tradition, if not the necessity, carried over into their more prosperous times in the 19th century. Besides practical considerations was the fear that useless ornament might encourage pride. Elder Frederick Evans of Mount Lebanon commented in 1875 that "the divine man has no right to waste money upon what you would call beauty, in his house or his daily life, while there are people living in misery."[5] The Shaker obsession with cleanliness also contributed to designs of simple, unadorned surfaces. Mother Ann, raised in the filthy slums, said, "Be neat and clean: for no unclean thing can enter heaven."[6] Dust and dirt could not accumulate on smooth unadorned surfaces. Drawers everywhere—in tables, under seats, built into walls—provided a place for everything (Figure IX–21).

Furniture of the Shakers also reflected the communal nature of their sect. Shakers adapted the medieval trestle table to seat up to 20 persons. It was lightened and the medial stretcher was placed up under the top to give more leg room (Figure IX–22). Sewing stands, ironing tables, and desks were designed to accommodate several workers. Chests of drawers and cupboards in large sizes served several persons.

Shaker furniture and, indeed, all their products exhibited a high standard of craftsmanship. From a lowly grain scoop used in a barn to a desk for the trustees' house, craftsmanship was of the highest quality. Mother Ann admonished, "Do all your work as though you had a thousand years to live on earth, and as you would if you knew you must die tomorrow."[7] Not only did excellent workmanship improve utility, but it was also a form of worship. Shakers built to last because they believed that their communities would survive forever. They believed that the millennium had come, so they worked to produce everything worthy of it. Their high standard of workmanship brought a premium in the marketplace of the World. Whether he bought seeds, chairs, or herbs, a customer could be sure of an excellent product.

Most Shaker furniture, even though made in widely scattered communities, exhibited a similarity of spirit. Some successful designs were passed around to other communities. Uniformity in all things, including furniture design, was important to promote a sense of community. Rotating from one craft to another, Shaker craftsmen were more likely to use only proven designs. Within the community, craftsmen worked with the same tools and produced the same designs. Uniformity, explained Elder Giles Avery in the 1860s, is necessary both economically and spiritually because it "contributes to peace and union in spirit."

But despite the ideal of uniformity, furniture varied slightly from village to village and particularly between the New England communities and the midwestern ones. The most obvious differences were in the woods employed. Whereas the New England settlements preferred butternut, pine, maple, and cherry, the western ones employed locally grown walnut, beech, and poplar. Further from the center of orthodoxy at Mount Lebanon, the communities in the west and also those in Maine exhibited a great degree of individuality. Western work was usually heavier and featured more embellishments, such as turnings on the pedestals of tables, in contrast to the austere, lighter furniture of New England. The Puritan ethic was still strong in New England, whereas the midwestern communities attracted converts from Virginia, Pennsylvania, and North Carolina who had different religious backgrounds.

Little concerned with changing style, Shakers produced furniture that is difficult to date. Their earliest work is quite similar to late Chippendale and Federal designs. Later, these designs became more simplified and plain. Early Shaker furniture is painted or finished with a thin red, blue, or yellow stain. Later, pieces were simply varnished. Chairs with cushion rails indicate a date after 1832. The earliest rocker had a one-piece front post topped with a turned mushroom reminiscent of a similar feature on 17th-century armchairs. Later ones had the applied mushroom turning on the top of the arm. Woven wool or cotton tape on list seats appear about 1830 and replace splint in popularity. Victorian elements, which crept into Shaker designs after the Civil War, indicate a date in the second half of the 19th century.

Only in a few instances did Shaker cabinetmakers sign their work. Clockmakers, such as Benjamin Youngs, continued the tradition of the World and signed most of their tall case clocks. Sometimes cabinetmakers would mark furniture with the name of the recipient. Orren Haskin inscribed a worktable he made for Sarah H. Winton:

Our Shaker sister
Worth her weight in gold:
Please accept this little token
of my approving love;
Altho' tis small it measures more
The half has not been told;
God Bless you ever ever more,
To rest in our clean fold
While on this mortal shore.
O.N.H., June 11, 1881, Mount
* Lebanon,*
Columbia Co., N.Y.[8]

FIGURE IX–22
Dining room with 19th century Shaker-made furniture in the home of Dr. Edward Deming Andrews, Pittsfield, Mass.
The through-tenon on the cross-brace of the table is typical of the extra-strong construction techniques employed by the Shakers. The sideboard was used in the dining room of the Canterbury, New Hampshire ministry. Originally painted red, this rare piece was made of walnut, birch, and pine. The Hancock table, dating about 1830, was made of maple and pine. In the corner, a tall tin cupboard held kitchen and tableware. It may have originally been built into a wall.
National Gallery of Art.

FIGURE IX–23

Washstand. Maple with butternut and pine. Hancock, Mass., Ca. 1825–1850.
A light red stain allowed the striped grain of the wood to show through the finish. The omission of feet on Shaker furniture, as on this piece, was common. The ubiquitous drawer and cabinet echo the Shaker insistence on cleanliness and neatness. Pieces similar to this stood in every retiring room or in a washroom or anteroom off the retiring room. The high backboard kept water from splashing on the wall when it was poured from a pitcher into a bowl.
Hancock Shaker Village, Shaker Community, Inc., Pittsfield, Mass.

FIGURE IX–24

Chest over drawers. Pine. New Lebanon, N.Y. Ca. 1825–1850.
Plain, simple, unadorned lines characterize this piece, which does not even have an escutcheon plate over the keyhole. A lock was unusual on Shaker furniture. The form was made throughout the 18th century in colonial New England and served as a model for these Shaker pieces, which simplified the shaping of the skirt with a flattened arch form. The exposed dovetails on each corner of the feet were also typical Shaker technique.
Hancock Shaker Village, Shaker Community, Inc., Pittsfield, Mass.

FIGURE IX–25

Sewing table. Maple. Hancock, Mass. Ca. 1825–1875.
The table, with typical Shaker rod-shaped legs and fine workmanship, served as a sewing table. The drawer in the end of the skirt held sewing paraphernalia, and scissors or other equipment hung from the handy pegs on the gate and the end of the skirt. The built-in drawers and cabinets were a common sight in Shaker dwellings. The emphasis on function is evident in the arrangement of the drawers and the size of the doors.
National Gallery of Art.

Other marks appearing on Shaker wood products included the last two digits of the year in which the piece was made or the number and letter code for the room where the piece belonged.

In 1841, a description of the furniture in the retiring room or bedroom, at New Lebanon included the following:

Green painted bed steads; plain chairs, with splint bottoms are preferable to any other kind, because they can be mended when they break. One rocking Chair, in a room, except where the aged reside. One table, or more, if necessary, according to the number of inmates and size of the room. One stand.[9]

Other items included looking glasses, chests, cupboards, and built-in drawers and closets (Figures IX–23, IX–24, and IX–25).

Beds were the simple, low-post variety with rope. Distinguishing many Shaker beds were casters that allowed the bed to be rolled out from the wall for ease of cleaning and making up. At first considered luxuries, mirrors gained acceptance by 1820 as a means of promoting cleanli-

FIGURE IX–26
Writing desk. Maple. New York. Ca. 1850–1875.
The fake set of drawers on the side and the secret compartment are unusual features on Shaker furniture. Such deception contradicted Shaker beliefs in honesty and forthrightness. A button hidden under the leather top released the writing surface, which pulled out on wooden rollers. Desks of any kind were rarely found among the Shakers and were confined primarily to the trustees until the second half of the century, when the Millennial Laws against writing were relaxed.
Hancock Shaker Village, Shaker Community, Inc., Pittsfield, Massachusetts.

ness. Nevertheless, the *Millennial Laws* were quite specific about them:

> *One good looking glass, which ought not to exceed eighteen inches in length, and twelve in width, with a plain frame. A looking glass larger than this, ought never to be purchased by Believers. If necessary a small glass may hang in the closet, and a very small one may be kept in the public cupboard of the room.*[10]

Since other Shaker laws discouraged writing among members, only a few lap and school desks were found. Sewing tables with drawers in the back under a broad table top sometimes doubled as desks. However, some of the most impressive pieces of furniture were the large desks used by the trustees, who were required to keep detailed accounts and journals (Figure IX–26).

Chests and cupboards were more common, though many were built into walls. Often constructed without feet, they simply rested on a protective base molding. A surprising number of Shaker pieces were fitted with locks despite *Millennial Laws* that forbade locking up private possessions.

Like all Shaker furniture, tables, with their clean lines and utilitarian designs, reflected the Shaker aesthetic. Tables for bedside or shop use rested on four square, tapered legs or simple, round spindles. Pedestal tables used for work stands, candle stands, or sewing were also common (Figure IX–27). The sewing table, which had drawers and was usually large enough so that two sisters might use it, was a Shaker specialty.

Shaker elders at first discouraged the use of clocks as an unnecessary luxury. Soon, however, Niskayuna and a few other com-

munities recognized their utility
in keeping the daily routine orderly (Figure IX-28). A tall case
clock was often found in the hall
of each family dwelling.

Chairs

Chairs were the most common
item of furniture produced by the
Shakers. Several types of rockers
were made for Believers, including ones with mushroom hand
holds, scrolled arms, rolled arms,
and cushion rails (Figure IX-29).
A special sewing rocker was
equipped with a drawer under the
seat. Rockers with rolled arms in
which the posts and arms were
made of one piece were typical of
Harvard and Shirley, although
they were occasionally found
elsewhere as well. Other types of
chairs included children's chairs,
invalid chairs, and high-legged
chairs for weaving or ironing (Figure IX-30). Low-back chairs for
dining quickly replaced benches
(Figure IX-31). One Shaker form,
the revolver, with a pedestal base
and either a wire- or wooden-spin-
dle back was reminiscent of
Windsor chairs.

Chairs made for Believers exhibited finer craftsmanship, were frequently made of special woods, such as curley maple, and were produced in greater variety than those for the World. Turned posts with acorn or simple flame finials marked most Shaker chairs (Figure IX–32). A nipple finial char- acterized chairs made at Watervliet, New York (Figure IX–33). Some chairs with flattened posts were indistinguishable from chairs made in the World. On some chairs appearing after 1825, a wooden tilting ball allowed Believers to lean back on the rear legs. A ball with a flat bottom ro-

tated in a socket and ensured that the legs remained flat on the ground (Figures IX–34 and IX–35). The Shakers patented a similar device made of brass and pewter in 1852, but the metal tilting ball is rarely seen.

Shaker Furniture after the Civil War

From the beginning of their establishment in America, Shakers had sold furniture to the World in order to raise money for the things that they could not make themselves. After the Civil War, the production of chairs became a major business. Robert M. Wagan of Mount Lebanon set up a large Shaker chair factory in the 1860s. At his death in 1883, Elder William Anderson and later Eldress Sarah Collins continued the business until the 1930s. The chairs came "with or without arms and rockers, or with neither arms nor rockers." A cushion rail on the crest could be had at no extra cost (Figure IX–36). Chairs were finished in "Mahogany, Ebony, or White finish—that is the natural color of the maple wood." Catalogs offered different chair sizes from 0 to 7 and 14 different woven cotton tape for list seats (Figure IX–37). Chair backs were either made of slats, webbed, or upholstered in 14 different colors

of plush (Figure IX–38). The Shakers also sold footstools.

Wagan's catalog declared that "we have spared no expense or labor in our endeavors to produce an article that cannot be surpassed in any respect, and which combines all the advantages of durability, simplicity and lightness."[11] In the first nine months of 1869, Wagan's factory tuned out 600 chairs. In order to ensure that the public received the genuine Shaker model, Wagan notified his customers as follows:

> *All chairs of our make will have a gold transfer trade-mark attached to them, and none others are Shakers' chairs.... Our trademark is a gold transfer, and is designed to be ornamental; but, if objectionable to purchasers, it can be easily removed without defacing the furniture in the least, by wetting a sponge or piece of cotton cloth with AQUA AMMONIA, and rubbing it until it is loosened.[12]*

Despite their fundamental belief in celibacy and the strict separation of sexes, the Shakers prospered and expanded in the first half of the 19th century. The number of Shakers peaked about 1830. Some 6,000 Shakers were gathered together in 18 communities in New England and the Midwest. However, after the Civil War, membership declined rapidly until fewer than a dozen Shakers were left in two locations at Canterbury, New Hampshire, and Sabbathday Lake, Maine.

A number of reasons contributed to the decline. Some communities, particularly Pleasant Hill, were devastated as a result of both Blue and Grey armies fighting across their farm lands during the Civil War. Some communities suffered mismanagement, incompetent leadership, and outright dishonesty, which compounded their economic difficulties. Economic problems undermined their self-sufficiency and forced them out of their isolation. Contacts with the World accelerated as their numbers diminished and as they hired hands to run their farms.

Economic difficulty was not the only travail that made Shaker life less attractive to potential converts. The earliest converts had sought meaning in their lives and an escape from poverty and hopelessness. In the era of prosperity that followed the Civil War, the ascetic Shaker way of life seemed to offer few compensating benefits. As their religious zeal abated, the Shakers inspired fewer and fewer proselytes. One pool of potential converts was lost as public orphanages took in many of the children once entrusted to the Shakers.

By the 1870s, the Shakers were buying furniture from the World. Even their own productions by such men as Henry Green at Alfred and Thomas Fisher at Enfield, Connecticut, betrayed the Victorian influence (Figure IX–39). Many Shakers even became addicted to changes in style and considered their furniture from the first half of the century "old fashioned." Shakers ignored many of the *Millennial Laws*, such as the prohibition against "beading mouldings and cornices," which had ensured simplicity in furniture design.

Just as the Shakers were abandoning their precepts and becoming more and more influenced by the World, the World was discovering the beauties of Shaker design. Gustav Stickley described the influence of Shaker designs on his work in the 1880s, recounting that he borrowed the use of a lathe "and with it blocked out the plainer parts of some very simple chairs made after the 'Shaker' model."[13] He had visited Shaker communities and was impressed by their simple designs. Indeed, the last pieces of furniture he made before his death in 1941 were three Shaker-style chairs for his granddaughter. Beginning in the 1920s, Shaker furniture

also influenced Danish designers, including Kaare Klint, an originator of the Scandinvian and Danish modern style.

The Shakers were 100 years ahead of their time in their concept of design. However, the simplicity of their furniture contrasted sharply with contemporary styles, and few Victorians were impressed. Charles Dickens spoke eloquently for the majority when he described his reactions during a visit to the Shaker community at New Lebanon in 1842:

We walked into a grim room, where several grim hats were hanging on grim pegs, and the

FIGURE IX–39

Desks. Butternut and maple. Alfred, Maine. Ca. 1880.

The elder's desk (left) and the eldress' desk (right) relate to one in the dwelling house at Sabbathday Lake, Maine, made by Henry Green. In 1883 Elder Otis Sawyer described three similar desks made by Green that contained "four larger and two smaller drawers, a folding leaf, partings for paper, and on top two shelves for books." Green was exposed to Victorian designs during his summer trips to resorts in the White Mountains and the sea coast, where he sold Shaker products. The four exposed drawers on the eldress desk are framed with dark contrasting wood in a technique found on other Maine Shaker furniture. The two desks are photographed at the site of the former Shaker community in New Lebanon, Connecticut.

Greenwillow Farm Shaker Gallery, Chatham, N.Y.

time was grimly told by a grim clock, which uttered every tick with a kind of struggle, as if it broke the grim silence reluctantly, and under protest. Ranged against the wall were six or eight stiff, high-backed chairs, and they partook so strongly of the general grimness, that one would have much rather have sat on the floor. . . .[14]

Yet despite the majority view, a surprising number of Victorians purchased Shaker chairs as a novelty or as a foil for their more ornate furniture.

NOTES

1. For this information, I am indebted to Monroe Fabian, a Pennsylvania German himself and the author of *The Pennsylvania German Decorated Chest* (New York: Universe Books, 1978).

2. Edward Deming Andrews and Faith Andrews, *Religion in Wood: A Book of Shaker Furniture* (Bloomington, Ind.: Indiana University Press, 1966), p. 7.

3. Andrews and Andrews, *Religion in Wood*, p. 8.

4. Andrews and Andrews, *Religion in Wood*, p. 8.

5. June Sprigg, *By Shaker Hands* (New York: Alfred A. Knopf, Inc., 1975), p. 100.

6. Sprigg, *Shaker Hands*, p. 107.

7. Sprigg, *Shaker Hands*, p. 33.

8. June Sprigg, "Marked Shaker Furnishings," *The Magazine Antiques* 115 (May 1979): 1054.

9. Edward Deming Andrews and Faith Andrews, *Shaker Furniture: The Craftsmanship of an American Communal Sect* (New York: Dover Publications, Inc., 1964), p. 54.

10. Andrews and Andrews, *Shaker Furniture*, p. 55.

11. "Illustrated Catalogue and Price List of Shakers' Chairs Manufactured by the Society of Shakers," p. 4, in Robert F. W. Meader, *Illustrated Guide to Shaker Furniture* (New York: Dover Publications, Inc., 1972).

12. Sprigg, "Marked Shaker Furnishings," p. 1055.

13. John Crosby Freeman, "The Forgotten Rebel" (Watkins Glen, N.Y.: Century House, 1966), pp. 13–14.

14. Charles Dickens, *American Notes* (New York: Books Inc., N.D.), p. 191.

X

VICTORIAN FURNITURE:
THE GOTHIC AND ROCOCO REVIVALS

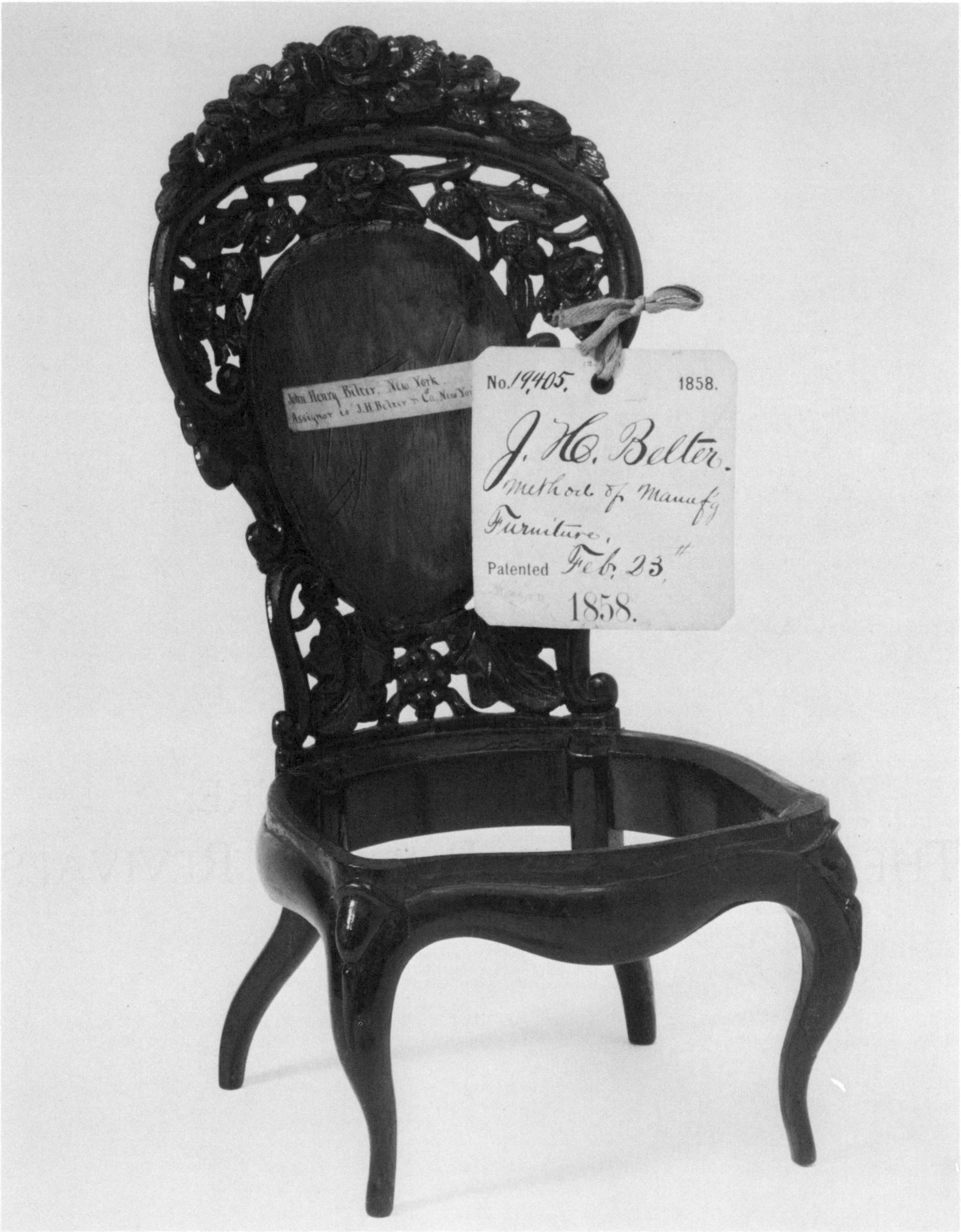
John Henry Belter, New York.
Assignor to J.H.Belter & Co. New York
No. 19,405. 1858.
J. H. Belter.
Method of Manufg
Furniture.
Patented Feb. 23th
1858.

FIGURE X–1
*Patent model. Rosewood. New York.
Dated 1858.*
**Standing just under a foot high, this
model illustrated John Henry Belter's
patent application for "dishing pressed
work." Pressed work referred to the
laminated wood, and dishing was the
process of adding a bulge to the back.
Except for the uniquely shaped back,
the chair with the carved fruit, flowers,
and nuts, the pierced back, and the
cabriole legs are typical of Rococo
revival chairs made by a number of
manufacturers working at this time.**
Smithsonian Institution Photo No. 70027.

VICTORIA BECAME QUEEN OF ENGLAND
in 1837 and ruled until her death
in 1901—the longest reign in
English history. Victoria lent her
name to an age during which
British power and prestige
reached their height. However,
with the principal exception of
the Gothic revival of the 1840s
and 1850s and the Eastlake style
at the end of the century,
France, not England, dominated
furniture design in Europe and
America. Nevertheless, the mag-
ical name of the queen has become associated with the dazzling array of revival styles and
substyles that characterized
most 19th-century furniture.

THE VICTORIAN ERA
IN AMERICA

Although the Industrial Revolution first began in England, it
reached the United States by the
mid-19th century. Even though
most Americans enjoyed a relatively high standard of living, an
average working class family in
New York had only about three
percent of its weekly budget left
over after paying for the necessities of food, clothing, and shelter to spend on home furnishings. And even to maintain that
standard of living, husbands la-
bored 12 long hours a day, and
often their working wives and
even sons and daughters supplemented that income. Manufacturers tailored their products to
the pocketbooks of this new
market.

Major shifts of population accompanied the Industrial Revolution. The mid-19th century
saw an accelerating immigration
from rural areas to the cities as
the United States grew from 17
million people in 1840 to 40 million in 1870. About a third of
this increase came from immigration, and Germans and Irish
made up about two-thirds of the
6.6 million new citizens. Over a
million Irish came to the United
States between 1847 and 1854
during the worst of the periodic
potato famines. The heaviest
German immigration occurred
between 1852 and 1854, when
nearly a half million landed in
the United States, and in the
five years after the Civil War,
when an equal number arrived.
Some of these newcomers were
cabinetmakers who plied their
trade in the major coastal cities
of Boston, New York, and Philadelphia. Others moved on to the
emerging midwestern cities of
St. Louis, Cincinnati, Pittsburgh,
and Grand Rapids to work in
factories opening there.

From the 17th to the early
19th centuries, furniture styles
had followed one after the other
in a neat progression. Beginning
in the 1840s, a cacophony of
styles blared their way into the

Side chair. Rosewood. American. Ca. 1840.

The legs do not depart radically from Empire chairs, but the back captures the essence of the Gothic. The pointed Gothic arch of the crest is repeated by the three arches of the back, and the tracery completes the effect. The painted decoration was added about 1860.

Margaret Woodbury Strong Museum.

home. It was an era of specialization—the Rococo revival in the parlor; Renaissance in the dining room; and Gothic in the den, library, or hall. Customers demanded comfort, which was epitomized by overstuffed chairs and sofas. Newly affluent clients wanted to show off their new-found wealth, and they purchased expensive furniture or, at least, furniture that looked expensive. The Victorians were fascinated by the machines that made the new largess possible. A reaction set in, but not until the end of the century.

Wives now took over the responsibility for furnishing the home as men became immersed in industrial enterprises. Earlier, the primary basis of wealth had been land and trade, and the more leisurely pace of an agricultural and mercantile economy gave husbands time to build and furnish their homes personally. Architecture was considered an important part of an 18th-century aristocrat's education. As education was extended to women in the 19th century, women acquired the knowledge,

once restricted largely to men, of how to furnish a house stylishly.

The lady of the house was not without help in discharging her newly acquired responsibility. She avidly read the latest issue of Godey's *Lady's Book,* which began publication in the 1830s, or one of the other domestic magazines that were the forerunners of *House and Garden* and *Better Homes and Gardens.* If she were still perplexed, and if she could afford the luxury, she hired an interior decorator. Not only could this specialist help wealthy patrons choose among the bewildering variety of furniture styles made increasingly available by mass production and factory techniques, but he could also help in the selection of factory-made carpets, statuary, wallpaper, tableware, and hundreds of other objects. A few 18th-century architects, such as the Adam brothers, had provided interior decorating services, but only for the English aristocracy. By the 1840s, however, some large cabinetmaking firms and a few interior decorators, such as George Platt of New York, advertised their decorating services for wealthy American clients. Patrons could choose from a warehouse full of furniture, or, for a substantially increased fee, Platt would design furniture to order. Although most people did their own decorating, the few who could afford decorator services tended to be style-setters.

A family had a large selection of architectural styles to select from as well. One architect noted that he could design houses in 14 different styles, including American Log Cabin, Swiss Cottage, Lombard Italian, Tuscan, Etruscan, Greek, and Castellated. The latter referred to the Gothic style that was popular in the 1840s and 1850s. It was a reaction against the "passionless repose" and "Godlessness" of the Greek revival. Perhaps because it was a British style, Gothic never achieved great popularity in America. Nevertheless, it freed American architects from the rigid, classically symmetrical floor plans of the 18th and early 19th centuries.

GOTHIC REVIVAL

Furniture, like architecture, carried a message. The Gothic style evoked an ecclesiastical image and fell receptively on those involved with the religious awakening characterizing this period. However, it spoke more clearly to Englishmen who could relate to a Gothic heritage. In the 18th century, furniture designers, such as Thomas Chippendale, revived the use of such Gothic elements for furniture. Gothic motifs crept into at least a few Federal and Empire designs. Sir Walter Scott's *Ivanhoe* and *The Lady of the Lake,* written at the beginning of the 19th century, vividly if fancifully described England in the Middle Ages and popularized the style. Gothic looked not to classical times but to the Middle Ages for inspiration, even though, early in the 19th century, these styles were grafted onto classical forms (Figures X–2 and X–3).

Augustus Charles Pugin, an English draftsman, published accurate examples of Gothic architecture in the 1820s. His son, A. W. N. Pugin, carried on the work in the 1830s, printing examples of medieval furniture in his book, *Gothic Furniture in the Style of the Fifteenth Century.* In America, one of the foremost exponents of the Gothic, Alexander Jackson Davis, opened his office in 1827 in New York. He had become steeped in Gothic ideas by exposure to English design books, such as those by the Pugins. Davis designed his first Gothic villa in 1832. His closest friend, Andrew Jackson Downing, America's first landscape architect, promoted the Gothic style through his book, *The Architecture of Country Houses,* published in 1850 (Figure X–4). In this first major book on taste in America, he declared the following:

A great beauty of this style, when properly treated, is the home-like expression which it is capable of, in the hands of a person of taste. . . . Those who love shadow, and the sentiment of antiquity and repose, will find most pleasure in the quiet tone which prevails in the Gothic style. . . .[1]

Since Americans had no medieval heritage, fewer Americans appreciated the Gothic style. In

FIGURE X–3
Side chair. Walnut and mahogany. American. Ca. 1845.
To the typical, late Empire side chair with saber legs and slip seat has been added three pointed Gothic arches cut into the underside of the crest rail, and the top of the crest rail shaped to a cusp. Applied pieces on the flat columns and the shaping of the stay rail above the seat repeat the pointed arch motif. The chair is an imaginative mixture of the Empire and Gothic elements common in the 1840s.
Margaret Woodbury Strong Museum.

FIGURE X–4
Center table. Rosewood and marble. Ca. 1845–1855.
The hexagonal top rests on six clustered columns and a triangular base. Andrew Jackson Downing illustrated a similar table in his *Architecture of Country Houses*, published in 1850. A related table has a history of ownership in the Rathbone family, who owned Kenwood near Albany, New York, in the 1840s. The table is composed of units of three and six—the six-sided top with six arches on each side and six legs, combine with a three-sided base with three-lobed trefoils.
E. J. Canton.

FIGURE X–5
Side chair. Walnut. American. Ca. 1845.
The intricate, rose window splat flanked by a series of well-carved crockets is surmounted by an unusual, five-lobed bow of inverted Gothic arches. The back rests on three other arches rising from the seat. The surface of the carved back is flattened so that the chair can actually be used comfortably. The rococo elements are confined to the serpentine seat rail and the cabriole legs.
Margaret Woodbury Strong Museum.

FIGURE X–6
Side table. Rosewood. American. Ca. 1845–1855.
The scroll-sawn stretcher and the pillar-like legs reveal the lingering influence of the late Empire. These details contrast nicely with the delicate Gothic arches on the skirt. The disk turnings on the top of the pillars, repeated on the drops, contribute to the sense of lightness.
Anne and David Sellin.

FIGURE X–7
Hall chair. Walnut. American. Ca. 1845–1855.
The walnut has a dark varnish, but the seat has been grained to simulate rosewood. The seat lifts up to expose a small well, as is typical of many hall chairs, which were made more for storage and show than for comfortable seating. Gothic rose windows inspired the famous "wheel"-back chairs by Alexander Jackson Davis at Lyndhurst, but the designer of these chairs departed from Davis's academic interpretation. Four quatrefoils whirl around a central medallion, all cut from one piece of wood, and a series of crockets and a central finial enliven the crest. Similar turned legs appear on English chairs of the 1820s and 1830s.
Anne and David Sellin.

on the Hudson River near Tarrytown, was one example. Alexander Jackson Davis designed the entire house and much of the furniture in the Gothic style. Produced in 1841, these pieces include the famous wheel-back chairs (patterned after rose windows), tables, sideboards, bookcases, beds, and pianos. Although the furniture of the 1830s exhibited only some elements of Gothic, Davis's furniture employed Gothic elements exclusively. He also embellished traditional furniture forms with details from various architectural design books, such as Gothic crockets, quatrefoils, cusps, pointed ogee arches, cluster columns, and rose windows.

Davis ordered his furniture custom made, but cabinetmakers, such as Joseph Meeks and Alexander Roux, also advertised Gothic styles. Robert Conner of New York illustrated Gothic furniture in a book published as early as 1842. Gothic furniture was most popular for halls and libraries. Hall chairs were meant more for decoration than for seating, so most were made with straight, carved backs

the United States, Gothic in its purest form connoted pretense and eccentricity. However, its scholastic and ecclesiastical associations made it particularly popular for colleges and churches, but few private houses had more than a room or two of Gothic furniture. Some, however, built Gothic castles to announce that they had arrived financially (Figures X–5 and X–6). Lyndhurst,

and wooden seats that raised up to expose a storage space (Figures X–7 and X–8). The use of oak evoked the Middle Ages. It was also suitable for the carving and piercing that was so much a part of the style. Gothic motifs were also common on iron furniture, particularly children's beds, which were indestructible, sanitary, and cheaply mass produced.

Related to the Gothic was Elizabethan- or Swiss-style furniture, characterized by ball, spool, bobbin, and spiral turnings (Figure X–9). These turned forms were based on furniture designs popular in the reigns of Charles I and II in the 17th century, but the Elizabethan name conjured up the glory of England and appealed to the romanticism of the 19th century. Beds with spool turnings were named for Jenny Lind, the Swedish opera star who toured America in the 1850s under the auspices of P. T. Barnum. The Salisbury Furniture Company of Vermont made a cradle named for Jenny Lind, and the term stuck. Spool and ball turnings, easily and cheaply turned out on lathes, also added interest to tables, washstands, and towel racks (Figure X–10).

FIGURE X–10
Side table. Pine. American. Ca. 1850–1860.

Similar to thousands of inexpensive tables made in the 1850s and 1860s, this table is distinguished only by the fact that the historic surrender of General Robert E. Lee to General Ulysses S. Grant took place around it in 1865. The spool turnings of the Elizabethan style were easily turned on lathes in large and small factories all over the country. The design provided a cheap alternative to the Gothic or rococo furniture popular at the same time.
Smithsonian Institution Photo No. 6218N.

Simple versions of the Gothic style, as well as low-priced lines of other revival styles, such as the Rococo and Renaissance, became known as cottage furniture. These pieces, usually made of a cheap wood and often painted, suggested, if faintly, the elegance of the high-style prototype. The name derived from the "Cottage Furniture Department," a column written by Sarah Hale that appeared in *Godey's* in 1849.

ALEXANDER ROUX

By the mid-19th century cabinetmakers, such as Alexander Roux, were producing a great diversity of styles. Downing, an influential advocate of the Gothic style, stated, in *The Architecture of Country Houses*:

> At the warehouse of M. A. Roux, Broadway, may be found a large collection of furniture for the drawing-room, library, etc.—the most tasteful designs of Louis Quatorze, Renaissance, Gothic, etc., to be found in the country.... The chairs and sofas are particularly elegant.[2]

Roux immigrated from France, where he had received his training as a cabinetmaker, and opened his own shop in New York in 1837. He used his background to advantage, trading on the popularity of French styles and craftsmanship. Roux's firm competed successfully with the best firms in New York, and by 1855, he employed 120 people in his factory.

Roux outgrew several locations during the 1850s, and in the 1860s, he operated from two adjoining four-story buildings on Broadway. As his business expanded, obtaining skilled labor became a problem, and he recruited in France. By the 1870s, at the peak of his success, he was producing a half million dollars of furniture annually. He retired in 1881, but his son continued to operate the firm until 1898. He handled the whole gamut of the furniture business, making furniture and importing some as well. In addition to furniture, he advertised mantelpieces, wainscoting, mirror frames, and cornices. He did interior decoration, including Rokeby, the Barrytown, New York, home of William B. Astor. The firm also replastered and painted the walls and ceilings of the Ballantine House in Newark, New Jersey, which is now part of the Newark Museum.

At the 1853 Crystal Palace Exhibition in New York, Roux displayed a fine black walnut sideboard and a rosewood sofa "elegant in its proportions ... highly finished in its workmanship [and] upholstered with gaily colored satin."[3]

ROCOCO REVIVAL

Even though Pugin had designed a medieval court for the Crystal Palace Exhibition in London in 1851, the Gothic style was never as popular as the Rococo, or Louis Quatorze, as it was called in the 19th century. The numerous international exhibitions held during the 19th century greatly stimulated and influenced the arts: Designers from all over the world gathered to exchange ideas and see the latest creations. Prince Albert conceived the idea of an international exhibition to encourage "most efficiently the application of the Fine Arts to our manufacturers" in order "to wed high art with mechanical skill." A great crystal palace of glass and iron rose up in Hyde Park in London; it enclosed 23 acres, including several full-grown elm trees. Queen Victoria opened the fair to the first of six million visitors who viewed 14,000 exhibits from all over the world.

The British hoped to show the world their cultural and technological supremacy. Much to their chagrin, the French again proved their cultural ascendency, particularly in the decorative arts. Even English observers proclaimed a grand sideboard in the Renaissance style by Henri Fourdinois of Paris as "one of the most superb specimens of cabinet-work to be seen in the Exhibition...."[4] A French artist, Eugene Prignot, even designed the most impressive piece of English furniture, a sideboard made by the London firm of Jackson and Graham.

The 1853 New York Exhibition confirmed the supremacy of French culture. The United States wanted the world to see that it had come of age. Critics praised American industrial products and rated them with the best the Europeans had to offer. But, although they were impressed by American technology, Europeans did not think much of American arts.

Although the Gothic, Renaissance, and other furniture styles were exhibited at both the London and New York exhibitions, the Rococo revival predominated. The style was given new life in the reign of Louis Philippe, who became king of France in 1830. Furniture designers during this period looked back to the reign of Louis XIV and the great age of France, but in reality the furniture was more inspired by styles during the reign of Louis XV, from 1715 to 1774. French craftsmen who came to America in the 1840s and 1850s were trained in the new style. They often maintained close relationships with shops in France and imported some furniture for sale in America. However, the influence of French cabinetmakers, such as Alexander Roux and Charles Baudouine of New York, was overshadowed by the much more numerous British and German craftsmen who came to America in the same period. More important than French cabinetmakers in the transmittal of the Rococo and Renaissance revival style were the numerous French publications on furniture available in America. Désiré Guilmard's bimonthly journal on furniture, which first appeared in 1839, was one of the most important. Another Frenchman, Victor Louis Quétin, published plates showing rooms of furniture. The French influence was also filtered through English publications, such as Blackie and Son's *The Cabinet-Maker's Assistant*, published in 1853. Common in America, this influential handbook showed many Rococo revival designs based on French sources.

Concurrent with the Rococo revival in furniture was the Italianate, or Tuscan, style in architecture. It was characterized by a sprawling asymmetrical floor plan with a square, flat-topped tower or cupola. Ignoring classical symmetry, architects frequently scaled and shaped rooms for function. The irregular skyline of Italianate houses appealed to the Victorian love of the picturesque, the delight in abrupt variations of form and line. Houses had an abundance of interesting details, such as gables, arched windows and doorways, cast iron balconies, marble fireplaces, frescos, Renaissance columns, balustrades, and cornices. All these elements contributed to a sense of roughness and rich texture, which also characterized the picturesque.

Godey's described Rococo furniture as decorated with the following:

Curves of artistic carving of some beautiful wreath, with the boldness, depth, and sharpness of a bouquet or cluster; in another, with the hanging foliage, budding flowers, and waving scrolls, many of which are triumphs of the chisel.[5]

Naturalistic carvings of roses, grapes, vines, and birds evoked aristocratic pretentions and the apogee of French culture in the 18th century. At the same time, the rich carving, matching in quality the best of the 17th and 18th centuries, proclaimed the newly acquired status of the wealthy industrialists and the rising middle class.

PARLOR FURNITURE

Style-conscious customers usually chose the Rococo, or "French antique," for the parlor and bedroom. By mid-century, every parlor required a seven-piece matched set consisting of an arm chair; a lady's chair, often with small bracket arms; a sofa; and four parlor chairs. Most chairs in the Rococo style were made with cabriole legs and had a balloon-shaped back, which was pinched in at the waist (Figure X–11). Cheaper seats used in the dining room had the same balloon-shaped back, but a single stay rail replaced the upholstered backs found on parlor chairs.

Chair design symbolized the rigid social hierarchy in the Victorian family. The husband, head of the household, sat in the throne-like armchair, whereas the smaller, less impressive lady's chair confirmed the subordinate position of women in the 19th century. Made without arms and with wider seats, these chairs also better accommodated the full dresses worn by women at mid-century. Children used the even less imposing parlor chairs.

The sofa, where visitors sat side by side with their hosts, symbolized hospitality and friendship (Figure X–12). These

sofas were either triple-arched, medallion-backed, or serpentine. Another variation was the meridienne, or short sofa (Figure X–13).

These parlor sets began to migrate from along the walls to permanent places in the center of the room; often they were grouped around a center table that usually held an astral or other type of lamp. In 1850, Downing wrote that "the center table is the emblem of the family circle." Often topped with white Tennessee marble, these circular, oval, or oblong tables rested on cabriole legs linked by arched stretchers supporting a simple or ornately carved, urn-like finial (Figure X–14).

Other furniture, serving in supporting roles, was scattered around the parlor. A new addition in this period, the étagère, or whatnot, usually consisted of four or five shelves, either free-standing or surmounting a table

FIGURE X–14
Center table. Laminated rosewood and marble. New York. Ca. 1855.
The standard series of S- and C-scrolls ornament the skirt and echo the lines of the legs. Flowers on the knees highlight the legs, which terminate in a variation of the 18th-century French whorled foot. The two fierce birds, whose wings cleverly spread to form the stretchers, confirm the inexhaustible creativity of the 19th-century furniture designer driven to create the unique.
Margaret Woodbury Strong Museum.

or cabinet (Figures X–15 and X–16). This piece held the personal knickknacks or bric-a-brac by which the Victorian housewife expressed her individuality in an age of increasingly standardized, factory production. Pier glasses stood between windows, and mirrors in the Rococo revival style, with heavily carved and gilded oval frames, hung from the walls (Figure X–17). One type, the oval or round mantel mirror with a carved, asymmetrical frame, hung over the fireplace.

FIGURE X–15 *(far left)*
Ladies writing desk. Rosewood. Brooklyn, N.Y. Ca. 1850–1860.
Thomas Brooks stenciled this piece with his name and his firm's address at 127 Fulton Street, Brooklyn, New York. The rococo scrolls combine with a Renaissance cartouche and split spindles applied to the front corners in a technique reminiscent of 17th-century joinery. The drawer, which has an applied wooden escutcheon, pulls out to expose a writing stand.
Anne and David Sellin.

FIGURE X–16
Étagère. Walnut. Boston. Ca. 1865.
Labeled by George Ware of Boston, this étagère, standing over seven feet tall, dominated a Victorian parlor. With the development of fret-cutting machinery in the mid-19th century, the intricate, flat, pierced panels appeared frequently on furniture. The carved bunch of fruit on the crest is a Rococo motif, but the rounded arch crest and the roundels applied above the mirror indicate elements of the Renaissance revival. The shelves held porcelains, wax flowers, shells, or other collectables popular in the 19th century.
Virginia Museum.

FIGURE X–17
*Pier glass. Gilt wood. American. Ca.
1860–1870.*
**Thomas Chippendale illustrated a pier
glass and table in his 1762 *Director*.
When this form was revived in the
mid-19th century, the table was reduced
in size. The carving, concentrated at
the top of the glass, contrasts with the
plain molded and beaded sides of the
common late Empire glasses. The low
console table at the base of the glass is
topped with white marble and rests on
elaborately carved brackets. The
somewhat more angular and stiffer
appearance of the glass, when compared
to earlier versions of pier glasses in the
pure Rococo revival, indicates the later
date. The carving of fruits and flowers,
including ears of corn, is extraordinary.**
*Christian Heurich Mansion, Columbia Historical
Society, Washington, D.C.*

Downing noted in 1850 that
"the piano-forte is the universal
accompanyment of the drawing-
room or parlor in America."[6] Its
ostentatiously carved Rococo
legs and the lattice tracery of the
music rack were frankly meant
to impress. Downing spoke with
exaggeration, but, increasingly, a
piano brought an aura of culture
and wealth into the parlor of
many upper-class families. In the
Renaissance style, the legs became massive turned and carved
supports (Figure X–18). By the
1870s, the more compact and
cheaper upright had passed the
square piano in sales. The
piano's popularity grew as factory production reduced prices.
Major furniture centers, such as
New York, supported specialists,
including carvers of legs, sound-
ing-board makers, felt dealers,
and key-board sellers.

The Steinway and Son's factory opened in New York in
1859, where the company occupied an entire city block in a
building rising five stories above
a basement. In yards adjacent to
the factory stood two million
feet of lumber and steam-heated
sheds for drying the wood properly. The factory employed 400
men who turned out 45 pianos a
week. A 50-horsepower Corliss
steam engine drove the machinery, most of which was located
in the basement. On the three
floors above, workmen as-
sembled the pianos. On the
fourth floor, others installed
sounding boards; and on the top
floor, away from the dust and
dirt, the cases were varnished—a

process which took several
months. In 1852, Jonas Chickering had begun construction of a
similar plant in Boston.

For the middle-class home,
the melodeon, or reed organ, provided a cultural center that sold
at half the price of a piano. The
melodeon operated on the principle of the accordion. Pedals
forced air across reeds that vi-
brated at different pitches. The
firm of Mason and Hamlin, established in Boston in 1854, produced the largest selection of
melodeons in the United States
(Figure X–19). Although the
more expensive piano sym-
bolized pretenses to culture, the
melodeon, with its ecclesiastical
overtones, capitalized on the religious revivals that swept the
country in the mid-19th century.

Furniture
as a Status Symbol

The quality of the parlor furniture symbolized the economic
status of the owner. Families at
the top of the economic scale
possessed extraordinary carved
creations in the richest mahogany or rosewood imported
from the East Indies, Africa, or
South America. Manufacturers
made such sets, which required
hours of expensive hand-carving,
to order. At the other end of the
scale, sets made of walnut or
stained maple had no carving—

cheaply made moldings on the
frame of a chair or sofa added
some interest to an otherwise
plain surface (Figure X–20). The
general shape of the furniture
was the same for expensive or
cheap furniture; part of the difference in cost was in the woods
and in the amount of carving.

The other variable was upholstery. Huge, automated textile
mills and the advent of sewing
machines reduced the cost of
fabric, which was found on all
but the plainest hall or dining-
room chair. However, elaborate
upholstering techniques could
transform the simplest chair into
a rich specimen costing twice as
much. As woodworking machinery reduced the cost of the
frame, obvious elegance was
achieved by costly upholstery
techniques. By mid-19th century,

upholstery began to cover the backs and arms of chairs as well as the seats; it even crept over crest and seat rails.

One of the cheapest and most common coverings was black horsehair. This upholstery produced many an unpleasant childhood memory when loose strands pricked the bare legs of children forced to sit quietly in a parlor. The most elegant chairs sported rich satin, silk, or plush finished off with tassels and fringes. Not until the 1860s did dark colors replace the preference for light lilac, yellow, and red and for delicate floral patterns. Tufting or buttoning in diamond or star patterns, often in combination with pleats and contrasting upholstery panels, added additional interest—and expense. Tufting held the mass of stuffing in place and also provided a way to use up short pieces of cotton and wool combings that were by-products of factory spinning. Cheaper sofas might have 50 buttons, and more expensive models employed over 125, involving considerably more labor and material. Other 19th-century upholstery techniques involved piping, a form of tufting that produced a ridge effect; and puffing, which employed pleated cloth usually of a contrasting texture around the edge of the seat. Many of these techniques were revivals of 17th-century upholstery practices. The overstuffed seats on chairs and sofas concealed coil

FIGURE X–21
Bed. Rosewood. Philadelphia. Ca. 1860.
This massive bed, about eight feet long and six feet wide, was probably part of a large quantity of furniture purchased by Mrs. Lincoln in 1861. Attributed to the Philadelphia firm of William and George Carryl, the bed, along with a center table, was purchased to redecorate the White House state bedroom in preparation for the visit of the Prince of Wales. The bed was designed to give an aura of a French state bed and was fitted with a half baldachin attached to the wall over the bed from which streamed purple satin trimmed in gold fringe. The vines, bunches of grapes, and birds—standard Rococo revival motifs—are applied rather than carved into the head and footboard. Although President Lincoln never slept in the bed, other presidents, including Woodrow Wilson and Theodore Roosevelt, did.
White House Collection.

220

springs, which came into widespread use about 1850.

Bedroom Furniture

A bedroom suite featured an ornately carved bedstead with a tall headboard, which was sometimes fitted with a half-tester, and a low footboard with rounded corners. Four-poster beds went out of style with the introduction of central heat (Figure X–21). Bed hangings were no longer necessary to ward off the cold. The Victorians thought that the heavy hangings cut off the circulation of air, which was unhealthy. As artificial light from gas lamps encouraged people to stay up late into the night, curtains over drafty windows became important. Except for children and servants, the supposedly prudish Victorians slept mostly in double beds. An elaborate dressing case with a looking glass attached, a washstand, and a chest of drawers completed the typical bedroom suite (Figures X–22 and X–23). Other furniture might include a shaving stand, a bedside table, a towel rack, a

night stand, and a dressing table. Wardrobes became less popular as more houses were equipped with built-in closets. Drawer pulls complemented the characteristic naturalistic motifs on other furniture. Carved by hand or with the aid of machines, they took the shape of fruit, leaves, or nuts. Cheaper versions made of composition sawdust can only be detected by a lack of grain.

The Rococo revival, as with all 19th-century revivals, was not a strict copy of a past style but an adaptation. Rococo furniture made in the 19th century was heavier and taller than its 18th-century predecessors. The rear legs of chairs were curved in a distinctive upside-down cabriole shape, and the front legs usually terminated in a cone rather than in the common 18th-century scrolled foot. Upholstery took on an overstuffed look, departing from the generally trim lines of 18th-century American work. The naturalistic carving of the 19th century recalled 18th-century Rococo carving but was often larger in scale and more lifelike (Figure X–24).

FIGURE X–22
Bureau. Rosewood. Baltimore. Dated 1857.
A label under the marble top reads, "Thomas Godey successor to John Needles 54 Hanover St. Baltimore." Another bit of paper reads "A. Webb Esq," who bought the piece. The delivery date slipped, as August is struck out and September, 1857 added. The piece was refinished in 1892 by Godey & Sons, the successor to the firm that made it. At that time, the brass pulls were added.
Anne and David Sellin.

FIGURE X–23 *(far left)*
Bureau. Walnut. Alexandria, Va. Ca. 1860.
James and William Green established Green & Brother in 1823, and the firm continued to make furniture until the 1880s, including pieces for the Supreme Court in Washington, D.C. This bureau, made in their "steam factory," combines thick carving on the supports for the looking glass and on the chamfered corners with a Renaissance cartouche. The carved wooden pulls are typical of much middle-class furniture at mid-century. One drawer is hidden in the skirt.
Private Collection.

FIGURE X–24
Side chair. Walnut. American. Ca. 1865.
Rosewood was the most expensive cabinetwood, and cheaper chairs, such as these, were often grained to simulate that wood. The carving of the bird, berries, vines, and flowers is exciting but not uncommon. The arched crest indicates a late date in the popularity of the Rococo revival. The double C-scrolls that form the legs were inspired by 17th-century examples and are less common than the cabriole leg. The upholstery is original.
Private Collection.

BELTER FURNITURE

John Henry Belter of New York City produced some of the best Rococo revival parlor furniture. The most ornate furniture in this style is known by his name, even though many other cabinetmakers produced similar furniture. Belter served his apprenticeship in Württemberg, Germany, before immigrating to New York about 1840. He produced stylish furniture, specializing in parlor sets, until his death in 1863. In the 1850s and 1860s Belter received patents on several processes relating to the production of furniture. He patented a laminated bedstead in 1856 that was made of two pieces of wood held together by an internal frame. Instead of a sharp break at the corners of the footboard, the laminated side rails curved gently into the footboard as one piece of wood. In 1860 he patented a bureau drawer made of laminated wood and fitted with an ingenious locking device.

His most famous patent, however, was for "dishing pressed work," which he received in 1858 (Figure X–1). The process entailed pressing strips of wood around a wooden form, using steam and pressure. Earlier, chair backs had been curved, but Belter's innovation involved the dishing of the upper section as well. The Patent Office rejected his initial application with the notation that the "principle of moulding wood into particular form is well known and in common use by Cabinet makers and others as admitted by your self."[7] Belter tried again. Among the documentation he submitted was a statement by Charles B. Hogg, a New York pattern maker, that the "process where by each veneer receives the bends in two contrary directions is not patent in his business and an art altogether novel."[8]

Although the Patent Office finally granted the patent, few documented chairs with the dished back are known. However, thousands of laminated- and curved-back chairs were made by Belter and others. Belter's dishing process involved fashioning staves of two plies of wood to fit around a heated form. Any number of staves could be glued together until a top layer of veneer was applied. After the laminated wood dried, a number of chair backs were then cut out of the molded wood. Any one of them could then have a seam running down the back where the veneer met.

FIGURE X–25
Sofa. Rosewood. New York City. Ca. 1852.

James Watson Williams purchased this sofa for his home, Fountain Elms, in Utica, New York, from Charles A. Baudouine of New York City. The bill read, "1 Suit of Rosewood Furniture in Green Tapestry viz. 2 Tete a tetes 4 chairs & 2 Fauteuils $340." Even though Williams preferred simple lines and restrained carving, he purchased his best parlor from stylish cabinetmakers in New York. The sofa still has its original muslin covering.
E. J. Canton.

Obviously, the recollections of the New York cabinetmaker, Ernest Hagen, were inaccurate when he stated that his employer, Charles Baudouine, infringed on Belter's patent by making his chairs with a seam, implying that Belter's chairs had no seams (Figure X–25).

The laminated chair back was then cut out in intricate designs, using a special saw Belter had patented. Additional pieces of wood were then glued to the surface and carved in the shape of fruits and flowers, such as grapes, pomegranates, morning glories, and roses (Figure X–26). Some Belter chairs had unpierced backs and Gothic ele-

ments. Belter either fused his chair backs with the seat rails without a break or installed braces rising from the seat rail to hold the chair backs. His competitors used similar techniques (Figure X–27).

Thomas Chippendale, as early as the 1770s, had employed the process of laminating chairs made for Osterley Park. However, cabinetmakers did not apply the technique extensively until after 1820, when Austrian chairmakers began to use the process. By 1830, Michael Thonet was also making chairs using veneered wood bent by steam heat in a method similar to Belter's. About the time

Thonet left southern Germany for Vienna, Belter was on his way to the United States. Both carried with them the idea of bending laminated wood for chair construction. Belter did not invent the technique of laminating wood; rather, he brought the idea with him from southern Germany.

GEORGE HENKELS

George Henkels was a contemporary of Belter's who worked in Philadelphia. Born in Harpers Ferry and trained as a chairmaker, Henkels began practicing his craft about 1843 in Philadelphia. By the 1850s, his trade card advertised "quick sales," "light profits," and "a fair Equivalent for your Dollars."[9] He produced furniture ranging from a $375 armoire made of rosewood, or a $350 high-post bed with canopy, down to 75 cents for a Windsor chamber chair. He also imported furniture from France.

Henkels owned two four-story brick buildings on Chestnut Street—"opposite Independence Hall"—where he made and sold his furniture. He stored his imported lumber in the basement. Lathes and other woodworking machinery occupied the first and second floors. Furniture was carved on the third floor and varnished on the top floor. On clear summer days, furniture dried on a sun roof. The adjacent building, which was almost twice as large, contained the showrooms on the first and second floors. The third floor had offices for the foreman and work areas for specialists, such as seamstresses and enamelers. Hardware and looking glasses were also stored there. The fourth floor was used for varnishing as well as for upholstering. The horsehair was stored in a single room on the roof. Clerks, bookkeepers, and salesmen toiled in the basement next to the furnace, and veneer took up the rest of the basement. In the 1850s, Henkels employed about 180 workmen and prided himself on not exploiting child labor, as many of his competitors did.

Henkels was a great promoter. He exhibited at most of the major trade exhibitions of the 19th century, including the 1853 New York Crystal Palace Exhibition and the Centennial of 1876. There, he showed a bedroom set made from a 200-year-old maple that had been felled at Independence Square in Philadelphia. Henkels also benefited from a close relationship with Samuel Sloan, the leading Philadelphia architect. Sloan's book, *Homestead Architecture*, published in 1861, contained sections on furniture contributed by Henkels. Henkels himself published several catalogs and treatises on furniture that he wrote for his customers.

CAST-IRON FURNITURE

Rococo revival motifs found their way into cast-iron furniture, which became increasingly popular in the 1840s. Blacksmiths fashioned wrought-iron furniture as early as the 16th century. By the early 19th century, iron was cast by pouring it into sand that had been shaped by pressing wooden molds into it. In the 1830s, cast-iron balcony railings and doorway ornaments were popular, and the material was soon used to make garden furniture. Pieces made by John B. Wickersham of New York and other manufacturers had grape, lily of the valley, rustic tree branches, fern, or Rococo scrolls; these sold the best (Figures X–28 and X–29). By the 1850s, cast-iron furniture was often cheaper than that made from wood. Painted black or bronze, it began to appear inside the house as well as in the garden and was used particularly for furniture that did not have to move, such as hat racks, umbrella stands, center tables, and plant stands (Figure X–30). Many people bought brass or iron beds made by such manufacturers as George Cornell and George R. Jackson, because they felt that iron did not harbor germs as wood did. Wire chairs were also popular (Figure X–31). The dramatic use of iron to frame the Crystal Palace in 1851 and to erect a dome over the United States Capitol during the Civil War boosted the popularity of iron, which was widely used in furniture until the end of the century.

FURNITURE OF PAPIER-MÂCHÉ

Exhibitions of papier mâché furniture in both the Rococo and Renaissance revival styles spread the popularity of that material. In 1772, Henry Clay in England patented a new process whereby sheets of paper were pasted together and baked in molds. The pieces were then lacquered or japanned and decorated with romantic motifs, such as birds, flowers, or pastoral landscapes. After 1825, many pieces were inlayed with mother of pearl. Most papier-mâché things were imported from England, particularly from Jennens and Bettridge of Birmingham, the largest English firm, but some objects were manufactured in the United States. Companies in Litchfield, Connecticut, Boston, and New York produced such items as clock cases, fire screens, tilt-top tables, and sewing stands. Papier-mâché furniture made before 1840 without a wooden or wire frame has not survived.

Papier-mâché cabinets, wrought-iron garden seats, and elegant bedroom and parlor suites all came under the spell of the Rococo revival. Gone were the archeologically correct styles of classical Greece and Rome. The revivals at mid-century were less revivals or copies and more mere suggestions, allusions, or improvements on the past. By the 1860s, customers had another major revival style to choose from or to combine with the others—the Renaissance revival.

FIGURE X–28
Garden chair. Cast iron. American. Ca. 1870.
The back, seat, and legs are cast separately and bolted together. The legs suggest branches and imitate rustic wooden garden furniture produced at the same time.
Margaret Woodbury Strong Museum.

FIGURE X–30
Hall stand. Cast iron. American. Ca. 1860–1870.
The term hall tree inspired this design, which is in fact a cast-iron tree. This design is similar to a piece that appeared in a catalog published by John A. Winn and Company of Boston, Massachusetts, in 1868. The loop held umbrellas and canes, and from the hooks hung hats and bonnets. The mirror, a standard feature, provided one last look before entering or leaving the house. The hall stand was largely passé by the 1880s, although debased examples continued to be made into the 20th century.
Margaret Woodbury Strong Museum.

FIGURE X–29 *(left)*
Armchair. Iron. Philadelphia. Ca. 1887–1905.
William Adams and Company cast their business address into the back of the chair to get a little free advertising. The chair was used in a cemetery, and J. B. Moery was the last owner. When the first catalogs of cast-iron furniture began to appear in the 1840s, naturalistic and rustic motifs were common. This design, however, combines a row of spindles and geometric shapes, typical of Eastlake furniture, with a stylized urn and lyre surviving from the Empire period. The wheel-like crest combines a Renaissance idea with an Eastlake execution.
Smithsonian Institution Photo No. 69437.

FIGURE X–31
Garden settee. Steel wire. American. Ca. 1890–1900.
This gossamer, wire settee hardly intruded on nature's beauty. The double S-scrolls were popular throughout the 18th and 19th centuries. The use of wire for furniture appealed to the 19th-century fascination with new materials, such as steel and wire. The unexpected use of a seemingly nonrigid material as a seat was an added novelty.
Margaret Woodbury Strong Museum.

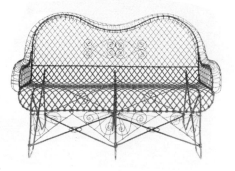

NOTES

1. Andrew Jackson Downing, *The Architecture of Country Houses* (New York: Dover Publications, 1969), pp. 387–88.

2. Downing, *Country Houses,* p. 432.

3. Dianne D. Hauserman, "Alexander Roux and his 'Plain and Artistic Furniture,'" *The Magazine Antiques* 93 (February 1968): 214.

4. Kenneth Ames, "The Battle of the Sideboards," Winterthur Portfolio 9 (Charlottesville, Va.: University Press of Virginia, 1974), p. 3.

5. Marshall B. Davidson, ed., *The American Heritage History of American Antiques from the Revolution to the Civil War* (New York: American Heritage Publishing Co., 1968), p. 234.

6. Downing, *Country Houses*, p. 429.

7. Rodris Roth, "A Patent Model by John Henry Belter," *The Magazine Antiques* 111 (May 1977): 1039.

8. Roth, "A Patent Model," p. 1040.

9. Kenneth Ames, "George Henkels, Nineteenth-Century Philadelphia Cabinetmaker," *The Magazine Antiques* 104 (October 1973): 641.

XI

VICTORIAN FURNITURE:
THE RENAISSANCE REVIVAL

STEEPED IN THE PRECEPTS OF THE MODern aesthetic that worshipped simplicity and condemned what they saw as useless ornament, Americans in the 20th century rejected high Victorian design and sought the simple lines of Queen Anne and Federal furniture. To the Victorians, however, classical simplicity meant dullness and boredom. They delighted in contrast, boldness, novelty, and surprise.

RENAISSANCE REVIVAL: EARLY STAGES

Exhibitors at London's Crystal Palace Exhibition in 1851 displayed furniture with both Rococo and Renaissance revival motifs. In contrast to the rounded silhouettes of the Rococo, the Renaissance revival presented an angular appearance with a jagged picturesque silhouette. The sharply vertical case pieces as well as the seating furniture terminated in elaborate pediments. The smooth, flowing lines of the Rococo contrasted with the segmented surfaces and broken lines of the Renaissance. This style evolved through three phases, although a single piece might include elements of all three. The first phase of the Renaissance style drew heavily on 16th-century French furniture designs, which featured Baroque cartouches, carved animal and human figures, and flattened arches. Even the preferred wood, walnut, was selected to emulate the 16th-century preference for that wood. The use of marquetry, ormolu, and porcelain insets added additional elegance and richness.

In the second phase, the Renaissance motifs soon merged with the Louis XVI revival style, which was based on furniture from 18th-century France. The Empress Eugénie, wife of Napoleon III, who ruled France from 1852 to 1870, had become interested in Marie Antoinette and, in the mid-1860s, decided to redecorate the Tuileries and other palaces in the Louis XVI style. The Empress had given her official blessing to the style, which had already been widely publicized by the growing number of furniture-design books and magazines. It had been displayed at the 1855 Paris Exposition and at the 1862 London Exhibition. The Louis XVI revival was characterized by gilt and ebonized surfaces, squarish backs with ear-like projections on the crests of chairs and sofas, turned and fluted legs, incised lines, and ormolu mounts (Figures XI–2 and XI–3). Beginning in the 1850s, angular flaps appeared on the fronts of seat rails and the bases of cabinets. Leon Marcotte, one

FIGURE XI–2

Sofa. Ebonized cherry. Possibly Philadelphia. Ca. 1850–1875.

Part of a seven-piece parlor suite, this sofa follows closely the neoclassical style of Louis XVI. The fire gilt mounts on the seat rail and the back supports, the brass stringing outlining the front seat rail, and the upholstered back are frequently found on other 19th-century Louis XVI revival furniture. Similar trim was found on 18th-century French case pieces, but seldom on chairs or sofas. Ebonized wood was used commonly in the 19th century, but the 18th-century designer would have painted the wood white, pastel, gold, or gilt. Ernest Hagen preferred this style, observing that it "is really the best of all and will never go out of fashion, and, if not overdone with decoration, is simply grand."

Virginia Museum.

FIGURE XI–3

Side chair. Ebonized cherry. American. Ca. 1870.

The clean, delicate lines of the Louis XVI style are evident in this chair, which has ormolu mounts on the stiles and at the base of the splat. The lyre-shaped splat was a common Empire motif, but the thick C-scrolls above and below the lyre are one indication of a later date.

Margaret Woodbury Strong Museum.

of New York City's most popular cabinetmakers in the 1860s, specialized in Louis XVI furniture. He may have brought the style to New York directly from Paris about 1849. In Philadelphia, the Lejambre family and other French émigrés were major exponents of furniture in the "French taste."

NEO-GREC

A third phase of the Renaissance revival style, the Neo-Grec, drew on Greek, Roman, and Egyptian motifs, as did the Empire style of the early 19th century (Figure XI–4). It was first prominently shown at the 1862 London Exhibition and was given further impetus at the Paris Exposition of 1867. In this phase, furniture took on a more two-dimensional look with less carving, more burl-veneer panels, and inlays of flowers and musical trophies. Egyptian motifs, such as sphinxes, lotus blossoms, and winged sun disks, became increasingly popular after the first exhibition of Egyptian artifacts in America in 1852 (Figures XI–5 and XI–6). Periodic archeological discoveries, particularly in Giza, continued to stimulate an interest in this exotic land. Greek and Roman motifs, such as angular pediments, medallions, columns, paneled plinths, paterae, and acroteria, replaced the carved fish, fowl, game, vegetables, and fruit on earlier Renaissance revival sideboards. Neo-Grec chairs and sofas often assumed the klismos or curule form (Figure XI–7).

American Neo-Grec was more inventive, less restrained, and

more diverse than European examples. However, there was less demand for quality construction, particularly for marquetry and boulle work, in America than in Europe. The difference in quality is understandable, since American factories offered a wider range of furniture to a large middle class, whereas the middle-range market in Europe was more limited. Giant American furniture factories catered to the needs of the middle class rather than concentrating on the high end of the scale. These factories sold flashy, if inexpensive, furniture to newly rich customers, whereas in France there was a more limited middle-class market.

Not everyone was enamored of the Neo-Grec style. Ernest Hagen, reminiscing about his career as a 19th-century New York cabinetmaker, commented that the firm of Rochefort & Skarren "done good work":

FIGURE XI–4
Armchair. Ebonized cherry. American. Ca. 1860–1875.
The winged sphinx arm supports, the winged sun disk, and the lotus blossoms carved at the top of the legs are obvious Egyptian revival motifs. Egyptian designs appear early in the 19th century on Empire furniture, but after the arrival of Egyptian artifacts in the United States in 1852, these motifs dominated some lines of furniture. The designers of this chair took liberties with Egyptian iconography by combining the winged sun disk with a star and flanking it by birds.
E. J. Canton.

FIGURE XI–6 *(left)*
Plant stand. Ebonized cherry. American. Ca. 1880.
The gilt incising stands out against the ebonized background. The anthemia, the arthritic paw feet, and the suggestion of a lyre on the supports flanking the central banister recall "Neo-Grec." The reeded rim of the top and the incising indicate the growing influence of the Eastlake style.
Margaret Woodbury Strong Museum.

FIGURE XI–7 *(below)*
Piano stool. Walnut. Cambridge, Mass. Ca. 1871–1876.
Labeled by Postawka and Company, this "X taboret piano stool," patented in 1871, won a prize at the Philadelphia Centennial in 1876. By turning the knob on the side, the height of the stool is cleverly adjusted up and down. The curule form is found on other Renaissance revival furniture. The upholstery is not original.
Anne and David Sellin.

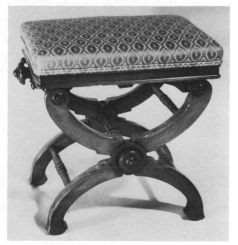

FIGURE XI–5 *(left)*
Safe. Iron. New York. Ca. 1860–1870.
Herring, Parrel, & Sherman sold safes from their store on Broadway in New York as both functional and ornamental additions to the parlor. The ball-topped obelisks, sphinx heads, and hoof feet show the strong influence of the Egyptian taste. The anthemia and nailheads on the brackets behind each obelisk and the acorn drops below them are all common Renaissance revival motifs. The crenelations on the skirt of the safe are repeated on the central portion of the baluster.
E. J. Canton.

Because of its high-quality workmanship and its similarity to two labeled pieces, this cabinet is attributed to Alexander Roux, one of New York's premier craftsmen in the mid-19th century. It is the grandest of the three examples since it has a third arched panel flanked by gilt cherubs. The three cabinets use standardized parts, including identical inlay of wheat stalks, feet, Ionic capitals, brass mounts, and projecting incised side brackets. The painted enamel porcelain plaques differ only in the scene depicted. Similar pieces were referred to as "French cabinets" or cabinets in the "Louis Seize" style. The form is basically Renaissance with its pseudo-Ionic capitals and prominent paneling. The ornamental brass and porcelain medallions follow the Louis XVI manner. The ebonized rosewood contrasts with the brass mounts, gilt carving, and multicolored inlay.
Margaret Woobury Strong Museum.

But their work was nearly all done in the "Neo Grec" most awfull gaudy style with brass gilt Spinx head on the sofas and arm chairs, gilt engraved lines all over with porcailaine painted medallions on the backs, and brass gilt bead moldings nailed on. Otherwise, their work was good; but the style horrible.[1]

ARCHITECTURE

By the 1870s, houses inspired by the Second Empire of Napoleon III, which revived 17th-century French Renaissance architecture, were popular. The hallmarks of this style were bay windows and the steep, dormered, mansard roof named for Francois Mansart, the 17th-century French architect who developed the idea. This style incorporated many architectural elements that were found on furniture of the period, such as cartouches, incised lines, and roundels. The stereotyped Victorian mansion was built in this style and furnished with Rococo and Renaissance revival

furniture. Interiors contained heavy moldings, abundant plaster medallions and ornaments, and arched black or white marble fireplaces. They were decorated with boldly patterned wallpaper, flowered carpets, and looping drapery. The LeGrand Lockwood mansion in Norwalk, Connecticut, finished in 1868, was one of the grandest houses in this style.

THE DINING ROOM

The dining room began to emerge as a separate room early in the 19th century. Victorians took every opportunity to show off their new-found wealth. Wasting an entire room for short periods of eating was one way of proclaiming their wealth. The sumptuous banquets that were so much a part of 19th-century social life were another. The furniture in the dining room, like that in the entire house, also confirmed their affluence. The Renaissance sideboards were not

the massive, costly, carved creations made for international exhibitions. Still, even the ordinary ones were quite impressive. The base consisted of two or three drawers above two doors resting on a raised plinth that sat directly on the floor. Above the top of the cabinet rose a wooden back that supported shelves and was topped with the characteristic Renaissance pediment (Figure XI–1). The more expensive cabinets for the dining room served little function, whereas the cheaper ones had only slightly more display and storage space (Figure XI–8). Incised, gilded lines and burl-veneer panels replaced costly carving or the abundance of applied ornament found on more expensive models.

Dining-room tables with center pedestals replaced the dropleaf type used at the beginning of the century. By mid-century, the extension table became fashionable and replaced earlier varieties, which were simply set side by side to form larger tables. The scrolled legs of the Rococo style were replaced by the more angular ones of the Renaissance and chairs were enhanced by veneered panels, rosettes, and roundels. Furniture manufacturers produced a great variety of dining chairs, from simple, caned ones to comparatively rare upholstered models. The Grecian chairs from the Empire period

continued to be popular as cheap dining room sets (Figure XI–9). Other dining room chairs had spindle-, slat-, or vase-shaped backs. The strengthening braces that joined the seat to the base of the back distinguished most dining-room chairs from parlor ones.

PARLOR SUITES

Both the parlor and the dining room featured a mass of seating furniture, but the best chairs furnished the parlor. The typical seven-piece parlor suite continued to enjoy popularity in the 1860s and 1870s. Some models retained the curves of the Rococo frame and simply added a few Renaissance ornaments. Others were completely redesigned in the new angular mode. The Renaissance sofa, squarish like the chairs, was sometimes divided into two parts rather than into three, as on most Rococo revival ones (Figure XI–10). The more common three-part Renaissance sofas with distinctive sections contrasted with the unified ovals of the Rococo. The square-back chairs with projecting ears had bulging U-shaped seats, triangular pendants on the seat rails, applied roundels, veneer, and incised designs to enliven the wooden frames (Figure XI–11). The legs were usually turned

FIGURE XI–9
Side chair. Walnut. Indiana. Ca. 1870.
Even the plainest chairs capture the essence of the Renaissance revival style. The triangular drop on the front seat rail and the turned front legs are simple suggestions of more elaborate creations. The crest, with its rectangular embossed panels and a central medallion, suggests the elaborately carved crests on expensive chairs. The back legs, which continue up to the crest, turn diagonally to give the impression of jutting ears.
Smithsonian Institution Photo No. 74–10567.

FIGURE XI–10
Sofa. Walnut. American. Ca. 1870.
The sofa, part of a parlor suite, exhibits the angular character of Renaissance revival furniture. The turned Roman legs, the tassel projections on the crest, and the triangular drops on the skirt are all in that idiom. The anthemia at the base of the wooden stiles rising from the back, the figures on the arm terminals, and the inset cameo on the crest all satisfy the Victorian love of the unexpected.
Margaret Woodbury Strong Museum.

FIGURE XI–11
Armchair. Walnut. American. Ca. 1870.
This armchair was made in the suite with the sofa shown in Figure XI–10. The crest, the drops on the corners of the crest, the carved figures on the arms, the seat rail, the turned feet, and the upholstery all match the sofa.
Margaret Woodbury Strong Museum.

FIGURE XI–12 *(right)*
Armchair. Walnut. American. Ca. 1876.
Rococo in form, with its cabriole legs and pinched-in back, this chair sported a special crest in honor of the Centennial. A carved medallion of George Washington rests in the middle, and an eagle with arrows and oak branches hovers overhead. The angularity of the crest, the cabochon medallion of Washington, and the pronounced drop on the skirt confirm the 1876 date.
Margaret Woodbury Strong Museum.

FIGURE XI–13
Detail of crest (Figure XI–12) with the carved medallion of George Washington.
Margaret Woodbury Strong Museum.

FIGURE XI–14 *(far right)*
Table. Walnut. American. Ca. 1876.
The walnut, maple, and painted wood inlay on the table top compares well with the finest 18th-century French work. Beneath the top are a riot of Neo-Grec images. Anthemia lay on the back of monopodal legs capped with exotic figures. An incised and gilded Greek key enlivens the skirt. Triglyphs are applied to each end of the astragal-shaped top. Although stiff and stylized, the turned legs recall Roman examples.
Margaret Woodbury Strong Museum.

and had a large wheel at the top set over a tapering leg and a ring on the cuff. The back legs curved in the reverse cabriole shape found on Rococo revival chairs. By 1876, the seven-piece parlor suite could cost from 60 to 400 dollars, and custom-made sets ran even more (Figures XI–12 and XI–13).

The center table continued to be a major focus of attention in the parlor. The most common marble-topped table, with four legs attached to a central pillar, resembled the earlier style but now took on the characteristic angular and jagged outline of the Renaissance. Roundels, panels of

veneer, and incising related to similar embellishments on chairs. The oval top, a holdover from mid-century designs, continued to be popular, but rectangular shapes with rounded ends became more stylish (Figure XI–14). Giant cup-like finials sometimes added interest beneath the table (Figure XI–15).

The upholstered chairs and sofa provided a focal point for the parlor, but a selection of specialized furniture was an important part of the decor. As with the other furniture, the étagère might reflect either a Renaissance or Rococo revival preference (Figure XI–16). Easels, not for painting but for the display of art, became more common (Figure XI–17). Sewing tables, music racks, and library or writing tables reflected the particular interests of the family (Figures XI–18 and XI–19).

John Jelliff of Newark was particularly known for his parlor sets in the Renaissance style. Jelliff set up his cabinet shop in Newark in 1843 and retired in 1860; the firm under his name continued in operation until 1890. Most of the company's work was custom done, and more than half the sales were to customers outside Newark, largely in New York City. Jelliff made the full range of furniture for parlor, library, and dining room as well as office furniture. Seldom veneered and often adorned with carved figures, tassels, and baskets of fruit, his furniture reveals his training as a

FIGURE XI-15 *(far left, top)*
*Center table. Ebonized wood.
American. Ca. 1875.*
The exquisite floral inlay on the table top is equal to the best inlay done in the 18th century. Next in interest is the turned urn encircled with an incised Greek key and flanked by acorns and other devices that give the element an extraordinarily complex silhouette. The turned pendant beneath the urn is typical of Renaissance revival furniture, as are the anthemia at the top of the legs and on the pendants around the skirt of the table. Gilt balls and applied roundels add further interest.
Margaret Woodbury Strong Museum.

FIGURE XI-16 *(far left, bottom)*
Étagère. Walnut. Rochester, N.Y. Ca. 1875.
Fine furniture was not confined to New York City in the 1870s, as this étagère attributed to Hunn, Smith & Spencer of Rochester attests. The inlaid panel on the door is as fine as anything found in New York City, although it was possibly shipped in from there. The repetition of the "hollow" corners on the top of the miror, in the crest, over each lower shelf, and in the base of the piece contrast with the diversity of the turned and carved ornaments.
Margaret Woodbury Strong Museum.

FIGURE XI-17 *(near left)*
*Easel and print rack. Walnut.
American. Ca. 1870-1880.*
Paintings are displayed on the upper section, and the lower compartment holds prints. Gold and ebony stain set off the geometric and foliate designs. The discovery of similar examples proves that the manufacturer changed the crest or the details of the surface decoration at will by the use of interchangeable parts. A wide variety of choices could be offered without retooling. The turned urn finials repeated on the tops of the front legs are holdovers from the earlier Renaissance style. Although the crest on this example is angular, in the Eastlake tradition, a piece with a Renaissance revival crest could be purchased at this same time.
Margaret Woodbury Strong Museum.

FIGURE XI-18
Canterbury. Walnut. American. Ca. 1865.
Sheraton, in his *Cabinet Dictionary*, published in 1803, describes a canterbury as a piece to hold relics of music. He claimed that the name derived from the Bishop of Canterbury, who supposedly ordered such a piece. By the mid-19th century, with the proliferation of books and magazines, the rack might be used to hold these publications as well.
E. J. Canton.

FIGURE XI–19
Writing table. Walnut. American. Ca. 1870–1875.
The small table top contrasts with the heavy, overengineered base, but the Victorians loved it. The leather top provided a good writing surface. The trefoil blocks applied to the legs and under the skirt echo the three-petaled flowers incised on the skirt. The turnings contrast with the square members.
Anne and David Sellin.

FIGURE XI–20 (right)
Pier glass. Walnut. American. Ca. 1865–1875.
Designed to fit between two windows, tall mirrors such as this added interest and elegance to halls and parlors. Burl walnut panels and paterae flank the glass instead of more common half-columns, even though the applied blocks suggest the pedestal and entablature of a column. The crest in the Renaissance manner is composed of semicircular ornaments, the central one flanked by miniature arcoteria. The stylized, pointed anthemia and other incised ornaments are commonly found on other Renaissance revival furniture.
Ronald A. F. Alvarez.

FIGURE XI–21 (left)
Overmantel mirror. Walnut. Baltimore. Ca. 1865–1875.
Layers of ornament have been applied to the basic frame, resulting in a visually exciting composition. Projecting anthemia sprout from the cornice. Drops surround a Renaissance shield in the center of the cornice. Gilt incising and burl veneer strips on the cornice and on either side of the glass contrast with the dark wood finish. Lotus blossoms, incised at each corner, suggest a touch of Egyptian exotica.
Anne and David Sellin.

FIGURE XI–22
Bed. Walnut. Grand Rapids, Mich. Ca. 1875.
This bed, identical to one advertised by Nelson, Matter & Company, is similar but not as elaborate as the one that firm exhibited at the Philadelphia Centennial. With only touches of carving on the crest of the head and footboards, the bed depends on a series of turnings and applied veneered panels and moldings for its interest. The columns flanking the head and footboards or the cartouche are repeated on the piece shown in Figures XI–25 and XI–29, which are part of this bedroom set.
Margaret Woodbury Strong Museum.

carver. Although he worked in all the styles, including Rococo, Gothic, and Elizabethan, he made his parlor suites mostly in the Renaissance taste.

Mirrors continued to add richness to the parlor. In the Renaissance style, severe pediments and flanking columns resting on stepped plinths replaced the richly carved mantel and pier glass frames of the Rococo period. Gilded incising and burl-veneer panels added touches of color and interest (Figures XI–20 and XI–21). Herman Fersenheim, a New York looking glass maker, aptly characterized the mirrors as the "column Style." These architectural designs, almost like floor-to-ceiling doorways, recalled the architectural mirrors of the 1820s but were much larger in scale and more fanciful in design.

FURNISHING A BEDROOM

Bedrooms, although private, still exhibited the Victorian penchant for conspicuous consumption. The center of attention in the bedroom was the massive Renaissance bed, which assumed monumental proportions. The elaborate headboard, which recalled a Renaissance church facade, loomed over a mattress with springs, and the footboard grew in importance in order not to be completely overshadowed. During the later phases of the Renaissance style, only the central cartouche was carved. Although based on the grand state beds of the 16th and 17th centuries, only a few Renaissance revival beds had canopies. Even so, their monumental size, along with a complicated array of moldings, turnings, and applied panels surrounding a carved central cartouche, made them the grandest pieces in the house (Figures XI–22 and XI–23).

The bureau tried to match the bed in elegance. These were surmounted by a looking glass, which had become progressively larger since the early 19th cen-

tury. Related to the bureau, a dressing case held an even larger mirror that encroached on the drawer space at the base of the mirror, depressing the central section and dividing the top into three parts (Figure XI–24). The lost storage space was made up by closets, which had become more fashionable by the 1870s. Bedroom suites usually had one or the other of these pieces, and gradually the dressing case became predominant. A gentleman's dresser was a tall chest without a mirror (Figure XI–25). A washstand with two doors below a drawer completed the bedroom suite (Figure XI–26). Other bedroom furniture included chairs; bootjacks; towel racks; shaving stands; bedside tables; and a somno, the less common, half-sized washstand (Figures XI–27, XI–28, and XI–29). Although varnished walnut was the most popular finish, cheaper painted bedroom sets of soft pine or poplar were made in abundance.

Drawer pulls were usually simple, turned wooden knobs or teardrop-shaped brass pulls reminiscent of early 18th-century William and Mary ones but much larger in scale. Richer furniture had pulls of brass and ebonized wood with a cross

FIGURE XI–23
Bed. Pine. American. Ca. 1875.
The state beds of the 16th and 17th century inspired mid-19th century beds in the Renaissance revival style. Whether simple or ornate, the typical bed had a Baroque cartouche on a high and imposing headboard. Instead of the more costly carving, this bed is ornamented with stenciling and hand-painted flowers and fruits similar to those on the washstand shown in Figure XI–26, of this set.
Margaret Woodbury Strong Museum.

FIGURE XI–24 *(far left)*
Dressing case. Pine. American. Ca. 1876.
This piece is part of the set that included the bed (Figure XI–23) and washstand (Figure XI–26). In contrast to the dresser or bureau, the dressing case had a mirror that encroached on the drawer space. The tear-drop pulls were generally found on less expensive furniture rather than the T-shaped ones, such as those on the more expensive piece shown in Figure XI–29.
Margaret Woodbury Strong Museum.

FIGURE XI–25
Gentleman's dresser. Walnut. Grand Rapids, Mich. Ca. 1875.
This piece and the ones shown in Figures XI–23 and XI–29 are part of the bedroom set associated with examples made by Nelson, Matter & Company. The arched veneer panels on the drawer fronts pleasantly repeat similar shapes on the crest and constrast with the rectangular shapes that include the drawers themselves, the veneered panels on each side of the drawers, and the side panels. A useful feature on the dresser is the side panel, which opens by means of a key inserted into the keyhole and serves as a locking bar.
Margaret Woodbury Strong Museum.

FIGURE XI–26
Washstand. Pine. American. Ca. 1875.
The plain washstand, part of a complete bedroom set that includes pieces in Figures XI–23 and XI–24, is enlivened with stenciling and hand-painted flowers against an ebonized background. Although originally more common and less expensive than the elaborately carved furniture of the time, much painted furniture has succumbed to the ravages of time and indiscriminate refinishers, so that painted furniture in good condition is now rare.
Margaret Woodbury Strong Museum.

FIGURE XI–27
Bootjack. Walnut. American. Ca. 1865–1875.
The anthemia, roundels, paterae, and other gilt incised lines adorning this mundane bedroom implement are the same motifs found on the grandest pieces of parlor furniture. The original needlework pouch held slippers. While one foot holds the jack down, the U-shaped notch holds the heel of the other boot and the foot is pulled out of the boot.
Smithsonian Institution Furnishings Collection.

piece piercing the enlarged teardrop, creating the shape of a fat cross.

HALL FURNITURE

Renaissance revival hall furniture replaced earlier Gothic or Rococo designs. An imposing hall rack first appearing in the 1840s served a number of functions. Pegs held coats and hats, and wet umbrellas dripped conveniently onto iron plates. Small mirrors in the center of the pieces gave departing residents one last chance to check their appearances before leaving the house. The rack also served as a table where guests could drop calling cards. Other hall furniture might include elegant pedestals to display sculpture, wooden chairs, a table or two, and possibly a clock (Figures XI–30, XI–31, and XI–32).

FIGURE XI–28
Shaving stand. Walnut. American. Ca. 1875.
Since the bureau or dressing case adequately filled the needs of a shaver, the shaving stand fell into the category of conspicuous consumption. The angular knees on the tripod base and the drop finial at the base of the baluster contrast with the smooth curves and absence of drops on most Rococo revival tripod tables.
Margaret Woodbury Strong Museum.

FIGURE XI–29
Night table. Walnut. Grand Rapids, Mich. Ca. 1875.
Also known as a "Somno," this type of night table was only rarely part of the standard parlor set. This one is associated with others made by Nelson, Matter & Company. Highly figured burl walnut veneer enhances the solid walnut frame. The veneered columns suggest the Ionic order but, like most Victorian revivals, are unique interpretations rather than copies of the original. The T-shaped brass pull is typical of the period.
Margaret Woodbury Strong Museum.

FIGURE XI–30 *(below)*
Pedestal. Rosewood. American. Ca. 1870.
The bronze plaques, carved swags, inlaid musical instruments, and burl walnut veneer panels are common Renaissance revival motifs. Furniture made for the Empress Eugenie, with metal plaques and porcelain corners, inspired similar motifs on American furniture. The incised flowers and overall angularity anticipate the coming of the Eastlake style and indicate a late date in the Renaissance revival style.
Lawrence L. Belles.

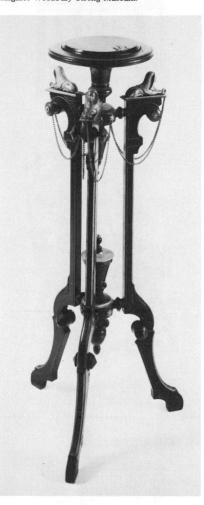

FIGURE XI–31 *(above)*
Plant stand. Ebonized pine. American. Ca. 1870–1875.
The Renaissance revival motifs include the turned pendant under the top and the turned vase with an acorn drop connecting the three legs at the base, the applied roundels, and the incised palmettes on the knees. However, none of these elements were found on actual furniture from the Renaissance. The gilt, white-metal sphinxes represent yet another element of Renaissance revival furniture not found on actual Renaissance furniture. The gilt chain, which added extra interest, suggests drapery in a durable and inexpensive medium.
Margaret Woodbury Strong Museum.

FIGURE XI–32
Tall case clock. Walnut. Ithaca, N.Y. Ca. 1870.
Henry B. Horton of the Ithaca Calendar Clock Company patented the improved calendar mechanism in this clock in 1866. The company sold over 200 variations of its calendar clocks during its 50-year history. Early in the 19th century, inexpensive mass-produced shelf clocks reduced the popularity of tall case clocks, but some customers continued to purchase the item for its novelty or its connotation of elegance. The angular pediment, which has a cartouche, and the applied roundels on the lower case signify the Renaissance revival style.
Margaret Woodbury Strong Museum.

FIGURE XI–33
Chair. Walnut. New York. Dated 1869.
The characteristic front stretcher braced by two vertical turnings under the seat rail and the pipe-like framing are present in this labeled George Hunzinger chair with the March, 1869 patent date. Although Hunzinger created distinctive designs, the projecting turned knobs, upholstered medallion-back, and the pair of roundels at the base of the back are all within the Renaissance revival tradition.
Anne and David Sellin.

FIGURE XI–34
Chair. Walnut. New York. Dated 1869.
George Hunzinger branded the seat of this chair, indicating that he had patented the model on March 30, 1869. The eclectic design combines mechanistic, pipe-like members, rococo sprigs flanking the upholstered medallion-back, roundels, nailheads, and an angular Renaissance crest. Some of his chairs did, in fact, fold up, but this one does not. The overstuffed seat with its original upholstery almost overshadows the light frame.
Smithsonian Institution Photo No. 79–3417.

FIGURE XI–35
Armchair. Maple. New York. Ca. 1876–1880.
George Hunzinger developed these chairs with seats and back of cloth-covered metal straps as a novel alternative to upholstery or cane. The metal outlasted the cloth, which wore through quite rapidly. The notches, necessary in order to recess the metal straps on the back and seat frames, are repeated on all the other turned members, creating a severe and mechanical feeling.
Margaret Woodbury Strong Museum.

INNOVATORS: HUNZINGER'S CHAIRS

The distinctive chairs of George Hunzinger illustrate another element of the Renaissance style, the delight in uniqueness and novelty. One of many German chairmakers working in New York in the 1860s, 1870s, and 1880s, Hunzinger produced some of the most creative chair designs of the century. He used many standard Renaissance motifs, such as acorn finials, nail heads, incising, and channeled lines. However, he usually designed his chairs with surprise twists. Although many of his chairs looked as if they would fold up, many of them did not. A distinctive pair of vertical stretchers usually joined the front stretchers to the seat rail but served no structural function. His wooden chairs took on the appearance of bizarre plumbing as one pipe-like member was joined to another with pseudo-couplings (Figures XI–33 and XI–34). He produced chairs in all price ranges, from a single eight-dollar maple or walnut rocker with an innovative cloth-covered wire seat to a $72 recliner in gilt and carved walnut upholstered in satin with silk fringes (Figures XI–35 and XI–36).

The numerous rocking chairs patented by Hunzinger and others were popular throughout the 19th century and appealed to people's desire for novelty and fascination with mechanical devices. If Americans did not make the first rocking chair, they certainly developed and popularized the device to an extent unknown to Europe. Americans had enjoyed the pleasures of rocking chairs since the 1740s. However, the first widely produced type, which was an American invention, was the Boston rocker, popular from 1825 to the end of the century. Also favored throughout the century was the Grecian rocker, which had a curved back and was based on Empire designs. The more expensive upholstered ones had carved mahogany arm supports in the form

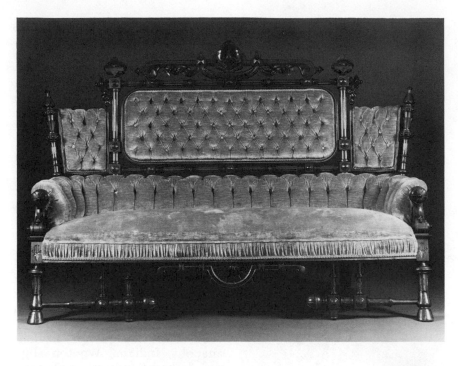

FIGURE XI-36
Sofa. Walnut. New York, Dated 1869.
The patent date of March 30, 1869, appears on this sofa by George Hunzinger. He specialized in chairs, but this sofa is part of one of his parlor suites. The sprigs of leaves dangling from either end of the rod across the top of the sofa are a surprising contrast to the severe, turned parts that frame the rest of the sofa.
Margaret Woodbury Strong Museum.

FIGURE XI-37 (center)
Rocking chair. American. Ca. 1850–1860.
President Abraham Lincoln was seated in this rocking chair when he was assassinated at Ford's Theater in Washington, D.C. The President was tired after a long series of cabinet meetings, and the chair was brought out of storage for the President's use. The publication of a picture of the chair early in the 20th century led antiquarians to call every rocking chair with Grecian volutes on the arms and sabre legs Lincoln rockers. The term applied either to upholstered chairs like this one or to the more common cane variety.
Greenfield Village and Henry Ford Museum.

of eagles, swans, or other Empire motifs instead of the more common scrolls. Cheaper styles, almost devoid of decoration and with caned seats, were made of maple and stained to simulate the more expensive rosewood, mahogany, or walnut. The so-called Lincoln rocker, a Grecian rocker updated with Rococo ornament, was named after the one in which Lincoln was assassinated (Figure XI–37). By mid-century, rockers began to exhibit the popular Rococo carving and balloon backs or the projecting ears and angularity of the Renaissance revival styles. Many rockers were simply parlor side chairs with rockers added. Others with shortened legs and no arms were known as nursing, sewing, or slipper chairs.

Inventors patented a variety of platform rockers by mid-century. Some patented chairs reclined as well as rocked. The American Chair Company of Troy, New York, showed one at the London Crystal Palace Exhibition of 1851. The earliest platform rocker tilted as well as rotated and was the forerunner of the modern office chair. The platform rocker rocked quietly on coil springs and yet looked like a stationary chair. By the 1870s, the rocking chair came out of

the bedroom and kitchen and became a respectable part of the parlor suite (Figure XI–38).

WOOTON DESKS

The mid-19th century brought forth an extraordinary number of creative designers. William S. Wooton had been a manufacturer of school desks, office furniture, and church pews when, in 1874, he took out a patent for an improved secretary. His invention consisted of a case of pigeonholes with a fall-front writing top. Large doors or wings

FIGURE XI-38 (below)
Platform rocker. Ebonized wood. Philadelphia. Ca. 1870–1880.
The original upholstery is complete, with tassels and fringes as recommended by Eastlake himself. The surface is incised with a variety of motifs cut by a shaper. These include anthemia on the arm terminations; a zigzag design found on a bookcase in *Hints on Household Taste*; and a series of circles, dots, and lines. The ears on the crest, which appear to be projecting tenons fastened with a wedge, and the roundels on the base beneath the arms survive from the Renaissance revival style.
Smithsonian Institution Photo No. 46660F.

FIGURE XI–39
Superior grade, the top of the line, Wooton desk illustrated in "Illustrated Catalogue of Wooton's Patent Cabinet Secretaries and Rotary Office Desks," published in 1876. The heavy doors roll open on casters. Marquetry, carving, and exotic woods distinguish the Superior Grade from the Standard.
Smithsonian Institution Photo No. 67057.

FIGURE XI–40
Desk. Walnut. Indianapolis, Ind. Ca. 1875.
Spencer Baird, secretary of the Smithsonian, ordered this "Standard Grade" Wooton desk in 1875. Applied burl walnut veneer panels enrich the surface of the case along with applied moldings, stylized anthemia, and spindles. The huge hinges that support the doors and protrude from each side of the desk are meant to be decorative as well as functional.
Smithsonian Institution Photo No. 16594.

FIGURE XI–41
Desk. Walnut. Indianapolis, Ind. Ca. 1875.
Except for the addition of a more elaborate skirt, this Standard Grade Wooton desk is virtually identical to the one shown in Figure XI–40. The interior view shows the contrasting light wood veneers on the drawer fronts and the numerous pigeonholes and shelves. The intricate patterns on the hinges, typically found also on household hinges of the period, add additional richness and interest.
Margaret Woodbury Strong Museum.

with pigeonholes and shelves were hinged to the central section so that the owner could close up the entire cabinet (Figures XI–39, XI–40, and XI–41). A typical newspaper advertisement summarized the virtues of the extraordinary desk:

> *One hundred and ten compartments, all under one lock and key. A place for everything and everything in its place. Order Reigns Supreme, Confusion Avoided. Time Saved. Vexation Spared.*[2]

By 1875, the company employed 150 men before moving to larger facilities. The next year the company turned out 150 desks a month.

From his headquarters in Indianapolis, Indiana, Wooton shipped desks by railway to all parts of the country. He sold to agents in England, Scotland, and Brazil as well. The massive desk became something of a status symbol, and such noteworthy customers as Spencer Baird, a Secretary of the Smithsonian Institution; John D. Rockefeller of Standard Oil; President Ulysses S. Grant; publishers Joseph Pulitzer and Charles Scribner; and Jay Gould, the railroad mag-

nate, owned them. So successful was the design that several companies, such as the Moore Combination Desk Company of Indianapolis and Henry H. Wiggers of Cincinnati, began to imitate the desk. By 1880, Wooton had left the company. Four years later, the original Wooton Desk Company disappeared from the records of Indianapolis, although other firms produced desks similar to Wooton's until the end of the century.

The desks came in four grades: Ordinary, Standard, Extra, and Superior. The Ordinary grade was the stripped-down model. The Standard grade added veneered panels and better locks. The Extra grade sported incised decoration and a more elaborate pediment. The Superior grade added marquetry and an interior of imported holly or satinwood. The desks were primarily in the Renaissance style. The pediment was often custom made: President Grant's desk was surmounted by an eagle.

MID-19TH CENTURY FURNITURE FACTORIES

Even the elaborate Wooton desks with their angular lines and largely applied ornaments could be produced using factory methods. On the other hand, the intricate carving that characterized the best of the Rococo revival furniture required considerable handwork and did not lend itself to mechanization. Other factors influenced the gradual shift in taste to the more angular furniture of the Renaissance revival, but its suitability for factory production certainly was a consideration for designers employed by factories to create the latest line of furniture.

Machinery did not take over furniture production as soon or as completely as was once thought.[3] As early as 1793, Sir Samuel Bentham was issued patents for almost all the modern woodworking machinery, including planing, molding, rabbeting, grooving, mortising, and sawing equipment. However, not until after the mid-19th century was the equipment in widespread use. Only then were enough factories producing practical woodworking machinery cheaply enough to make it widely affordable. A lack of coal to provide the steam to drive the equipment also hindered the development of large furniture factories. As late as 1870, small cabinetmaking establishments in Boston, Philadelphia, and New York continued to make a significant amount of furniture for large wholesalers in those areas.

The first successful Wentworth planer using a revolving drum cutter was built in 1828. The competing Daniels planer employed a rotating blade like a lawn mower to do the same job. The bandsaw was not widely used until after 1865, when high-grade steel was available to make the saw blade durable enough so that it would not snap under the strain. Circular saws were common by the 1840s and 1850s, but only large factories that ran by steam or water power could employ them efficiently. Numerous patents were issued for boring and mortising machines in the 1830s, but many of these were pedal operated. An individual craftsman could cut six mortises a minute with the machine. The Blanchard lathe, which could cut irregular shapes, such as gunstocks, could also shape cabriole legs. Multiple carving machines were invented in England in the 1840s, but work still required hand finishing. More often, highly skilled operators used spindle carvers with tiny rotating burrs to do freehand carving. Some machines used templates clamped to the work as patterns. The table was raised to a revolving blade that cut along the edge of the template, tracing the design in the wood. Numerous templates combined with differently shaped cutters could produce a wide variety of designs easily and quickly. By the 1880s, designs could also be embossed on furniture by pressing wood between two revolving cylinders with raised designs on them.

The introduction of machinery occurred most widely in the newly settled midwestern towns, such as St. Louis, Cincinnati, and Grand Rapids. These towns grew up near supplies of timber and adjacent to rail and water transportation routes so that furniture could be easily shipped to markets. They also did not have to compete with already entrenched cabinetmaking establishments. As a result, most of the largest factories were located in the Midwest.

MITCHELL AND RAMMELSBERG

The furniture factory of Mitchell and Rammelsberg that opened in Cincinnati in 1849 became one of the largest in the country. An English visitor to the United States in 1854 recorded that the factory was as large as a Manchester cotton mill and employed 260 workers, "native Americans and Germans, the English and Scotch being rejected on account of their intemperance."[4] By 1859, the factory spread over two buildings, one for the machinery and one for finishing the furniture. Two steam engines on the first floor drove more than 80 different machines. Also on the ground floor were 16 lathes, a tin-punching machine for making pie safes, three dovetail cutting machines for making bedsteads, and the blacksmith shop. On the second and third floors, the rough wood was dressed and cut to size, using such machinery as planers; jointers; scroll saws; tenoning machines; frieze-cutting machines; molding cutters; miter, rip, and crosscut saws; grooving cutters; and boring machines. Elevators carried the furniture parts to the next floor for assembly. On the fifth floor, 36 carvers turned out ornaments, such as crest rails and pediments. The adjacent building was used for

Figure XI–42
Folding arm chairs. Walnut. Worcester, Mass. Ca. 1880.
This chair and the one shown in Figure XI–43, patented by E.W. Vaill, illustrate the 19th-century furniture manufacturer's use of interchangeable parts to achieve diversity. Although the overall appearance of the two chairs is similar, they differ significantly in details. The original upholstery on each chair is the most obvious difference. Even the turning of the balls and spindles on the backs of the two chairs is slightly different. Production of these chairs was standardized, but within narrow limits; details were altered to broaden the appeal.
Margaret Woodbury Strong Museum.

Figure XI–43 (center)
Folding arm chair. Walnut. Worcester, Mass. Ca. 1880.
This chair has an E.W. Vaill label.
Margaret Woodbury Strong Museum.

Figure XI–44
Sewing table. Rosewood. Cincinnati, O. Ca. 1857–1868.
The stenciled label, "Mitchell & Rammelsberg, Makers, No. 99 W. 4th St., Cincinnati, O," was used only between 1857, when the firm moved to that location, and 1868, when the company was incorporated. This was one of their cheapest sewing tables, with only a touch of carving on the skirt and the escutcheons. It is similar to a lady's workstand "with silk bag and scroll leg, carved" in either mahogany or rosewood, which the firm sold at wholesale for $35 in 1863. The cloth bag on this example is missing. Both the expensive and cheap version used the same templates for the major parts.
Margaret Woodbury Strong Museum.

varnishing. Woods, such as black walnut, cherry, oak, pine, ash, maple, mahogany, and rosewood, were stored behind the factory in a 75,000-square-foot lumberyard.

The factory turned out a half million dollars worth of furniture a year on the eve of the Civil War. This included over 60 types of furniture and nearly 500 individual patterns, more than two-thirds of them in the low-priced category. A close look at the furniture revealed the use of interchangeable parts, and the same ornament often appeared on different types of furniture (Figures XI–42 and XI–43). The firm's production included étagères, hat racks, music stands, bedsteads, cribs, willow chairs, gilt fancy chairs, bentwood chairs, desks, chests, work tables, and secretaries (Figure XI–44). The company even produced tables and chairs for offices and saloons. The warehouses stocked most of the cheaper furniture, but the very expensive pieces were still made to order. The firm sold from branch warerooms in New Orleans, St. Louis, and Memphis. When the Civil War destroyed its lucrative trade with the south, it began to cater to newly wealthy midwesterners. In 1881, Mitchell dropped the Rammelsberg name, and the company survived until the 1930s.

Furniture factories, such as Mitchell and Rammelsberg, turned out a plethora of children's furniture. Only a few children's pieces have survived from the 18th century, but by the 19th century, chairs, beds, cradles, and children's beds were made. The abundance of such furniture reflects the changing attitude toward children. In the 18th century, aristocrats viewed childhood as a stage in the development toward adulthood that must be tolerated. Children were viewed as miniature adults. In the 19th century, a rising middle class who did not view themselves as perfect aristocrats looked at childhood as a stage in life on a par with adulthood.

The introduction of labor-saving machinery, even in small cabinet shops, and the growth of large-scale factories considerably reduced the price of furniture. As a result, furniture that looked fancy, even if not expensively hand-carved, was priced within reach of the middle-class customer. He could buy the standard seven-piece parlor set, an act that reaffirmed his affluence. Few prosperous merchants in the 18th century had been able to afford such an expensive purchase all at one time.

THE GRAND RAPIDS FURNITURE INDUSTRY

The furniture produced by these large midwestern factories has come to be called, generically, Grand Rapids furniture. It was characterized by incised lines, the use of walnut, of scrolled pediments rather than carved ones, and of 1/40-inch-thick veneer panels. Turned roundels and urn finials were familiar ornaments. Shallow carving was done by shapers with little hand finishing. Seats were often caned rather than upholstered. The furniture was turned out rapidly. In 1851, one Grand Rapids producer boasted that he could toss "whole trees into the hopper and grind out chairs ready for use" to fill an order for 10,000 chairs in Chicago.[5] The use of much identical woodworking machinery by factories across the country resulted in similar products and strikingly uniform designs. Despite the similarities, the subtle variations possible within the broad Renaissance idiom were infinite.

The furniture industry began in Grand Rapids when William Haldane established a cabinet-making shop there in 1836. Not until the 1870s, however, with the establishment of the three major firms—Berkey and Gay; Phoenix Furniture Company; and Nelson, Matter and Company—in the city did Grand Rapids become a major factor in the national furniture market. By 1880, the city ranked seventh nationally in furniture production. Berkey and Gay traced its origin back to 1859 and, by the 1870s, operated from three large factory buildings in Grand Rapids. Showing a willingness to adopt new technology, the company installed steam-powered elevators to move furniture easily from floor to floor. They also installed studios where furniture could be photographed for salesmen's catalogs. The Phoenix Furniture Company, incorporated in 1870, also displayed innovative management. Its new factory included a sawmill and drying kiln for 90,000 feet of lumber, which would assure it of a steady supply of raw materials. The factory also incorporated elaborate precautions to make it fireproof and thus reduce the usually high insurance payments for furniture factories. The third major furniture company in Grand Rapids, Nelson, Matter and Company, was also innovative in its use of railroad tracks that ran right through the building and were used to move furniture.

The three firms expanded their markets by supporting semi-annual trade fairs, beginning in 1878 in Grand Rapids. The Philadelphia Centennial, where all three exhibited and won awards, publicized their work. Soon after the Centennial, the three firms were selling their merchandise from showrooms in New York City. Their furniture was shipped all over the world as well as all over the country. By 1880, a total of 15 firms in Grand Rapids employed over 2,200 workers and sold nearly two million dollars worth of furniture a year. The Phoenix Company alone employed about 520 workers and produced a half million dollars worth of furniture.

THE PAINE FURNITURE COMPANY IN BOSTON

Factory-made furniture was a boon for the middle-class housewife trying to furnish her house on a limited budget, but these new factories accelerated the demise of many small furniture manufacturers in the old cabinetmaking centers. What happened in Boston was repeated in varying degrees in other Eastern cabinetmaking centers. Until mid-century, Boston continued as a major furniture-manufacturing center. The proximity to textile mills in Lowell, Waltham, and Lawrence gave Boston firms an advantage over others, who had to pay shipping rates for a major component of their furniture. A steady stream of immigrants supplied a cheap source of labor, and the railroads that fanned out from Boston provided access to a wide market.

The Paine Furniture Company, established in 1835 in Boston, prospered by using these advantages. Leonard B. Shearer, the founder, at first delivered unfinished furniture to local farmers, who decorated and finished the furniture during their off-seasons. By the 1840s, he began to mechanize his factory and established branch sales offices in New York, New Orleans, and Chicago. However, by the 1860s, he could not compete with furniture shipped to Boston from western factories. The firm survived by specializing in types of furniture those factories did not produce in abundance—such as office, school, and church furniture. The company also purchased unfinished furniture from midwestern factories and added its own decorations and fancy extras. Many other firms were not so clever and simply went out of business.

Throughout the 19th century, the shift accelerated from small cabinetmaking shops selling to a local market to large-scale factories that distributed their products nationally. Although a number of small entrepreneurs, such as Hunzinger, Wooton, and Leonard B. Shearer, carved out small niches in the furniture market, the large furniture manufacturers took over more and more of the job of supplying the middle class. But the dramatic Gothic, Rococo, and Renaissance style furniture from these factories, which had complemented the dominant mood of romanticism in the 19th century, was not without a mounting chorus of critics. These critics were largely responsible for a new direction in furniture design in the last decades of the 19th century.

NOTES

1. Elizabeth A. Ingerman, "Personal Experiences of an Old New York Cabinetmaker," *The Magazine Antiques* 81 (November 1963): 579–80.

2. Betty Lawson Walters, "The King of Desks: Wooton's Patent Secretary," *Smithsonian Studies in History and Technology*, 3 (Washington, D.C.: Smithsonian Institution Press, 1969), p. 1.

3. Polly Anne Earl, "Craftsmen and Machines: The Nineteenth-Century Furniture Industry," *Winterthur Conference Report* (1973) *Technological Innovation and the Decorative Arts* (Winterthur: Henry Francis du Pont Winterthur Museum, 1973), pp. 307–29.

4. Donald C. Peirce, "Mitchell and Rammelsberg, Cincinnati Furniture Manufacturers, 1847–1881," *Winterthur Portfolio* 13 (Chicago: University of Chicago Press, 1979), p. 211.

5. Marshall B. Davidson, ed., *The American Heritage History of Antiques from the Civil War to World War I* (New York: American Heritage Publishing Co., 1969), p. 70.

XII

The Eastlake
and Other Revivals

FIGURE XII–1
Ladies writing desk. Ebonized cherry. New York. Ca. 1870–1880.
Branded on the back is the maker's name, "Herter Bros." The exquisite inlay of grape vines, stylized chrysanthemums, and a beautiful butterfly and the typical piston feet enliven this and other fine pieces produced by this firm. The gallery of spindles flanking the shelf above the writing surface is a motif found on even the cheapest Eastlake furniture. The light satinwood or maple inlay on the fall-front and on the interior contrasts with the dark, ebonized cherry. Ebonizing connoted richness because hard ebony was an exotic and expensive wood, difficult to work with. The light green, patterned velvet behind the shelf adds an additional touch of color.
Ronald A. F. Alvarez.

A POLITICAL AND ECONOMIC MALAISE characterized the years between the 1870s and the 1890s. As the 1870s opened, the United States was approaching the end of a speculative boom touched off by the production demands of the Civil War and the frenzied railroad construction that followed. The bubble burst with the depression of 1873. One of the longest periods of economic contraction in American history followed, reaching its nadir in the depression of 1884 and the panic of 1893. Similar economic woes hit Europe. The political corruption of President Grant's administration also cast a pall across the country between 1868 and 1876. With the economic and political problems depressing the nation, it is not surprising that a new style of furniture, called Eastlake, with less exuberance and fewer elements of conspicuous consumption should be-come popular between the 1870s and 1890s. The passing of the "Brown Decades" and the return of prosperity after 1897 contributed to the interest in Art Nouveau and Arts and Crafts style furniture, as epitomized by the Greene brothers in California and Charles Rohlfs in New York.

ORIGINS

The 1870s represented a watershed decade in the development of furniture. The bizarre creations of the Rococo and Renaissance revival styles, which had dominated the furniture designs of the mid-19th century, gave way to a growing simplicity. By the 1880s, the jagged silhouette of furniture became generally smoother and squared off. Incised lines replaced heavy carving. The change did not occur all at once but was a gradual toning down of the Renaissance and Rococo exuberance.

With few exceptions, such as the neoclassical style of the Adam brothers, French culture had dominated Europe throughout the 18th and 19th centuries. Even when England exerted a cultural influence on America, it was often an Anglicized version of French culture. Early in the 19th century, some English reformers vowed to correct the situation. The English School of Design was established in 1837, and the South Kensington Museum, now the Victoria and Albert, was opened in 1844 under Henry Cole, its first director. The new school trained English designers who began to replace imported Frenchmen, and the museum collected furniture and other decorative arts to serve as models for industrial designers. Whereas Cole pushed for design reform, others—such as the Oxford art critic, John Ruskin, and the architect, Augustus Welby Northmore Pugin—criticized the products of machines. They recommended a return to handcraftsmanship. Rejecting Renaissance classicism, they took the English Middle Ages as their model. They idealized the Gothic furniture, which was produced by individual craftsmen and resulted in simple, honest construction devoid of ornament.

At the same time, England, under Queen Victoria, grew in international stature. She had hoped to show the world her newly acquired power in the London Crystal Palace Exposition in 1851. The world admired her industrial achievements, but France captured the cultural and artistic honors. Only briefly, at the end of the 19th century, did England challenge French cultural dominance. France's defeat by Germany in the Franco-Prussian War in 1871 symbolized the decline of France as an international power.

WILLIAM MORRIS

The best-known English designer in the second half of the century was William Morris, who built on the teachings of Ruskin. When Morris began to furnish his English country house in Bexleyheath, he was appalled by the monstrosities of commercially made furniture. He thought the problem resulted from the unfortunate division of labor between the craftsman and the designer that had occurred in the 1830s with the arrival of the Industrial Revolution. Therefore, in 1861, he established a company organized like a medieval guild to produce household furnishings, including wallpaper, textiles, stained glass, and furniture. An early advertisement explained his purpose:

A company of historical artists had banded themselves together to execute work in a thoroughly artistic and inexpensive manner; and that they determined to devote their spare time to designing for all kinds of manufacture of an artistic nature. [1]

Morris and a number of other Englishmen, such as architects William Burges and Ernest Gimson, and industrial designer Bruce Talbert, produced simple, sturdy oak pieces that suggested medieval English furniture. Their products, devoid of veneer and ornament, stood in sharp contrast to currently popular, heavily ornamented styles. These designers believed that craftsmanship should show, that joints should be visible; this was in contrast to the French idea—that materials should be manipulated in order to mask the hand of the craftsman. Morris first exhibited his revolutionary furniture in 1862 at the International Exhibition in London. By 1881, he had gained an international following and even had showrooms in New York City. Morris hoped to rescue the craftsman from the oblivion of the assembly line and, at the same time, sell cheap furniture of "artistic nature." However, only the famous Morris and Sussex chairs reached a mass market. On the former, the sloping sides of the seat rails formed the rear legs. The hinged back reclined by moving an iron bar from notch to notch along the seat rails. The Sussex chair, based on local Sussex County prototypes, had a rush seat, a spindle back, and delicately turned and splayed legs. Other furniture, often decorated with original paintings by Morris himself and Edward Burne-Jones, the pre-Raphaelite painter, was much too expensive for any but the richest clients.

ARCHITECTURE: RICHARDSON

Like their contemporaries in the decorative arts, architects also drew heavily on English medieval traditions. In the 1870s and 1880s, Americans built houses in the new Queen Anne style inspired by the English cottages erected at the 1876 Centennial Exposition at Philadelphia. Really closer to the architecture of Elizabethan and Jacobean structures, Queen Anne houses took on irregular shapes with round or octagonal towers. The sharply pitched roofs pierced by dormers and turrets contributed to the jagged outlines. The turned spindles on verandas and upper-story balconies replaced earlier Gothic gingerbread and echoed similar turnings common on furniture of the period. Stained-glass windows, colored brick, and patterned shingles created additional visual interest.

In the 1870s and 1880s, the Boston architect, Henry Hobson Richardson, developed his Romanesque style. Before he died in 1886, his characteristic half-circle Romanesque arches, clustered pillars, and massive stone construction influenced architects all over the country and inspired a truly national style that was the beginning of the modern period. Richardson also designed furniture to blend with his medievally inspired buildings. Produced by the Boston firm of Irving and Casson and Davenport, the furniture included high, spindle-back dining-room chairs and tables with spiral turnings or heavy angular legs.

CHARLES EASTLAKE

Richardson's expensive custom-made furniture, like that produced by Morris, never reached a mass market. However, the ideas of the reformers struck a responsive chord, and popularizers, such as Charles Locke Eastlake, had already carried the message to the public. Eastlake incorporated many of Morris's ideas into his decorating handbook, which was entitled *Hints on Household Taste*, and was first published in England in 1868. The first American edition appeared in 1872, and seven more printings proved its widespread influence in the United States.

One of Eastlake's most avid disciples, Harriet Prescott Spofford, writing in 1878 in *Art Decoration Applied to Furniture*, declared that his book "has done a great work toward revolutionizing the manufacture of furniture." Clarence Cook illustrated Eastlake-inspired furniture in *The House Beautiful*, published in New York in 1878. A critic in Cincinnati, however, was not impressed. He declared that "Of all the clumsy, ugly inventions, or rather copies, the sort advocated by Eastlake deserves most to be condemned." He rejected Eastlake's medievalism and declared that comfort and beauty were more important than simplicity.

There may be some use of medievalising household articles in England where this movement is but parallel to the reassertion of conservatism as proclaimed by the recent parliamentary elections—but whereas in our country comfort and beauty are the only guides, the manifest incongruity and unsuitableness of the fashion give it but small chance of being extensively adopted.[2]

Eastlake's purpose was to "improve taste in objects of modern manufacture" and "encourage a discrimination between good and bad design...." In addition to furniture, his book offered advice on all the decorative arts, including picture-framing, floor coverings, glassware, cutlery, dress, jewelry, and architecture. In fact, Eastlake's book contained fewer than 30 designs of furniture and only a couple of these were his own. He warned that his illustrations were not sufficiently detailed to permit cabinetmakers to actually work from them (Figures XII–2, XII–3, and XII–4). And he added the following:

I think it the more necessary to state this, as I find American tradesmen continually advertising what they are pleased to call "Eastlake" furniture, with the production of which I have had nothing whatever to do and for the taste of which I should be very sorry to be considered responsible.[3]

However, Eastlake would have approved of the custom-made furniture of such manufacturers as Leon Marcotte and Christian Herter of New York and Daniel Pabst of Philadelphia. These firms catered to the wealthy few who could still afford custommade furniture. One of the outstanding specialty shops in New York in the 1880s was the firm of Christian Herter. Born in

FIGURE XII–2
Library bookcase. Walnut. American. Ca. 1880.
This is one of the few pieces of American furniture based directly on a plate from Eastlake's *Hints on Household Taste*. Instead of the ornamental hinges on the doors, the American manufacturer has carved a Renaissance revival cabochon. The iron hinges on the roof of the Eastlake design have been replaced by wooden imitations. Even the vent holes on the side and the decorative incising have been copied. The scalloped leather strips on each shelf are suggested by wooden moldings at the top of the doors and above the doors in the bottom section.
Margaret Woodbury Strong Museum.

FIGURE XII–3 *(far left)*
Plate XXV from Eastlake's *Hints on Household Taste*, first American edition, 1878.

FIGURE XII–4
Side chair. Ebonized wood. American. Ca. 1880.
This side chair, one of a set of 30 used in a home in Washington, D.C., is based directly on an illustration in Charles Eastlake's *Hints on Household Taste*. Eastlake declared that "I know no better examples of dining-room chairs than some made in the early part of the seventeenth century which still exist in excellent preservation at Knole...." As was typical, 19th-century designers have embellished Eastlake's rendering by the addition of more boldly turned legs, serpentine stretchers, a row of spindles on the back, and metal inlay. The original light green upholstery follows the Eastlake illustrations closely.
Smithsonian Institution Photo No. 73–6083.

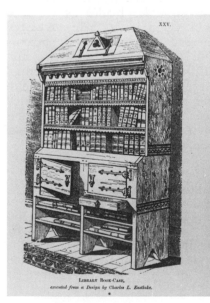

FIGURE XII–5
Side chair. Walnut. American. Ca. 1890.
Spindles, reeding, and the overall rectangular lines of the chair place it firmly in the Eastlake tradition, but the exquisite back places this chair in the Aesthetic category. The gentle curve of the oval is repeated in the crest and in the vines, with their stylized leaves traversing the back.
Margaret Woodbury Strong Museum.

Stuttgart, Germany, in 1840, Herter attended the Ecole des Beaux-Arts in Paris and, about 1860, came to New York to work in his brother's cabinet-making business. Ten years later, he bought out his brother and established his reputation as the head of one of the foremost firms in the city. The company catered to clients such as William H. Vanderbilt, J. Pierpont Morgan, Mark Hopkins, and Jay Gould. The bulbous, carrot-shaped legs tapering to a large ring and flaring into a trumpet-shaped foot appeared on a number of Herter pieces (Figure XII–1). High-quality Herter furniture involving a great amount of hand work in inlay, carving, and finishing deserved to be called Art or Aesthetic Furniture, a name applied to top-of-the-line furniture that typically combined Eastlake's medieval precepts with strong Oriental and naturalistic elements (Figure XII–5).

Few middle-class customers could afford the rich, custom-made furniture produced by the most stylish New York firms. However, furniture manufacturers marketed less expensive lines embodying real or imagined elements of the popular Eastlake precepts to a receptive middle-class clientele. Cheap, but not always poorly designed, furniture often had just enough of the Eastlake ethos to make it palatable. Middle-class customers were happy to be able to afford at least the suggestion of elegance and stylishness preached by Eastlake, Godey, and other voices of the popular culture. This huge mass of furniture was produced in centers such as Grand Rapids, which had 60 factories in the 1890s.

Eastlake blamed poor workmanship on "an unhealthy spirit of competition" that resulted in "a cheap and easy method of workmanship. . . ." He did not disavow factory methods even though he admired hand-craftsmanship like that practiced in the Middle Ages. He declared that "the evidence of human handiwork. . . will always be more interesting than the result of mechanical precision." But, unlike Morris, he recognized that the "division of labour and perfection of machinery have had their attendant advantages, and it cannot be denied that many articles of ancient luxury are by such aid now placed within reach of the millions."[4]

Eastlake went on to describe ways to embellish furniture for the masses. He recommended ebonizing if cheaper woods other than oak were used. He approved the use of walnut veneer since the price of solid walnut was so high. However, he cautioned that the veneer must be a quarter of an inch thick in order to resist blistering. The edges of the ground should be left plain to show honest construction and so that "no thin edges would be exposed to injury . . ." He also approved of geometric or naturalistic marquetry, but he added that "it is quite possible for furniture to be well designed, independently of this or any other mode of surface decoration. . . ." Carving was also acceptable, especially on cabinets, though less so on chairs and tables, where it might interfere with comfort. He recommended the low-relief variety—sawtooth, geometrical, or stylized naturalistic lotus buds or papyrus—rather than the "knot of carving, which chafes our shoulder blades as we lean back upon it. . . ." He suggested instead "a few incised patterns and turned mouldings" as substitutes for the lumpy carving.[5] American manufacturers employed many of these suggested embellishments to create their own interpretation of the Eastlake style.

MEDIEVAL INSPIRATION

The overall appearance of Eastlake style furniture reflected its medieval inspiration. Indeed, the style was sometimes marketed as "modern Gothic." Trained as an architect, Eastlake early became fascinated with medieval buildings. His book, *A History of the Gothic Revival*, acknowledged his debt to the Gothicism of Ruskin. Eastlake's angular architectural furniture with plain oaken surfaces, sometimes enlivened by reeding, and the prominent use of turning, all recalled medieval designs. Eastlake's illustrations of chairs in that tradition, such as wainscot and Cromwell chairs, confirm his fascination with old styles.

Implicit in Eastlake's nostalgia for medieval England was a strong current of cultural nationalism. He reserved his strongest criticism for things French. He railed particularly against the curves of the "bad and vicious" Louis Quatorze and instead recommended rectangularly shaped furniture. He argued against the meaningless curve on the back of a sofa and pointed out that it "is manifestly inconvenient, for it must render it either too high in one place or too low in another to accommodate the shoulders of a sitter." And "chairs were invariably curved in such a manner as to ensure the greatest amount of ugliness with the least possible comfort." Curves made tables "inconvenient to sit at, and always rickety." He complained that the curves weakened furniture and were at the same time more expensive to make. But some American critics, less sensitive to Eastlake's underlying nationalistic motivations, complained that "perhaps in decoration it was too simple . . . and in construction too much like a packing case."[6]

Likes and dislikes are culturally conditioned. No eternal truths decree that a curve is less desirable than a straight line. Morris, Ruskin, and Eastlake were trying to condition the public to appreciate the English cultural heritage and to escape from cultural bondage to France. Cultural nationalism was just another manifestation of the competition between nations that was seen most clearly in the renewed scramble for colonial empires after 1870. According to many English designers, the straight line was good because it suggested England's heritage; curves were bad because they suggested France, her traditional competitor.

THE ORIENTAL CRAZE

English designers drew heavily on their medieval heritage, but they were also influenced by exotic cultures as well (Figure XII–6). They saw in Japanese design the same virtues of simplicity, honesty of construction, and handwork that they praised in the Middle Ages. Interest in Japan began when the American, Commodore Matthew Perry, opened relations with that country in 1854. The major impact of Japanese designs dates from the 1862 London Exhibition, at which the Japanese had their first overseas exhibit. At the Philadelphia Centennial Exhibition of 1876, similar displays of Japanese bronzes, porcelain, and other objects in an authentic Japanese cottage heightened American interest. The Western world was fascinated with the boldness, yet delicacy, of Japanese designs. By the 1880s, Japanese fretwork often replaced the turned spindles of earlier pieces, and inlaid or painted cranes, rushes, butterflies, cherry blossoms, fans, and chrysanthemums cascaded over the surface of custom-made furniture (Figure XII–7).

The designs for inset ceramic tiles in furniture and the vogue for a highly polished lacquer finish also had Japanese origins. Architect Edward W. Godwin's catalogs of designs for art furniture issued in 1877 illustrated Japanese latticework and brackets. Talbert, in his book, *Gothic Forms Applied to Furniture, Metal Work, and Decoration for Domestic Purposes*, advocated the use of inset tiles, and such firms as Herter Broth-

FIGURE XII–6
Table. Ebonized wood. American. Ca. 1880–1890.
The designer of this table creates an aura of the Orient by the use of exaggerated corner brackets on the skirt, on each corner of the top, and on the stretcher. The hoof foot on Chinese furniture usually turns inward, but on this interpretation, the foot turns outward. The wooden studs at each corner of the shelf beneath the top show the influence of the Arts and Crafts movement and the emphasis on obvious joinery.
Ronald A. F. Alvarez.

ers and Kimbel & Cabus of New York picked up the idea for their best furniture (Figure XII–8). The highly polished Japanese lacquer cabinets with mother-of-pearl inlay shown at the 1876 Centennial Exhibition produced a spate of imitations.

BEDROOM FURNITURE

Trading on the Japanese craze, companies, such as J. E. Wall in Boston and Nimura and Sato in Brooklyn, sold complete sets of bamboo bedroom furniture imported from the Orient. They also sold American imitations made of maple turned to simulate bamboo (Figures XII–9 and XII–10). An 1886 issue of *The Decorator and Furnisher* declared that bamboo bedroom suites created a "light and bright, summery and inviting" atmosphere. These bedroom pieces were characterized by rectangular shapes; veneered panels; and the repeated use of spindled galleries on the head- and footboards, on the tops of

dressers, and around the tops of tables. More often, the bed was of oak accented with walnut veneer. The overhanging cornice on fancier beds suggested a roof and security. Both Morris and Talbert used this idea, which was based on medieval church niches. Carved panels in floral or geometric motifs often substituted for the overhanging cornice on the headboard. Eastlake recommended four-poster beds, but American versions are rare.

Beds that folded out of the way were known from the 17th century, but by the 1880s and 1890s, as more people moved into small apartments, such furniture became increasingly popular. Specialty manufacturers, such as the Empire Parlor Bedstead Company of Chicago, designed beds that folded into organs, desks, pianos, sideboards, and chests. The Chicago firm advertised in 1872 a bed "being a cabinet combination bedstead, which represents at pleasure, when closed, an elegant bookcase, marble sideboard, étagère dressing-case or desk...."[7] (Figures XII–11 and XII–12).

FIGURE XII-9

Rocking chair. Maple. New York. Ca. 1880–1890.

This chair is attributed to the Novelty Manufacturing Company of Syracuse, New York. Almost identical chairs appear on the labels of the Niles Chair Works of Niles, Michigan and of Alfred E. Stacey of Elbridge in Onondaga County, New York, who advertised "East Lake and Bamboo" in the 1880s. This chair has little relationship to anything in *Hints on Household Taste*; nor does it resemble bamboo. It is reminiscent of Hunzinger furniture, which was still being made in the 1880s. The upholstery is original, although the customer did not order the long fringe for the front rail, as shown in the Niles and Stacey advertisements. *Private Collection.*

FIGURE XII-10 *(top right)*

Bed. Maple. New York. Ca. 1880.
Bauman Brothers of New York was one of a number of firms specializing in imitation bamboo furniture, primarily bedroom sets. The customer could purchase the bed separately or order an entire suite to match including a dresser, a dressing table, and a side chair. No bamboo was used in this example, but turned maple admirably created the effect. The designer combined the suggestion of the Orient in the bamboo turnings with elements typical of reform furniture of the late 19th century, including the rectilinear lines, the decorative veneer panels, and the beehive-like turnings on the head and foot posts. *Margaret Woodbury Strong Museum.*

FIGURE XII-11 *(right, center)*

Folding bed. Oak. Chicago. Ca. 1880.
Paine's Furniture Company of Boston, Massachusetts sold this bed made by A. H. Andrews & Company of Chicago, who patented the design in 1880. Ideal for cramped apartment living, this bed folded into a slant-front desk. The plain surface is relieved with several burl veneer panels and the ubiquitous reeding of the Eastlake style. The brass knobs on either side of the drawers drop down to form legs when the bed is opened. *Smithsonian Institution Photo No. 64944.*

FIGURE XII-12

Detail of folding bed (Figure XII-11). The label, pasted to the underside of the slant-top, gives instructions on how to open the bed. By the 1880s, coil springs such as were used on this bed were in common use. *Smithsonian Institution Photo No. 64958.*

FIGURE XII–13
Icebox. Walnut. American. Ca. 1875–1885.
This portable model could be placed in a bedroom to eliminate trips to the kitchen for cold water or food. The base, a holdover from the Renaissance revival, contrasts with the angular icebox. The reeding flanking the front door and on the molding around the base of the box suggests similar work on medieval furniture. The stylized leaves and flowers on the crest conform to Eastlake's dictum against the naturalistic portrayal of plant forms.
Smithsonian Institution Photo No. 72–6912.

FIGURE XII–14 *(below)*
Bureau. Ebonized cherry. Philadelphia. Ca. 1876.
This is part of the bedroom set attributed to Allen & Brothers of Philadelphia. The bed that goes with the set is pictured in Figure XII–8. The diamond motif flanking the drawers and the lower section of the mirror is inspired by designs of tile illustrated in Eastlake's *Hints on Household Taste.* The geometric motifs contrast with the naturalistic, brass escutcheons and inset Minton tile.
Smithsonian Institution Photo No. 46660B.

FIGURE XII–15 *(below, right)*
Tête-à-tête. Ebonized wood. American. Ca. 1880.
The tête-à-tête, or "conversational," was a Rococo revival innovation that usually had carving and asymmetrical curves. Eastlake versions were made as well. This interpretation, with its geometrically shaped seats, turned spindles, original upholstery, and tassels and fringe, is typical of other Eastlake seating furniture.
Margaret Woodbury Strong Museum.

In addition to an occasional icebox, other bedroom furniture included matching wardrobes and dressers or bureaus (Figure XII–13). The wardrobe, usually with one or two drawers beneath long doors in the upper section, had a flat top and looked as if it could be turned over without changing the design. Others rested on small square or flattened ball feet and were crowned with spindles. Bureaus, equipped with small drawers below the mirror, served as toilet tables (Figure XII–14). As recommended by Eastlake, simple projecting moldings at each corner of the front stiles relieved the box shape. Chests rested on raised plinths, or short turned, or block-shaped feet. A high five- or six-drawer chest, sometimes known as a "gentleman's chest," was made with or without small mirrors. Tops on fancier ones had flanking drawers or small compartments and ubiquitous spindle galleries. The pulls were rectangular embossed brass ones or oversized drop pulls, recalling the William and Mary style.

PARLOR SEATING

Parlor and dining-room furniture tended to be more ornate than less public bedroom suites. Upholstered parlor chairs were more impressive than the more numerous dining-room chairs, which often had caned or plank-bottom seats. Invariably, on both types, a crest rail filled with turned spindles echoed the spindly turned legs. Some parlor chairs had angular, straight, or flaring legs. Shallow carving, reeding, or geometric or floral marquetry enlivened the seat rails and other exposed wooden parts. Back legs continued to be simple, angular, unadorned stumps. By the 1880s, elaborate

FIGURE XII–16
*Settee. Walnut. American. Ca.
1870–1880.*
**Flowers, such as the giant sunflower
that rises in the center panel of the
back, were favorite motifs on Eastlake
furniture, but, as on this piece, were
stylized in accordance with Eastlake's
disapproval of the naturalistic excesses
of the Rococo revival. This piece has
great rhythm in the crenellated head
rests and in the repetition of the gentle
arches flanking each side of the central
panel and crest ornament.**
Anne and David Sellin.

FIGURE XII–17
Couch. Walnut. American. Ca. 1880.
**Specialized couch-makers, such as
Martyn Brothers, the firm that incised
its label on the frame, produced
reclining couches by the thousands in
the 1880s and 1890s. The incised
anthemia and other decorations on the
crest and skirt are picked out in gilt
against an ebonized background. The
brass roundel on the headrest contrasts
with the usual wooden ones on couches
of lesser quality. The flowered carpet
upholstery is original.**
Margaret Woodbury Strong Museum.

fretwork inspired by Japanese designs was an acceptable alternative for crest rails and the area
beneath the arms. The gender
distinction between parlor chairs
continued. The man's chair had
arms, whereas the woman's
chair was lower and armless to
accommodate the fuller femi-
nine costumes. The chairs of the
1870s still betrayed vestiges of
the Renaissance revival in the
triangular drop on the seat rail
and the heavily turned legs.
However, the flattened crest rail
and the absence of heavy carving
marked them with the new Eastlake style. The popularity of
elaborate tufting continued on
Eastlake furniture even though
Eastlake himself eschewed such
fripperies. Lightness distinguished boudoir chairs, which often
had upholstered seats; thinly
tapered, turned legs; and crest
rails with marquetry or spindles.
Tête-á-têtes, sofas, and settees
exhibited similar characteristics
(Figures XII–15 and XII–16). The
Eastlake couch was a pale reflection of the bold Empire models.
A few squiggles were scratched
into bracket feet. Carving on the
angular stepped-down crest
flanked by wheel-like crowns
and simple scrolls repeated the
shallow work on the feet (Figure
XII–17). Other sofas approx-

FIGURE XII–18
Child's chair. Birch or maple laminated veneer seat and back on walnut frame. New York. Ca. 1880.
Simple, turned front legs and stretchers and plain rear legs support the typical Gardner & Company laminated seat. Only 17 inches high, this chair was designed to lure a doting parent by its expression of endearment in the word, "pet," punched into the back.
Private Collection.

FIGURE XII–19 *(far right)*
Side chair. Ebonized and gilt wood. New York. Ca. 1872.
At the top of the Gardner line, this chair exhibits touches of elegance in the gilt incising on the crest, seat rails, and legs. To cut expenses, it appears only on the front of the legs and the tops of the stretchers, since the backs and bottoms are not visible. The Gardner trademark of a laminated seat and back is punched in a simple design, but the center of attention is the bouquet of flowers painted on the back.
Smithsonian Institution Photo No. 77–15067A.

FIGURE XII–20
Table. Walnut. American. Ca. 1875–1885.
The Eastlake style has come to connote cheap, unadorned furniture. In the late 19th century, however, elegant carved furniture in this style was produced for the elite. This furniture owes more to the Aesthetic, or Art Furniture, Movement than to Eastlake. This table, likely used in a library, exemplifies the best of this furniture style. The flat gadrooning, the lion's paw feet with acanthus leaf above, and the lion's head drawer pulls are derived from Empire motifs. The stylized leaves and flowers repeated on the skirt of the table and on the stretcher and the panels beneath are similar to carving found on other pieces of the period, though not in such abundance.
E. J. Canton.

imated the Renaissance style and were Eastlake only in their sparse carving, incising, and reeding.

Even without Eastlake's praise, the light and durable Windsor chairs would have enjoyed a great popularity throughout the 19th century. The so-called firehouse Windsor, or captain's chair, descended from the 18th-century low-back variety. Windsors with a hoop-shaped back were also similar to 18th-century prototypes but were constructed of oak with thinner seats and little shaping. Double stretchers reinforced lighter legs with little splay. The rod back, usually with a wide crest rail, also survived from the early 19th century.

Windsors could not compete with more stylish cane chairs, but in 1872, George Gardner of New York patented a chair design that afforded both the stylishness of cane and the durability of Windsors. The three layers of wood glued together at right angles to each other made a strong, durable seat. The plywood could also be bent into a continuous seat and back. The secret of their success, however, was the pierced designs that the Gardner Company drilled in the seat—everything from circles and geometric designs to fraternal lodge slogans (Figures XII–18

and XII–19). The chairs were suitable for home use as well as for railroad stations, schools, offices, churches, and any establishment that needed a large number of cheap, durable chairs. Multiple boring produced an infinite variety of patterns, and painted decorations added yet another dimension. By 1888, when the name of the company disappeared from the New York City directories, numerous competitors imitated the perforated seat idea. Some had the spindles and angular silhouette of the Eastlake, but others were devoid of style except for the drilled geometrical designs.

TABLES AND CASE FURNITURE

Tables, like chairs, were scattered throughout the house, and each had a special purpose. Boudoir tables descended from the 18th-century dressing tables and became more common toward the end of the 19th century. Larger, heavier tables with drawers often served in libraries. These had paneled sides joined by turned or pierced stretchers that supported the top (Figure XII–20). Dining-room tables, usually with a central pedestal flanked by rectangular-shaped legs, showed the angularity so characteristic of the Eastlake style. Serving tables, also angular and plain, augmented impressive sideboards in the dining room.

Housewives continued to spend the biggest portion of their furniture budget on cabinets, desks, and sideboards (Figure XII–21). Many cabinet doors swung on engraved strap hinges inspired by medieval hardware as illustrated by Talbert and others. Ebonized and painted geometrical or floral decorations marked top-of-the-line cabinets, but even the cheapest ones were often crowned with the familiar gallery of spindles (Figure XII–22). One line of cabinets had

FIGURE XII–21
Ladies' writing desk. Cherry. American. Ca. 1885.
The rectilinear Eastlake style was often transformed into the Anglo-Japanese, as on this desk. The spindle gallery, common on Eastlake furniture, has been replaced by Oriental fretwork, and the incised decorations are Oriental instead of classical or medieval motifs. As in the 18th century, the Oriental motifs are fanciful interpretation that have very little relationship to actual Oriental designs.
Margaret Woodbury Strong Museum.

FIGURE XII–22
Cabinet. Ebonized wood. Probably Philadelphia. Ca. 1875–1880.
Related to Renaissance revival sideboards with its stop-fluted classical columns and dentil moldings, the cabinet is overlaid with Eastlake ornament, such as the spindle gallery across the back and the row of stylized sunflowers over the central niche, which is paneled with bird's eye maple. The eglomise door panels on either side of the niche and above it draw on Egyptian, medieval, Japanese, and Italian sources for the designs.
Virginia Museum.

FIGURE XII–23
Fire screen. Maple. American. Ca. 1880.
With the advent of central heating in the 19th century, the fire screen lost its utilitarian function but continued in use as a decorative accessory. This screen, with its simulated bamboo turnings and angular lattice design, brought a touch of the Orient into a stylish home. Firelight streaming through the glass panel, lighting up the pressed ferns and flowers, created a striking effect.
Margaret Woodbury Strong Museum.

frames enlivened the facades of both cabinets and sideboards. Eastlake style desks and secretaries of the cylinder or slant-front varieties showed similar motifs.

The angular Eastlake style with incised decorations, inlay, veneer panels, turned legs, and reeding appeared on most of the other accessories common in houses of the late 19th century. With the flood of cheaply printed books, bookcases became a necessity, even in middle-class homes. Washstands and shaving mirrors were common bedroom furniture, and easels, mirrors, music racks, firescreens, occasional tables, plant stands, and pedestals for sculpture contributed to the fashionable cluttered look in the drawing room (Figures XII–23, XII–24, and XII–25).

tiered, open shelves above an enclosed base, and other cabinets were surmounted by rectangular boxes flanked by pierced fan-like fretwork. As illustrated by Eastlake, panels set diagonally into

FIGURE XII–24
Occasional table. Ebonized maple. American. Ca. 1880.
The bamboo turnings place this table firmly under the influence of the Anglo-Japanese style. The red felt applied to the top is heavily embroidered in polychrome wools. The wooden pendants dangling from links of chain suggest Oriental bells or tassels and create additional interest with a minimum of expense.
Margaret Woodbury Strong Museum.

FIGURE XII–25 *(far right)*
Pedestal. Ebonized cherry. American. Ca. 1875–1885.
Carving, still done by hand and expensive, was found only on the best work. No machine could cut under the leaves to make them stand out, as was done on this baluster. The designer combined stylized, naturalistic flowers and leaves with classical motifs, such as the triglyphs on the rim of the top, the reeding on the baluster, and crenellated incising on the base.
E. J. Canton.

In the 1850s and 1860s, decorators tried to furnish rooms in a single style—Rococo for the parlor, Renaissance for the dining room, Gothic for the library. Few people achieved that goal because comfort, whim, nostalgia, convenience, and expense all combined to disrupt the scene. By the 1880s, the cluttered look, sanctioned by Eastlake and others, became fashionable, and the ideal of the matched parlor suite was downplayed. Decorators tried to portray the unique personality of the homeowner by using personal touches, such as an old-style chair or table, Oriental vases, family pictures hanging on the wall, or collections of everything imaginable. The overall effect was more important than individual pieces of furniture.

THE TURKISH CORNER

Some people sought an exotic effect by installing Turkish corners, which suggested romance and a touch of promiscuousness. The Turkish bazaar at the Philadelphia Centennial Exhibition popularized the fad. Overstuffed chairs and sofas, Turkish rugs, and brass tables created slightly risque pleasure alcoves in otherwise prim and proper Victorian houses. Lockwood de Forest set up a shop in India where he commissioned Indian wood, stone, and brass articles that he sold in his New York decorating shop. Another firm, Pottier and Stymus, installed the famous Moorish smoking room in John D. Rockefeller's New York apartment about 1885. Competing firms, such as A. A. Vantine & Company, specialized in creating the Oriental effect. Those who could not afford an entire Turkish room achieved at least a suggestion of the effect with overstuffed chairs, divans, sofas, and couches (Figure XII–26). Other popular exotic themes included the Moorish and Egyptian.

FIGURE XII–26
Armchair. American. Ca. 1880–1890.
The frame of the chair has disappeared at the hands of the upholsterer. The thick, overstuffed seat suggesting the Turkish style conceals coil springs. The embroidered pastoral scene with the shepherd feeding a lamb reflects 19th-century romanticism. The decorative cord on the seat rail and the arms and the elaborately knotted fringe are examples of the wide range of upholstery techniques available in the late 19th century.
Smithsonian Institution Photo No. 71–2208.

FIGURE XII–27

Armchair. American. Oak and maple. Ca. 1875–1880.
This chair design is based on a 17th-century chair in Pilgrim Hall at Plymouth, Massachusetts. In reproducing the chair in the late 19th century, the designer simulated age by omitting a second top rail and the second row of spindles below the front seat rail. Rear stretchers have been omitted altogether. The spindles have been misinterpreted. Instead of an elliptical shape between two pointed shapes, the 19th-century turner made a vase and urn. The original chair may have had a turned finial at the top of the front stile but certainly did not have the meager disks seen on this chair.
Courtesy, The Henry Francis du Pont Winterthur Museum.

FIGURE XII–28 (right)

Rocking chair. Baltimore. Ca. 1875–1885.
The splat design is typical of 18th century Philadelphia chairs, although the straps are stiff in contrast to the flowing lines of the 18th-century prototype. In fact, the chair was labeled by C. F. Meishahn & Company of Baltimore. Although coarse, the carving on the knees is close to 18th-century prototypes. The droopy shell on the skirt indicates that the designer never saw a scallop shell. And, of course, rockers were never attached to ball and claw feet in the 18th century.
Smithsonian Institution Photo No. 71–2154.

FIGURE XII–29

Platform rocker. American. Ca. 1876.
New spinning-wheel parts were produced for the purpose of assembling them into this chair. The maker was appealing to the same market that purchased Colonial revival suggestions of 18th- and early 19th-century furniture. However, this chair carried a more personal message in the reminder that the chair was similar to "Our Mother's." In an 1886 edition of *The Decorator and Furnisher*, William B. Savage of Boston advertised "The Old Flax Spinning Wheel Chair...Novel, Artistic, Durable."
Margaret Woodbury Strong Museum.

COLONIAL REVIVAL

Just as Europeans glorified their past, Americans expressed their nationalism by favoring Colonial revival furniture. By the 1870s, homeowners brought down from the attic at least one or two old 18th-century chairs or tables. Indeed, the term Colonial revival, applied indiscriminately to Queen Anne, Chippendale, Federal, and even Empire-style furniture manufactured after 1876. Revivals of these styles are often referred to erroneously as Centennial furniture (Figures XII–27, XII–28, and XII–29). Although the New England kitchen at the Centennial Exhibition, housed incorrectly in a Middle Atlantic style log cabin, encouraged the taste, it did not gain great popularity until after 1876. By 1884, the *Cabinet Making and Upholstery* magazine, in an article entitled "The Antique Craze," declared that "The manufacture of antiques has become a modern industry...." Such firms as the Barnard & Simonds Company of Rochester, New York, prospered at the turn of the century by specializing in "thoroughly correct Colonial Reproductions." The passion for American furniture of the 18th century continues to the present.

The widely popular Colonial style in architecture paralleled the similar interest in furniture. As early as the 1870s, architects, such as McKim, Mead, and White, were using Colonial architecture as a basis for their designs. By the 1890s, revivals of other historic styles became part of the repertoire of the architects influenced by the French Ecole des Beaux-Arts, and classical architecture of the World's Columbian Exposition of 1893 in Chicago reflected this influence. Architects copied French chateaus, Italian palazzos, and German castles as well as 18th century American Colonial mansions. The Biltmore, a French chateau recreated in Asheville, North Carolina, and The Breakers, an Italian palace built in

Newport, Rhode Island, are two of the most impressive examples. Decorators furnished these great mansions with reproductions of Spanish, Italian, English, French, and American furniture, mostly from the 17th and 18th centuries. These revivals differed from earlier ones in that they were more historically correct. Although mid-19th-century styles were derived from earlier designs, they did nothing more than suggest the style, add on to it, and improve it, at least in the mind of the designer. By the 1890s, good American reproductions of Louis XIV, XV, and XVI and Renaissance styles closely recreated the real thing.

The widespread availability of pattern books allowed firms, such as A. H. Davenport and Company of Boston, to offer a wide variety of furniture. Between 1880 and 1906, the year the owner died, the firm produced furniture for such places as Iolani Palace in Honolulu and the White House in Washington, D.C. They also worked for prominent architects, such as McKim, Mead, and White. Whether the style was Federal, Colonial, William and Mary, Gothic, or Eastlake, Davenport could fill the order by consulting his large library of source books.

WICKER, HORN, AND RUSTIC FURNITURE

Wicker had no such historical associations and appealed for other reasons. Wicker furniture, made from the rattan plant and woven on bentwood frames, evoked the exotic Far East where the plant flourished. Photographers capitalized on its exotic connotation by frequently using wicker chairs as props. The natural material also appealed to the late 19th-century interest in plants and nature, of which the profusion of house plants was but one symptom. Wicker had an ancient history. It was used by the Egyptians, the Greeks, and the Romans, and the Pilgrims brought a wicker cradle with them on the *Mayflower*. After a wicker chair was exhibited at the 1851 Crystal Palace Exhibition, wicker grew steadily in popularity. Lightweight and cool, it was suitable for porch and outdoor use. (Figure XII–30).

Rattan had served as a packing material for exotic Oriental imports. Cyrus Wakefield

FIGURE XII–30
Chair. Wicker. American. Ca. 1885–1895.
Sometimes used as a photographer's props, these chairs were even more common in the home. The original gilt paint on this chair proves that white was not the only color for wicker. The swirling lines of the back and seat and the curls confirm Gervase Wheeler's observations in his style book, Rural Homes, published in 1852, that wicker has "durability, elasticity, and great facility of being turned and twisted into an almost endless variety of shapes. . . ."
Smithsonian Instituion Photo No. 69901.

FIGURE XII–31
*Armchair. Steer horn. American. Ca.
1875.*
**Numerous horns were rejected before
suitable shapes could be found. The
graceful horns combine in a sensuous,
writhing riot of curves. The upholstered
seat and back fulfill the demand for
comfort, which was sometimes
overlooked on other horn chairs.**
Margaret Woodbury Strong Museum.

FIGURE XII–32
*Plant stand. Wood branches. American.
1850–1900.*
**Made of branches, twigs and roots, this
planter blended perfectly with furniture
for a country cottage or summer retreat.
Rustic furniture was popular in the
18th century, but the jagged outline
also appealed to the Victorian love of
the picturesque. The vertical limbs
nailed to the legs suggest the jagged
outline of legs on high-style
Renaissance revival tripod tables.**
Margaret Woodbury Strong Museum.

brought some home with him
from the docks of Boston. Real-
izing its potential for furniture,
he established the Wakefield
Rattan Company, which opened
its first factory in 1855. The
company received an award for
its displays of wicker at the 1876
Centennial. By 1885, the company's catalog illustrated 71 designs for wicker rockers alone
plus countless stands, divans, tea
tables, library tables, bookstands,
étagères, music stands, piano
seats, lounges, couches, footstools, and ottomans. Star patterns, sunbursts, feathers, fans,
and hearts added interest to
these pieces. Braiding, twisting,
pleating, or winding the wicker
cane into scroll patterns
achieved further diversity. By
the 1880s, the more angular
Eastlake-inspired chairs, painted
yellow, green, and red as well as
white, replaced chairs with
curlicues. Competing with natural wicker, by the early 20th
century, was a process of winding twisted paper treated with a
glue sizing around a wire core.

Like wicker, furniture of animal horn and hide appealed to
people because of its romantic
associations and its novelty.
Such pieces evoked the wild
west and the frontier (Figure
XII–31). Chairs made of steer,
buffalo, or elk horns were the

most common. Judges at a fair in
New Jersey called a buffalo-horn
hat rack made by William
Thompson of New York "the
lightest and handsomest hat rack
ever made." Abraham Lincoln
accepted a gift of an elk-horn
chair from an admiring western
trapper, and the popularity had
not abated when Teddy Roosevelt received a horn chair for his
home at Sagamore Hill at the
turn of the century.

A number of 18th century pattern books inspired by Chinese
furniture, illustrated rustic furniture made of natural tree
branches. If Americans indulged
in the fad in the 18th century,
no examples have survived. The
idea was revived in the 1830s for
garden seats, summer houses,
and cottages. A. J. Downing recommended it in *The Hor-
ticulturist*. The Renaissance tradition, which had dominated
furniture design throughout the
18th and early 19th centuries, demanded that man master the
natural materials. In contrast,
rustic furniture was constructed
with a minimum of alteration to
the wood. The alternative system appealed to the Victorians'
love of novelty. It also evoked
the romanticism of the strong
back-to-nature movement (Figure XII–32). Several firms specialized in rustic furniture. In
1874, O'Brien Brothers of
Yonkers, New York, advertised
that they would ship rustic furniture anywhere in the country.
The Laurelton Rustic Manufacturing Company sold quantities
of furniture in New York City in
the 1870s, and the Old Hickory
Furniture Company did a large
mail-order business from Mar-
tinsville, Indiana, beginning in
the 1890s. In such places as the
Adirondacks, local inhabitants
produced distinctive rustic furniture for the numerous woodland
camps of wealthy city dwellers.
Split twigs nailed onto boards in
geometrical patterns created a
striking effect. Other artisans
fashioned crude bentwood chairs
that resembled ones by Michael
Thonet.

BENTWOOD

Thonet, working in Austria in the 1840s, refined his process for bending wood into gentle curves. He exhibited at the 1851 Crystal Palace Exhibition in London and soon expanded his market by shipping the chairs in parts to sales offices all over the world. By 1871, the year of Thonet's death, factories in Germany, Austria, and Eastern Europe manufactured chair parts for such destinations as New York, where children assembled the chairs before they went on sale (Figure XII–33). The chairs were made of beech stained to imitate rosewood, walnut, or mahogany. Thonet added a rocking chair to his line in 1860. The bentwood chair has been the most popular piece of furniture ever designed. The Thonet firm continues to manufacture furniture in a Pennsylvania factory where it relocated on the eve of World War II.

ART NOUVEAU

The sensuous, curving lines of bentwood foreshadowed the arrival of Art Nouveau in the 1890s. Sold in America in the two decades before World War I,

FIGURE XII–33
Armchair. Beech. Austrian. Ca. 1875–1880.
This example with the common cane seat is based on the design for a chair sold to a Viennese cafe in 1849 that was Thonet's first major commission. The Thonet patent expired in 1869; more than 50 companies were imitating bentwood furniture by the end of the 19th century, including the Kohn brothers in Europe and the Sheboygan Chair Company in America. The chairs were produced by cutting beech logs into poles that were soaked or steamed and fixed into iron forms until dry. All the joints were screwed together so that when disassembled, the parts would lay flat for ease of shipping. Distributors all over the world, including a New York office opened about 1873, assembled and sold the imported furniture.
Anne and David Sellin.

the style takes its name from the sign Siegfried Bing hung outside his interior decorating shop in Paris in 1896. Drawing on nature for abstract forms, Art Nouveau was the only 19th-century style not based on historical precedents. Sensuous, writhing, elongated shapes based on plants, waves, and flowers, characterized Art Nouveau (Figure XII–34). English designers, such as C. F. A. Voysey, A. H. Mackmurdo, and Charles Rennie

FIGURE XII–34
Card table. Mahogany. Chicago. Ca. 1900–1910.
This table combines sweeping lines with deep, swirling carving. The carving merges into a smooth, flaring trunk and again bursts forth on the underside of the top like a breaking wave. A brass seal on the underside of the base is the Tobey Furniture Company label. Several identical tables are known. The firm had produced an expensive, high-quality line of furniture, since 1888, when a subsidiary was established for that purpose. By the 1890's the firm was considered the leading furniture and decorating company in Chicago, and its reputation had spread nationwide.
Anne and David Sellin.

FIGURE XII–35
Table. Cherry. American. Ca. 1880–1890.

Few pieces of American Art Nouveau furniture are known. This simple table has the sensuous lines of the Art Nouveau style with only a touch of carving on the bracket attaching each buttress to the underside of the top.
Margaret Woodbury Strong Museum.

FIGURE XII–36
Side chair. Oak. Buffalo, N.Y. Dated 1905.

Charles Rohlfs was trained as a designer at the Cooper Union in New York and began his career designing iron stoves. He later became an actor, but in 1884 promised his new wife to give up the stage and turned to his hobby of woodworking. He exhibited his custom-made furniture at a number of national and international exhibitions and frequently lectured to the Roycrofters at East Aurora, New York. The notched frame and angular forms of this chair characterized much of Rohlfs' work. The prized Rohlfs' mark, an R within a saw frame, is burned into the side of the left rear chair leg.
Nancy and Fred Starr.

Mackintosh of Glasgow, Scotland, first experimented with the style. It soon spread to the Continent and to America, where it took on a more erotic and naturalistic flavor. Louis Comfort Tiffany was an internationally acclaimed master of the new style. He worked primarily in glass and metal, but he also produced some furniture. Only a few American designers matched the graceful and imaginative furniture produced in Europe. Most American Art Nouveau furniture manufactured by such Grand Rapids firms as the Bishop Furniture Company was a pale rendition of Continental design (Figure XII–35). Some firms, however, especially the Gorham Manufacturing Company of Providence, Rhode Island; George C. Flint of New York; Charles Rohlfs of Buffalo, New York; and Edward Colonna of Dayton, Ohio, produced extraordinary naturalistic pieces (Figure XII–36). S. Karpen and Brothers Furniture Company of Chicago and New York publicized over 1,000 designs of Art Nouveau furniture. Even so, its elite associations restricted the influence of Art Nouveau in America.

THE ARTS AND CRAFTS MOVEMENT: STICKLEY

In contrast to Art Nouveau, the furniture inspired by the English Arts and Crafts Movement was much more popular in the United States. This movement grew out of the same criticisms by William Morris and John Ruskin that had influenced the development of the Eastlake style. Their idea was to reunite art and craftsmanship, which had been separated about 1830. According to these critics, as a result of the Industrial Revolution, the craftsman no longer designed his own work. In the 1880s, a number of guilds and communes were established to change that. The Century Guild, established by English architect, A. H. Mackmurdo, in 1882 was the first. Magazines, such as *Hobby Horse*, publicized the work of these groups, and the Arts and Crafts Exhibiting Society, from which the movement derived its name, exhibited the results of their work periodically from 1888 on. These exhibitions showed the public the range of experimental furniture, but only a few wealthy patrons could afford to buy anything. One critic wrote that "the exhibition is full of things which seem to have been done because the designer and maker enjoyed doing them—not because they were calculated to sell well."[8]

Voysey and other English reformers directly influenced the American furniture manufacturer, Gustav Stickley, during his trip to England in 1898. Upon his return, Stickley began making simplified furniture. *The Craftsman* magazine, which he began publishing in 1901, became the oracle of the Arts and Crafts movement in America. A 1907 advertisement for his furniture summed up his philosophy of functionalism:

The piece . . . is first, last and all the time a chair, and not an imitation of a throne, nor an exhibit of snakes and dragons in a wild riot of misapplied wood-carving.

The fundamental purpose in building this chair was to make a piece which would be essentially comfortable, durable, well proportioned and as soundly put together as the best workmanship, tools and materials make possible.[9]

Like Eastlake, Morris, and other reformers, Stickley rejected the use of ornament: "Again, the structural lines should not be subjected to the indignity of applied ornament, which, in its nature as a parasite, never fails to absorb the strength of the organism on which it feeds. . . "[10] (Figure XII–37).

Stickley called his work Craftsman furniture, but his imitators popularized the term "Mission." A story in the March 1915 issue of *Good Furniture* recounted that Joseph P. McHugh designed a line of furniture based on a chair received from California in 1894. An architect, inspired by the Spanish missions along the California coast, had designed the chairs. Stickley, however, vehemently maintained that European designs, and not the California missions,

influenced his furniture. He believed that commercial advertisers merely used the term "mission" to capitalize on the public's fascination with California.

After viewing Stickley's furniture at the 1900 Grand Rapids Exposition, *The House Beautiful* wrote that "the day of cheap veneer, of jig-saw ornament, of poor imitations of French periods, is happily over."[11] His furniture for bedroom, dining room, or parlor had a rhythmic quality in its repetition of slats on chairs, in the mullions on secretaries, and in the radiating stretchers of tables. Believing in honesty of construction, Stickley used exposed tenons, dovetails, and butterfly joints, and wrought-iron or hammered copper pulls and hinges, which relieved the warm expanses of golden oak (Figures XII–38 and XII–39). Between 1903 and 1904, Stickley's designer, Harvey Ellis, convinced him to use metal inlay in stylized plant designs, but when Ellis died in 1904, Stickley abandoned the idea. Stickley most frequently used leather and

FIGURE XII–37
Armchair. Oak. Grand Rapids, Mich. Ca. 1900–1910.
Very similar to Gustav Stickley Mission furniture, this chair made in Grand Rapids is actually labeled "Limbert's Arts and Crafts furniture." The plain, broad expanses of oak; the exposed tenons on the arms; the dark wooden pegs securing the tenons of the stretchers; and the seat rail are all features found on Stickley furniture and copied by his numerous competitors. The cushion is removed to expose the slats and corner braces of the seat. The furniture is purposely overengineered.
Ronald A. F. Alvarez.

FIGURE XII–38
Sideboard. Oak. Eastwood, N.Y. Ca. 1905–1915.
A drawer is branded "Als ik Kan/ Stickley"—As I Can. The grainy oak is relieved by the use of hammered copper pulls and long strap hinges. The rail at the back of the sideboard held plates. The extra work on the hardware, such as the hammer marks and the shading, often distinguished Gustav's furniture from his competitors. The U-shaped bail was usually found on Stickley's early work. This piece sold for $50 in 1910.
Virginia Museum.

canvas upholstery, but he also recommended linen stitched with delicate floral patterns (Figure XII–40).

Stickley had a wide following. His furniture was popularized by *The House Beautiful* magazine. Stickley supported vocational training, and school manuals showed plans for his furniture. *Popular Mechanics* published a do-it-yourself book, *How to Make Mission Furniture*. Others, however, vulgarized the concept

(Figure XII–41). Louis Brigham, for example, described how to imitate the style with orange crates and scrap lumber. Stickley had a number of competitors, including his five brothers, who were all in the furniture business. The Grand Rapids firms of Charles P. Limbert Company and Lifetime Furniture Company also made furniture in the Mission manner, as did the flamboyant Elbert Hubbard of the Roycroft Shops in East Aurora, New York (Figure XII–42). Stickley wrote, immodestly, as follows:

Most of my furniture was so carefully designed and well proportioned in the first place, that even with my advanced experience I cannot improve upon it.[12]

Be that as it may, the public got tired of his furniture, and by 1915, he was bankrupt. The flock of imitators drew business away from the Stickley firm, but his bankruptcy resulted more from the shift in public preference to Colonial revival styles.

THE GREENE BROTHERS

Many of Stickley's imitators skimped on quality by such expedients as using plain-sawn instead of quarter-sawn oak or stamped pulls rather than hand-wrought ones. However, the furniture designed by several prominent American architects and designers—particularly in California and in the Prairie school of architects and designers in Chicago and the Midwest—usually equalled Stickley's pieces in quality. Many of these firms, such as Henry and Charles Greene in California, recommended Stickley's furniture for clients who could not afford their custom-made furniture. The Greene Brothers employed Peter Hall to execute many of their designs, which featured inlaid floral motifs in fruit woods and semiprecious stones (Figures XII–43, XII–44, and XII–45). The Greenes used ebony pegs as a

FIGURE XII–43
Armchair. Mahogany. Berkeley, Calif. Ca. 1909.
The Greenes designed this armchair for the William R. Thorsen house in Berkeley, California. Craftsmen from Peter Hall's shop in Pasadena made the furniture in the basement of the Thorsen house. The exposed, square, ebony pegs; the inlay on the crest rail; and the twisted arms are repeated on many other pieces of Greene furniture. The pegs covered countersunk brass screws.
Private Collection.

FIGURE XII–44
Writing desk. Ash. Pasadena, Calif. Ca. 1904.
The furniture for Adelaide Tichenor's house in Long Beach, California represented a departure from the angular furniture inspired by Gustav Stickley (Figure XII–39) and the emergence of a distinctive Greene style derived from the Greenes' interest in Oriental design. Subtle, curved forms replaced the linearity of Mission furniture. The drop-front rests on the drawers. The rear, vertical bar on the side of the desk raises up, allowing a panel to slide out, giving access to a hidden compartment behind the pigeonholes.
Private Collection.

FIGURE XII–42
Magazine pedestal. Oak. East Aurora, N.Y. Ca. 1908–1912.
This piece is related to Stickley's work in the use of oak and the through-tenon fastened with a key, but the incised design similar to Chinese characters on the side of the piece was a technique Stickley did not use. This piece is labeled as made by Roycroft Shops, whose furniture is less massive and employs incised carving to relieve the oak surfaces.
Virginia Museum.

FIGURE XII–45 (right)
Desk. Mahogany. Pasadena, Calif. Ca. 1907.
Peter Hall executed this Greene design for Robert R. Blacker. The corner brackets reveal a direct Oriental influence. Oak inlay on the sides of the desk and on the lid adds considerable interest to the plain mahogany surface. The lid rests on leather pads applied to the edges of the lid. Traditionally, the backs of case pieces were left unfinished because they rarely showed, but on later cabinets designed by the Greenes, the backs are finished as nicely as the fronts.
Private Collection.

Figure XII–46
Armchair. Oak. Milwaukee, Wis. Ca. 1904.
Frank Lloyd Wright designed a set of these chairs for the living room, dining room, and library of the Darwin D. Martin House in Buffalo, New York. The chair, along with other furniture and woodwork, was produced by the Matthews Brothers Manufacturing Company of Milwaukee, Wisconsin. The use of circular and semicircular forms in this chair departs from Wright's earlier chairs with rectilinear forms. The curved back and arm rests were designed for comfort in contrast to his earlier chairs with straight backs.
Albright-Knox Art Gallery, Buffalo, New York. Gift of Mr. Darwin R. Martin, 1968.

Figure XII–47 *(right)*
Desk. Oak. Milwaukee, Wis. Ca. 1910.
The Niedecken–Walbridge Company made this desk under the direction of Frank Lloyd Wright for the Avery Coonley House that Wright built near Chicago. Wright designed the architecture and furnishing to be in harmony. He even designed dresses for Mrs. Coonley to harmonize with the interior. The desk echoes the interior and the exterior design both in spirit and in detail. The cantilevered lamps on either side of the desk recall the outdoor lamps attached to the house. The four doors repeat the form of the casement windows in the living room. The intersecting planes of the desk are repeated in the interior and exterior architecture.
The Art Institute of Chicago.

decorative touch to relieve their plain expanses of oak, mahogany, teak, walnut, ash, rosewood, or maple. One observer, after visiting a house designed and furnished by the Greenes, commented as follows:

It is all in keeping with the style of architecture and the wall fittings but there is not a deep, soft chair or sofa in the house. . . . It is studio furniture.[13]

THE PRAIRIE SCHOOL: FRANK LLOYD WRIGHT

The Greene Brothers' furniture resembled pieces by other notable architects and designers in the Chicago area, such as George Washington Maher, George Grant Elmslie, and Frank Lloyd Wright. The custom-made furniture by these men represented only a small part of the burgeoning furniture trade in Chicago. Chicago manufacturers, such as the Tobey Furniture Company, had taken advantage of the city's central location near wood supplies and at the hub of transportation arteries that linked the city with markets all over the United States. By the 1890s, the city had surpassed even New York as the center of the furniture-making industry in America.

Although he was an architect who catered only to a small, affluent clientele, Wright has become the best known of the Chicago furniture designers. Wright pioneered the use in America of tall slats for chair backs, an idea inspired by the Japanese and used earlier by English designers (Figure XII–46). The horizontal effect of Wright's tables, with their heavy tops and massive square legs, contrasted with the high backs of his chairs (Figure XII–47). These flat, straight designs lent themselves to construction by machines that could cut only straight lines. Wright commissioned most of his early furniture in the 1890s from the small Chicago cabinet shop of John Ayers. Wright, like Eastlake and Stickley, did not object to the use of machinery if the designs were well drawn. On this point he split with many in the American Arts and Crafts movement, who, like Morris and Ruskin, rejected the machine altogether in favor of hand-craftsmanship.

Designers, such as Frank Lloyd Wright, the Greene brothers, and others, served as a bridge between the Victorian era and the 20th century. On the eve of World War I, the Arts and Crafts movement, which had captured only a small but important part of the American furniture market, had been completely engulfed by a new wave of revival styles (Figure XII–48). However, many of the precepts of these early reformers, such as simplicity of design, honesty of construction, and functionalism, were soon rediscovered and provided the departure point for modern design in the 20th century.

NOTES

1. Elizabeth Aslin, *Nineteenth Century English Furniture* (New York: Thomas Yoseloff, 1962), p. 58.

2. Elizabeth Aslin, *The Aesthetic Movement: Prelude to Art Nouveau* (New York: Frederick A. Praeger, 1969), p. 62.

3. Charles L. Eastlake, *Hints on Household Taste* (New York: Dover Publications, Inc., 1969), p. xxiv.

4. Eastlake, *Hints*, pp. 4, 105–106.

5. Eastlake, *Hints*, pp. 58, 164–165, 182.

6. Aslin, *Nineteenth Century English Furniture*, p. 61.

7. Kenneth Leroy Ames, *Renaissance Revival Furniture in America* (Ph.D. Dissertation, University of Pennsylvania, 1970), pp. 399–400.

8. Aslin, *Nineteenth Century English Furniture*, p. 70.

9. Robert Judson Clark, ed., *The Arts and Crafts Movement in America 1876–1916* (Princeton, N. J.: Princeton University Press, 1972), p. 40.

10. John Crosby Freeman, "The Forgotten Rebel" (Watkins Glen, N.Y.: Century House, 1966), p. 107.

11. Carol Lorraine Bohdan and Todd Mitchell Volpe, "The Furniture of Gustav Stickley," *The Magazine Antiques* 111 (May 1977): 986.

12. Berry B. Tracy, ed., *19th-Century America: Furniture and Other Decorative Arts* (New York: Metropolitan Museum of Art, 1970), Plate 295.

13. Clark, *The Arts and Crafts Movement in America*, p. 83.

FIGURE XII–48
Armchair. Walnut. American. Ca. 1890–1910.
Used in a dining room, this chair evoked the hunt with the two hounds baying the stag. Cupids, one with a bow and arrow and the other with a staff, flank the crest. The spiral turnings on the arm supports and stretchers recall the twist turnings of 17th-century furniture. The smoothly sculptured dogs on the arm terminals contrast with the wild carving on the back.
Margaret Woodbury Strong Museum.

XIII
THE CONNOISSEURSHIP
OF AMERICAN FURNITURE

FIGURE XIII–1
Side chair. Mahogany. American. Ca.
1900–1925.
**The unlikely combination of fully
developed Queen Anne with equally
developed Chippendale elements raises
immediate questions about the 18th
century origins of this chair. The
Queen Anne characteristics of the
compass seat and S-curved stiles are
embellished with Chippendale ears and
elaborate rococo carving, a highly
unlikely combination. The combination
of ideas in this chair, recarved in the
early 20th century, fights with one
another, and the results are
unsatisfying.**
*Courtesy, The Henry Francis du Pont Winterthur
Museum.*

CHARLES MONTGOMERY, FORMER CU-rator for the Garvan Collection at Yale University and one of the greatest professors of American furniture and decorative arts, explained that the goal of the connoisseur "is to determine the date and place of manufacture; the author, if possible; and where within the range of its fellows the object stands in terms of its condition, excellence of execution, and success as a work of art."[1] The major elements to consider when evaluating a piece of furniture in this manner include design, color, tool marks, wood, shrinkage, hardware, finish, and wear. The interaction of form and ornament, proportion, the excellence of craftsmanship, and the color and figure of the wood determine quality. Once a piece of fine furniture has been identified, it is the responsibility of the connoisseur to preserve that piece through enlightened conservation practices.

DESIGN

Design is paramount in determining country of origin, date, authenticity, and quality. Jonathan Richardson, who wrote the first tract in English on the subject of connoisseurship in 1719, declared that "to judge the degrees of goodness of a picture or drawing it is necessary that the connoisseur should be thoroughly acquainted, and perpetually conversant with the best...."[2] The same advice applies to the evaluation of the quality and authenticity of furniture.

Charles Montgomery concluded that "anyone who aspires to become a connoisseur must first learn to see, and then he must look and look and look, and remember what he sees."[3] The old saw, "You will never see another one like it," is seldom true. Furniture in any given style period falls within a general range of form and ornament. If a piece of furniture deviates from these general dimensions, the explanation may be that the piece has been altered or made entirely in a different period than is at first apparent (Figure XIII–2).

Is IT AMERICAN?

Design helps the connoisseur to identify the country of origin. Particular difficulty arises in distinguishing between English and American furniture in the 17th and 18th centuries because of the predominant influence of the English culture in America. Is-

FIGURE XIII–2
Armchair. Oak. North Scituate, Mass. 1969.
This chair was sold to the Henry Ford Museum as a 17th-century Brewster-type turned chair. Several years after the sale, the maker, Armand LaMontagne, admitted that he had made the chair himself in the late 1960s. LaMontagne copied almost exactly a turned chair in the Metropolitan Museum of Art. The only major difference was in the number of spindles, six across the front and four across the back, versus three on the back and five in the front of the Metropolitan Museum chair. Two of the lower spindles were omitted to simulate wear. Other subtle differences from 17th-century practice abound. The feeble turnings of the LaMontagne chair are not crisp and fluid like the 17th-century one. A dull, grayish color of the modern chair clearly indicates the product of a stain rather than natural aging. X-rays confirmed the presence of modern gimlet-bit drills instead of the old-fashioned pod drill, which makes a cup-shaped hole.
Greenfield Village and Henry Ford Museum.

FIGURE XIII–3
Side chair. Mahogany. American. Ca. 1880–1890.
Designed in the manner of an 18th-century Philadelphia chair with a Gothic splat, this chair reveals its late 19th-century origin in a number of details. Instead of volutes, the outside straps terminate in eight-petaled flowers suspiciously like those on Eastlake furniture. The inner straps do not flow gracefully into the crest, but instead, double back on themselves just under the crest. The carving on the stiles also reveals the influence of Eastlake designs, particularly in the half-moon ornament at the base of the splat and elongated rectangle at mid-section. The carving on the knees is coarser and less graceful than the best 18th-century examples.
Mrs. Thomas L. Wattles.

rael Sack, the founder of one of the major antique shops in America, was once asked the difference between English and American furniture. He replied, "English furniture speaks with an accent." And, in fact, a comparison of high-style English and American furniture reveals that, in most cases, the English work is much richer and more ornate. Although a few pieces of Ameri-can furniture are as elaborate as any English furniture, most American work has an appealing simplicity and directness. Relatively few American patrons could afford the high cost of carving, gilt, and other enrichments. American furniture is much closer to English rural cabinetmaking than to high-style London work.

In comparing these areas, the differences are much more subtle; often, only differences in wood distinguish the English work from American. American cabinetmakers typically selected thick boards of pine; poplar; or, occasionally, chestnut for drawer bottoms, corner blocks, backboards, and other spots where the wood did not show. English furniture-makers usually chose the familiar oak or deal as a secondary wood and cut the boards thinly. Even in the 17th century, when both areas used oak, microscopic analysis can distinguish between English white oak and American red oak.

REVIVAL VERSUS PERIOD

Design can also help connoisseurs with another difficult problem: distinguishing revivals from period pieces. After the Philadelphia centennial celebration in 1876, the popularity of Colonial revival furniture styles based on 18th- and early 19th-century American furniture increased dramatically. Accurately designed copies are often difficult to distinguish from period models. Philadelphia Chippendale furniture and Baltimore Federal pieces, along with Empire furniture from the first half of the 19th century, were the most commonly reproduced American styles (Figure XIII–3).

Many 19th-century revivals fail to capture the subtleties of the earlier styles, and a familiarity with the principal design motifs of each period will often betray the later date. For example, an Empire style bed with typical Eastlake reeded molding or an Empire style chest with

18th-century-style bail pulls indicates a late date. Proportion is also a dating clue. Since 19th-century cabinetmakers often worked from lithographs rather than actual examples, many Colonial revival pieces appear taller and thinner than the actual 18th-century prototypes. Carving and inlay often reveal a lack of understanding of the classical principles of unity that dominated design in the 18th century. A design might duplicate 18th-century forms, but construction techniques frequently reveal actual age. The use of machine-made dovetails and the characteristic double-ogee curved corner blocks are sure indications of a late 19th- or 20th-century date (Figures XIII-4 and XIII-5).

In many of these examples, the hand of a later craftsman is revealed by the evidence of a modern cultural influence that was unconsciously incorporated into his design and workmanship. Wallace Nutting's reproductions, popular in the 1920s and 1930s, illustrate this phenomenon. Nutting studied 17th- and 18th-century furniture and carefully designed his line of

reproductions. But the furniture he produced never existed in the 17th or 18th centuries. His pieces are often too perfect, combining the best elements from several 18th-century pieces into one piece (Figure XIII-6). Another example of cultural conditioning is the practice of the early 20th-century collectors, steeped in the traditions of the Arts and Crafts movement, which worshiped natural wood surfaces, to strip furniture down to the bare wood. In fact, most furniture other than those pieces

FIGURE XIII-4 *(left)*
Detail of drawers from 18th- and 19th-century chests.
The two drawers on the bottom, made in the 18th century, have handmade dovetails. The scribe marks indicate the depth of the saw cuts. Highly regular and comparatively small dovetails on the top two drawers were made by machine. The crescent shape with the dowels is an easily recognizable machine-made variation.
Author's Collection.

FIGURE XIII-5
Detail of Figure XIII-3.
The rear seat joints are reinforced by the typical double-ogee corner blocks sawn out with a band saw. Another indication of factory construction is the slight deflection of the line of the sides of the seat rails where they join the legs. The top of the front legs are cut square, and the sides of the seat rail extend at an angle. In most well-made 18th-century chairs, this line would be perfectly straight.
Mrs. Thomas L. Wattles.

FIGURE XIII-6
Chest. Oak. American. Ca. 1920–1930.
Wallace Nutting copied a Connecticut sunflower chest in his own collection for this example. The original chest is now in the Wadsworth Atheneum (see also Figure I-11). The reproduction was advertised for $275 in Nutting's 1928 catalog. The most obvious difference between the 17th-century prototype and the Nutting piece is the lack of wear and softening of edges. It does not look 200 years old. A close comparison of the two pieces reveals subtle differences of design, particularly in the carving. The sunflowers, for example, on the early piece are flanked by tulips, not the amorphous designs of the Nutting reproduction. Nutting's penchant for bolder turnings and deeper carving than that of his models is not as apparent on this chest as it is on some of his other pieces.
Margaret Woodbury Strong Museum.

FIGURE XIII–7
Desk and bookcase, upper section walnut, Philadelphia; lower section mahogany, Massachusetts. Ca. 1760–80.
The use of different woods for the upper and lower sections is a strong indication that these two parts did not start life together. Although the piece was heavily stained to disguise the marriage, with time, natural aging has revealed the different wood colors. An even more obvious sign of a marriage is the difference in design of the top and bottom. The reverse serpentine base is a common Massachusetts form, while the petaled rosettes and flame finials are typical of Pennsylvania work. A shell carved at a late date on the desk interior's central door matches the one in the bonnet but was intended to create the illusion that the two parts belonged together.
Yale University Art Gallery, Mabel Brady Garvan Collection.

made of mahogany and walnut was painted or stained in the 17th and 18th centuries. In another example of cultural influences, skirts on close stools—chairs fitted with chamber pots—disappeared at the hands of Victorians, who could not stand the idea of a toilet in their parlors.

MARRIAGES AND EMBELLISHMENTS

Alterations present another problem. One of the most common examples is the married piece in which the top and bottom sections from old but different pieces are brought together (Figure XIII–7). Large case pieces, such as desk and bookcases, high chests, and chest on chests, were made in two parts for ease of handling. These parts often became separated in the course of their history. On original pieces, workmanship usually will not vary from top to bottom. The dovetails on drawers should have similar dimensions. The same woods should be found in upper and lower sections. Pegs securing tenons should be inserted in similar configurations at each joint. The distance between holes for posts to hold brasses should be the same. If additional

holes are present, indicating several sets of brasses, the pattern should be consistent from drawer to drawer. The technique used to attach the drawer runners to the case should be the same.

The connoisseur also has to contend with unscrupulous craftsmen who alter the original design to increase the price. In some cases, a totally new piece is made from old wood or furniture parts (Figures XIII–8 and XIII–9). In a more subtle technique, an old but simply designed piece is embellished in order to create a more expensive one. (Figure XIII–1).

The list of embellishments is endless. Bonnets are added to flat-top high chests. Blockfronts are applied to straight-front chests. Arms are added to side chairs. Ball and claw feet are carved from plain pad feet. Inlay or carving is applied to the surface of drawer fronts, chair knees, and table skirts (Figure XIII–10). More desirable settees are made from sofas. Sideboards are cut down to smaller sizes. Tilt-top tables are dished and the tops scalloped. In most of these examples, the new design clearly violates the classical principle of proportion (Figures XIII–11 and XIII–12). A familiarity with the standard motifs and techniques peculiar to each period can often reveal the work of a later hand.

FIGURE XIII–8
Table. Walnut. American. Ca. 20th century.
The popular Queen Anne style dropleaf table is one of the most commonly altered 18th-century forms. Few of the 18th-century ones have survived unaltered, the rigors of hard use. This is an example of the most common alteration—the addition of a new top to an old base.
Private Collection.

FIGURE XIII–9
Detail of underside of top (Figure XIII–8).
The hinge marks on the edge of the table indicate that leaves from several tables were used to make the new top. Each leaf is made up of four pieces of wood. Leaves on 18th-century tables were generally one or two pieces, but seldom more. No glue blocks have been used to attach the center board to the frame, as was the practice in the 18th century. Glue blocks often fall off, but the light-colored spot where they were once attached should be apparent.
Private Collection.

FIGURE XIII–10 *(above)*
Table. Mahogany. American. Ca. 1780.
The heavy, stop-fluted baluster and snake feet with a broad knee are not sympathetic with the Federal carving of bow knots and grape leaves. The incompatibility of the carving and the style of the baluster suggests that the carving was added later.
Private Collection.

FIGURE XIII–11 *(above)*
High-post bed. Maple. New England. Ca. 1800.
The cleaner lines of the bed without the footboard may explain why it was removed. A close look at the footposts reveals the plugged mortises that secured the original footboard. The plugs were stained red along with the rest of the bed to hide the removal. The chamfering of the posts, which stops just above the old mortises, indicates that a footboard was originally present, and not something added later and then removed.
Private Collection.

FIGURE XIII–12
Detail of foot posts (Figure XIII–11).
Private Collection.

FIGURE XIII–13
Base of tripod table. Walnut. Ca. 1860.
One leg is removed to show the dowel joint common on furniture in the second half of the 19th century. The round hole was easier to drill than cutting a rectangular mortise.
Private Collection.

FIGURE XIII–14
Tall case clock. Cherry. Massachusetts. Ca. 1800–1810.
The case is typical of a group found in Roxbury, Massachusetts and throughout New England with its brass ball finials, spaghetti fretwork on the bonnet, reeded corner columns, and French flared feet. The molding on the bonnet is one piece of wood, not three with mitered joints, as would be expected.
Private Collection.

The unity is destroyed when carving and inlay that deviate from the original decoration are added. If the top of a tea table is scalloped, it may be much too fancy for the plain baluster and base. Later carving applied to a drawer or other surface can also be detected when the board is not thick enough to take it. The result is a paper-thin board or very shallow carving. Tilt-top tea tables can easily be dished on a lathe, but the craftsman starts with an appropriately thick piece of wood so that the end result is still amply thick. Knees and feet on rough-cut legs will be large enough to provide surface to accommodate the carved design.

CONSTRUCTION AS A GUIDE

Not only the evolution of design but also the evolution of construction techniques helps to date furniture. The primary 18th-century technique for fastening stiles and rails was the mortise and tenon joint, often secured by a peg. Such a joint is still used today on the best handmade furniture. In the mid-19th century, however, a more easily made joint with a dowel that fit into a drilled hole became popular (Figure XIII–13). Clock cases always

FIGURE XIII–15
Detail of clock face (Figure XIII–14).
The American-made works, with an imported English dial by Wilson, are typical of the period but probably not original to this case. Cases were made to order for the works and usually fit exactly. The wide space between the face of the works and the frame indicates a case and works that were not originally together.
Private Collection.

FIGURE XIII–16 *(far right)*
Detail of clockworks and platform (Figure XIII–14).
Clockworks rest on a platform. This platform has been cut down about one inch to accommodate the slightly different size of these works. A remnant of the piece cut off the top of the platform is visible directly behind the platform, and the saw cut is also evident.
Private Collection.

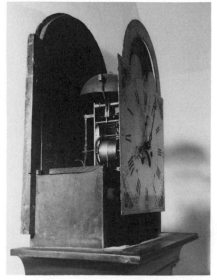

fit the case exactly since they were custom-made for the works. A cut-down platform on which the works rest or a clock face that does not fit flush with the inside of the bonnet raises suspicions (Figures XIII–14, XIII–15, and XIII–16). Moldings were usually nailed on in the 18th century, whereas glue was more often used to attach the molding in the 19th century.

Stretchers on most 18th-century chairs were made flush with the edge of the leg (Figure XIII–17). When the joint was secured with a pin, the flush stretcher provided extra reinforcement to the leg so that the pin would not split the leg. By the 19th century, the original reason for the design was lost because the pin was omitted, and the custom of placing the stretcher in the middle of the leg began (Figure XIII–18).

TOOL MARKS

Although most of the cabinet-making tools used even today are similar to those employed by the Greeks, Romans, and Egyptians, several new tools were developed by the mid-19th century, and others were refined. An awareness of these changes can be extremely useful for dating furniture. Although patented in England in the 1790s, the circular saw was not widely used in America until the 1840s. When the unmistakable arc-shaped kerf appears on a piece of wood, it probably dates after that time (Figure XIII–19). Likewise, the distinctive marks of the band saw, developed somewhat later than the circular saw, betray a mid-19th-century date. The parallel kerf marks can be confused with the marks of the up-and-down mill saw used in America as early as the 1650s (Figure XIII–20). However, the latter makes marks that are spaced about a half-inch apart and are not as clean looking. The kerf on hand-sawn boards is also similar to that made by the band saw

FIGURE XIII–17 *(above)*
Detail of stretcher of easy chair. Mahogany. Massachusetts. Ca. 1770–1780.
Most chairs with Marlborough legs in the 18th century were made with the stretcher flush with the side of the chair leg as in this example.
Author's Collection.

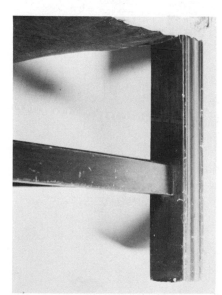

FIGURE XIII–18 *(above)*
Detail of stretcher on easy chair. Mahogany. 20th century.
The stretchers of most straight-legged 20th-century chairs and those of reproductions of 18th-century chairs are made with the stretcher entering the leg in the middle.
Author's Collection.

FIGURE XIII–19
Underside of tilt-top table. Walnut. American. Ca. 1860.
The presence of distinctive circular saw marks indicates that the piece of wood was worked after about 1840. The kerf of the circular saw is a series of parallel curves.
Author's Collection.

FIGURE XIII–20 *(below)*
Top: Detail of backboards of secretary. New England. Ca. 1815.
Showing up-and-down saw marks.
Bottom: Detail of back of drawer. American. Ca. 1900.
Showing band saw marks.
Author's Collection.

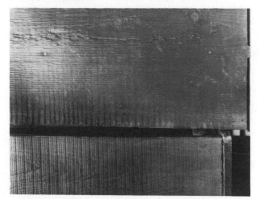

FIGURE XIII–21 *(above)*
Detail of backboards on desk shown in Figure IV–58.
The pit-saw marks are not parallel, as is apparent in the marks on the backboards of this 18th-century desk. On exterior surfaces, these marks are planed and sanded out, but on the backs of desks and chests and in other places where the marks do not show, they are usually left untouched.
Author's Collection.

FIGURE XIII–22 *(top, right)*
Back of chest. Cherry and pine. New England. Ca. 1760.
The curved blade of the fore or jack plane makes a distinctive concave furrow across the surface of the wood.
Author's Collection.

FIGURE XIII–23 *(center, right)*
Lathe marks on an 18th-century side chair.
The slow revolution of the tredle or cranked lathe caused the turner's chisel to make faint ridges on the wood.
Author's Collection.

FIGURE XIII–24
Detail of finial on slat-back chair. Maple. Pennsylvania. Ca. 1750–1800.
Wear is apparent on the back of the finial where rubbing against the wall has flattened it. Shrinkage of the wood has caused the peg holding the slat to protrude from the surface. The faint scribe mark above the peg indicates to the chairmaker the top of the mortise, which accepts the top slat.
Author's Collection.

but is easily distinguishable by marks that are not exactly parallel (Figure XIII–21).

The first step facing the 18th-century cabinetmaker, and the modern wood craftsman as well, is to dress the wood or plane it to a uniform thickness. In the 18th century, this was accomplished by a 16- to 18-inch-long fore, or jack plane, with a slightly cupped blade that could take a bigger bite than a straight blade. The cupped blade produced a wavy texture on the board (Figure XIII–22). Outside surfaces were smoothed out by the even longer trying plane and the short smoothing plane, both of which had straight blades. Even on finished surfaces, however, fingers can sometimes feel the evidence of the jack plane, and the marks are generally visible to the eye on the backboards of chests and other hidden surfaces. Nineteenth-century machine planes cut a smooth surface. A machine for planing was patented in England as early as the 1790s, but such devices were not in common use in America until the middle of the 19th century.

The slow hand-cranked or treadle-powered 18th- and early 19th-century lathes produced slight ridges on the wood (Figure XIII–23). Although the turner would smooth out most of these ridges, some would remain in the crevices of the turnings. The modern, high-speed, electrically driven lathes leave no such marks. However, if the faker uses a slow-speed lathe to duplicate the marks, his chisels will tear the fibers of the wood, leaving a fuzzy surface. The early turners avoided the problem by using green wood.

Molding planes also left their distinctive marks. Operated by hand, the plane, no matter how skillfully used, could not be made to cut a completely straight line. By sighting down the length of a piece of molding, a slight waviness is easily apparent. From the mid-19th century on, mechanical planers employed blades that revolved at a fixed point, and the wood was pushed through them, giving unerringly straight results.

Other 18th-century tools, called pod and spoon drills, made a rounded bottom on holes bored into the wood. By the 19th-century, the gimlet drill, which had a threaded tip to start the hole, was common. The result was a squared-off bottom with a screw hole in the center. The hole made by a gimlet drill should not be confused with a similar hole made by an 18th-century center bit, which was used only for large, shallow boring. X–ray can reveal which tool was used without breaking apart the joint.

COLOR

It is possible, although unlikely, that an extremely knowledgeable and competent craftsman could duplicate the design and workmanship of the 18th century. However, it would be more difficult to accurately duplicate the coloration of the wood, as it has changed over the years. Wood oxidizes with age and darkens. New wood or wood that is freshly cut has a lighter color. Exposure to sunlight bleaches the wood; dirt discolors it. Walnut changes from a dark brown to a honey gold color after a century of exposure. Pine is almost white when freshly cut but ages to a mellow tobacco brown. Tulip poplar turns to a grayish color. The exterior surfaces of a piece, even though stained and finished, reflect the natural aging. Two different woods stained to match will change color at different rates and within several decades will begin to appear very different in color. But the most dramatic color changes occur on the unfinished surfaces such as the underside of tables and chest tops and the backs of high chests. If top and bottom belong together, the color of the upper and lower boards will match. A light outline where a drawer covers the underside of a table top proves that the drawer is original to the piece and not a recent addition. If the color of rails, supporting blocks, and feet matches, then the feet have not been restored. A light outline on the wood duplicating the shape of the brass pulls is evidence that they are original. The outline on the underside of a table top, resulting from its protection from air and light, should match the outline of the frame that supports it.

Changes in the color of wood caused by age cannot be accurately duplicated. In the 18th century, cabinetmakers did not finish unseen surfaces, such as the undersides of tables, the insides of drawers, and the backs of chests. Occasionally, these surfaces have been sealed at a later date, but more often stains on hidden surfaces cover up alterations. The presence of new wood is easily detected, and the addition of old wood can be detected because even wood of the same species will discolor differently and not match other old boards. Often, fakers will use old wood, but when it is cut, new wood is exposed, since surface discoloration penetrates less than a sixteenth of an inch. To cover up alterations, fakers have used black washes, ammonia gases, tea, and coffee stains. A sharp and experienced eye familiar with the natural process of discoloration of old wood can usually detect these subterfuges. The gas treatment, for example, produces a uniform color over the wood without the variations caused by natural differences in exposure to light and air. Other variations, such as those caused by grease from hands grasping for knobs, and under table tops or the crest rails of chairs, will also be obliterated by such techniques.

WOOD

The quality of the wood is also a clue to age. Boards 18 to 30 inches wide and cut from virgin forests were not uncommon in the 18th century. Today, however, the standard 17-inch-wide boards are usually spliced together from several thinner boards cut from trees only 20 or 30 years old. Even in the 18th century, two boards were sometimes used for table tops, the sides of chests, or other places that required a wide board, but the advice to beware of three-board tops is good. With an abundance of wood to choose from, cabinetmakers selected knot-free boards and frequently used highly figured wood in order to enhance their design. Boards were typically one inch thick compared to the standard three-quarter or five-eighths-inch thickness of modern wood. Plywood, of course, was not widely used until after the 1860s when the first patents for the process were granted.

SHRINKAGE

Wood is composed of 80 to 90 percent water. As it ages, it gives up water and shrinks. This process is a clue to age. Wood tends to shrink across the grain. Thus, on a table top, the dimensions across the grain may be half an inch less than a measurement with the grain. Shrinkage is also apparent on turned balusters or ball feet, which flatten slightly across the grain. When the top of a chest shrinks, the molding around the edge protrudes slightly behind the chest. The two separate strips of wood on either end of a desk lid will protrude slightly beyond the edge of the top. Shrinkage also affects veneer. Since different woods shrink at different rates, veneer will tend to crack or pop off altogether as the two woods shear past one another.

Pegs in joints tend to protrude as the surface of the wood recedes across the grain, whereas the peg shrinks very little with the grain (Figure XIII–24). Flush pegs may indicate that the pegs are new. Many chairs have, at one point, been reglued, a job that requires drilling out the ir-

regularly cut old pegs in order to take the chair apart so that the joints can be cleaned and reglued. New, round pegs are driven in flush.

WEAR

Does the piece look two or three hundred years old? Even the most cherished heirloom will show signs of wear (Figure XIII–25). Drawer runners will wear more deeply on the front and curve upward toward the back in a concave arc, as the drawer dips when pulled out. By opening and closing a drawer on the average of twice a day, the runner will travel as much as 50 miles in the course of its 250-year history. Similarly, chairs and tables dragged back and forth across a gritty floor often lose an inch or two of height to wear, so that some are actually resting on their stretchers. The front edges of the feet are rounded over as a chair is tilted and slid across the floor. Stretchers are also worn flat from boots scraping on them. Finials on the backs of chairs are smoothed as they rub against walls. Arm supports are worn where hands nervously rub them. Fingernails and keys that

missed their mark scar the areas around latches, escutcheons, and pulls. Desk tops are marred by ink and the pressure of pencils.

Chains, sandpaper, and rasps can simulate wear, but such techniques produce random distressing. Wear should make sense. The edges of wood erode and are smoothed down by handling. The soft appearance of old furniture is a result of this abrading process. New carving is sharp; only after years of polishing and wear does it take on a soft quality.

HARDWARE

The examination of hardware is at the same time the best and worst way of determining the age of furniture. Nails and screws reveal their age by the way they are made. Nails were hand-forged until about 1790, and the marks of the blacksmith's hammer are visible on the head of the nails, often giving them the appearance of a rose. Nails were so valuable in the 17th century that unscrupulous arsonists sometimes even burned down houses just to recover the nails. Even so, by the 18th century, nails became fairly common and were used to attach drawer runners, backboards, drawer bottoms, and even corner blocks. The 18th-century economist, Adam Smith, studied the English nailmaking industry in 1776 and reported that a skilled nailmaker could pound out over 2,000 nails a day. About the same time, the first cut nails were snipped out of an old lock plate by a blacksmith in Cumberland, Rhode Island. The heads on such cut nails had hammered heads until about 1815, when machinery was developed to cut a waist into the nail and fashion a crude head. Using a nail-cutting machine in 1789, William J. Folsome of Harrisburg, Pennsylvania, could produce 120,000 nails a week. Cut nails produced after 1840 are indistinguishable from modern ones. The modern wire nail was developed about the middle of the 19th century, although cut nails continued to be made as well.

Most early iron smelters extracted only the purest iron from high-grade bog ore. On hardware made from such ore, oxidation built up a black crust on the surface that is impervious to further rust. Although it is easy to drive old nails into a piece of wood, original nails, particularly in oak with a high tannin content, will often discolor or bleed on the wood around the nail hole, indicating that the nail has been in place for a long time.

Screws were used sparingly in the 17th and 18th centuries because of the considerable expense necessary to make them. The earliest ones were forged and had hand-filed threads and blunt ends. A cold chisel cut a slightly off-center, V-shaped slot in the irregular head. Screws were used primarily for fastening hinges and locks and, later, for attaching the tops of tripod tables to frames. Not until late in the 18th century were screws commonly used to replace the earlier glue blocks to fasten dropleaf table tops to frames. Lathes to make screws were employed in England in the 1760s, but machine-made screws were not widely used in America until after the Revolution. Machine-made screws had regular threads and a rectangular slot cut dead center. However, the tips continued to remain blunt until about 1850, when the now familiar gimlet point came into widespread use.

The style of the hardware, particularly the drawer pulls—if original—is an excellent guide to age. Extra holes behind the pulls, however, are a sure sign of replacements (Figure XIII–26). Not only is brass soft and susceptible to breaking, but pulls were frequently replaced to update the style of furniture. Cotter pins attached the earliest metal pulls. By the Queen Anne period, cast plates fastened by posts, with hand-cut threads and square shanks, were common. Reproduction stamped brasses have a smooth back instead of the rough texture of the original sand-cast brass (Figure XIII–27). File marks on the edges and a greater thickness, as compared to stamped brass, indicate sand-casting techniques common in the 18th century. This evidence of age is not infallible, however, since custom-made brass can be cast in sand even today. Federal style pulls were stamped like modern ones, but the posts were still cast and the threads hand-cut. Until the Victorian period, the posts were usually square or chamfered and can easily be distinguished from the round posts fashioned by machines after the mid-19th century. Brass is a mixture of copper and zinc. The greater portion of zinc used in 18th-century formulas gives 18th-century brass a yellower color.

PAINTED FINISHES

Original, untouched painted surfaces from the 18th century are extremely rare because of the ravages of time and overzealous collectors of the late 19th and early 20th century who were imbued with the Arts and Crafts movement's love of bare wood. Although early collectors once wanted refinished and brand-new-looking pieces, now, the desire is for untouched surfaces. The look of old paint is often simulated. Soft paint indicates a recent application, and even brittle paint may prove to be no more than 10 years old. Milk-based or casein paints, which resist chemical strippers, indicate a date after 1800. Casein paint had been used since ancient times, but oil-based paints, invented in the 15th century, for a time overshadowed its use. The best clue to the authenticity of a paint is a mottled appearance. Since painted surfaces age with slight variations, a perfectly uniform surface is the sure sign of a recent paint job.

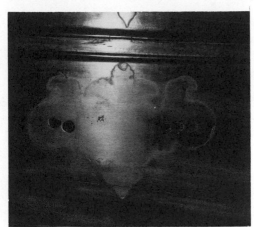

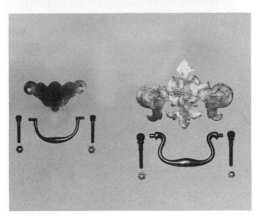

FIGURE XIII–26 *(top)*
Detail of wood surface behind drawer pull of desk (Figure IV–58).
The presence of several sets of holes indicates several sets of brass pulls. The original pulls probably made the faint, circular outline centered on the outer holes. The outline of the present Chippendale style pulls is also clearly visible.
Author's Collection.

FIGURE XIII–27 *(bottom)*
Left: Detail of 20th-century reproduction brass pull. Right: Detail of 18th-century Chippendale style pull.
The reproduction pull has a completely smooth back since it was cut from a rolled sheet of brass. The 18th-century example has a rough surface resulting from sand casting. The posts on the reproductions are completely round, whereas the shanks of the 18th-century examples are square. The nuts of the reproductions are perfectly symmetrical, whereas the holes in the 18th-century nuts are slightly off-center.
Author's Collection.

Conservation of Fine Furniture

Once the connoisseur has authenticated and evaluated a piece of furniture, it is his responsibility, be he a collector or a curator, to preserve that bit of America's cultural heritage in his charge. Thus furniture should be preserved and protected in as close to the original condition as possible. Alter a piece as little as possible. Antiques have bumps and scratches that are part of their history and that prove their authenticity. Repair only damage that seriously interferes with function or appearance.

When repairs and refinishing are unavoidable, use techniques that can be reversed. Avoid epoxy glues and polyurethane finishes, that cannot easily be removed without damage to the wood surface. Nails and screws to tighten joints soon work loose and cannot be removed without gouging the wood. Many old finishes can be saved by a good cleaning with varsol or a waterless hand cleaner. If stripping is absolutely necessary, remove only the finish and be careful not to remove the surface of the wood itself. Machine sanders will remove not only the color of the wood but the tool marks and other evidence of age and authenticity as well. Even fine sandpaper and steel wool may remove more wood than is desirable.

When a new finish is necessary, select a varnish, lacquer, or shellac, all of which can be easily removed. Water-based aniline dyes are preferable to oil-based ones for the same reason. Linseed oil, tung oil, and other oil-based finishes, which bind to the wood, cannot be removed without sanding away some of the wood. These oil finishes will also darken with age. They should be avoided. The famous, or infamous, museum finish of turpentine and boiled linseed oil is no longer used by knowledgeable museum curators because the finish blackens furniture as it ages and then cannot be removed without losing some of the surface of the wood.

Waxing can provide some protection of the finish against wear and spills, but it can be overdone. Too frequent waxing will result in a wax buildup that will eventually have to be removed. Paste waxes provide the most protection and can last six months to a year. Liquid waxes are more oil and less wax, and the oil will absorb dirt. Some even contain silicone, which, over a long period of time, can abrade the finish like sandpaper.

The key to the preservation of furniture is constant temperature and humidity control. In winter, houses and museums with hot-water or forced-air heat must have a humidifier in order to maintain an ideal humidity of about 50 percent. When the humidity falls drastically as the air is heated, wood shrinks as it gives off moisture. Splitting occurs when a board cannot move to accommodate the shrinkage. Glue dries out, and joints loosen. Veneer cracks or pops off as the soft-wood ground shrinks more than the hard-wood veneer. Warping occurs, and a piece can literally fall apart.

The connoisseur of American furniture has studied the evolution of American furniture styles and has learned to appreciate and evaluate the work of the cabinetmaker. He can determine the authenticity of a piece and place it within a proper historical perspective. He can also judge its quality. And, through the application of sound conservation principles, he can preserve for posterity an important part of America's cultural heritage.

Notes

1. Charles F. Montgomery, "Some Remarks on the Practice and Science of Connoisseurship," in *The Walpole Society Note Book* (New York: The Walpole Society, 1961), p. 58.

2. Jonathan Richardson, as quoted in *The Walpole Society Note Book* (New York: The Walpole Society, 1961), p. 52.

3. Montgomery, "Remarks", p. 58.

APPENDIX

In the Historical Society of Pennsylvania is a list of *Prices of Cabinet & Chair Work* that belonged to Benjamin Lehman, a lumber merchant who lived in Germantown, on the outskirts of Philadelphia. Dated January 1786, this price book records the variety of furniture available to customers in the late 18th century and their relative cost in Pennsylvania currency.

The Henry Francis du Pont Winterthur Museum holds the catalog of furniture sold by George J. Henkels of Philadelphia about 1850. Similar furniture was no doubt sold in most major cities of America at mid-century.

These two important documents offer significant insights into comparisons between cabinetmaking in the 18th century and factory-made furniture of the mid-19th century.

PRICES OF CABINET & CHAIR WORK
BINJAMIN LEHMAN JANUARY 1786,

N.B. The First Column is of Mahogany the Second of Walnut, and Third the Journeymans Wages

DESKS

	Mohogany	Wallnut	Jurnyman
	£ S d	£ S d	£ S d
Desk winged	14— 0—0	10— 0—0	4—10—0
Dito with Skolloped Drawrs beLow and Shell drawers obove	13—10—0	9—10—0	4—21—0
Dᵒ with Collumns, Drawers, & Sliding Prospects	13— 0—0	9— 0—0	4—21—0
Dᵒ with Collumn Drawers	12—10—0	8—10—0	3—10—0
Dᵒ with two rows of Skolloped Drawers ...	11— 5—0	8— 0—0	3— 5—0
Dᵒ with a Prospect & Swelled Brackets ...	11— 0—0	7—10—0	3— 0—0
Dᵒ without a Prospect & Straight Brackets	10— 0—0	7— 0—0	2—12—0
Note Add for Quater Columns 10 Shillings			

BOOK-CASES

	Mohogany			Wallnut			Jurnyman		
	£	S	d	£	S	d	£	S	d
Book Case with Scroll pedimt head & Door's Pannel	12—	0	—0	9—	0	—0	3—	10	—0
Do with Dentils and Fret	7—	10	—0	5—	0	—0	2—	5	—0
Do Square Head, Pannels or Sash Door's with Sliding Shelves only	6—	0	—0	4—	0	—0	1—	15	—0
Do Pitch pediment without Din¹ on fret— and Plain Balls	7—	10	—0	5—	0	—0	2—	5	—0
Do with Dintils, fret, and Shield	10—	0	—0	7—	0	—0	3—	0	—0
Do with Arch Doors	10—	10	—0	7—	10	—0	3—	5	—0
Do with Skolloped Doors	11—	0	—0	8—	0	—0	3—	5	—0
Do with Chinese Doors	12—	0	—0	9—	0	—0	3—	10	—0
Book Case with Scroll pediment head and Chinese Doors	13—	0	—0	10—	0	—0	4—	0	—0
Add for Quater Columns 20 Shillings .	———			———			0—	10	—0

N.B. the above Doors are without
Gleasing Carv'd work not to exceed
25 Shillins.

HIGH CHEST OF DRAWRES

	£	S	d	£	S	d	£	S	d
Chest on a Frame head and Corners and Plain Feet	13—	0	—0	9—	0	—0	3—	10	—0
A Table to Suit Ditto	4—	10	—0	2—	5	—0	1—	5	—0
Ditto. Chest on Chest and Swell'd Bracke's	13—	0	—0	9—	0	—0	3—	10	—0
Tables Sutt Ditto	5—	0	—0	3—	5	—0	1—	7	—0
Do Draers: on a Frame Clawfeet & quater Coluns	15—	0	—0	11—	0	—0	4—	0	—0
A Table to suit Do	5—	0	—0	3—	15	—0	1—	7	—6
Do Drawers Chest on Chest and Swelled Brackets	15—	0	—0	10—	10	—0	4—	0	—0
A Table to Suit Do	6—	0	—0	4—	0	—0	1—	10	—0
Drawers Pitch pediment Head Square Corners Plain feet without dentils or fret Plain Ball	16—	0	—0	11—	10	—0	4—	0	—0
A Table to Suit Do	4—	0	—0	2—	15	—0	1—	5	—0
Do Drawers Chest on Chest	16—	0	—0	11—	10	—0	4—	0	—0
A Table to suit Do with straight Brack:	5—	0	—0	3—	0	—0	1—	5	—0
Do Drawers with Quarter Columns	17—	0	—0	12—	10	—0	4—	10	—0
A Table to suit Do	6—	0	—0	4—	0	—0	1—	10	—0
Do Drawers on a frame and Claw feet	17—	0	—0	13—	0	—0	4—	10	—0
A Table to suit Do	5—	0	—0	3—	5	—0	1—	5	—0
Do Drawers with Dent¹ fret & Shield	19—	0	—0	14—	0	—0	5—	0	—0
A Table to suit Do	6—	0	—0	4—	0	—0	1—	10	—0
Do Drawers Chest on Chest	20—	0	—0	15—	0	—0	5—	0	—0
A Table to suit Do	6—	0	—0	4—	0	—0	1—	10	—0
Chest on a Frame Claw feet leaves on the knees and Shell Drawers in the Frame	20—	0	—0	15—	0	—0	5—	0	—0
A Table to suit Do	6—	0	—0	4—	0	—0	1—	10	—0
Ditto Drawers Scroll Pedimt. head Carvedwork not to Exceed £3—10	21—	0	—0	16—	0	—0	5—	10	—0
Table to suit Do	6—	0	—0	4—	0	—0	1—	10	—0
Do Drawers Chest on Chest, a Table Do	21—	0	—0	16—	0	—0	5—	10	—0

Add for a Desk Drawer to any of the above Draws: 3£

LOW CHEST OF DRAWERS

	£	S	d	£	S	d	£	S	d
Low Chest of Drawers with 3 long & 5 small Dr.	———			4—	10	—0	18—	12	—6
Do with 4 long & 5 small Drs	———			5—	0	—0	19—	15	—0
Do on Frame 18 Inches high without a Drawer	———			5—	10	—0	110-	17	—6

CHAIRS WITH CROOKED LEGS

	Mohogany £ S d	Wallnut £ S d	Jurnyman £ S d
Chair with Plain feet & Banister with leather Bottoms	1—14—0	1— 5—0	0— 9—0
Arm D°	2—18—0	2— 5—0	0—16—0
D° without through Banister	1—16—0	1— 7—0	0—10—0

CHAIRS

	Mohogany	Wallnut	Jurnyman
Arm D°	3— 0—0	2—12—0	0—17—0
D°, with Claw feet	2— 0—0	1—10—0	0—10—0
Arm D°	3— 3—0	2—13—0	0—17—0
D° with Shells on the Knees & Front Rail,	2— 3—0	1—13—0	0—10—0
Arm D°, ...	3— 7—6	2—16—0	0—17—0
D° with Leaves on the Knees	2— 6—0	1—15—0	0—10—0
Arm D°, ...	3—11—0	2—18—0	0—17—0
D° for fluting or ogee Backs	2—10—0	1—15—0	0—10—0
Arm D°, ...	3—15—0	3— 0—0	'0—17—0
For relieving the Banisters add according to the worth of them			
For extraordinary Carved work add in Proportion .... work			
For Damask Bottoms add 2 Shi¹, ...			
For Hair 2ˢ—6ᵈ			
Add to any arm chair made for a Close Stool with a cover to the pan—framed 7ˢ—6ᵈ	————	————	0— 3—9
D° not framed 5 Shillings	————	————	0— 2—6

CHAIRS, MARLBOROUGH FEET,

	Mohogany	Wallnut	Jurnyman
Chairs plain open Banisters with Bases or Brackets with Leather Bottoms	1—12—0	1— 5—0	0— 9—0
Arm D°	2—18—0	2— 5—0	0—16—0
D° with fluted or ogee Backs bases & Brackets	2— 5—0	1—15—0	0—10—0
Arm D°			
D° Add for releving the Banister and for Damask or hair Bottoms or Close as in the Crook leg Chairs			
For any Chair as above Stuffed over the rails & Brass nails add 8 Shillings			
For fluted or ogee Back feet add to the Journeman	————	————	0— 1—0

CORNER CHAIRS FOR CLOSE STOOLS

	Mohogany	Wallnut	Jurnyman
Corner Chair plain Feet and Banister	2—10—0	2— 0—0	0—12—6
D° Claw feet and open Banister	3—10—0	2—15—0	0—14—0
Corner Chairs with the upper part the Legs workᵈ Crooked	3—15—0	3— 0—0	0—16—6
For Commode front Add	0—12—0	0—10—0	0— 5—0

EASY CHAIRS,

	Mohogany	Wallnut	Jurnyman
Easy Chair frame plain feet and knees without Casters	2—10—0	2— 5—0	0—18—0
D° with Claw feet	2—15—0	2—10—0	0—18—0
D° with Claw feet and Leaves on the Knees	3— 5—0	3— 0—0	0—18—0
D° Marlborough Feet Bases & Brackets ...	2—10—0	2— 5—0	0—18—0

CHAIR FRAME,

	Mohogany	Wallnut	Jurnyman
Chair frame for Stuffing over back and Feet with Marlborough Feet	1— 5—0	1— 0—0	0— 6—0
D° Arm D°	2— 0—0	1—10—0	0—10—0
Folding Cabbin Chair frame for Stuffing ..	1— 5—0	1— 0—0	0— 6—0
D° Stools	0—12—0	0— 8—0	0— 2—0
D° of Oak	————	0— 5—0	0— 1—6
Add for Brackets to any Chair	0— 2—6	0— 2—6	0— 1—3
and Bases to any Chair	0— 2—6	0— 2—6	0— 1—3
Aand for Carved Mouldings	0—12—0	0—12—0	0— 1—3

SUFFAS MARLBOUROUGH FEET

	Mohogany			Wallnut			Jurnyman		
	£	S	d	£	S	d	£	S	d
Suffa plain feet and Rails without Casters	4	10	0	4	0	0	1	0	0
D° with Bases and Brackets	5	0	0	4	10	0	1	5	0
D° with a fret on the feet	7	10	0	7	0	0	1	15	0
D° with a fret on the Feet & Rails and Carved Mouldings	10	10	0	9	10	0	2	10	0

SUFFAS WITH CROOKED LEGS

	Mohogany			Wallnut			Jurnyman		
Suffa plain feet and Knees without Casters	5	0	0	4	10	0	1	5	0
Claw feet Suffa	5	10	0	5	0	0	1	5	0
D° with Leaves on the Knees	6	10	0	6	0	0	1	5	0
Add for Casters 10 Shillings									
D° with Carved Mouldings	7	10	0	7	0	0	1	7	6

SETEES,

	Mohogany			Wallnut			Jurnyman		
Setees plain Crooked Legs feet & Banisters without Casters with hair or Damask Bottoms	6	10	0	5	0	0	1	6	0
D° Marlborough with bases and Brackets cut through banisters	6	10	0	5	0	0	1	6	0
D° with Claw fect & Knees Carved	8	0	0	5	15	0	1	6	0
D° with fluted or ogee Baks	8	10	0	6	5	0	1	8	0
Add for Carved Mouldings 20 S & to the Jour^(ma):	———			———			0	2	0

COUCHES WITH CROOKED LEGS,

	Mohogany			Wallnut			Jurnyman		
Couch frame plain Knees feet & Banisters without bottoms or casters	4	10	0	3	0	0	1	4	0
D° with Claw feet & open Banister	5	5	0	3	15	0	1	4	0
D° with leaves on the Knees	6	0	0	4	10	0	1	4	0
D° with fluted or ogee Backs	6	5	0	4	15	0	1	5	0
D° with Marlborough feet without bases or Brackets	4	10	0	3	0	0	1	0	0
D° with Bases and Brackets	5	0	0	3	10	0	1	4	0
D°, with fluted or ogee Backs	5	5	0	3	15	0	1	6	0
Add for Carved Mouldings 20 S, add to the Jorneymans Wages	———			———			2	0	0

DINING TABLES

	Mohogany			Wallnut			Jurnyman		
Dining Table plain feet Crooket or Marlbeorough with Bases 3 feet in the Boad	3	5	0	1	17	6	1	0	0
D° 3 feet 6 Inches	4	0	0	2	5	0	1	0	0
D° 4 Feet	4	10	0	2	15	0	1	2	6
D° 4 feet 6 Inches	5	0	0	3	10	0	1	5	0
D° 5 Feet 6 Inches with 6 Legs	8	0	0	4	10	0	1	15	0
For Tables with Claw feet add 2^s—6^d per Claw									
For Tables with Straight legs without bases Deduct 5S & 3S in ye Journ^y. wages ..									

CARD TABLES WITH CROOKED LEGS

	Mohogany			Wallnut			Jurnyman		
Card Tables plain feet & Knees	3	10	0	2	5	0	0	17	6
D° with Claw feet	4	0	0	2	15	0	0	17	6
D° with Carved Knees and Mouldings	5	0	0	3	15	0	0	18	6
Add for Coviring without finding the Cloth 7S. 6d & to the Journeymans Wages for sinking the Top 2—6	———			———			0	7	—

CARD TABLES WITH MARLBOROUGH FEET

	Mohogany			Wallnut			Jurnyman		
Card Table with a Drawer with out bases or Brackets	3	0	0	2	0	0	0	15	0
D° with bases and Brackets	3	10	0	2	5	0	0	17	6
D° with Carved Mouldings	4	0	0	2	15	0	0	17	6
Add for the Tops 10S & to the Jorney^n: wages	———			———			0	5	0

CARD TABLES WITH ROUND CORNERS

	Mohogany			Wallnut			Jurnyman		
	£	S	d	£	S	d	£	S	d
Claw feet & plain Knees	5—	0—	0	_____			1—	2—	6
Dº lined with Green Cloth	6—	10—	0	_____			1—	10—	0
Dº leaves on the Knees & Carv'd Mouldings	8—	0—	0	_____			1—	10—	0
Dº with Carved Rails	10—	0—	0	_____			2—	0—	0

PEMBROKE OR BREAKFAST TABLES

	Mohogany			Wallnut			Jurnyman		
Breakfast Tables plain	2—	15—	0	1—	15—	0	0—	12—	6
Dº with a Drawer	3—	0—	0	2—	0—	0	0—	14—	6
Breakfast Table with Bases & Brackets	3—	5—	0	2—	5—	0	0—	17—	6
Dº with a plain Stretcher, ...	3—	10—	0	2—	10—	0	1—	0—	0
Dº with open Stretcher & low Drawers ...	4—	0—	0	3—	0—	0	1—	2—	6
Dº with Crooked Legs and plain Feet	3—	5—	0	2—	5—	0	0—	17—	6
Dº with Claw feet									
Add for Scolloping the Top 4S & to the Jour.	_____			_____			0—	2—	0

CORNER TABLES

	Mohogany			Wallnut			Jurnyman		
Corner Table/ˢ Crooked Legs or Marlbourough feet with Bases 3 feet Square	3—	10—	0	2—	10—	0	1—	0—	0
Dº Claw Feet	4—	10—	0	3—	0—	0	1—	0—	0

TEA TABLES

	Mohogany			Wallnut			Jurnyman		
Plain Top & feet	2—	15—	0	1—	15—	0	1—	0—	0
Plain Tea Table with Claw feet	3—	5—	0	2—	5—	0	0—	12—	6
Dº Leaves on the Knees	4—	0—	0	2—	15—	0	0—	12—	6
Dº Scollop'd Top & Carv'd Billar	5—	15—	0	_____			1—	2—	6
Add for fluting the pillar 5 S, & to the Jorⁿ.	_____			_____			0—	2—	6

FOLDING STANDS

	Mohogany			Wallnut			Jurnyman		
Stand 22 inches Diameter with a box plain Top and feet	1—	15—	0	1—	5—	0	0—	11—	
Dº plain Top and Claw feet	2—	2—	6	1—	12—	6	0—	11—	0
Dº with Leaves on the Knees	2—	10—	0	2—	0—	0	0—	11—	0
Dº fixed 18 Inches Diameter	1—	4—	0	0—	16—	0	0—	7—	6
Add for fluting the Pillar as at the Tea Table	_____			_____			0—	2—	6

SIDE BOARD TABLES

	Mohogany			Wallnut			Jurnyman		
Side Board Table with Bases & Brackets 6 feet by 2 feet 6 Inches	5—	0—	0	3—	0—	0	1—	2—	0
Dº 5 feet by 2 feet 6 Inches	5—	0—	0	3—	0—	0	1—	2—	0
Do 5 feet by 2 fe/6 In	4—	5—	0	2—	10—	0	0—	18—	0
Do 4 feet by 2 Fe—6 In	3—	5—	0	2—	0—	0	0—	14—	0
Do 3 feet 6 inches by 2 Fe—3 I	3—	0—	0	1—	15—	0	0—	12—	0
Add for Carved Mouldings 2 Shilling per foot for fret round the Rails 5 Shillings per foot and to Jorneymans wages	_____			_____			0—	2—	6

TEA KETTLE STANDS

	Mohogany			Wallnut			Jurnyman		
Tea kettle Sand with Gallery Top & plain feet	2—	10—	0	_____			0—	15—	0
Do with Claw feet Leaves on the knees Carved & fluted, Pillar with Turned Banister	3—	10—	0	_____			0—	15—	0
Bason Stand with 3 pillers & 2 Drawers ..	2—	10—	0	1—	15—	0	0—	15—	0
Do Square and tow Drawers	1—	10—	0	1—	2—	6	0—	12—	0

SQUARE TEA TABLES

	Mohogany			Wallnut			Jurnyman		
Tea Table square top plain feet & Rails ..	3—	0—	0	2—	5—	0	1—	5—	0
Do Claw feet	3—	10—	0	2—	15—	0	1—	5—	0
Do leaves on the Knees	4—	10—	0	3—	10—	0	1—	5—	0
Do with Carv'd Rails £6—0—0 and Jorneyⁿ the Same	_____			_____			1—	5—	0

COMMODE DRESSING TABLES

	Mohogany	Wallnut	Jurnyman
	£ S d	£ S d	£ S d
Commode Dressing table with four long Drawers without a Drising Drawr	14— 0—0	_____	4—10—0
Add for a Dresing drawer from 30 to 80 Shilln and for the Jorneymans wages in Porprotion			

WRITING TABLES

	Mohogany	Wallnut	Jurnyman
Writing tables with one top to raise on the Side only Front to Draw out	7— 0—0	_____	_____
Do with one top to raise on Both Sides ...	7—10—0	5—10—0	2— 0—0
Do with tow Tops to rase on both Sides work in the Drawers excluded	8— 0—0	6— 0—0	2— 0—0

BUREAU TABLES

	Mohogany	Wallnut	Jurnyman
Bureau Table with Prospect Door and Square Corners	7—10—0	6— 0—0	2— 7—6
Do with quater Colums	8—10—0	7— 0—0	2—15—0

CHINA TABLES,

	Mohogany	Wallnut	Jurnyman
China Tables plain Legs and Stretcher three feet long with Bases brackets & fret Top	4—10—0	_____	1—15—0
China Tables open Stretcher Top three feet Long Bases and Brackets	5— 0—0	_____	1—15—0
Do with fret Frame	8— 0—0	_____	3—10—0
Add for Commode Ditto 2 £—10 S. To Jorney[n]:	_____	_____	1—15—0
Ditto 5 Feet, with 6. Legs	6—10—0	_____	_____

PLAIN NIGHT TABLE

	Mohogany	Wallnut	Jurnyman
Plain night Table	4— 0—0	3— 5—0	1— 5—0

FRAMES FOR MARBLE SLABS

	Mohogany	Wallnut	Jurnyman
Frame for Marble slab Marlborough feet without Bases or Brackets about 4 feet long	2—10—0	1—10—0	0—12—0
Do with Bases and Brackets Commode Rails	3—10—0	_____	0—17—0
Do with plain Knees & Claw feet	4— 0—0	_____	1— 0—0
Do with Leaves on the knees & Carved Mouldings	5— 0—0	_____	1— 0—0
Do 5 feet with 6 Legs	6—10—0	_____	_____

PINE KITCHEN TABLES

	Mohogany	Wallnut	Jurnyman
Pine Kitchen Tables full Frame with two Leaves hung with Rule Joint 4 feet long	_____	1—17—6	0—15—0
& two Drawers	_____	1—10—0	0—12—6
Do with one Leaf and one Drawer	_____	_____	_____
Do 3 feet 6 Inches Long with two Leaves .	_____	1—10—0	0—12—6
Do with one Leaf	_____	1— 5—0	_____
Do with one Leaf	_____	1— 5—0	_____
Do single Frame 3 F: 6 Inches with a Drar.	_____	0—16—0	0— 7—0

JOINT STOOL

	Mohogany	Wallnut	Jurnyman
Joint Stool with a Drawer & Sliding Top 3 feet Long	_____	0—12—0	0— 5—6
Do without a Drawer	_____	0—10—0	0— 4—6
Do fixed with a Drawer	_____	0—10—0	0— 4—6
Do fixed without a Drawer	_____	0— 7—6	0— 3—3
Stool for a Store of Walnut	_____	0—12—0	0— 5—6
Do of Pine	_____	0— 7—0	0— 3—0

FIRE SCREENES

	Mohogany	Wallnut	Jurnyman
	£ S d	£ S d	£ S d
Fire Screene with plain feet	1—15—0	1— 5—0	0—11—0
Do with Claw feet	2— 2—6	1—12—6	0—11—0
Do with Loaves on the Knees	2—10—0	2— 0—0	0—11—0
Add for fluting the Pillars 5 S and to the Jorneymen	_____	_____	0— 2—6

HORSE FIRE SCREENES

without a fret	2—10—0	2— 5—0	0—17—6
Do with a fret under the Stretcher	3— 0—0	2—15—0	1— 5—0

DUMB WAITERS,

Dumb waiter with four Tops plain feet ...	5— 0—0	_____	1— 0—0
Do with Claw feet	5—10—0	_____	1— 0—0
Do with Leaves on the Knees	6— 0—0	_____	1— 0—0

CLOATHS-PRESSES

Cloathe Press in two parts upper Part about 4 feet Square in the front the Doors hung with Rule Joints and Sliding Shelves with 3 Drawres in the Lower part in Side work of Red Ceder	15— 0—0	11— 0—0	3—10—0
Do inside work not Red Ceder	13—10—0	9—10—0	3—10—0
Do in one part without Drawers inside work of Red Ceder	12— 0—0	8— 0—0	2—10—0
Do inside work not Red Ceder	10—10—0	7—10—0	2—10—0
Do with tow Drawers inside blow and Pins above with Doors hung in the Common way	8—10—0	6— 0—0	2— 0—0
Do of Pine	_____	4— 0—0	1—10—0
N.B. Add to any of the Presses with a Pitch Pediment, Dentils fret & Shield	6— 0—0	5— 0—0	2— 0—0
Do without Dentils fret or Shield	3—10—0	2—10—0	1— 2—6

CORNER CUPBOURDS

Corner Cupbord in two parts about 7 feet high Square Head & stright Pannels ..	9—10—0	6—10—0	2— 0—0
Do with common Sash Doors	9—10—0	6—10—0	2— 0—0
Do with square Head Dentills Fret and pain Pannel Doors	10—10—0	7—10—0	2—10—0
Do with Pediment head Dentil Cornice fret Shield Roses and Blazes with plain Pannel Doors	15— 0—0	10—10—6	3— 0—0
Do with Common Sash Doors	14— 0—0	10—10—0	3— 0—0
flat Pannels with Skolloped Doors	16— 0—0	11—10—0	3—10—0
Do with Chinese Doors	15— 0—0	11—10—0	4— 0—0
N.B. Deduct in a Pitch Pediment for any of the above Cupboards 15 S and to the Journeymans wages	_____	_____	0— 7—6

SINGLE CUPBOARDS

Cupboard about four feet high and Three feet wide Square head and common sash doors	4—15—0	3—15—0	1— 5—0
Do with Dentil Cornice plain Pannels	5—10—0	4— 0—0	1—10—0
Do without Dentil and Plain Pannel	4—15—0	3—15—0	1— 5—0
Do with Common Sash Doors Dentil Cornice	5—10—0	4— 0—0	1—10—0
Cradle plain without Carving	2—15—0	1—10—0	0—12—6

PINE CUPBOARDS

Double Pine Cupboards about 7 feet high	_____	4—10—0	1— 5—0
Single pine Cupboard about 4 feet high and 3 wide	_____	2— 0—0	0—15—0
N.B., The Prices to any of the above Cupboards are without Glasing			

CLOCK CASES

	Mohogany			Wallnut			Jurnyman		
	£	S	d	£	S	d	£	S	d
Clock Case with Square head & Corners	6—	0—0		4—	0—0		1—	15—0	
Do with Scroll pediment head without fret Dentil or Carved and Square Corners	8—	0—0		5—	0—0		2—	5—0	
Do, with Column Corners	10—	0—0		7—	0—0		3—	0—0	
Do, with fret Dentils Shield Roses & Blases	12—	0—0		9—	0—0		4—	0—0	
Do without fret or Dentils	11—	0—0		8—	0—0		3—	5—0	

N.B., The above prices without Glazing

TEA BOARDS

Tea Board Scolloped at 15 d per Inch	————			————			0—	7—6	
Do, Plain Turned from 15 I to 22 I at 6d per Inch									
Hand Boards from 6 I to 12 I at 4 per Inch									
Decanter stands lined at 5 S per pair									

BEDSTEADS & C.

Bedstead Low Posts, Tow Posts Mahogany Clawfeet & plain Knees	2—	5—0		————			0—	10—0	
Do high Posts all Poplar stained except feet Posts of Mohognay Claw feet & Plain Knees	4—	0—0		————			0—	12—0	
Do all Mahognay Claw feet & Plain Knees	7—	0—0		————			1—	0—0	
Do Head Posts Popler	6—	10—0		————			0—	15—0	
Do Claw Feet Leaves on the Knees not fluted with brass Caps	————			————			————		
Do Knees to move fluted pillars a mamber Carved or Capital and Base	10—	0—0		————			————		
Gothic Pillers and & Strait feet Beadsteads	————			————			1—	10—0	
Beadstead Popler staned towo feet posts Mahogany with Bases	3—	0—0		————			0—	12—0	
Do all Mahogany Plain turned Pillers and Bases	5—	0—0		————			0—	15—0	
Do Gothic pillers & Fret on the feet	10—	10—0		————			2—	10—0	
Mahogany Field Beadsteads with Canopy Rails	6—	0—0		————			1—	0—0	

POPLAR BEDSTEADS

Poplar Corded Bedstead	————			0—	18—0		0—	5—0	
Do Low posts with four Screws	————			0—	18—0		0—	5—0	
Do Claw feet to two Pots	————			1—	5—0		0—	/—0	
Do high Posts plain turned	————			2—	0—0		0—	9—0	
Do with bases & caps Claw feet	————			2—	12—6		0—	12—6	
Poplar field Beadsteads canopy Rails	————			2—	15—6		0—	13—0	
Do Strait Rails	————			2—	0—0		0—	10—0	

Add for Fluting the Posts 15 Shl. and to the Jorneymans wages 7 s—6 d.

CHINA TRAYS

Fret China Trays 18 inches by 24	1—	15—0		————			0—	18—0	
Commode Do	2—	15—0		————			1—	8—0	
Trays for Pewter 18 Inches by 24	1—	0—0		0—	14—0		0—	4—6	
Do for Knives and forks 15 by 9	0—	10—0		0—	7—0		0—	3—0	

GEORGE J. HENKELS'
CITY
CABINET WAREHOUSE,
173 Chestnut Street,
Opposite Independence Hall,
PHILADELPHIA.

CATALOGUE
OF
FURNITURE
IN EVERY STYLE
COMPRISING
LOUIS XIV, LOUIS XV, ELIZABETHAN AND ANTIQUE,
With Sculpture Carving and Modern Style,
IN ROSEWOOD, WALNUT, MAHOGANY, SATINWOOD & MAPLE

**All of Superior Construction and Finished in the Best Style, Equal to,
if not Excelling in Quality the Goods of any
Establishment in the United States.**

Employing none but experienced workmen (apprentices being positively excluded,) and using the best materials, the work cannot fail to give satisfaction to purchasers.—Amongst the many advantages offered to purchasers, is the facility for furnishing a house, either in elegant or plain style, completely, from one establishment; by which means all the articles in each room correspond in style and quality, and the IMMENSE STOCK always on hand being so various in design, enables purchasers to please their taste in a selection without the delay necessarily caused in ordering Furniture.

To give an idea of the finished Furniture on hand, I need only inform you that my Rooms are 175 feet long, by 27 feet wide, 4 floors in number; with shops contiguous, sufficient to employ 200 hands, which is a guarantee that the work is all done under my own immediate inspection.

The Packing is all done in the Store, and Furniture warranted to carry safely any distance. Visitors to Philadelphia, are respectfully invited as purchasers or otherwise, to call and examine the Goods.

ROSEWOOD DOORS AND WINDOW FRAMES.

GOTHIC ORNAMENTING, FOR WAINSCOTTING AND VESTIBULES.

PLEASE EXAMINE THE CATALOGUE.

296

CATALOGUE.

ROSEWOOD
DRAWING-ROOM FURNITURE,
STYLE ANTIQUE.

		Each.
Trio Tete-a-Tete, elaborately carved, Satin covering,		$350 00
Arm Chair to match,	Medallion,	125 00
Lady's Arm Chair to match,		85 00
Chairs,	Stuffed backs,	50 00
Centre Table to match,	Sienna Marble,	250 00
Consol do. do.	do. do.	175 00
Cabinet Etagere,	do. do.	120 00
Do. do.		350 00
Corner do.		100 00
Reception Chairs,		28 00

The prices of the Tete-a-Tetes and Chairs might be varied either way be the Style of covering selected, the above prices being for Brocatelle. The Carving on the above is done by the best European Artists.

ROSEWOOD
BOUDOIR FURNITURE.

		Each.
Tete-a-Tete, elegantly carved, Satin covering,		$95 00
Fauteuil, do. do. do.		55 00
Work Table, do. do.		55 00
Tabouret,		20 00
Centre Table,	Velvet top,	75 00
Boquet Table,	Sienna Marble top,	35 00

The Ladies' Boudoir has been heretofore much neglected in our country, and it is creditable to the growing taste of the Ladies, that this most comfortable Room in the house should be furnished tastefully.

ROSEWOOD
PARLOR FURNITURE.
STYLE OF LOUIS XIV.

			Each.
Tete-a-Tete, rich carving, Large size, Plush covering,			$60 to 75
Do. do. Medium,			50 to 65
Do. do. Large size, Hair cloth,			45 to 60
Do. do. Medium,			42 to 57
Arm Chairs,	Richly carved, Plush,		30 to 45
Do. Lady's do. do. do.			25 to 30
Do. do.	Hair cloth,		22 to 32
Do.	Large size,		28 to 40
Centre Tables to match,	White Marble,		30 to 65
Do. do.	Black do.		35 to 75
Do. do.	Sienna do.		40 to 90
Reception Chairs,	Satin covering,		6 to 18
Do. do.	Cane Seat,		3 to 4 50
Parlor do. Spring seat,	Plush,		9 to 16
Do. do. do.	Hair cloth,		8 to 15
Do. do. Medallion back,	do.		14 to 20
Do. do. do. do.	Plush,		16 to 22
Sociables,	Plush,		22 to 35
Do.	Hair cloth,		18 to 30
Etagere or What Not, Plain,			15 to 30
Do. do. Elaborate,			35 to 120
Etagere, Cabinet, very elegant, with Mirror back, and Lined with Satin wood,			100
Consol Table,	White Marble,		25 to 45
Do.	Sienna Marble,		35 to 60
Consol Table, Black and Gold Marble, Pink or Yellow Lisbon Marble,			30 to 55
Corner Etagere, very neat,			40 to 45
French Secretary, very handsome,			60 to 135

All of the above are finished in Superb Style, and of the Latest French Designs which are regularly received from Paris. Purchasers can have made to order without delay, any selections from the Book of Patterns.

ROSEWOOD
DINING ROOM FURNITURE.

	Each.
Extension Tables, Rich Pattern, the loose leaves all Rosewood, the table 16 feet long, and 4 feet 6 inches wide, (Brigg's Patent,)	$150 00
Same Table, 12 feet long, 4 feet wide,	120 00
Do on legs, 12 by 4 feet,	75 00
Do do 16 by 4 feet 6 inches,	90 00
Arm Dining Chairs, leather cushions,	18 00
Do do plain style,	7 00
Do do cane seat imitation,	4 50
Etagere Buffets, Mirror backs and doors, White Marble, very elegant,	60 to 150
Do do Sienna Marble,	75 to 250
Do Plain with White Marble,	45 to 60
Wine Coolors, (Cellerets,)	20 to 75
Lounge to hold Table Leaves,	40 to 60

The above Extension Dining Table has taken the Premiums at the National Fair at Washington, at the Boston Fair, and at the Franklin Institute, in Philadelphia, and it is acknowledged to be the best in use. The extension being formed by cross-arms working at right angles on metal hinges, preserves it from the objections to all other Tables, viz:—swelling and shrinking with the weather in our variable climate. The difference in price of Tables does not interfere with the construction, as the same extension is used in the lowest price as in the most expensive, the difference being only in the ornamental part.

ROSEWOOD CHAMBER FURNITURE.
RICH ORNAMENTAL STYLE.

	Each.
Single Armories, Mirror doors, rich carving, lined with Satinwood, richly polished, per pair,	$375 00
Double Wardrobe, very handsome,	100 00
Do do plainer,	90 00
Do do	45 00
Bureaus, very imposing and Richly carved, with Mirror,	95 00
do rich, plain style, do	65 00
do do	40 00
French Bedsteads, very elaborate,	275 00
do do very handsome,	100 00
do do plainer,	70 00
do do	45 00
High Post Bedstead, Cornice and Canopy, very rich,	350 00
do do do do elegant style,	175 00
do do without Cornice,	75 00
do do plain,	45 00
Toilet Tablet, very elegant, style Louis XIV.,	150 00
do plain,	90 00
do	55 00
Bidet Washstand, Marble tray top,	60 00
do plain style,	40 00
Enclosed Washstand, do,	35 00
Open Scroll Washstands, plain style,	25 00
do do plain Marble,	18 00
Tete-a-tete, fancy covering,	90 00
do plain,	45 00
Chamber Chairs, cane seat,	3 50
do do rich, comfortable style,	16 00
Commode Chairs, handsome style,	45 00
do do plain,	20 00

CURTAINS
For Bedsteads, Drawing Room, Bed Room,
AND DINING ROOM WINDOWS.

The price will be regulated altogether by the quality of goods selected, (of which there is a full assortment always on hand,) and by the design. The French Bedstead Curtains are attached either to a gilt or wooden cornice, fastened to the wall or ceiling. The latest designs for all kinds of curtains are regularly received; and the proprietor, by employing the best workmen in the upholstery line, is enabled to fit up curtains in the most tasteful manner, equal, if not superior to any establishment in the country.

SPRING MATTRESSES.

There have been so many varieties of Spring Mattresses patented within the last few years, and purchasers have been so much disappointed in their quality and utility, that it becomes a delicate matter to offer anything new to your notice. But trusting your discrimination, I would ask the favor of calling and examining for yourselves.

The mattress spring-frame is so constructed, that it can be used either for a hair mattress or a feather bed, and its simplicity is its greatest recommendation. The price of a spring-frame for feather bed is $25 for large size, and $20 for medium; the mattress furnished at 50 cents per pound for the best curled hair, as I use no other kind. I cannot supply of my own manufacture any of the cheaper mattresses, but will sell them according to size and quality, as low as any upholsterer in the trade.

Persons sending the size of their bedsteads, can have a spring-frame made to fit, and shipped to their order immediately.

TO THE READER.

The previous articles enumerated in the Catalogue are always kept on hand, and the assortment being so varied, the prices are of course regulated by the style. I would again impress on you the fact that the quality of the furniture is equal to any in the country, and the proprietor being a practical cabinet maker and designer, is enabled to understand an order as a purchaser intends it, and also, to suggest alterations which will benefit the construction, with the details of which a purchaser is frequently unacquainted.

A word as regards the durability of furniture. I hold it to be sound doctrine, that nature has adapted the wood growing in any country to the wants of its inhabitants. The continent of North America produces for furniture, Walnut, Maple and Oak for fine outside wood, and Poplar and Pine for interior wood: and for veneering with the finer woods, South America and the Islands in the same latitudes produce Rosewood, Mahogany and other fine woods, but none of them used to any extent in the manufacture of furniture, except those above enumerated. Experience has taught us that the Rosewood of Brazil will not adhere with glue for any length of time, unless the oil contained in it is removed by exposure to the weather, or by a process of steaming, therefore, the importance of the workman understanding the nature of the wood he works, and the positive necessity of having the wood prepared for a length of time previous to using it, and not as is generally the case, procuring it for immediate manufacture when it happens to be wanted. Mahogany, which is used *more than any other wood throughout the world for furniture*, is less liable to difficulties in manufacturing than Rosewood, but it still requires the utmost care in preparing, a proof of which you have every day before you. Look through your furniture, on one piece the veneering has cracked and come off, the wood is dark and blotched, caused by not being properly prepared. Another piece is perfect, the wood sound and of a beautiful rich color, produced only by age in this fine wood. See the contrast!—One piece was made by a practical thinking man, the other by one of those, of which class there are unfortunately too many, who make work for sale only.

In making Rosewood furniture to insure its durability, it must be worked as much as possible in connection with the woods of our own country, with very strong glue, and the grain of the wood thoroughly filled up with varnish to protect it from the atmosphere, when it is as durable as any furniture can be made, and retains its beauty for a century. The furniture made in Europe of Rosewood and Mahogany, where it is veneered, will not stand our climate, on account of the soft wood on which the veneer is glued, not being adapted to this country, and the French polish, (in France they do not varnish as we do, but polish with Gum Shellac and Spirits of Wine, forming but a slight coating which is not sufficient protection for the wood here,) soon admits the atmosphere, destroying the grain of the wood, and the adhesive qualities of the glue. To protect the wood we must have all the pores filled with varnish, which is made of Gum Copal, Linseed Oil, and Spirits of Turpentine, each one of which component parts resist the humidity of the atmosphere. The wood when well varnished and polished, should not show an open pore, but be as it were, cased in glass. It is often remarked that furniture does not wear so well as it did in olden times. The reason is very plain. Furniture used to be *wax-polished*, and servants were instructed to rub it well, keeping the grain of the wood well filled with wax, which was as much protection as varnish. A careful examination of my furniture will show that there has been full attention paid to these important matters; and, as a matter of course, I must be paid more for furniture of the character I make, than an inferior article can be purchased for; and as it is a well established fact, that goods are always sold at a certain rate of profit on the cost, you will see on reflection, that you are paying as much per cent. profit to a manufacturer of *common furniture*, as you do to one who understands his business, and takes a pride in selling an article creditable alike to your taste it the selection, and his skill in the construction.

WALNUT AND MAHOGANY PARLOR FURNITURE. STYLE ANTIQUE.

			Each.
Tete-a-tete, hair cloth, large size and elegantly carved,			$65 00
do	do	medium,	50 00
do	do	plainer,	40 00
do	do	for recess,	33 00
do	plush,	do	38 00
do	satin,		41 00

On a Tete-a-tete, large size, the covering with Plush, would be $12 extra, and in proportion for the other sizes.

Arm Chairs, elegant finish, hair cloth,			45 00
do	medium,	do	30 00
do	plainer,	do	25 00
do	sewing,		15 00
Chairs, spring seat, hair cloth, carved to match Tete-a-Tete,			12 00
do	do	do medium,	8 00
do	do	do plainer,	6 00
do	do	do	3 50
Occasional Tables, Black and Gold Marble, elegantly carved,			76 00
do	White	do do	65 00
Centre Tables, richly carved, White Marble,			55 00
do	do	Black Marble,	65 00
do	medium,	do	45 00
do	do	White Marble,	35 00
Boquet Table, medium,		do	16 00
do	do	Black Marble,	21 00
Etagere, very elegant,			80 00
do	medium,		35 00
do	plainer,		18 00

PLAIN STYLE MAHOGANY OR WALNUT PARLOR FURNITURE.

			Each.
Sofas, hair cloth covering, spring seat, handsomely tufted,			$25 to 48
Divans	do	do	20 to 35
Rocking Chairs, do		do	6 to 18
Parlor Chairs, do	spring seats,		5 to 8
do	do	without springs,	3 50 to 7
do	cane seats,		1 50 to 3
Parlor Rocking Chairs, cane seat,			3 to 7
Centre Tables, Black Marble,			25 to 45
do	White Marble,		18 to 35
Pier Tables,	do		20 to 30
do	Black and Gold Marble,		26 to 38

Furniture of this style is equal in construction to the most expensive, and the style of Tufting Hair Cloth is the richest ever offered in this city. I have always on hand a large stock of this kind of Goods, which enables Merchants to fill their orders without delay.

It must not be presumed because my store is on Chestnut Street, at a high rent, that an extra price is charged to help to pay the expenses; as the contrary can easily be shown. If a manufacturer can afford to pay a moderate rent, with a light business, and save money, it is fair to suppose that another can pay a larger rent with a much larger business. The theory of heavy expenses in great establishments causing the proprietors to have large profits, has exploded, and is only used by those Tradesmen who, not having enterprise enough to embark extensively into business, are jealous of those who undertake anything out of the ordinary way, and whose short-sighted policy can never teach them to invest One Dollar to gain Ten. Trusting to the discernment of an enlightened public, I cordially invite all to call as purchasers or otherwise, and judge if the above remarks are worthy of credit.

MAHOGANY OR WALNUT
DINING-ROOM FURNITURE.

	Each.
Extension tables, 12 ft. long, 4 ft. wide, leaves all polished, elegant pattern, suitable for Centre Table,	$65 00
do same size, with Octagon worked legs,	45 00
do do plain legs,	40 00
Sofa to hold table leaves, plain style,	30 00
do do elegant,	60 00
Chairs with arms, very comfortable,	7 00
do do stuffed backs,	10 00
Chairs, plain style, stuffed seats,	4 00
do do cane seats,	1 75
Buffet or Sideboard, plain style, Marble top,	45 00
do do etagere top,	70 00
Butler's Trays, solid Mahogany,	6 00

MAHOGANY OR WALNUT
PLAIN CHAMBER FURNITURE.

	Each.
Bedsteads, High-Post, with Cornice and Canopy,	$90 00
do do plain Tester Frame,	65 00
do Octagon Post,	30 00
do French, 5 feet wide, elegant,	60 00
do do do plain,	30 00
do do 4 feet 6 inches wide, handsome,	25 00
do do do plain,	16 00
Dressing Bureaus, Marble top and Mirror,	65 00
do do do plain,	30 00
do	20 00
Wardrobes, Mirror Doors, extra size,	100 00
do medium,	55 00
do do	40 00
do do	28 00
Washstands, enclosed, Tray top, extra,	30 00
do do do medium,	18 00
do do Marble top,	12 00
do open, do	7 00
do do Tray top,	14 00
do do do extra	18 00

WALNUT OR MAHOGANY
LIBRARY FURNITURE.

	Each.
Secretary and Bookcase, elegant style,	$75 00
do do mirror doors,	60 00
do do silk plaiting,	45 00
do do plain style,	35 00
Library Tables, handsome finish,	40 00
do do plain,	20 00
Library Chairs, stuffed backs,	10 00
do do plain,	4 00
do do cane seat,	2 75
Recumbent Chairs, very comfortable,	36 00
do do plain,	25 00

Bookcases to fit recesses made to order at reasonable prices.

CHAMBER FURNITURE.
ORDINARY.

	Each.
Plain Bureaus,	$12 to 18
Plain Washstands,	2 50 to 6
Wardrobes, stained wood,	18 to 28
Cherry Post Bedsteads, Mahogany headboard,	10 to 25
Chamber Chairs, cane seat,	1 50 to 2 50
do do Windsor	75 cts. to 1 00
Servants' Bedsteads, elastic bottom,	5 50 to 7 00

Mattresses are fully described in another part of this Catalogue.

OAK, WALNUT OR MAHOGANY
HALL FURNITURE

	Each.
Hat Stands, Florid Gothic, with mirror,	$45 00
do medium style, do	22 00
do plain, do	15 00
do without mirror,	9 00
Hall Chairs, Gothic, to match,	12 00
do medium,	9 00

DIRECTIONS
FOR CLEANSING AND RE-POLISHING
FURNITURE.

Which apply only to the best quality, where superior varnish is used,
and the grain of the wood is thoroughly filled up with
varnish, rendering it impervious to water.

First, if there is any paint or grease on the surface, with a woolen rag moistened with Spirits of Turpentine, rub it gently until the blemish is removed; next, with a soft rag rub the Turpentine entirely off. Take a soft sponge wet with clean cold water, wash over well, then wipe off with a soft Chamois or very fine buckskin, which must be wet in clean cold water and rung as dry as possible—afterwards, if any places are scratched or bruised, apply a very small quantity of boiled Linseed Oil to the injured places; rub it off well with a piece of silk, being careful to leave no oil on the furniture, as it unites with the varnish and makes a hard rough surface; when dry you will find this process makes the furniture look as well as new. If your furniture should not be well varnished, or be discolored by water, the Linseed Oil applied as above will restore the color.

Above all things beware of *quack nostrums for polishing old furniture,* as I have never known any to be of service, and have always found them injurious. If your furniture needs varnishing, take fine ground pomice stone, with a piece of cloth wet well with water, and rub the surface, being careful not to rub through to the wood; then with a flat varnish brush, put on a coat of very fine Copal Varnish; if it does not look well after the first application, renew it in three or four days by the same process.

Furniture should be cleaned with water as above directed, once every three months, by which means it will always look well.

BIBLIOGRAPHY

Any bibliography is, at best, arbitrary and selective. To list all the books and articles consulted, even ones of marginal value, would clutter an already long list. Primarily, publications since 1960 have been favored under the assumption that earlier research that has stood up under repeated scrutiny has been incorporated into recent studies. Some earlier studies, however, are included if they were particularly helpful. General histories for the most part are omitted in favor of monographic work.

Since the text is sparingly footnoted, the bibliography serves as both a guide to important sources and a tacit recognition of the many scholars to whom I am indebted. Documentary collections, reprints of contemporary design books, exhibition catalogs, and books on major furniture collections were used whenever possible.

Several periodicals were cited time after time. *The Magazine Antiques* and the *Winterthur Portfolio* contain much of the published research in the field of furniture history. Many of these articles were written by Winterthur fellows whose research was heavily relied upon. *Art & Antiques* (formerly *American Art & Antiques*) and *Nineteenth Century*, two relatively new periodicals, proved indispensable, particularly on the 19th century. The *Journal of Early Southern Decorative Arts* contained much of the latest research on southern cabinetmaking emerging from Frank Horton and the Museum of Early Southern Decorative Arts.

The work of several scholars was consulted repeatedly. Benno Forman at Winterthur and several of his former students, including Robert Trent and Patricia Kane, have delved into Jacobean and William and Mary furniture to an extent that finally surpasses Irving Lyon's classic book first published in 1891. William Hornor's *Blue Book* was indispensable on the 18th and early 19th centuries, as were specialized studies by Brock Jobe on the 18th century upholsterer, Nancy Goyne Evans on Windsor chairs, Charles Montgomery on the Federal Period, John Kirk on regional aesthetics, and Dean Fales on painted furniture. On the 19th century, such scholars as Kenneth Ames, Page Talbot, David Hanks, and Robert Smith have illuminated that era far beyond the pioneering essay in the exhibition catalog of 19th-century decorative arts published by the Metropolitan Museum of Art in 1970. Special studies by Monroe Fabian on the Pennsylvania German chest, Lonn Taylor and David Warren on Texas furniture, and Charles Hummel on the Dominy craftsmen contained much useful information.

Following a section on general works, the bibliography is organized by chapter. In cases where sources cover more than one subject, the item is listed under the chapter where it contributed the most to the text.

GENERAL

ARONSON, JOSEPH. *The Encyclopedia of Furniture*. New York: Crown Publishers, Inc., 1965. A revised edition of his 1938 encyclopedia, with over 2,000 illustrations. Some of the scholarship has been superseded, and it is weak on the 19th century but is still the best encyclopedia on furniture available.

ARTZ, FREDERICK B. *From the Renaissance to Romanticism*. Chicago: University of Chicago Press, 1962. Useful background on philosophy and world outlook in the 17th and 18th centuries.

DAVIDSON, MARSHALL B. ed. *Three Centuries of American Antiques*. New York: American Heritage Publishing Company, Inc. 1979. Reprint of the three-volume history published in 1967 (*The American Heritage History of Colonial Antiques*), 1968 (*The American Heritage History of American Antiques from the Revolution to the Civil War*), and 1969 (*The American Heritage History of American Antiques from the Civil War to World War I*). Beautifully illustrated. Covers the major 17th-, 18th-, and 19th-century American crafts, including cabinetmaking. Sees the craftsman in a larger social and cultural milieu. An excellent source, but it is chopped up into many short essays.

FALES, DEAN A. *American Painted Furniture 1660-1880*. New York: Dutton and Company, Inc., 1972. The most comprehensive and well-illustrated look at an important segment of American furniture.

GOWANS, ALAN. *Images of American Living*. New York: Harper and Row, 1976. Excellent essay on the changing styles of architecture and furniture to the 20th century. The major focus is on architecture, but this is an interesting interpretation of furniture styles, particularly in the 18th century. A pioneering effort at a broad interpretation.

HAYWARD, HELENA. *World Furniture*. New York: McGraw-Hill, 1965. Best general history of world furniture. American sections by Robert Smith and Joseph Butler.

KANE, PATRICIA E. *300 Years of American Seating Furniture*. Boston: New York Graphic Society, 1976. Careful and solid survey of American chairs through three centuries, using examples from the Yale University collection.

NAEVE, MILO M. *The Classical Presence in American Art*. Chicago: The Art Institute of Chicago, 1978. Useful focus on a major element in American furniture design, although the essay encompasses silver, painting, and sculpture as well.

PALMER, BROOKS. *The Book of American Clocks*. New York: The Macmillan Company, 1950. Brief introduction to clockmaking with a listing of makers. Also contains illustrations of various clock-case styles.

PETERSON, HAROLD. *Americans at Home*. New York: Charles Scribner's, Sons, 1971. American interiors are documented through several centuries of contemporary paintings and prints.

PYE, DAVID. *The Nature and Art of Workmanship*. New York: Van Nostrand Reinhold Publishing Company, 1968. Stimulating discussion of what makes an antique.

RAMSEY, L.G.G. ed. *The Complete Color Encyclopedia of Antiques*. New York: Hawthorn Books, Inc, 1975. Useful sections on American furniture and the Aesthetic Movement. The article on "American Mirrors" is particularly useful.

18th Century

American Antiques from Israel Sack Collection. 6 Vols. Washington, D.C.: Highland House Publishers, Inc., 1957–1979. Indexed illustrations of several thousand pieces of some of the finest American furniture that has passed through one of the foremost antique shops in the country.

BATTISON, EDWIN A. AND PATRICIA E. KANE. *The American Clock 1725–1865*. Greenwich, Conn.: New York Graphic Society, Ltd., 1973. The development of clockmaking in America is illustrated by clocks from the Yale University collection. Both the cases and movements are illustrated and described in detail.

BJERKOE, ETHEL HALL. *The Cabinetmakers of America*. Garden City: Doubleday and Company, Inc., 1957. Standard, though by no means exhaustive, listing of cabinetmakers.

COMSTOCK, HELEN. *American Furniture: Seventeenth, Eighteenth and Nineteenth Century Styles*. New York: The Viking Press, 1962. General introduction and description of each major period of American furniture design through about 1850. Weak on Victorian furniture. Now dated.

COOPER, WENDY. *In Praise of America*. New York: Alfred A. Knopf, 1980. Excellent summary of recent research on the decorative arts, with a major focus on furniture, written to accompany the 1980 Exhibition at The National Gallery of Art.

EDWARDS, RALPH. *The Shorter Dictionary of English Furniture*. London: Country Life, 1964. Mostly on English furniture but is germane to the origin of furniture styles and craftsmanship of American furniture as well.

KIRK, JOHN T. *Early American Furniture*. New York: Alfred A. Knopf, 1970. The subtitle tells the story: How to recognize, evaluate, buy, and care for the most beautiful pieces of high-style, country, primitive, and rustic antiques. Kirk looks at furniture as art and explains how he evaluates quality and excellence in furniture design.

MARSH, MORETON. *The Easy Expert in American Antiques: Knowing, Finding, Buying & Restoring Early American Furniture*. Philadelphia: J. B. Lippincott, Company, 1978. Reprint of the 1959 edition, which contains much common-sense information about evaluating and restoring American furniture.

MILLER, EDGAR G. JR. *American Antique Furniture*. New York: Dover Publications, Inc., 1966. Picture source-book first published in 1937, with over 2,000 illustrations of furniture found mostly in the Baltimore area.

MONTGOMERY, CHARLES AND BENNO M. FORMAN. *Joseph Moxon's Mechanick Exercises*. New York: Praeger Publishers, 1970. Reprint of an 18th-century guide to handling cabinetmaker's tools and the implements of other crafts.

NUTTING, WALLACE. *Furniture Treasury*. New York: The Macmillan Company, 1963. First printed in 1928, it is still a useful compendium of American furniture, with over 5,000 photographs. Nutting's caveat—"mostly of American origin"—should be noted.

ORMSBEE, THOMAS H. *Field Guide to Early American Furniture*. New York: Bonanza Books, 1951. Useful handbook of types, styles, and relative value, although some of his information has been surpassed by recent scholarship.

SACK, ALBERT. *Fine Points of Furniture: Early American*. New York: Crown Publishers, Inc., 1950. Comparing "good, better, and best" in various forms. Sack shows what to look for in order to determine quality.

WARD-JACKSON, PETER. *English Furniture Designs of the Eighteenth Century*. London: H. M. Stationery Office, 1958. A selection of printed sources used by English as well as American furniture makers in the 18th century.

19th Century

ASLIN, ELIZABETH. *Nineteenth Century English Furniture*. New York: Thomas Yoseloff, 1962. A solid survey of 19th-century English furniture that also influenced American designs.

BUTLER, JOSEPH T. *American Antiques: 1800–1900*. New York: The Odyssey Press, 1965. About 100 pages on furniture, with some illustrations. By the curator of the Sleepy Hollow Restorations.

LEA, ZILLA RIDER, ed. *The Ornamented Chair: Its Development in America, 1700–1890*. Rutland, Vt.: Charles E. Tuttle, 1960. The seven essays are mostly on 19th-century developments.

McCLINTON, KATHARINE MORRISON. *Collecting American Victorian Antiques*. New York: Charles Scribner's Sons, 1966. About 100 pages on furniture; good pictures and information. Still a useful introduction to the period.

ORMSBEE, THOMAS. *Field Guide to American Victorian Furniture*. New York: Bonanza Books, 1952. Uses the same format as his earlier volume on 18th-century furniture. A useful handbook for identifying Victorian sub-styles.

OTTO, CELIA JACKSON. *American Furniture of the Nineteenth Century*.

New York: The Viking Press, 1965. An excellent pictorial history of Victorian furniture. Brief essays on each period.

TRACY, BERRY B. *19th Century America: Furniture and Other Decorative Arts: An Exhibition in Celebration of the Hundredth Anniversary of the Metropolitan Museum of Art*. New York: Metropolitan Museum of Art, 1970. Catalog of the pioneering exhibit of 19th-century decorative arts. Excellent introductory essay and informative commentary on the pieces that represent the best of the century.

CHAPTER I

Books, Catalogs, and Theses

CHINNERY, VICTOR. *Oak Furniture: The British Tradition*. Woodbridge, Suffolk, England: Baron Publishing, 1979. Excellent survey of English 17th-century furniture and its close relationship to American furniture of this period.

FORMAN, BENNO M. "The Seventeenth Century Case Furniture of Essex County, Massachusetts, and Its Makers." Master's Thesis, University of Delaware, 1968. Preliminary research on 17th-century New England furniture that will be incorporated into a forthcoming book on 17th-century American furniture.

KANE, PATRICIA E. *Furniture of the New Haven Colony: The Seventeenth-Century Style*. New Haven: The New Haven Colony Historical Society, 1973. Catalog of a 17th-century furniture exhibit; based on her Winterthur thesis.

LYON, IRVING W. *The Colonial Furniture of New England*. New York: E. P. Dutton, 1977. First published in 1891, this book is still the best general study of 17th- and early 18th-century furniture.

TRENT, ROBERT F. "The Joiners and Joinery of Middlesex County, Massachusetts, 1630–1730". Master's Thesis, University of Delaware, 1975. One of the best studies of 17th-century furniture.

Articles

KIRK, JOHN T. "Sources of Some American Regional Furniture, Part I" *The Magazine Antiques*

88 (December 1965): 790–98. Traces many common American regional characteristics to English origins, particularly the painted and carved chests of the late 17th and early 18th centuries in England.

KIRK, JOHN T. "The Tradition of English Painted Furniture, Part I: The Experience in Colonial New England." *The Magazine Antiques* 117 (May 1980): 1078–83. Excellent study of the sources of American painted furniture in England.

ST. GEORGE, ROBERT BLAIR. "Style and Structure in the Joinery of Dedham and Medfield, Massachusetts, 1635–1685." in *Winterthur Portfolio 13, American Furniture and Its Makers*: 1–46. Chicago: University of Chicago Press, 1979. Another piece in the 17th century furniture story; based on his Winterthur thesis.

SYMONDS, R. W. "The Evolution of the Cupboard." *Connoisseur* 112 (December 1943): 91–99. Succinct, enlightening account of the evolution of the cupboard, which was the most impressive piece of furniture in American homes of the 17th-century.

TRENT, ROBERT. "The Endicott Chair: American Classics." *Maine Antiques Digest* (March 1979): 1B–2B. Best essay on what are now known as Cromwellian chairs.

WARREN, WILLIAM L. "Were the Guilford Painted Chests Made in Saybrook?" *Bulletin of The Connecticut Historical Society* 23 (January 1958): 1–10. Most up-to-date work on the subject.

CHAPTER II

Books, Catalogs, and Theses

HENDRICK, ROBERT E. P. "John Gaines II and Thomas Gaines I, 'Turners' of Ipswich, Massachusetts." Master's Thesis, University of Delaware, 1964. Good study of late 17th- and early 18th-century turners and their work.

WILLS, GEOFFREY. *English Lookingglasses: A Study of the Glass, Frames and Makers (1670–1820)*. New York: A. S. Barnes and Co., 1965. The best study of the looking glass, with particular emphasis on manufacturing processes.

Articles

O'DONNELL, PATRICIA CHAPIN. "Grisaille decorated *Kasten* of New York," *The Magazine Antiques* 117 (May 1980): 1108–11. Pulls together the current information on this impressive early form.

RANDALL, RICHARD H. JR. "'Boston Chairs.'" *Old-Time New England* 54 (Summer 1963): 12–20. Defines a chair type popular in the first half of the 18th century.

CHAPTER III

Books, Catalogs, and Theses

DOW, GEORGE FRANCIS. *The Arts & Crafts in New England: 1704–1775.* Topsfield, Massachusetts: The Wayside Press, 1927. A basic source of published 18th-century advertisements relating to the crafts and particularly to cabinetmakers.

GOTTESMAN, RITA SUSSWEIN, comp. *The Arts and Crafts in New York, 1726–1776.* New York: New York Historical Society, 1938. A collection of advertisements and notices concerning New York craftsmen and their products.

JOHNSON, J. STEWART. "New York Cabinetmaking Prior to the Revolution." Master's Thesis, University of Delaware, 1964. Based primarily on the Delaplaine account books, this thesis illuminates the least understood major style center in America in the 18th century.

KATES, GEORGE N. *Chinese Household Furniture.* New York: Dover Publications, Inc., 1962. Reprint of the 1945 edition.

KIRK, JOHN T. *American Chairs: Queen Anne and Chippendale.* New York: Alfred A. Knopf, 1972. Uses the same approach as his earlier survey of furniture but focuses on chairs. An excellent study of the regional characteristics of both Queen Anne and Chippendale styles.

PENN, THEODORE ZUK. "Decorative and Protective Finishes, 1750–1850: Materials, Process, and Craft." Master's Thesis, University of Delaware, 1966. One of the best surveys of a highly technical subject.

THOMAS, GERTRUDE Z. *Richer than Spices.* New York: Alfred A. Knopf, 1965. A study of the influences of Catherine Braganza, wife of Charles II, on English culture.

WHITEHILL, WALTER MUIR, ed. *Boston Furniture of the Eighteenth Century.* Boston: The Colonial Society of Massachusetts, 1974. Report of a conference on this subject attended by some of the top experts on 18th-century furniture. Good chapters on upholsterers, japanning, 17th-century Massachusetts furniture, and Boston bombe and blockfront furniture.

Articles

FORMAN, BENNO M. "Delaware Valley 'Crookt Foot' and Slat-Back Chairs: The Fussell-Savery Connection." *Winterthur Portfolio* 15 (Spring 1980): 41–64. A carefully researched account of where William Savery got his training.

GOYNE, NANCY A. "American Windsor Chairs: A Style Survey." *The Magazine Antiques* 95 (April 1969): 538–43. The best account of Windsor chairs that takes the story to the early 19th century.

HECKSCHER, MORRISON H. "Form and Frame: New Thoughts on the American Easy Chair." *The Magazine Antiques* 100 (December 1971): 886–93. An illuminating study on regional stylistic and construction characteristics of easy chairs. Based on an exhibition at the Metropolitan Museum of Art.

McELROY, CATHRYN J. "Furniture in Philadelphia: The First Fifty Years" in *Winterthur Portfolio* 13, *American Furniture and Its Makers*: 61–80. Chicago: University of Chicago Press, 1979. Fills the gap in Hornor's *Blue Book*, which emphasizes Queen Anne and Chippendale furniture.

PHILBRICK, TIMOTHY. "Tall Chests: The Art of Proportioning." *Fine Wood Working* 9 (Winter 1977): 39–43. A stimulating essay on the proportions of 18th-century high chests.

SCHOELWER, SUSAN PRENDERGAST. "Form, Function, and Meaning in the Use of Fabric Furnishings: A Philadelphia Case Study, 1700–1775." *Winterthur Portfolio* 14 (Spring 1979): 25–40. Chicago: University of Chicago Press, 1979. A statistical study of inventories

that concludes that textiles declined as a symbol of status and richly carved furniture rose as the century progressed.

SMITH, ROBERT C. "China, Japan, and the Anglo-American Chair." *The Magazine Antiques* 96 (October 1969): 552–58. Presents evidence for the influence of the Orient on English and American chairs, particularly the ball and claw foot, the yoke crest, and the vase-shaped splat. Still, however, not the final word.

CHAPTER IV

Books, Catalogs, and Theses

BAKER, HOLLIS S. *Furniture in the Ancient World.* New York: The Macmillan Company, 1966. A solid account of ancient furniture that shows many of the classical motifs that appear on 18th-century American furniture.

BRIDENBAUGH, CARL. *The Colonial Craftsman.* New York: New York University Press, 1950. A classic social history of the colonial craftsmen, including cabinetmakers.

CARPENTER, RALPH E. *The Arts and Crafts of Newport, Rhode Island, 1640–1820.* Newport: Preservation Society, 1954. Clear illustrations and good commentary on Newport furniture.

CHIPPENDALE, THOMAS. *The Gentleman and Cabinet-Maker's Director.* New York: Dover Books, 1966. Latest reprint of the third edition of 1762.

COMSTOCK, HELEN. *The Looking Glass in America, 1700–1825.* New York: The Viking Press, 1968. An illustrated survey of the important styles of American and English looking glasses.

CUMMINGS, ABBOTT LOWELL. *Rural Household Inventories.* Boston: The Society for the Preservation of New England Antiquities, 1964. An indispensable reference and research tool to understanding 18th-century furniture.

DOWNS, JOSEPH. *American Furniture: Queen Anne and Chippendale Periods.* New York: The Macmillan Company, 1952. Classic survey by the first director of Winterthur. Illustrated with 400 pictures from the Winterthur collection.

FALES, DEAN A., JR. *The Furniture of Historic Deerfield.* New York: E. P. Dutton and Company, Inc., 1976. A survey of one of the great collections of American furniture; written in a lively style.

GILBERT, CHRISTOPHER. *The Life and Work of Thomas Chippendale.* New York: Macmillan Publishing Company, Inc., 1978. The definitive book on Thomas Chippendale.

GREENLAW, BARRY A. *New England Furniture at Williamsburg.* Williamsburg, Va.: Colonial Williamsburg Foundation, 1974. A scholarly catalog of a major collection of New England furniture.

HIPKISS, EDWIN J. *Eighteenth Century American Arts: The M. and M. Karolik Collection.* Boston: Museum of Fine Arts, 1941. Excellent pictures, description, and comments on furniture in the Boston Museum of Fine Arts.

HORNOR, WILLIAM MACPHERSON JR. *Blue Book Philadelphia Furniture: William Penn to George Washington.* Washington, D. C.: Highland House Publishers, 1977. First published in 1935, this is still the best source for 18th-century Philadelphia furniture, particularly the Queen Anne and Chippendale styles.

MONTGOMERY, CHARLES F. AND PATRICIA E. KANE, eds. *American Art: 1750–1800, Towards Independence.* New Haven: Yale University Art Gallery, 1976. A landmark bicentennial exhibition catalog with excellent essays on American furniture and other decorative arts. Montgomery's essay on regional preferences is particularly useful.

OTT, JOSEPH K. *The John Brown House Loan Exhibition of Rhode Island Furniture.* Providence, R.I.: The Rhode Island Historical Society, 1965. Catalog of an important exhibition of Rhode Island furniture by one of the major specialists in that subject.

PRIME, ALFRED COX, comp. *The Arts & Crafts in Philadelphia, Maryland, and South Carolina 1721–1785.* Series One. Topsfield, Mass.: The Wayside Press, 1932. A compilation of the notices and advertisements of craftsmen.

RANDALL, RICHARD H. JR. *American Furniture in the Museum of Fine Arts, Boston.* Boston: Museum of Fine Arts, 1965. One of the best catalogs of 18th- and early 19th-century furniture, mostly of Massachusetts origin, with informative descriptions of pieces in this major collection.

WARREN, DAVID B. *Bayou Bend: American Furniture, Paintings and Silver from the Bayou Bend Collection.* Houston: The Museum of Fine Arts, 1975. The catalog of one of the great American collections of decorative arts.

Articles

GOYNE, NANCY A. "The Bureau Table in America." In *Winterthur Portfolio* 3 (1967): 24–36. Winterthur, Del.: The Henry Francis du Pont Winterthur Museum, 1967. A thorough study of the popular 18th-century form now known as a kneehole desk.

HECKSCHER, MORRISON H. "The New York Serpentine Card Table." *The Magazine Antiques* 103 (May 1973): 974–83. A definitive survey of one of the most impressive 18th-century New York furniture forms.

MOOZ, R. PETER. "The Origins of Newport Block-front Furniture Design." *The Magazine Antiques* 99 (June 1971): 882–86. A recent attempt to pin down the origins of the Newport blockfront.

SMITH, ROBERT C. "Finial Busts on Eighteenth-century Philadelphia Furniture." *The Magazine Antiques* 100 (December 1971): 900–05. Attempts to identify the carvers of characteristic finials on Philadelphia furniture.

WEIL, MARTIN ELI. "A Cabinetmaker's Price Book." In *Winterthur Portfolio* 13, *American Furniture and Its Makers*: 175–92. Chicago: University of Chicago Press, 1979. A rare 18th-century document that lists many of the period terms for furniture elements and embellishments.

CHAPTER V

Books, Catalogs, and Theses

BROWN, MICHAEL. "Duncan Phyfe." Master's Thesis, University of Delaware, 1978. A fresh look at Phyfe that produces some new information and corrects a few errors of past research.

CORNELIUS, CHARLES O. *Furniture Masterpieces of Duncan Phyfe.* New York: Dover Publications, Inc., 1970. The life and times of Phyfe as well as an analysis of his style. A reprint of the 1922 study now dated.

GOTTESMAN, RITA SUSSWEIN, comp. *The Arts and Crafts in New York, 1800–1804.* New York: New York Historical Society, 1954. Sequel to an earlier compilation.

HECKSCHER, MORRISON H. "The Organization and Practice of Philadelphia Cabinetmaking Establishments, 1790–1820." Master's Thesis, University of Delaware, 1964. A detailed study of the subject.

HEPPLEWHITE, GEORGE. *The Cabinet-Maker and Upholsterer's Guide.* New York: Dover Publications, Inc., 1969. Reprint of the 1794 edition of his design book, which had a major impact on American furniture design of the Federal period.

MCCLELLAND, NANCY. *Duncan Phyfe and the English Regency, 1795–1830.* New York: Dover Publications, Inc., 1980. Reprint of the classic 1939 study of Duncan Phyfe and early 19th-century American furniture.

MONTGOMERY, CHARLES F. *American Furniture: The Federal Period.* New York: The Viking Press, 1966. The definitive work on Federal furniture; illustrated with 500 photographs from the Winterthur collection. The author was the director at Winterthur and then curator of the Garvan Collection at Yale University.

NONEMAKER, JAMES AULTON. "The New York Town House, 1815–1840." Master's Thesis, University of Delaware, 1958. Useful survey of inventories to determine the types of furniture popular in the early 19th-century and their room placement.

PRIME, ALFRED COX, comp. *The Arts & Crafts in Philadelphia, Maryland, and South Carolina, 1786–1800.* Series Two. Topsfield, Mass.: The Wayside Press, 1932. A companion to a compilation of earlier craftsmen's notices.

SHERATON, THOMAS. *The Cabinet-Maker and Upholsterer's Drawing-Book.* New York: Dover Publications, Inc., 1972. Reprint of his design book first published in the 1790s.

SHERATON, THOMAS. *Thomas Sheraton's Cabinet Dictionary.* New York: Praeger Publishers, 1970. Reprint of the 1803 London edition of the dictionary, with a wealth of detail on late 18th- and early 19th-century furniture terms, practices, and design.

STONEMAN, VERNON C. *John and Thomas Seymour, Cabinetmakers in Boston, 1794–1816.* Boston: Special Publications, 1959. An interesting study on the Seymours, but many of his illustrations cannot be firmly attributed to Seymour.

Articles

CANDEE, RICHARD M. "The Rediscovery of Milk-based House Paints and the Myth of 'Brickdust and Buttermilk' Paints." *Old-Time New England* 58 (Winter 1968): 79–81. Shows that milk-based paint was not commonly used on furniture until the 19th-century.

CLUNIE, MARGARET BURKE. "Joseph True and the Piecework System in Salem." *The Magazine Antiques* 111 (May 1977): 1006–13. An important study of Salem cabinetmaking that fills a gap in Montgomery's classic study of Federal furniture. Based on her excellent Winterthur thesis.

GOLOVIN, ANNE CASTRODALE. "Daniel Trotter: Eighteenth-Century Philadelphia Cabinetmaker." In *Winterthur Portfolio* 6 (1970): 151–84. Charlottesville: University Press of Virginia, 1970. Detailed monograph on an important Philadelphia chairmaker.

CHAPTER VI

Books, Catalogs, and Theses

GRANDJEAN, SERGE. *Empire Furniture, 1800 to 1825.* New York: Taplinger Publishing Company, 1966. One of the best summaries of French Empire furniture, which influenced the American Empire style.

HALL, JOHN. *The Cabinet Maker's Assistant.* Baltimore: John Murphy, 1840. A rare book that contains useful illustrations of the late Empire pillar-and-scroll type furniture.

HOPE, THOMAS. *Household Furniture and Interior Decoration.* New York: Dover Publications, Inc., 1971. Reprint of the 1807 edition that influenced the development

of the Empire style in England and America.

KENNEY, JOHN TARRANT. *The Hitchcock Chair.* New York: Clarkson N. Potter, Inc., 1971. A sketchy biography of Hitchcock, but the outline of the story is there.

MUSGRAVE, CLIFFORD. *Regency Furniture, 1800–1830.* New York: Thomas Yoseloff, 1961. One of the best sources for English Empire furniture, with useful background on the development of the style.

SMITH, GEORGE. *A Collection of Designs for Household Furniture.* New York: Praeger Publishers, 1970. Reprint of the 1808 book that influenced the development of the Empire style of America.

TRACY, BERRY B. *Classical America 1815–1845.* Newark: Newark Museum Association, 1963. Catalog of one of the few exhibitions of Empire furniture and other decorative arts in this period. An excellent introductory survey.

Articles

CATALANO, KATHLEEN M. "Cabinetmaking in Philadelphia, 1820–1840: Transition from Craft to Industry." In *Winterthur Portfolio* 13, *American Furniture and Its Makers*: 81–138. Chicago: University of Chicago Press, 1979. An excellent study of Philadelphia cabinetmaking in this period, with emphasis on shop practices and the business of cabinetmaking.

HOLLIS, HELEN RICE. "Jonas Chickering: The Father of American Pianoforte-making." *The Magazine Antiques* 104 (August 1973): 227–30. A good biography by a specialist in the division of musical instruments at the Smithsonian.

OTTO, CELIA JACKSON. "Pillar and Scroll: Greek Revival Furniture of the 1830's." *The Magazine Antiques* 81 (May 1962): 504–07. A succinct definition of this phase of the Empire style.

PEARCE, JOHN N., LORRAINE W. PEARCE, AND ROBERT C. SMITH. "The Meeks Family of Cabinetmakers." *The Magazine Antiques* 85 (April 1964): 414–20. Pioneering study of an important New York cabinetmaking firm.

PEARCE, LORRAINE W. "The Distinctive Character of the Work of Lannuier." *The Magazine Antiques*

86 (December 1964): 712–17. A good account of the important New York cabinetmaker. Based on her Winterthur thesis.

RALSTON, RUTH. "The Style Antique in Furniture, I: Its Sources and Its Creators." *The Magazine Antiques* 47 (May 1945): 278–81; Part II, "The Style Antique in Furniture: Its American Manifestations and Their Prototypes." *Ibidem* 48 (October 1945): 206–09. Pioneering essays on the source of Empire furniture.

RANDALL, RICHARD H. JR. "Sources of the Empire Style." *The Magazine Antiques* 83 (April 1963): 452–53. An alternate view that the Empire style is based on 18th-century interpretations of classical Greece and Rome rather than on 19th-century studies of those ancient cultures.

SMITH, ROBERT C. "The Classical Style in France and England 1800–1840." *The Magazine Antiques* 74 (November 1958): 429–33; "Late Classical Furniture in the United States, 1820–1850." *Ibidem* 74 (December 1958): 519–23. Good definitions of the classical and Empire styles.

SMITH, ROBERT C. "John Hall, A Busy Man in Baltimore." *The Magazine Antiques* 92 (September 1967): 360–66. Hall published a major collection of Empire furniture designs in 1840, and Smith illuminates this obscure man.

SMITH, ROBERT C. "The Furniture of Anthony G. Quervelle: Part I: The Pier Tables." *The Magazine Antiques* 103 (May 1973): 984–94; "The Furniture of Anthony G. Quervelle: Part II: The Pedestal Tables." *Ibidem* 104 (July 1973): 90–99; "The Furniture of Anthony G. Quervelle: Part III: The Worktables." *Ibidem* 104 (August 1973): 260–68; "The Furniture of Anthony G. Quervelle: Part IV: Some Case Pieces." *Ibidem* 105 (January 1974): 180–93; "The Furniture of Anthony G. Quervelle: Part V: Sofas, Chairs, and Beds." *Ibidem* 105 (March 1974): 512–21. An excellent five-part series on the furniture of this major Philadelphia cabinetmaker.

TALBOTT, PAGE. "Boston Empire Furniture, Part I." *The Magazine Antiques* 107 (May 1975): 878–87; "Boston Empire Furniture, Part II." *Ibidem* 109 (May 1976): 1004–13. An excellent study of a little-known subject. Based on her Winterthur thesis.

TRUMP, ROBERT T. "Joseph B. Barry, Philadelphia Cabinetmaker." *The Magazine Antiques* 107 (January 1975): 159–63. The best study of this important Philadelphia cabinetmaker.

WAXMAN, LORRAINE (Lorraine Pearce). "The Lannuier Brothers, Cabinetmakers." *The Magazine Antiques* 72 (August 1957): 141–43. A study of one of the most important New York cabinetmakers. Based on her Winterthur thesis.

CHAPTER VII

Books, Catalogs, and Theses

BULKELEY, HOUGHTON. *Contributions to Connecticut Cabinet Making.* Hartford, Conn.: The Connecticut Historical Society, 1967. One article disproves the theory that John Townsend was in Connecticut. Other entries include notes on Aaron Roberts and Benjamin Burnham.

GARVIN, JAMES L. *Plain & Elegant, Rich & Common.* Concord, N.H.: New Hampshire Historical Society, 1979. An excellent catalog of an exhibit of documented New Hampshire furniture made mostly in the early 19th century.

HUMMEL, CHARLES F. *With Hammer in Hand.* Charlottesville: The University Press of Virginia, 1968. An exhaustive study of the Dominy family of cabinetmakers on Long Island. A pioneering work on country cabinetwork.

KIRK, JOHN T. *Connecticut Furniture: Seventeenth and Eighteenth Centuries.* Hartford, Conn.: Wadsworth Atheneum, 1967. More information and analysis of the furniture than most catalogs.

MORSE, JOHN D., ed. *Country Cabinetwork and Simple City Furniture.* Charlottesville: The University Press of Virginia, 1970. Stimulating thoughts on a difficult subject by well-known scholars in American cultural history.

PARSONS, CHARLES S. *The Dunlaps & Their Furniture.* Manchester, N.H.: The Currier Gallery of Art, 1970. The best work on the Dunlaps, with illustrations of pieces in a 1970 exhibit of southern New Hampshire furniture.

RIPPE, PETER M. "Daniel Clay of Greenfield, 'Cabinetmaker.'" Master's Thesis, University of Delaware, 1962. One of the best monographs on a rural cabinetmaker.

TRENT, ROBERT F. *Hearts & Crowns.* New Haven: The New Haven Colony Historical Society, 1977. Presents a significant new look at the development of the heart-and-crown chair.

Articles

BULKELEY, HOUGHTON. "Benjamin Burnham of Colchester, Cabinetmaker." *The Magazine Antiques* 76 (July 1959): 62–63. The best monograph on this important Connecticut craftsman.

COMSTOCK, HELEN, et al. "Country Furniture: A Symposium." *The Magazine Antiques* 93 (March 1968): 342–71. Eight essays by Charles Montgomery, Richard Randall, Nina Fletcher Little, and others on the definition of country furniture.

FORMAN, BENNO M. "The Crown and York Chairs of Coastal Connecticut and the Work of the Durands of Milford." *The Magazine Antiques* 105 (May 1974): 1147–54. A precise definition of the origins and migration of a common chair form in New York and Connecticut.

KANE, PATRICIA E. "Samuel Gragg: His Bentwood Fancy Chairs." *Yale University Bulletin* 33 (Autumn 1971): 27–37. Best study of this innovative craftsman.

SNYDER, JOHN J., JR. "The Bachman Attributions: A Reconsideration." *The Magazine Antiques* 105 (May 1974): 1056–65. A careful study of Lancaster as a major cabinetmaking center where over 160 wood craftsmen worked between 1760 and 1810. Bachman was only one of many working in this school.

SNYDER, JOHN J., JR. "Carved Chippendale Case Furniture from Lancaster, Pennsylvania." *The Magazine Antiques* 107 (May 1975): 964–75. Illuminates cabinetmaking in Lancaster and places Bachman in perspective.

CHAPTER VIII

Books, Catalogs, and Theses

BURTON, E. MILBY. *Charleston Furniture, 1700–1825.* Columbia, S.C.: University of South Carolina Press, 1955. A pioneering work on Charleston furniture. Based primarily on Thomas Elfe's account book, but includes no documented furniture.

CRAIG, JAMES H. *The Arts and Crafts in North Carolina, 1699–1840.* Winston-Salem, N.C.: The Museum of Early Southern Decorative Arts, 1965. A useful compilation of the newspaper notices placed by southern craftsmen.

ELDER, WILLIAM VOSS, III. *Maryland Queen Anne and Chippendale Furniture of the Eighteenth Century.* Baltimore: October House, Inc., 1968. The exhibition catalog by a specialist on Maryland furniture who is curator at the Baltimore Museum of Art.

ELDER, WILLIAM VOSS, III. *Baltimore Painted Furniture, 1800–1840.* Baltimore: Baltimore Museum of Art, 1972. Catalog of some of the flamboyant Maryland furniture.

GREEN, HENRY D. *Furniture of the Georgia Piedmont before 1830.* Atlanta: The High Museum of Art, 1976. Catalog of a major exhibit on Georgia furniture.

GROSS, KATHARINE WOOD. "The Sources of Furniture Sold in Savannah 1789–1815." Master's Thesis, University of Delaware, 1967. An important survey of the relationship between northern cabinetmaking centers and Savannah.

GUSLER, WALLACE B. *Furniture of Williamsburg and Eastern Virginia 1710–1790.* Richmond: Virginia Museum, 1979. An innovative study of a heretofore little-understood cabinetmaking center.

HIND, JAN GARRETT. *The Museum of Early Southern Decorative Arts.* Winston-Salem, N.C.: Old Salem, Inc., 1979. The introduction by Frank Horton, the director of MESDA, is one of the best overviews of Southern furniture.

HORTON, FRANK L. AND CAROLYN J. WEEKLEY. *The Swisegood School of Cabinetmaking.* Winston-Salem, N.C.: Museum of Early Southern Decorative Arts, 1973. Catalog of an exhibition of this important North Carolina cabinetmaker.

POESCH, JESSIE J. *Early Furniture of Louisiana 1750–1830.* New Orleans: The Louisiana State Museum, 1972. Catalog of a major exhibition on Louisiana furniture by the man who has done more research in the area than any other.

TAYLOR, LONN, AND DAVID B. WARREN. *Texas Furniture: The Cabinetmakers and Their Work, 1840–1880.* Austin: The University of Texas Press, 1975. One of the best regional studies that made heavy use of census records to identify cabinetmakers. Their descendents were then queried to locate documented furniture.

WINTERS, ROBERT E., JR., ed. *North Carolina Furniture, 1700–1900.* Raleigh, N.C.: North Carolina Museum of History Associates, Inc. 1977. A good general survey of North Carolina furniture.

Articles

BARTLETT, LU. "John Shaw, Cabinetmaker of Annapolis." *The Magazine Antiques* 111 (February 1977): 362–77. An updated and refined study of Annapolis' most important cabinetmaker.

BEASLEY, ELLEN. "Tennessee Furniture and Its Makers." *The Magazine Antiques* 100 (September 1971): 425–31. One of the few studies of this area.

BIVINS, JOHN, JR. "A Piedmont North Carolina Cabinetmaker: The Development of a Regional Style." *The Magazine Antiques* 103 (May 1973): 968–73. A documented account of Jesse Needham, who worked in North Carolina from 1793–1839.

BIVINS, JOHN, JR. "Baroque Elements in North Carolina Moravian Furniture." *Journal of Early Southern Decorative Arts* 2 (May 1976): 38–63. Identifies German Baroque influences in the Moravian furniture of North Carolina.

COMSTOCK, HELEN. "Furniture of Virginia, North Carolina, Georgia, and Kentucky." *The Magazine Antiques* 61 (January 1952): 58–100. Pioneering catalog of the first major exhibition of Southern furniture.

COMSTOCK, HELEN. "Southern Furniture Since 1952." *The Magazine Antiques* 91 (January 1967): 102–19. An update of her 1952 article on Southern furniture.

DAHILL, BETTY. "The Sharrock Family: A Newly Discovered School of Cabinetmakers." *Journal of Early Southern Decorative Arts* 2 (November 1976): 37–51. A preliminary study of a family of cabinetmakers in the Albemarle area of North Carolina.

DIBBLE, ANN W. "Fredericksburg-Falmouth Chairs in the Chippendale Style." *Journal of Early Southern Decorative Arts* 4 (May 1978): 1–24. A convincing study of the distinctive chairs produced in this region.

HORTON, FRANK L. "The Work of an Anonymous Carolina Cabinetmaker." *The Magazine Antiques* 101 (January 1972): 169–76. A study of a related group of Carolina furniture with putty inlay and pierced comb finials.

HORTON, FRANK L. "William Little, Cabinetmaker of North Carolina." *Journal of Early Southern Decorative Arts* 4 (November 1978): 1–25. A small group of furniture signed or attributed to Little is the basis of this study.

McCLINTON, MARY CLAY. "Robert Wilson, Kentucky Cabinetmaker." *The Magazine Antiques* 103 (May 1973): 945–49. Documentation on an important Kentucky cabinetmaker.

OLCOTT, LOIS L. "Kentucky Federal Furniture." *The Magazine Antiques* 105 (April 1974): 870–82. A preliminary survey of Kentucky furniture.

RONSTROM, MAUD O'BRYAN. "Seignouret and Mallard, Cabinetmakers." *The Magazine Antiques* 46 (August 1944): 79–81. Outdated by research now in progress, but still an important study of these men who sold so much furniture in the lower South.

SNYDER, JOHN J., JR. "John Shearer, Joiner of Martinsburgh." *Journal of Early Southern Decorative Arts* 5 (May 1979): 1–25. A thorough survey of Shearer and his furniture.

WEEKLEY, CAROLYN. "James Gheen, Piedmont North Carolina Cabinetmaker." *The Magazine Antiques* 103 (May 1973): 940–44. A study of an important craftsman, with emphasis on construction techniques.

CHAPTER IX

Books, Catalogs, and Theses

ANDREWS, EDWARD DEMING AND FAITH ANDREWS. *Shaker Furniture: The Craftsmanship of an American Communal Sect.* New York: Dover Publications, Inc., 1964. Sees Shaker furniture as reflecting a complete way of life. Reprint of the classic 1937 study on Shaker crafts.

ANDREWS, EDWARD DEMING AND FAITH ANDREWS. *Religion in Wood: A Book of Shaker Furniture.* Bloomington, Ind.: Indiana University Press, 1966. Classic work on Shaker furniture.

EMERICH, A. D. *Shaker: Furniture and Objects from the Faith and Edward Deming Andrews Collections Commemorating the Bicentenary of the American Shakers.* Washington, D.C.: Smithsonian Institution Press, 1973. Catalog of Shaker furniture and other objects that stimulated recent interest in Shakers. Good essays on Shaker design and an interview with Faith Andrews about her life-long study of Shakers.

FABIAN, MONROE H. *The Pennsylvania-German Decorated Chest.* New York: Universe Books, 1978. The definitive work that debunks many of the myths about the best-known Pennsylvania-German furniture form.

KAUFFMAN, HENRY J. *Pennsylvania Dutch American Folk Art.* New York: American Studio Books, 1946. Brief on furniture, but offers good background on the people.

LICHTEN, FRANCIS. *Folk Art of Rural Pennsylvania.* New York: Charles Scribner's Sons, 1946. This book has some errors but is still the best general book on Pennsylvania-German folk art.

MEADER, ROBERT F. W. *Illustrated Guide to Shaker Furniture.* New York: Dover Publications, Inc., 1972. A useful survey by a former director at the Shaker Museum, Old Chatham, New York, with illustrations from that collection.

MELCHER, MARGUERITE FELLOWS. *The Shaker Adventure.* Old Chatham, N.Y.: The Shaker Museum, 1975. A reprint of the classic history of the Shakers; first published in 1941.

SHEA, JOHN G. *The American Shakers and their Furniture.* New York: Van Nostrand Reinhold Publishing Company, 1971. Good background and overall history on Shakers and their furniture. Also contains measured drawings.

SPRIGG, JUNE. *By Shaker Hands.* New York: Alfred A. Knopf, 1975. A topical description of the Shakers and their philosophy with excellent drawings by the curator at Hancock Shaker Village.

Articles

CARPENTER, MARY GRACE AND CHARLES H., JR. "The Shaker Furniture of Elder Henry Green," *The Magazine Antiques* 105 (May 1974): 1119–25. Documents one group of Shaker furniture with a Victorian flavor.

FRASER, ESTHER S. "Pennsylvania German Dower Chests Signed by the Decorators, Part I." *The Magazine Antiques* 11 (February 1927): 119–23; "Pennsylvania German Dower Chests, Part II." *Ibidem* (April 1927): 280–83; "Pennsylvania German Dower Chests, Part III: Some Problems of the Chests." *Ibidem* (June 1927): 474–76. Three-part series on Selzer and Pennsylvania-German chests. "Dower chest" is a misnomer, but the other information is valid.

NEAL, JULIA. "Regional Characteristics of Western Shaker Furniture." *The Magazine Antiques* 98 (October 1970): 611–17. One of the few descriptions of furniture in the midwestern Shaker communities.

RAY, MARY LYN. "A Reappraisal of Shaker Furniture and Society." In *Winterthur Portfolio* 8: 107–32. Charlottesville: University Press of Virginia, 1973. A persuasive thesis that Shaker furniture in the second half of the 19th century was heavily influenced by the secular world.

SPRIGG, JUNE. "Marked Shaker Furnishings." *The Magazine Antiques* 115 (May 1979): 1048–58. Explodes the myth that Shakers never marked their work.

WALTERS, DONALD. "Johannes Spitler, Shenandoah County, Virginia, Furniture Decorator." *The Magazine Antiques* 108 (October 1975): 730–35. A study of the painted furniture tradition in the Valley of Virginia.

WEISER, FREDERICK S. AND MARY HAMMOND SULLIVAN. "Decorated Furniture of the Mahantango Valley." *The Magazine Antiques* 103 (May 1973): 932–39. The best study of this distinctive school.

CHAPTER X

Books, Catalogs, and Theses

BLACKIE AND SON'S. *The Victorian Cabinetmaker's Assistant.* New York: Dover Publications, Inc., 1970. A reprint of the influential book of designs published first in 1853 in England.

DOWNING, ANDREW JACKSON. *The Architecture of Country Houses.* New York: Dover Publications, 1969. Important primary source on the Gothic and other mid-19th-century furniture styles that he recommended for his houses. Reprint of 1850 edition.

DREPPERD, CARL W. *Victorian: The Cinderella of Antiques.* Garden City: Doubleday and Company, Inc., 1950. Illustrated with drawings. Brief introduction to the various styles, with some good information.

HOWE, KATHERINE S. AND DAVID B. WARREN. *The Gothic Revival Style in America, 1830–1870.* Houston: The Museum of Fine Arts, 1976. Catalog of an exhibition that included other decorative arts as well as furniture. Suggests the magnitude of the Gothic influence in America.

LICHTEN, FRANCES. *Decorative Arts of Victoria's Era.* New York: Charles Scribner's Sons, 1950. An excellent social history of all the decorative arts of the Victorian period.

MAASS, JOHN. *The Gingerbread Age: A View of Victorian America.* New York: Rinehart and Company, Inc., 1957. Focuses primarily on architecture but relates to furniture as well.

SCHWARTZ, MARVIN D., EDWARD J. STANEK, AND DOUGLAS K. TRUE. *The Furniture of John Henry Belter and the Rococo Revival.* New York: E. P. Dutton, 1981. Essays on Belter and his furniture with interesting technical analyses of his furniture. The illustrations are primarily from the Gloria and Richard Manney Collection.

SEALE, WILLIAM. *The Tasteful Interlude: American Interiors Through the Camera's Eye, 1860–1917.* New York: Praeger Publishers, 1975. An introductory essay and contemporary photographs document typical house interiors in the second half of the 19th-century.

TOLLER, JANE. *Papier-mâché in Great Britain and America.* London: G. Bell & Sons, Ltd., 1962. A good general survey of the subject.

Articles

AMES, KENNETH L. "George Henkels, Nineteenth-century Philadelphia Cabinetmaker." *The Magazine Antiques* 104 (October 1973): 641–50. A definitive study on a major Philadelphia cabinetmaker. Based on work in his Ph.D. dissertation.

AMES, KENNETH L. "Designed in France: Notes on the Transmission of French Style to America." In *Winterthur Portfolio* 12: 103-14. Charlottesville: University Press of Virginia, 1977. A perceptive essay on the influence of French designers on American furniture in the mid-19th-century.

DAVIS, FELICE. "Victorian Cabinetmakers in America." *The Magazine Antiques* 44 (September 1943): 111–15. An early analysis of Victorian taste.

DEVOE, SHIRLEY SPAULDING. "The Litchfield Manufacturing Company, Makers of Japanned Papiermâché." *The Magazine Antiques* 78 (August 1960): 150–53. A study of a major American papiermâché company.

DOUGLAS, ED POLK. "Rococo Roses." *New York-Pennsylvania Collector* (January–February 1979) Part I; (April 1979) Part II; (August 1979) Part III; (September 1979) Part IV; (December 1979) Part V; (January–February 1980) Part VI. Fact-filled series of articles reflecting the growing understanding of the Rococo revival; based on continuing research.

GREENE, LESLIE A. "The Late Victorian Hallstand: A Social History." *19th Century* 6 (Winter 1980): 51–53. Excellent interpretation of a now passé object.

HAUSERMAN, DIANNE D. "Alexander Roux and His 'Plain and Artistic Furniture'." *The Magazine Antiques* 93 (February 1968): 210–17. The best study of this major New York cabinetmaker.

JANDL, H. WARD. "George Platt, Interior Decorator (1812–1873)." *The Magazine Antiques* 107 (June 1975): 1154–57. An interesting account of an early interior decorator and his role in the furniture business.

MAASS, JOHN. "On the Myth of Victorian Prudery." *19th Century* 3 (Autumn 1977): 42–49. Thought-provoking but overstated.

MORNINGSTAR, CONNIE. "Fact and Fancy: A Belter Update." *The Antiques Journal* 35 (June 1980): 12–17, 45. Debunks a number of the myths that have grown up around this cabinetmaker.

ROTH, RODRIS. "A Patent Model by John Henry Belter." *The Magazine Antiques* 111 (May 1977): 1038–40. A scholarly look at Belter's patents.

SMITH, ROBERT C. "Gothic and Elizabethan Revival Furniture, 1800–1850." *The Magazine Antiques* 75 (March 1959): 272–76. A good description of the sources of these important revival styles.

SMITH, ROBERT C. "Rococo Revival Furniture, 1850–70." *The Magazine Antiques* 75 (May 1959): 471–75. A good summary of this revival style.

SMITH, ROBERT C. "'Good Taste' in Nineteenth-century Furniture." *The Magazine Antiques* 76 (October 1959): 342–45. Interesting essay in a series on 19th-century furniture.

VINCENT, CLARE. "John Henry Belter's Patent Parlour Furniture." in *The Journal of the Furniture History Society* 3 (1967): 92–99. A careful study of Belter's German background and style as it developed in New York.

VINCENT, CLARE. "John Henry Belter: Manufacturer of All Kinds of Fine Furniture." In *Winterthur Conference Report* (1973): 207–31. *In Technological Innovation and the Decorative Arts.* Charlottesville: University Press of Virginia, 1974. One of the best studies of this key figure in Rococo revival furniture production in New York.

CHAPTER XI

Books, Catalogs, and Theses

AMES, KENNETH L. "Renaissance Revival Furniture in America." Ph.D. dissertation, University of Pennsylvania, 1970. A comprehensive study of the mid-19th-century furniture style. Available through University Microfilms of Ann Arbor, Michigan.

BROOKLYN MUSEUM. *The American Renaissance, 1876–1917.* Brooklyn: The Brooklyn Museum, 1979. The essay on the decorative arts by Dianne H. Pilgrim of the Brooklyn Museum is a useful survey of the late 19th-century styles. Published in conjunction with an exhibition on the subject.

DENKER, ELLEN AND BERT DENKER. *The Rocking Chair Book.* New York: Mayflower Books, Inc., 1979. A comprehensive survey of a peculiarly American furniture form.

ETTEMA, MICHAEL JOHN. "Technological Innovation and Design Economics in American Furniture Manufacture of the Nineteenth Century." Master's Thesis, University of Delaware, 1981. Excellent analysis of 19th-century woodworking machinery and its effects on furniture design.

GIEDION, SIEGFRIED. *Mechanization Takes Command.* New York: Oxford University Press, 1948. A classic interpretation of the influence of machinery on design, using the development of patented furniture as one example.

PERRY, ANN G. *Renaissance Revival Victorian Furniture.* Grand Rapids: Grand Rapids Art Museum, 1976. The introductory essay and catalog entries provide an excellent survey of the Renaissance revival style.

Articles

AMES, KENNETH L. "The Battle of the Sideboards." In *Winterthur Portfolio* 9: 1–27. Charlottesville: University Press of Virginia, 1974. A convincing thesis on the influence of international expositions on decorative arts.

AMES, KENNETH L. "Grand Rapids Furniture at the Time of the Centennial." In *Winterthur Portfolio* 10: 23–50. Charlottesville: University Press of Virginia, 1975. One of the first scholarly looks at Grand Rapids furniture by a major figure in the field of 19th-century decorative arts.

AMES, KENNETH L. "What is the Neo-Grec?" *Nineteenth Century* 2 (Summer 1976): 13–21. The best definition of the Neo-Grec style.

AMES, KENNETH L. "Sitting in (Neo-Grec) Style." *Nineteenth Century* 2 (Autumn 1976): 51–58. The Neo-Grec style as exemplified in chairs. Amplifies his earlier article on the subject.

BOHDAN, CAROL. "Egyptian-inspired Furniture 1800–1922." *Art & Antiques* 3 (November/December 1980): 64–71. First comprehensive survey of the Egyptian influence on American 19th- and early 20th-century furniture.

EARL, POLLY ANNE. "Craftsmen and Machines: The Nineteenth-Century Furniture Industry." In *Winterthur Conference Report* (1973): 307–29. *Technological Innovation and the Decorative Arts.* Winterthur: Henry Francis du Pont Winterthur Museum, 1973. One of the few studies of machinery used in the furniture industry in the 19th century.

FLINT, RICHARD W. "George Hunzinger, Patent Furniture Maker." *Art & Antiques* 3 (January/February 1980): 116–23. A well-researched study of the man and his furniture.

INGERMAN, ELIZABETH A. "Personal Experiences of an Old New York Cabinetmaker." *The Magazine Antiques* 84 (November 1963): 576–80. Ernest Halen's account of 19th-century cabinetmaking in New York is a major source but it must be used critically.

JOHNSON, J. STEWART. "John Jelliff, Cabinetmaker." *The Magazine Antiques* 102 (August 1972): 256–61. Important study of a major cabinetmaker in Newark, New Jersey.

PEIRCE, DONALD C. "Mitchell and Rammelsberg, Cincinnati Furniture Manufacturers, 1847–1881." In *Winterthur Portfolio* 13, *American Furniture and Its Makers*: 209–29. Chicago: University of Chicago Press, 1979. One of the few studies of a 19th-century furniture factory.

SEIDLER, JAN. "The Furniture Industry in Victorian Boston." *Nineteenth Century* 3 (Summer 1977): 64–69. The fruits of a study of 19th-century Boston furniture-makers by the Boston Museum of Fine Arts. Shows that much hand-work continued in the face of mechanization.

SMITH, ROBERT C. "Architecture and Sculpture in Nineteenth-century Mirror Frames." *The Magazine Antiques* 109 (February 1976): 350–59. Illustrates the alternation between architectural and sculptural approaches to mirror frame design.

STRICKLAND, PETER L. "Furniture by the Lejambre family of Philadelphia." *The Magazine Antiques* 113 (March 1978): 600–13. Another in a growing list of studies on 19th-century Philadelphia cabinetmakers. This family worked mainly in the Renaissance revival style.

WALTERS, BETTY LAWSON. "The King of Desks: Wooton's Patent Secretary." *Smithsonian Studies in History and Technology* 3. Washington, D.C.: Smithsonian Institution Press, 1969. A thorough study of the Wooton Desk Company.

CHAPTER XII

Books, Catalogs, and Theses

ASLIN, ELIZABETH. *The Aesthetic Movement: Prelude to Art Nouveau.* New York: Praeger Publishers, 1969. Useful in defining Eastlake and art furniture on both sides of the Atlantic in the last decades of the 19th century.

CLARK, ROBERT JUDSON, ed. *The Arts and Crafts Movement in America, 1876–1916.* Princeton: Princeton University Press, 1972. The catalog of the first major exhibition of decorative arts from this movement, which offers a solid introduction to decorative arts of the East, Midwest, and the Pacific Coast.

CORBIN, PATRICIA. *All about Wicker.* New York: E. P. Dutton, 1978. A useful survey of the interest in wicker furniture, with many illustrations.

EASTLAKE, CHARLES L. *Hints on Household Taste.* New York: Dover Publications, Inc., 1969. An unabridged reprint of the 1878 American edition; indispensable to an understanding of late 19th-century furniture.

FREEMAN, JOHN CROSBY. *The Forgotten Rebel.* Watkins Glen, N.Y.: Century House, 1966. An in-depth study of Stickley and his furniture.

HANKS, DAVID A. *The Decorative Designs of Frank Lloyd Wright.* New York: E. P. Dutton, 1979. A broad study of Wright's household designs that grew out of an exhibition at the Renwick Gallery in Washington, D.C. in 1978.

HANKS, DAVID A. *Christian Herter and the Aesthetic Movement in America.* New York: Washburn Gallery, 1980. Brief catalog of a show on Herter and the Aesthetic Movement in America.

MACKINSON, RANDELL L. *Greene and Greene: Furniture and Related Designs.* Layton, Ut.: Peregrine Smith, Inc., 1979. A survey of the major houses and furnishings attributed to the Greenes; by the curator of the Gamble House, which was designed by the Greenes, in Pasadena, California.

MADIGAN, MARY JANE SMITH. *Eastlake-Influenced American Furniture, 1870–1890.* Yonkers, N. Y.: The Hudson River Museum, 1974. An important exhibit catalog that de-

fines a major 19th-century furniture style.

RHEIMS, MAURICE. *The Flowering of Art Nouveau.* New York: Harry N. Abrams, 1966. Excellent background on the many influences on the new style at the end of the 19th century.

SAUNDERS, RICHARD. *Collecting & Restoring Wicker Furniture.* New York: Crown Publishers, Inc., 1976. One of the few solid studies of wicker.

Stickley Craftsman Furniture Catalogs. New York: Dover Publications, Inc., 1979. Reprint of a 1910 catalog of Gustav Stickley and an undated catalog of the L & J. G. Stickley furniture company. A basic source for Mission furniture, with a good introduction and analysis of the style progression of Gustav Stickley furniture.

STICKLEY, GUSTAV. *The Best of Craftsman Homes.* Salt Lake City, Ut.: Peregrine Smith, Inc., 1979. Most of the articles reprinted from Stickley's magazines deal with architecture, but several are key documents in explaining and describing his furniture designs.

THONET BROTHERS. *Thonet Bentwood & Other Furniture: The 1904 Illustrated Catalogue.* New York: Dover Publications, Inc., 1980. This reprinted publication contains most of the Thonet designs produced by the company since its founding, plus a succinct essay on the company itself.

Articles

AMES, KENNETH L. "Gardner & Company of New York." *The Magazine Antiques* 100 (August 1971): 252–55. A thorough study of an innovative furniture company of the late 19th-century.

BOHDAN, CAROL LORRAINE AND TODD MITCHELL VOLPE. "The Furniture of Gustav Stickley." *The Magazine Antiques* 111 (May 1977): 984–89. One of several important articles on Stickley by the dealers specializing in the decorative arts of the Mission period.

BORDES, MARILYNN JOHNSON. "Christian Herter and the Cult of Japan." in "Aspects of the Arts and Crafts Movement." Robert Judson Clark, ed. *Record of the Art Museum* 34. Princeton University (1975): 20–27. Additional information about Herter that shows how his furniture reflected the Oriental taste.

FARNAM, ANNE. "A. H. Davenport and Company, Boston Furniture Makers." *The Magazine Antiques* 109 (May 1976): 1048–55. An interesting study of a firm specializing in revival styles at the end of the century.

GILBORN, CRAIG. "Rustic Furniture in the Adirondacks, 1875–1925." *The Magazine Antiques* 109 (June 1976): 1212–19. The director of the Adirondacks Museum defines this unique style.

HANKS, DAVID A. "The Nineteenth Century Furniture Manufacturing in Chicago." *Nineteenth Century* 1 (January 1975): 18–19. A summary of the development of the furniture companies that made Chicago the leading center of furniture-manufacturing in the Midwest.

HANKS, DAVID A. "Daniel Pabst, Philadelphia Cabinetmaker." *Art & Antiques* 3 (January/February 1980): 94–101. The best study of one of Philadelphia's finest cabinetmakers in the second half of the 19th-century.

HANKS, DAVID A. "Kimbel & Cabus: 19th-Century New York Cabinetmakers." *Art & Antiques* 3 (September/October 1980): 44–53. Another in the growing list of monographs on an important New York furniture-making firm that produced important examples of "Modern Gothic" furniture.

MADIGAN, MARY JEAN SMITH. "The Influence of Charles Locke Eastlake on American Furniture Manufacture, 1870–90." In *Winterthur Portfolio* 10: 1–22. Winterthur: Henry Francis du Pont Winterthur Museum, 1975. A good analysis of the Eastlake style. Based on her Winterthur thesis.

MARKS, ALAN. "Greene and Greene: A Study in Functional Design." *Fine Wood Working* 12 (September 1978): 40–45. An analysis of the construction techniques and designs of Greene and Greene furniture.

MENZ, KATHERINE. "Wicker Furniture: Four Centuries of Flexible Furniture." *American Art & Antiques* 1 (September/October 1978): 84–91. A documented survey of the wicker craze. Based on her Winterthur thesis.

ROTH, RODRIS. "The Colonial Revival and 'Centennial Furniture.'" *The Art Quarterly* 1 (1964): 57–80. A close look at the origins of Colonial revival furniture and a persuasive argument against the use of "Centennial Furniture" as a term to describe this important Victorian style.

SANDERS, BARRY. "Gustav Stickley: A Craftsman's Furniture." *American Art & Antiques* 2 (July/August 1979): 46–53. An overview of Stickley furniture with emphasis on the style and variety of the furniture as well as background on the company.

SMITH, ROBERT C. "Furniture of the Eclectic Decades, 1870–1900." *The Magazine Antiques* 76 (July 1959): 50–53. Not quite as thorough as earlier articles in his series on 19th-century furniture, but still useful.

TELLER, BETTY. "American Furniture in the Art Nouveau Style." *Art & Antiques* 3 (May/June 1980): 96–101. A clear overview of the Art Nouveau style in America and a summary of its major exponents.

WILK, CHRISTOPHER. "Michael Thonet and Bentwood Furniture before the First World War." *Art & Antiques* 3 (November/December 1980): 84–91. The best summary of the history and furniture of Thonet.

CHAPTER XIII

Books, Catalogs, and Theses

CESCINSKY, HERBERT. *The Gentle Art of Faking Furniture.* New York: Dover Publications, Inc., 1967. Reprint of the original 1931 classic.

EDLIN, HERBERT L. *What Wood Is That? A Manual of Wood Identification.* New York: The Viking Press, 1969. Contains a good system for identifying wood and includes 40 actual wood samples.

GAMON, ALBERT T. *Pennsylvania Country Antiques.* Englewood Cliffs, N.J.: Prentice-Hall, 1968.

One useful feature of this book is the chapter on "Signs of Age."

PETERSON, HAROLD L. *How Do You Know It's Old?* New York: Charles Scribner's Sons, 1975. A practical handbook on evaluating the authenticity of wood, metal, and ceramic objects by the former Chief Curator of the National Park Service.

SYMONDS, R. W. AND T. H. ORMSBEE. *Antique Furniture of the Walnut Period.* New York: Robert M. McBride Co., 1947. Mostly on English and American furniture of the Queen Anne period but includes an excellent chapter on "Spurious Walnut Furniture."

YALE UNIVERSITY ART GALLERY. *The Eye of the Beholder: Fakes, Replicas and Alterations in American Art.* New Haven: Yale University Art Gallery, 1977. Catalog of an exhibit at the Yale University Art Gallery on the subject of fakes.

YATES, RAYMOND F. AND MARGUERITE W. *A Guide to Victorian Antiques.* New York: Harper and Row, 1949. Has errors but lots of good information, too. The theme is how to detect fakes in 19th-century decorative arts.

YATES, RAYMOND F. *Antique Fakes and Their Detection.* New York: Harper & Row, 1950. On the gentle art of faking; by a cabinet-maker who has also written on reproducing antiques.

Articles

MONTGOMERY, CHARLES F. "Some Remarks on the Practice and Science of Connoisseurship." *The Walpole Society Note Book.* New York: The Walpole Society, 1961, pp. 56–69. Excellent advice on evaluating furniture.

NELSON, LEE H. "Nail Chronology." *Technical Leaflet* No. 48. Nashville: American Association of State and Local History, 1968. An excellent description of the changing methods of manufacturing nails to aid in dating objects.

INDEX